America the Almighty

The Maverick Hyperpower

Stephen L. Damours

Bookman LLC
Publishing & Marketing
Providing Quality, Professional
Author Services

www.BookmanMarketing.com

ISBN: 1-59453-349-0

For Paramahansa Yogananda

Contents

From *America the Almighty*

If there is a worthy vision for the United States and for human civilization at this stage in history, it is larger than avoiding various possible disasters, though that is a first step. It's about exercising the courage and imagination to build a tremendously difficult future, about taking off our nationalistic blinders, letting go of our tribalistic selfishness and doing the hard-headed work of creating transnational laws and institutions to bring an entire planet into increasing rather than diminishing harmony and cooperation. It's about the world's most powerful nation supporting the establishment of global institutions such as the International Criminal Court and renouncing violence as a tool of foreign policy except in defense against attack or imminent threat of attack. It's about creating and reinforcing democratic global structures that make human rights and justice realities for all humanity, mirroring progress that has already taken place within the boundaries of the great democracies. And it's about leading global efforts to treat this fragile planet on which we depend for our lives, not as a disposable resource to be pillaged and despoiled for the enrichment of the few, but as a treasure to be preserved for our children and our grandchildren.

ACKNOWLEDGEMENTS

I owe to one of my most treasured friends, Scott Hoffman, special appreciation for opening doors for me into organizations personal contacts that in turn created access to an abundance of information on the issues and conceptual perspectives that dominate this book. Without the intellectual stimulation and the opportunities and contacts Scott provided, I would never have embarked on the fourteen-year odyssey that led to this book and made it possible. Standing next to Scott as a major contributor to my education in international affairs and as a connecting link to helpful people, organizations and information is Don Kraus, Executive Vice President, Citizens for Global Solutions. Debbie Metke, Heather Hamilton, Justina Grubor, and all of the staff of this invaluable organization have also made vital contributions to my background knowledge relevant to the book.

Special thanks are due to Joy Frey, who demonstrated her versatility by doing and outstanding job in the triple roles of research assistant, substantive editor, and eagle-eyed copy editor. She made the book more informative, more factually and logically accurate, more nearly error-free, and easier for the reader to assimilate.

Three colleagues made special contributions to my understanding of women's issues. Sarah Albert and Kit Cosby, co-chairs of the Group on Ratification of the UN Convention on the Elimination of All Forms of Discrimination Against Women (CEDAW), provided research materials that were valuable in developing my understanding the treaty and the issues surrounding it. Many thanks to Thesil Morlan, who provided a careful reading and astute comments on an early draft of the chapter on women's rights.

Tom and Jackie Valone made much-appreciated special contributions by sharing their experiences in the twists, turns, pitfalls, and opportunities in getting books published, distributed, and publicized. Joan Jungfleisch deserves appreciation for challenging and vibrant lunch conversations that sharpened and stimulated my thinking on the issues in the book. Special thanks to Joanne Damours for inspiring me to work with her and her risk-analysis software company, Bayesian Systems, in developing and testing the

Peace-War knowledge base, a component of a computer program that calculates probabilities on whether a country will be engaged in peace, civil war, anarchy, or international war in the near-to mid-term future. Developing the knowledge base forced me to think and research probingly and comprehensively about the causes of peace and war and the different kinds of war. The insights I derived from that experience have been invaluable in my understanding the forces at work in the Iraq war and other conflicts and potential conflict situations around the world.

Cecilia Fuentes deserves thanks for making a special effort to provide me with her paper on the diplomatic history of the Ottowa landmine convention and particularly the shifting role relationships between Canada and the United States during the evolution of the convention.

To my father, Leon W. Damours I owe special thanks not only for the many things a father does for a son, but specifically for his worldwide travel, curiosity and frequent picture-taking and home-slide shows that piqued my curiosity about other countries and cultures at an early age and made me feel that the whole world was my home, not just a single country, however admirable that country may be.

The United States must resist basing foreign policy on hegemonic power. Many of the problems affecting world order are not susceptible to solution by military means. History shows that sooner or later every powerful country calls into being countervailing forces. And at that point—and I would insist even now—the United States will not be able to sort out every international problem alone without exhausting itself physically and psychologically.... The ultimate challenge for U.S. foreign policy is to turn dominant power into a sense of shared responsibility.

Henry Kissinger, "A Dangerous Divergence" *The Washington Post,* 12/10/02

A fortress on a hill can only stand alone, casting a menacing shadow over all beneath. As such, America would become the focus of global hatred. A city on a hill, by contrast, could illuminate the world with the hope of human progress—but only in an environment in which that progress is both the focus of a vision and an attainable reality for all. "A city that is set on a hill cannot be hid....Let your light so shine before men, that they may see your good works." So let America shine.

Zbigniew Brzezinski, *The Choice: Global Domination or Global Leadership.* Basic Books, 2004, p.232

Chapter One

THE WORLD'S GREATEST PROBLEM

What we see now is the tragedy of a great country, with noble impulses, successful institutions, magnificent historical achievements and immense energies, which has become a menace to itself and to mankind.

—Anatol Lieven, Carnegie Endowment for International Peace Senior Associate[1]

What are the key elements in the role of the United States in the world at the beginning of the twenty-first century? No one disputes that we are different from other countries, that we have a unique place and unique power in the world. How we play our unique role and use our power in this new century will determine not only America's future, but also the world's.

The United States is the richest single country in the world as measured by the size of its economy. It has by far the most powerful military establishment in the world. The $400 billion per year the U.S. budgeted in 2003 for our military, without counting the expense of the war on Iraq, was six times the spending of the world's second biggest military spender, Russia, and greater than the military spending of most of the world's other countries combined. It seems only natural to expect a democracy with such overwhelming power to lead the world and be in the vanguard of global progress on numerous fronts. Yet there is a profound and growing problem with American leadership in the world. More often than not, U.S. foreign policy is either backward or bullying or both, halting global progress on multiple fronts and instilling fear and loathing in the populations and leaders of other countries, including our allies. We think of ourselves as a leader, but often we are a "leader" with no followers, and many resentful detractors.

1

Our disproportionate power tempts our leaders to demand exceptions for ourselves from international law as we have with the International Criminal Court, and to use military force and economic arm-twisting to get our own way in the short term, with little regard for long-term consequences to ourselves and other countries. The adverse consequences include deep popular resentment in other countries, cynicism in our own, and irreversible environmental damage. The siren song, "Go it alone, it's easier!" is often irresistible music to the ears of our leaders. The backup siren song, less alluring but still tempting, is "If we subject them to enough pressure, they will cave." The recipients of all-but-coercive pressure sometimes give this approach the ugly label of "bullying." Who can argue with them? The United States stands out at the beginning of the 21st century, with the Cold War more than a decade behind us, not only for its extraordinary power among nations, but also for its extraordinary resistance to international cooperation and international law. If this statement sounds extreme, read on. The whole book substantiates it.

Our American values and traditions call us to a higher and more benign use of our power. The U.S. has a tremendous responsibility and opportunity to work for the creation of a better world—one in which global peace and stability rely increasingly on international cooperation, including international laws and institutions and widely accepted values, and decreasingly on military brute force, economic clout, and win-lose games. When we invest in a more law-abiding, orderly world, gradually our own security as well as that of other countries is enhanced. When we undermine such a world and reinforce international anarchy, our own security is undermined, regardless of the "protection" of our raw, coercive power.

The values for which America stands have inspired the world and made it a better place. However, our recent, surprisingly frequent suspensions or reversals of our historic national commitments to peace, human rights, justice, arms control, and environmental protection not only represent failures of national character, but also create unacceptable political and economic costs in the long run. Without the foundations of these values, the freedom our politicians stress in their Fourth of July speeches cannot endure.

To the many patriotic Americans who sincerely and in many ways rightly believe that "we are the good guys" in the international arena, U.S. foreign policy since the end of the Cold War must come as an unpleasant shock. A shock, that is, if they are aware of the increasingly stark pattern of our leaders' selfish disregard for international teamwork and cooperation and the alienation and anti-American feeling this behavior pattern has generated

2

outside the U.S. Most Americans seem blissfully unaware of the extent to which the behavior of our government alienates the rest of the world and clashes with our American values. These two gaps are huge and seem to be growing. The consequences for our integrity as a nation and our relationships with the rest of the world are deeply disturbing. Consider the following specifics on our relationship with our most consistent allies, the Europeans.

In an article on the deteriorating relationship between the U.S. and Europe, Jessica Matthews, one of the nation's foremost foreign policy analysts and president of the Carnegie Institute for International Peace, points out, "In a solid bloc, the European Union (EU) approved, and the United States did not, the creation of the International Criminal Court (ICC), the Kyoto Protocol on climate change, the ban on antipersonnel land mines, the biodiversity treaty, and a verification mechanism for the Biological Weapons Control Treaty."[2]

To these I add, among many others, America's refusal for years to pay our UN dues. Whatever one may think of the United Nations, this longstanding insult was intensely irritating to other countries, who justifiably asked why the world's richest nation was a deadbeat, but still participated in UN debates and voting and threw its considerable weight around in the corridors of UN power. We finally paid some of our back dues when President Bush went to the UN Security Council to push for renewed weapons inspections in Iraq, a move which he loudly and repeatedly announced was a prelude to war. He knew he could expect no cooperation from other nations on weapons inspections in Iraq in the context of resentment for U.S. non-payment of dues. So at last we paid them—partially.

In the human rights arena, the U.S. Senate has refused to ratify two major international treaties on the rights of women and the rights of children, treaties ratified by all the major democracies and most other countries as well. In our rejection of the rights of women treaty (Convention to Eliminate All Forms of Discrimination Against Women, or CEDAW) we have found ourselves in the unsavory company of morally backward dictatorships with atrocious records in treatment of women such as Iran and Libya. We have no recent record of gender-based oppression remotely comparable to theirs, and nothing to lose by ratification, but still we don't ratify the treaty. We thereby send a signal to the world of indifference to moral principle and to human suffering. What's wrong with this picture? Why is the U.S. government behaving this way? This is one of the many disturbing questions about U.S. foreign policy this book tackles.

A leader is ahead of the pack, showing the way toward improvements, working to formulate or crystallize agreement and promote consensus among disparate political forces. Does the U.S. act as a leader among other nations? Matthews adds to her observations:

Washington has repeatedly found itself on the wrong side of lopsided international judgments. The vote on the landmine ban was 142 to 0, with 18 abstentions; on the ICC [International Criminal Court] it was 120 to 7, with 21 abstentions; and on Kyoto [protocols on global warming] in 2001 it was 178 to 1, with only the United States opposed... [On human rights and justice,] The United States has found itself in uncomfortable company with the likes of China, Cuba, Libya, Iraq, and Iran.... The pattern is unmistakably not in the U.S. interest. No country, no matter how strong, will remain a legitimate leader for long when it is odd man out on so many decisions that command the support of the vast majority of the world's countries.[3]

Jessica Matthews is not alone in sounding this alarm. In a few sentences excerpted from his article, "The Troubling New Face of America," former President Jimmy Carter sums up the same problem more broadly:

Formerly admired almost universally as the preeminent champion of human rights, our country has become the foremost target of respected international organizations concerned about these basic principles of democratic life.

* * *

We have thrown down counter-productive gauntlets to the rest of the world, disavowing U.S. commitments to laboriously negotiated international accords. Peremptory rejections of nuclear arms agreements, the biological weapons convention, environmental protection, anti-torture proposals, and punishment for war criminals have sometimes been combined with economic threats against those who might disagree with us. These unilateral acts and assertions increasingly isolate the

4

United States from the very nations needed to join in combating terrorism.

* * *

It is crucial that the historical and well-founded American commitments prevail: to peace, justice, human rights, the environment and international cooperation.[4]

In addition to these decisions to opt out of global cooperation on matters of fundamental moral and legal principle, the most spectacular instance of America's leaders "jumping the tracks" of global law and cooperation is launching the Iraq war. In this book I have explored in depth the rationales for the war and its consequences for the U.S. and the world. I've done so first because of the war's enormous current importance in world affairs and second because it was a straight-up violation of international law, launched in the absence of any one of the three explicit essentials for legality of war: response to an attack or an imminent threat of attack, or sanction by the UN Security Council. I have spoken with people who sneer at international law as insignificant, but in effect they are saying it's O.K. for the U.S. to be an outlaw nation like Iran and North Korea. I don't believe that most Americans would find the U.S. being a pariah or outlaw acceptable. Those who denigrate international law are also ignoring the decades of striving to establish it by some of America's greatest leaders. We are not the victims of rules created by others, we ourselves are among the foremost creators of international law.

A third reason this book explores the rationales and consequences of the Iraq war is that it was a clear and extreme instance of the militarizing of American foreign policy. The evidence suggests that the civilian American leaders who controlled the Pentagon were tempted by our enormously disproportionate military power to a kind of imperial overreach. The "opportunity" provided by U.S. military power seduced them into undermining American security by starting a destabilizing war. Furthermore, the Department of Defense had the political power to "call the shots" and overcome the reluctance of the State Department, the agency tasked by the Constitution with responsibility for managing U.S. foreign policy. The war illustrates dramatically the ironic title of this book. America's leaders displayed a pronounced lack of "decent respect for the opinions of mankind," acting with dismissive indifference to global and even domestic public opinion. A majority of the people in every nation in the world, except the U.S. itself and Israel, opposed the war.

As a result, when the leaders of other democracies did support the Iraq war militarily, against the will of their populations, they risked the political futures of their governments. England's Tony Blair has survived politically, although his approval ratings in Britain have dropped significantly; Aznar's People's Party of Spain has not fared so well. It has been replaced by a socialist government—hardly an outcome American conservatives are ready to celebrate. Currently, Koizumi of Japan is in deep political trouble over one of the consequences of sending troops to Iraq—the abduction by Iraqi insurgents of three Japanese civilians and threats by their captors to burn them alive if Japanese troops don't pull out of Iraq. (The three Japanese prisoners were subsequently freed, much to the relief and joy of their countrymen and the world. But civilians from other countries continue to be abducted, making cooperation with the U.S. in the war more dangerous for the leaders of other countries.) Following the lead of Spain's new socialist Prime Minister, the Dominican Republic and Honduras have also expressed their intention to withdraw troops from Iraq as soon as possible.

Are We "the Good Guys"?

We Americans like to see our country as benign and noble, a city on a hill, an example and leader to the rest of the world. Much in the historical behavior of the U.S. supports the view that it is indeed a constructive force in the world. And we like to believe we are the leaders of the world. Every few nights on the TV news, one news anchor or another refers to the U.S. as the "leader of the free world," a strangely antiquated Cold War term that still exists in the American consciousness.

However, since the end of the Cold War and much more since the run-up to the Iraq war, the views of the rest of the world on the role of the U.S. have evolved into something radically different. Most educated people in the rest of the world feel that America's misuse of its power generally, and especially under the leadership of George W. Bush, is one of the world's greatest problems, if not *the* greatest problem. This misuse of power has a pervasive effect on most other global problems. The U.S. is increasingly seen as an obstacle, even an aggressor against global progress and stability. When we create serious problems for others, eventually resentment surfaces and those problems come back to hit us in the face. What a nation sows, it reaps. When we incur widespread resentment, we incur danger to ourselves.

"Why is so much of the world so hostile toward us?" This has become an increasingly urgent question. The Iraq war brought it to a head, but it has been brewing for some time. This book is an attempt to answer that question with particular attention to what the U.S. does to create the situation, and what we as American citizens can do to change it for the better. As Pogo, the wise cartoon character famously said, "We have met the enemy and he is us." There is much to be deplored in American foreign policy since the end of the Cold War, and much of it could be different without significant sacrifices for the American people or costs to American economic and security interests. In most cases the security benefits to the U.S. from changing these policies would far outweigh the costs of the changes. The changes would reduce both the incentives to terrorism and some of the assumed requirements for huge military expenditures.

In every case I have analyzed in this book, the American policies and behaviors that have angered the rest of the world and left us more vulnerable to overt and covert attacks are also clear betrayals of treasured American values enshrined in our founding documents and embraced by a substantial majority of American citizens. As a country, we are shooting ourselves in the foot without any necessity to do so, and in the process contradicting our own core values and sacrificing our integrity as a nation. The problem is one of character, not just political judgment.

One somewhat snooty theory on why the rest of the world resents us so much is that America's critics are merely envious of our success. After all, foreigners are standing in line to emigrate to this country legally and risking their lives to do so illegally. Those who cite envy as the problem are correct in claiming that the U.S. is a great country and people the world over wish to live here. No doubt some of our overseas critics are envious of our success. But this viewpoint overlooks the serious faults of U.S. behavior toward the rest of the world and its major contribution to anti-American hostility.

It is not our prosperity and our domestic lifestyle the rest of the world dislikes; it is the overbearing and domineering behavior of our leaders in the international arena. Two paradoxical realities exist side-by-side: the U.S. is a great country and a wonderful place to live—a country that inspires well-justified patriotism—and concurrently there is much to deplore and correct in its foreign policy. There is no contradiction in making both of these statements any more than there is a contradiction in recognizing the faults of an admirable friend or of oneself. People and countries are complex entities, neither wholly good nor wholly bad. Recognizing our country's faults and striving to correct them is the patriotic approach to this duality. Sweeping the faults under a carpet of denial and flag-waving is not.

After September 11, 2001, George W. Bush repeated over and over the theory that "they," the al Qaeda terrorists, hate us for our freedoms. For the morally blinded extremists who perpetrated this atrocity, there may be some truth in the statement. Clearly some of the freedoms we have and the way we use them are anathema to al Qaeda. But polls show that most people all over the world admire the U.S. for its freedoms; it's the foreign policy they dislike. They see not leadership, but arrogance, coercion and dominance. American citizens and government policy-makers would do well to pay attention to the distinction.

Some ultra-liberals tend toward the opposite extreme. They not only reject jingoistic rationalizations of an aggressive and domineering foreign policy, but fall into the "blame America first" trap. Accepting responsibility for our actions and their consequences is a first step toward constructive change, but it's possible to develop a toxic overdose of self-criticism by engaging in self-hatred and self-flagellation. Vietnam era flag burning is not the answer. In this regard, an especially sensitive point is "moral equivalence." We need to recognize that there is not necessarily any moral equivalence between specific U.S. actions and the direct adverse consequences we incur in the international arena. To look for moral equivalence in every case of causality is a major mistake.

For instance, when the September 11 attack devastated the U.S., it was vital that we as a country search not only for the perpetrators, but also for the underlying causes of the event. The two searches are quite distinct, but of course deeply interlinked. We found that Osama bin Laden's terrorist organization, al Qaeda, was behind the attack. They were the perpetrators. Without knowing that, we could not have learned the underlying causes. We found out that bin Laden's anger with the U.S., his wealth and organizational skills, plus numerous other factors were at work in his strike against the U.S.

One of the chief things he was angry about, a key proximate cause of his attack on the U.S., was the U.S. military presence on the sacred soil of Saudi Arabia, home of the Prophet. Here is where we need to make a huge distinction. *Proximate causes and moral equivalence can be light years apart.* Establishing military bases in Saudi Arabia was a common-sense move by the U.S. as a part of the effort to roll back Saddam Hussein's aggression against Kuwait. It was done with the concurrence of the Saudi government and was partly to protect Saudi Arabia (and U.S. access to its oil) from further aggression by Saddam. But in the mind of a religious fanatic, it was an atrocity, a defilement of sacred territory. Let us not confuse causality with moral equivalence. They are not remotely the same thing.

However, looking at the narrow issue of U.S. bases in Saudi Arabia misses the larger picture. A number of American policies and actions seem hostile to the Arabs and the Muslims of the world (not least of which is our current one-sided support for Israel), and some of these are unnecessary provocations. As a result they serve as recruiting tools for terrorists. In a number of cases we have failed to do the common sense political analysis needed on the relationship between some of our actions and their costs in terms of the anger they trigger in the Arab or the Muslim world. Basing troops in Saudi Arabia is only one of several examples, and one that might not have been avoidable. Many of the cost and risk calculations about our actions are not primarily moral issues, but rather are matters of common-sense politics and competent diplomacy.

This book is not primarily about such practical calculations. It is mainly about something graver and more ominous: our leaders' frequent—indeed, almost consistent—foreign policy violations of the deeply held moral values of Americans and of the whole world. Violations of these values cause profound alienation of much of the rest of the world, undermining the moral high ground on which this country has struggled to stand since its founding. As noted earlier, these values cluster into four broad categories: peace, justice, human rights, and sustainable prosperity. (The importance of the latter is just dawning on the world. It boils down to exercising stewardship and avoiding reckless behavior that threatens the existence of a livable planet and a viable economy for our future and that of our children and grandchildren.) When the behavior of a nation that is far more powerful than any other on earth is far out of alignment with all these values, the problem is monumental; it threatens the well-being of the entire world.

Although I will undoubtedly be accused of the "blame America first" viewpoint, I intend throughout to acknowledge and embrace all that is positive in American values and the positive actions of the U.S. Government, and to draw clear distinctions between causal links and moral equivalence. That said, the subject matter of this book is *what's wrong* morally, legally, politically and even militarily, with American foreign policy, mainly since the end of the Cold War, and what we citizens need to do to change it. The book is primarily a critique and a call for change. I intend it to be a balanced and fair-minded one, but I also intend to pull no punches in stating my case.

9

Why focus on what's wrong? Isn't that unpatriotic? To use a simplistic analogy, if your car won't start, you focus on things related to starting the car, e.g., the battery, the starter mechanism, etc., not the tires or the brakes. You have to know what's wrong before you can fix it. Focusing on what's wrong does not constitute disloyalty to the car, it constitutes a precondition for repairs. Fixing what's broken with U.S. foreign policy will benefit not only the driver and passengers, the U.S. Government and citizens, but also the rest of the world.

There are two more boundaries on the scope of this book. First, it is extremely current. It deals mainly with U.S. foreign policy since the end of the Cold War. For the sake of brevity I have tried to avoid going into long (in most cases even short) historical explanations of the current circumstances except briefly in this introductory chapter. The reason for the exclusive focus on the post-Cold War period is that its essential dynamics are completely different from those of the Cold War itself. During the Cold War virtually everything that happened was seen and decided through the lens of the life-and-death rivalry between the Soviet Union and the United States. All that American leaders did, for better or for worse, could be rationalized in terms of the struggle to contain the Soviet Union.

When the USSR collapsed at the end of the 1980s, a new era was born. It became the era of the lone superpower, the United States struggling to cope with a new global anarchy and with an explosion of formerly submerged nationalism in countries that had previously been pushed around as pawns in the Cold War. It also became an era in which the rest of the world struggled to cope with the new reality of a single superpower or "hyperpower" unrestrained by competition with a roughly comparable opponent.

Suddenly the U.S. had a dominant free hand in shaping the world we would all live in, replete with a sea of troubles to swim in. We could choose to use that free hand to strengthen and democratize the embryonic and very weak global order that existed at the time or we could undermine global order and seize advantages for ourselves when no one had the power to oppose us. We could act like a global statesman or we could act like a planetary thug. A remarkably prescient scholar of international relations, Stanley Hoffman, recognized this choice for the U.S. ten years in advance, in 1978, and summarized it in the title of his book, *Primacy or World Order: American Foreign Policy Since the Cold War.*[5] The leaders of the United States increasingly acted out the former alternative, primacy or dominance for the U.S. at the expense of world order, though they never made the choice explicit. However, the second Bush administration did make it explicit when it announced its policy of preemptive warfare—a policy that depended on American military preeminence, intensified it, undermined world order, and directly contradicted a half-century's cultivation of international law. The Iraq war is the test case for this policy, and the chaos it is promoting speaks for itself.

One final boundary on the scope of this book: it is not primarily about what's wrong with our innumerable relationships with individual countries or groups, e.g., Israel and the Palestinians, North Korea, or China. Some of these problems are being handled badly and desperately need a change of approach. Some are going fairly well. They have been discussed thoughtfully in a number of books and op-ed pieces published since the turn of the millennium, and they need not be the subject of this book. I am mainly concerned with a comparatively neglected subject: the indifference to international law and moral principle and the preference for military and economic coercion America's leaders have increasingly often displayed since the end of the Cold War. In particular, this involves how these preferences affect the world as a whole, especially through multilateral treaties[6] and international organizations.

Treaties, the Bedrock

Strangely, at the present moment in American history, the dawn of the 21st century, it is necessary to begin a book targeting the public, not the academic experts, on the U.S. role in the world with a reminder of how critical treaties are to global stability and cooperation. The fact that treaties are essential should be obvious, even banal, but it is not. As with government, so with international law; there has been a great deal of ill-considered political rhetoric bashing and trashing the foundations of the social order on which we now stand. We need a brief reminder of what we're standing on, and why a solid foundation is better than quicksand.

As the world is presently constituted, treaties are the bedrock of international cooperation. Without them, relations between nations would be chaotic, a continual war of all against all. With treaties, it is possible not only to have orderly and stable bilateral relations between pairs of nations, but also to have increasingly orderly and cooperative multilateral relationships among large numbers of nations. Treaties serving as founding charters have made possible the establishment of all international institutions such as the United Nations and the North Atlantic Treaty Organization (NATO).

The United Nations, a favorite whipping boy for American conservatives, has promoted dialogue rather than violence between nations and has organized over one hundred peace negotiations among warring nations and groups. It played a key role in defusing the Cuban Missile Crisis and thereby preventing World War III. Through the Security Council, the UN has also legitimized military action to restore order among nations such as the rollback of Saddam Hussein's invasion of Kuwait. Lacking any coercive power, the UN's influence stems exclusively from its legitimacy, which in turn stems from the nobility of its goals and the fact that 191 nations— virtually all the earth's nations—have chosen to join it, signing and ratifying its Charter and participating in its debates, discussions, programs, and voting processes. No other institution on the planet has such unanimous support. The UN's flaws are many and conspicuous, but its vital contributions should not be forgotten. NATO, for its part, protected Europe militarily for over a half-century during the Cold War. Whatever the questions about NATO's present usefulness and relevance, there was little doubt about the danger of Soviet aggression during the 1950s through the 1980s. And there is little doubt about the key roles the UN and NATO contributed in containing that danger.

International covenants such as the Universal Declaration of Human Rights (UDHR) define bedrock human rights that virtually all nations can agree on, much like the Bill of Rights in the American Constitution. At the dawn of the 21st century, a network of multilateral treaties, the institutions they charter and the human rights they articulate, constitute the foundations of a developing but still fragile and less than stable world order. While dangerously imperfect, that order has prevented a third world war for over 50 years. It has also provided the relative stability that has permitted world trade to flourish.

Since the end of World War II and well before that, the United States has been a key player in advocating, negotiating, and enforcing the existing network of treaties and in building the world order they have defined. The Cold War and the shadow of nuclear weapons in some ways stunted and in some ways promoted the growth of order through treaties and institutions, but the threat of nuclear annihilation constantly dangled by a metaphorical thread, like the legendary sword of Damocles, over the survival of the human race for nearly 50 years. The end of the Cold War was the end of a 50-year migraine headache, almost certainly the greatest political development in a half-century, and possibly in all human history, given the stakes.

Since the end of the Cold War it has become the ultimate trite statement, repeated *ad nauseam*, to call the U.S. the world's lone superpower. I remember vividly the euphoria that spread over the world and especially the U.S. when the Berlin Wall fell and we all began to realize that it really is true that the Cold War is over, and the threat of nuclear annihilation has receded to the background of human affairs. I shared that feeling of joy and relief, but I also experienced a less welcome feeling of unease and discomfort.

The devil hadn't died and evil hadn't passed from the human heart, so what was the next form it would take at the global level? Were we suddenly thrust into a global utopia, a glorious and happy end of the dismal history of war and conflict? I doubted it. One of several questions that haunted me was, where would all that fear, anger, and paranoia go that Americans had focused on the Soviet Union? Would it just disappear like a mist in the morning? I didn't think so. Free-floating paranoia, like a loose cannon, is dangerous stuff. And politicians love to use fear to mobilize the public against their pet enemies and thereby attract votes. Fear, whether rational or irrational, and the politicians who exploit it were not likely to disappear.

I didn't have to wait long to find out where the free-floating paranoia would focus. Politicians had always found the bureaucracy of the U.S. Government's Executive Branch a convenient whipping boy, but something much more extreme was afoot. The extreme right formed militias and focused their hatred, fear and loathing, on the U.S. Federal Government. Waco, Ruby Ridge, and ultimately Timothy McVeigh's bombing of the Murrah Building in Oklahoma City were painful demonstrations of the effects of fear and paranoia turning on themselves, or American citizens turning on their own government.

But another focal point of hatred and fear, equally irrational but much more popular with some American politicians, was the United Nations and to a lesser extent other global organizations, the fragile and cumbersome but sometimes helpful world order that contributed to a non-catastrophic end to the Cold War. The UN became the target of those politicians of the far right who were irresponsible but not quite so radical as the militias. The U.S. virtually stopped paying its UN dues, and conservative politicians took turns using the UN as a rhetorical piñata, vying for supremacy in bashing it at every opportunity. The facts of its valuable contributions were completely submerged in the festival of scapegoating and hatred.

13

National sovereignty was the central rallying cry and motive, but a few specific issues such as funding for birth control (possibly including abortions) and hostility toward Israel in the General Assembly became grist for the powerful anger and alienation mill. The UN was portrayed as a huge, dangerously powerful organization out to control the world by mobilizing black helicopters to take over the U.S. at any moment. It was also portrayed as a weak, bloated and ineffectual bureaucracy. The two views clearly contradicted each other. The grand thinkers who projected these images could hardly be accused of suffering from consistency, the "hobgoblin of little minds."

Although there has been no explicit rhetorical attack on treaties as an object of fear or scorn, another element in the ultra-conservative hostility to the outside world was an almost complete ban on approval of multilateral treaties. The U.S. Senate has always been slow to ratify them, especially human rights treaties, but under Senator Jesse Helms's dictatorial control of the Senate Foreign Relations Committee, virtually all important multilateral treaty ratifications came to a stop. Sometimes it appeared that the more benign the treaty, the more intransigent was Helms's opposition. Although President Bill Clinton was a moderate-to-strong practitioner of global cooperation in practice, those parts of his foreign policy that required Senate approval were filtered through Jesse Helms, giving them a radical go-it-alone cast in the end.

When President George W. Bush moved into the White House, from a foreign policy point of view it was as if Jesse Helms had become President. Not only would the U.S. stiff-arm the rest of the world in its efforts to negotiate progressive treaties, but existing arms control treaties that had long served the cause of global stability would also be summarily abrogated. With regard to treaties, the stabilizing structures of global cooperation, the U.S. Government—particularly the Executive Branch—became the great wrecking ball, smashing down walls at an unprecedented pace. The rest of the world justly became alarmed.

Starting before the Bush administration but dramatically accelerating when he took office, the U.S. Government has either refused to sign, refused to ratify, "unsigned," violated, or abrogated more than thirteen major treaties, most of which were products of decades of delicate negotiations among scores of nations and many of which were especially negotiated to accommodate U.S. concerns. Several of these have been mentioned above. The following is a more complete list: the Convention to End All Forms of Discrimination Against Women (CEDAW), the Convention on the Rights of the Child, the Rome treaty establishing the International Criminal Court, the Kyoto Protocols on Global Warming, the treaty to ban landmines (Mine Ban Treaty), the Antiballistic Missile Treaty, the Comprehensive Nuclear Test Ban Treaty, the Biological Weapons Convention, the Chemical Weapons Convention, the Nuclear Nonproliferation Treaty, a protocol to strengthen the 1987 Convention Against Torture, the Law of the Sea Treaty, and the Geneva Conventions on treatment of prisoners of war.

This book delves into the pros and cons of several of these, though there is not enough space for all of them. They are all in various ways embodiments of the basic principles of human rights, justice, sustainable prosperity, peace and security, and finally, cooperation in use of two of the most vital global commons, the oceans and the atmosphere. They each represent epochal progress in human cooperation and goodwill. Rejection of a single one might be driven by concerns about specific provisions, but rejection or violation of all of them constitutes a clear and systematic negation of global moral and legal norms and progress.

In reviewing this list, we encounter the spectacle of the U.S. repeatedly standing against global progress while other nations have taken the lead and struggled to cope with American non-cooperation. In a series of positive ventures that have massive global support, the U.S. is not only failing to lead, it is refusing to cooperate. In so doing American leaders have in effect declared the country, for highly dubious reasons, to be an over-muscled maverick if not a rogue state, a nation waging an undeclared war on international law and order. This is the exact opposite of a team player or a constructive force in the world. It certainly is not the behavior of a global leader.

Patriotism and Tribalism

In conversations with friends, when I outline this record of American global non-cooperation, much of it on matters of basic moral principle, they immediately ask one question. "Why does the U.S. behave this way? Why?" They are baffled. In my experience most American citizens are genuinely horrified when they see the dots connected. Why is a nation they love and believe in, a nation that has been a global leader in establishing human rights and justice and prides itself on being peaceful, turning away from these principles and betraying them?

This question cropped up so persistently I eventually realized I would have to tackle the "why," not just the "what" of the problem. I wanted to dig deep, not just toss off glib, superficial answers. Theories of international relations are the ideological faces of something deeper—some of the most basic drives and impulses of human nature. I wanted to get at these, not just their ideological trappings.

In a very brief nutshell, the answers I've been driven to by much thought and reading are a synergism between three closely related psychological forces: (1) the negative side of tribalism or group selfishness, including outright greed and indifference to the well-being of others; (2) the temptations of excessive power, particularly military power, i.e., arrogance and willingness to use coercion and violence routinely, covering it with the fig leaf of a noble cause; and (3) a strong cultural habit of thinking and acting in terms of win-lose games, rather than win-win strategies. This latter mental habit seduces the American public and leaders into unconsciously assuming that the world is set up so that we gain at the expense of others or vice-versa; the global "pie" is fixed and therefore if others get more, we get less and vice-versa. In many cases this assumption is the exact opposite of the reality. At this stage in a crowded and deeply interdependent world, international relations must be played as a win-win game or it will inescapably become a lose-lose game.

These three forces—tribalism, the arrogance of power, and win-lose games—are deeply interrelated and work together. And they all conflict with something that seems to be still deeper in human nature, the essential humanness that moves us to empathize with others and recognize their lives as valuable, regardless of cultural, religious or national differences. The human race might well have destroyed itself by now if these benign forces had not been marginally stronger than the forces causing wars, genocides, and hatred. The universality of each of the great religions, their ability to reach across national and cultural boundaries, is based on this bedrock reality of human nature, often obscured by the viruses of tribalism, greed, racism, sexism, etc. My own view is that this essential humanness is partly spiritual, but one could argue that it is merely a biological imperative toward preservation of the whole species. Whichever way one interprets it philosophically, it is a powerful counterweight to the most destructive tendencies in human nature.

By "tribalism," I mean the negative side of a universal human impulse that expresses itself positively as group solidarity, and at the national level, as patriotism. The single most frequent criticism of this book is likely to be that it is unpatriotic to launch such a far-reaching indictment of American foreign policy. Ironically, it will be the extreme conservatives who have

16

created this tribalistic and destructive foreign policy in violation of our nation's most treasured values who will undoubtedly cry, "Unpatriotic!" They need to be reminded of some basics. First, let's consider what patriotism is and is not.

It's almost self-evident that patriotism—loyalty to one's country—its values and institutions and people, is not just a good thing; it is essential. It is vital to the health of a country and even to its survival. It is a key component in the glue that holds a country together. When patriotism declines, civil war, anarchy and the breakup of a country can readily follow. The opposite extreme from patriotism, treason—betrayal of one's country by actions such as spying for others—is justly considered one of the most heinous of crimes, comparable to mass murder. Traitors seldom get much leniency from the American judicial system. The U.S. is notable for inspiring in its citizens a strong patriotism and a sense of belonging and pride in belonging. It has led the world in establishing human rights (the Bill of Rights in the Constitution), impartial justice, and representative democracy as foundations of legitimate government. Moreover, Americans treasure these foundations. They form a solid basis for legitimate patriotism.

The U.S. has earned the loyalty of its citizens many times over by its benign and just treatment of a majority of its people. However, it's important to acknowledge terrible exceptions such as slavery before the Civil War and the Jim Crow laws after it, the genocidal treatment of Native Americans, the internment of Japanese Americans during WWII, and the long delay in giving women the vote. These ugly and major exceptions have been recognized in retrospect as deeply wrong and have been partially but not fully corrected. They have resulted in less rebellion and disloyalty on the part of the victimized populations than one might have expected, considering the nature of the offense. Having acknowledged these exceptions, it is vital to recognize again that they stand out precisely because they are exceptions to the norm in the U.S. Government's behavior toward its citizens, which is the natural foundation of American patriotism.

If some loyalty is good, isn't more loyalty better? Terms like jingoism and chauvinism remind us that the patriotism can be carried too far, like a toxic overdose of an essential vitamin. So where does genuine patriotism end and these excesses begin? I would suggest that they begin when Americans (or any group of people) think and act in terms of win-lose games in the international arena, when we begin to look for American advantage at the expense of other people and nations, and when we suppress dissent about policies that at least some Americans believe to be destructive.

Jingoism or chauvinism begins when we betray our most treasured values (all are created equal and are endowed with certain inalienable rights) using violence or economic leverage to gain advantage over other people and other nations to their disadvantage, acting as if their lives and well-being don't matter as much as ours do. When the U.S. stops being a "team player" concerned with win-win outcomes on the world stage and starts being a "me first" player—an arrogant superstar that can legitimately elbow aside lesser people and nations—jingoism and chauvinism have taken over. I would suggest that any gains made at the expense of others will in the long run generate a backlash of resentment and prove to be self-destructive. For every action there is an equal and opposite reaction. This law that governs the physical world has its own close analogy that governs the human world. Whatever a nation sows, it reaps. Only win-win gains will provide lasting benefits.

Throughout this book I use the term "tribalism" to refer generically to a deeper and more all-inclusive phenomenon than jingoism, chauvinism, or nationalism. It is the psychological root of these phenomena, plus others as well, including religious exclusiveness. National selfishness is a part of tribalism, but not the whole of it. (By the word "tribalism" I'm *not* referring merely to the divisions of people into literal extended families or tribes that arise at the earliest stages in the evolution of social complexity.) In the context of this book, by "tribalism" I mean a widespread, all-but-universal psychological and social impulse whose benign expression is the deep-seated emotional need for a sense of belonging to a larger group. The wish to get together with one's extended family for Thanksgiving dinner is a classic benign example. People are willing to spend money and time and travel great distances to fulfill this desire; it is deep rooted and powerful, no matter how urbane and sophisticated the individual may be.

The negative side of tribalism is the powerful and virtually automatic tendency to put the well-being of one's own group before the survival and well-being of other groups and their members. It is partly a result of evolution; in a cutthroat world of competing species and tribes, group cohesion and effective group defense against threats lead to group survival. Groups that don't do this successfully may not survive. So genes that promote tribalism get passed on more often, and genes that don't promote tribalism get passed on less often as less successful groups die off. As a result, the "tribalistic" impulse can be seen again and again in the animal kingdom. Viewed psychologically, tribalism in humans is also a natural projection of egotism onto the group. "We" are the good guys, but "they" are

18

the bad guys. "Our" lives matter, but "their" lives don't. "Our" prosperity matters, but "theirs" doesn't. In short, "we" are special. The group in this psychological context may be any social grouping, real or imagined—a nation, a religion or cult, a genetic or ethnic grouping, an organization, a gang, or a team involved in a sport. In the case of major groupings such as religions or nations, the implicit assumption of inequality that says "their lives don't matter" is usually unconscious; a great many people automatically act on this unstated assumption who would firmly reject it on rational grounds if it were offered to them as a proposition.

The American news media report every American death in Iraq, but certainly not every Iraqi death. During the initial fighting, counts of American deaths were routinely reported by the military and the news media. However, when asked about numbers of Iraqi deaths during the most active part of the military operation, even Colin Powell, one of the less blatantly tribalistic members of the Bush team, didn't say, as he could have, that those numbers are hard to obtain and that we're not sure what the Iraqi casualty rate is. Rather, he stated emphatically that he was not interested in a count of Iraqi deaths. Human rights groups were disturbed, but there was no great outcry against this attitude. Iraqi lives matter less, or hardly at all. Of course, the far more numerous Iraqi lives destroyed by Saddam mattered greatly; they were mourned and emphasized. Grisly pictures of Saddam's mass graves were repeatedly displayed on the U.S. news media. Those Iraqi deaths helped to demonize the enemy and support the war, so they mattered. Only when Iraqi deaths might have the effect of causing Americans to question their government's foreign policy do they not matter.

The frenzied cheering at a football game is a playful form of win-lose tribalism, not to be taken too seriously and not especially harmful to the participants. It is designed to whip up excitement and to make one feel more passionately involved in the game and the local community, maybe as an antidote to boredom. People the world over seem to love to play at tribalism by creating win-lose games and cheering one side or the other as if the fate of the world were at stake. So far, little harm is done except maybe the occasional heart attack from too much excitement or occasional rioting and destructive pranks. Paradoxically, at times win-lose games have been successfully used to cultivate peace between nations. Ping-pong was used to help bring China and the U.S. together, and soccer is helping to bring India and Pakistan together. But the malevolent extreme of tribalism has motivated some of the worst crimes ever perpetrated by human beings, the wars and genocides in which national, "racial" or religious groups try to annihilate or totally subdue and enslave an "out group" of heretics or hated nationalities or "races."

In this context, jingoism or chauvinism can be seen as destructive or toxic tribalism applied to the nation-state. A number of ultra-conservative American leaders have a bad case, judging from their behavior, though their rhetoric is too politically correct to expose the full extent of it. Universal opposition by extreme conservatives to almost every multilateral treaty being hammered out by the international community (including efforts by negotiators from the U.S.), no matter how benign and principled the treaty, is just as eloquent a statement of jingoism in its less-visible way as would be an impassioned speech denouncing foreigners or foreign influences. It is jingoism flying under the radar screen of political correctness.

Religious fanaticism that motivates terrorism, genocide, or religious wars is an all-too-common instance in which religion is infested with an acute case of the virus of tribalism. This is the virus that infects Osama bin Laden and his followers and that drove Christians to commit the atrocities of the Spanish Inquisition and the Crusades. (The two are linked; the Muslim world has a long historical memory, and many see the American wars in Afghanistan and Iraq and its support for Israel as modern revivals of the medieval crusades.)

It cannot be emphasized enough that religion itself does not create these horrors. All the great religions of the world have attracted millions of adherents in a variety of countries and cultural contexts precisely because these religions are essentially universalist, valuing the lives and well-being of all human beings, rather than tribalist, valuing only a certain group. When tribalism infects religions and is used as a rationale to kill "infidels" or "heretics," it is acting like a virus in a computer. It commandeers religious symbols, beliefs, and rituals (key elements of the operating system) and perverts them to bring about the exact opposite of their intended use. It generates cruelty, killing and conquering instead of the intended products of religion—kindness, respect, and justice.

"Win-Win" or "Win-Lose"?

An important source of power for the United States, perhaps the most important of all, is the attractiveness of American values. The political advantage of this attractive force is diffuse; it can be difficult to quantify and to use politically in a focused way. Yet it constitutes a background, a context, for more specific actions and events. Perhaps for this reason Joseph Nye has labeled it "soft power" in his notable book, *The Paradox of American Power: Why the World's Only Superpower Can't Go it Alone.*[7] I find the term "soft power" unfortunate since the word "soft" implies weakness in most contexts. Mr. Nye clearly does not intend to convey weakness by this term. He simply uses it for contrast with the "hard" power of military force. One of the purposes of his book is to emphasize the neglected importance of this dimension of American power and show how we are in fact contradicting and squandering this legacy of goodwill with our arrogance and over-use of military power.

The power of higher values than national egomania and greed is often denied or ignored in foreign policy theory. Much of this theory has an extremely Machiavellian flavor, particularly in the "realist" school that focuses exclusively on ruthless and amoral power-jockeying among the nations that are major global powers. Along with neoconservatism, which touts itself as a more moral alternative but advocates violence as a means toward benign ends, this kind of thinking is influential in the foreign policy outlook of many who call the shots in current U.S. foreign policy. However, higher values than greed and raw coercive power are far from weak. Values are the foundation of human action, the wellspring of human motivation. They drive all action, including the use of military force and the patriotism that keeps countries united. When the U.S. acts internationally in ways that violate the values it claims to treasure domestically, not only is the hypocrisy evident and grating to the rest of the world, but support for U.S. actions comes grudgingly, if at all. Under these conditions coalitions are harder to build and more fragile, and support for U.S. proposals in the UN quickly fades away.

The Paradox of American Power makes a convincing case that the U.S. will lose the multi-dimensional chess game in the international arena if we ignore the vital dimension of power that stems from the attractiveness of our values. When those same values—justice, human rights, democracy, etc.— manifest in the international arena, we trample on them at our peril. Nye makes a valid and terribly important point. However, in calling attention to this danger he uses as his central metaphor a win-lose game, chess. The title of the book focuses on power, reinforcing the image of a win-lose power game that the U.S. should play to win, using our values as a weapon of seduction along with our more coercive hard power. The call to emphasize and use the attractive power of our values and to avoid overusing coercion and military force, which contradict and undermine the attractive power of our values, is the admirable core of Nye's message. I agree with it heartily and recommend it highly.

However, this basic win-lose metaphor and orientation, which is almost universal in American foreign policy thinking, is both misleading and extremely dangerous. Win-lose thinking is one of the root causes of our increasing political isolation from the rest of the world. In a tightly interdependent world, the most powerful nation playing win-lose games (as with the Kyoto Protocols on Global Warming) creates an all-around destructive lose-lose game for everyone.

In his fascinating book, *Nonzero*, Richard Wright tracks the effects of win-win versus win-lose survival "games" through millions of years of biological evolution and thousands of years of human evolution. He shows convincingly that the major advances in complex cooperation among cells, organisms, and finally human societies, are instances of win-win cooperation rather than destructive win-lose or lose-lose competition. Among human societies, the modern nation-state is a fairly new invention, less than three hundred years old. This invention is hugely successful and popular because it has empowered large numbers of people over large land areas to cooperate in ways that produce mutual benefit. A national government exists primarily to pool human resources for cooperative, win-win public enterprises such as schools, police, hospitals, equitable markets, hydropower and irrigation projects, national defense, and so on.

Of course, this is not to say that win-lose competition has no place within a nation. In the Darwinian struggle for survival among competing businesses, win-lose competition is still the predominant mode of operation. The beneficial result is that only strong performers, the most successful businesses, survive. The winnowing out of relative losers has an energizing, if harsh effect overall on economic activity. Lacking this bracing dynamic, communist countries allow appalling inefficiencies to go on indefinitely. The results stifle initiative and cripple effectiveness in delivering economic benefits to their citizens. So the interaction between benign win-lose, or zero-sum dynamics and win-win, or nonzero sum dynamics is a complex one. I am not arguing that all win-lose competition is bad, by any means.

At the global level, we still cling to intractable and destructive forms of win-lose competition between nations. Some nations stay poor; others get rich. The poor ones don't thereby cease to exist, as businesses do. They just become huge problems. Some nations gain power at the expense of others. At worst, wars result. And wars increasingly have become lose-lose games in which vast resources and countless human lives are wasted by both sides to the ultimate benefit of neither. Human misery is the main end-product of wars. The realignments of power they produce are temporary because they are brought about by coercion rather than voluntary cooperation; they don't last. They set the world up for the next round of war.

With fast-growing realities such as proliferation of weapons of mass destruction and the industrial capacity to destroy the planet's ecosystem, it's becoming clear that the overarching challenge for the human race for the next century is to develop global win-win relationships between nations and within nations that permit successful management of the planet for the benefit of all. This goal may sound utopian, but a few moments of thought will reveal it to be a stark necessity. And carrying it out, as we must, will always be a work in progress. There will never be a utopian end-point, an "end of history," in this monumental task. The task is much bigger and more difficult at the global level than at the regional or national level, but not much different in principle from governing a large nation-state, a task which is always a work in progress.

Essentially, the logic or principle behind this imperative to successful planetary management is simple. The more interdependent the parts of a system are, the more cooperation and coordination among them becomes the road to success and the more problematic failures of cooperation become. In a tightly and complexly linked system, conflict and isolation are roads to failure and breakdown. This basic principle applies to the world as a whole in the long run, no less than to the United States and Europe. The world as a whole, economically and ecologically, is becoming extremely tightly linked. If we, the U.S., trash the global environment, everybody loses, Americans included. If we resist the establishment of legal and institutional mechanisms to improve cooperation, we undermine the functioning of the entire system, and in the end adversely affect ourselves as well as others. If we initiate destabilizing wars in the name of a theoretical self-defense against possible future hazards, the resulting instability causes everybody to lose, including the U.S.

Just as the American colonies once united for mutual benefit, with huge beneficial consequences for themselves and the world, so the European nations have traveled far in the past fifty years in institutionalizing a new win-win game among themselves. In the evolving European Union they pool their power and some degree of sovereignty to achieve mutually beneficial goals they could not hope to achieve alone. As a result, the kind of war among the European nations that twice devastated the world in the first half of the twentieth century is now unthinkable.

This sensible approach to international power and cooperation horrifies conservatives in the U.S. who seem obsessed with national sovereignty and win-lose games among nations, as if these were guarantors of human freedom rather than the guarantors of chaos and misery they have proven to be. But the kind of systematic cooperation Europe is exploring and the U.S. established among its own states at its founding over two centuries ago is bound to be the wave of the future in an increasingly interdependent world. Contrasting Europe with the U.S., Zbigniew Brzezinski suggests, "Imbued with neither missionary zeal nor self-righteous fanaticism, the Europe of tomorrow could become the example of, as well as the impulse for, the responsible multilateralism the world ultimately needs."[8]

The success of this approach is demonstrated by the strong desire of Eastern European countries and Turkey to join the European Union. Their primary concern is not fear of some external tyranny, but rather, they long for the economic benefits conferred by the union. At the global level the benefits of increasing political union are also demonstrated by the virtually universal practice of applying for membership in the UN by new nations who are seeking to establish their legitimacy and integration into the international scene. They prefer the benefits of inclusion to the "freedom" of exclusion. At the opposite extreme, when a nation such as North Korea isolates itself, its isolation is disastrous in every respect.

The dominant pre-World War I and II paradigm of nation-states in cutthroat competition and often on the verge of war will eventually have to yield to a new paradigm of global cooperation in which nations agree to establish supra-national institutions and laws to solve intractable global problems such as terrorism, global warming, war, genocide, and the proliferation of weapons of mass destruction. These problems cannot be solved by individual nations working separately and at cross-purposes. This change is already taking place at the global level on multiple fronts, but the U.S. is dragging its feet, and often aggressively blocking progress. For the longer term the existing institutional mechanisms such as the UN and the cumbersome treaty-making traditions of international law will prove too weak, too slow, and too undemocratic for efficient and effective progress. Still, these mechanisms are better than nothing, and they're all we have at present.

Is "Human Nature" the Problem?

It is worth digressing for a moment to note that a popular, simplistic response to major global evils such as war, anarchy, genocide, terrorism, industrial pollution and the like is that "you can't change human nature," i.e., human nature is inherently evil and is the root cause of all problems. The implication or assertion is that legal and institutional structures are not the problem and cannot affect it; the problem is basic human nature. It creates all the other problems. Only by a miraculous change in the world or in the natures of individuals (usually the idea is by religious conversion) can we change the world.

One extreme variation of this view is the apocalyptic religious belief of a significant minority of American citizens. They strongly disagree with the claim that it's up to us humans (guided by God, if you're a theist) to use our own free choice to create a better world. They believe that all such human effort is to no avail because of the irretrievable evil of human nature and the imminent "second coming of Christ." They envision this highly dramatic, miraculous external event—the rapture—as taking the form of people suddenly disappearing from cars, airplanes, and desk chairs along with Christ's dramatic appearance in the sky and other wondrous events. The world as it is presently set up will abruptly end with various unpleasant after-effects for those who are left behind. Apparently millions of Americans believe this.

A series of six novels about these projected events is said to have sold some fifty million copies. In these novels the United Nations is pictured as the Antichrist. As the term hints, the UN plays a rather less than constructive role in the world, its remarkable record of humanitarian aid and its negotiations of over 100 peace treaties forgotten or ignored. One wishes that people were better able to distinguish between fiction and reality, and between the profound religious symbolism in the Bible and literal fact. This apocalyptic belief system is not only radically disconnected from reality; it is very unhelpful in establishing the kind of civilization we need to build in order to manage the planet we live on. But like black helicopters and fantasized UN takeovers of the U.S., it actually, and tragically, affects votes.

Aside from apocalyptic visions, there is an important germ of truth in the belief that human nature, collectively, is the root of the problem. It might be instructive to illustrate with a thought experiment positing two extreme examples. One example, a nation or a world populated by nothing but violent and undisciplined thugs, would certainly be a chaotic, essentially

25

ungovernable mess. No set of institutions could rescue such a population from self-created chaos. In order to prosper, successful societies rely completely on a strong majority of voluntarily law-abiding citizens. At the opposite extreme, a (hypothetical) nation or world populated by saints would be easily governed by democratic means. It would still need a government; even saints need agreed-upon rules to guide their voluntary cooperation. Even saints disagree sometimes among themselves, as the early history of the Christian church demonstrates. But a world of saints wouldn't need jails and it certainly would avoid wars. So human nature—whether corrupted or exalted or somewhere in between—does of course have a profound effect on the nature of a society and of the world.

It is also vital to recognize that without religion there would be a lot more thugs and a lot fewer saints and law abiding citizens in the world. Religions provide widespread beliefs and practices that promote cooperative behavior; they are critically important to human civilization. However, most nations and the world as a whole contain a mixture of thugs and saints and a majority of people in between. Turning everybody into saints may be a splendid goal (aside from the idea that it can be done by proselytizing for a particular religion) but it is not going to happen any time soon. As a solution to immediate problems, it is not an option. For the longer term, we can all hope and pray. For the shorter term, we need to organize our ordinary, non-saintly selves for improved global cooperation and democratic international order.

The answer to the problem of social disorder, "It's just human nature," fails to explain why we had two world wars in the first half of the twentieth century and none in the second half. It fails to explain why we have (relatively) successful nations as well as failed nations. Despite cultural differences, *essential* human nature is the same in different countries. Yet some countries succeed and others fail. Predominantly secular nations such as those of Western Europe succeed as well as more religious nations such as the U.S. Some of the successes and failures can be explained by natural resources and location (e.g., whether a country has a temperate climate, fertile farmland, and/or a port on an ocean). But other critical differences between nations are their governments and economies. These differences are structural. Structural factors (democracy, adequate security, orderly business practices, etc.) have the huge advantage of being partially controllable by human action, and provide far better explanations for the observable successes and failures of societies than do individual good or evil, though these play a part.

It is helpful to recognize that there is a powerful interplay between governmental and economic structures and civic virtue. A relatively well-ordered, prosperous society such as the United States or Finland tends to produce a population that is, on the whole, law-abiding. There is little incentive to the contrary. In such a society it "pays" to obey the law and does not "pay" to violate it. People learn and adapt accordingly.

Contrast these countries with a chaotic society such as Haiti, in which people struggle desperately for survival and grab however they can the minimal necessities like food and clothing. Desperately poor and disorganized societies like this more often produce people who are easily bribed or tempted to steal; citizens and officials alike are corrupted by their harsh environment. If survival depends on looting or bribery, it's obvious who's going to still be standing at the end of the day. Under these circumstances, converting people to a particular set of religious beliefs would probably do little (at least in the short run) to change the dire poverty and systemic corruption within which they struggle to survive. Haiti's elected leader, Aristide, was a priest but in the context of a country all but impossible to lead, he apparently succumbed to the temptations of corruption to maintain power.

The key point here is that "human nature" is not incorrigible; people are trained by their environments to practice greater or lesser degrees of integrity and willingness to function as law-abiding citizens. An environment can shape people for better or for worse.

The same observations are true at the planetary level. Where human civilization at the global level lacks the legal and institutional tools to solve certain key global problems, these problems will remain unsolved and will wreak havoc, regardless of how good or evil individuals or even nations may be. Moreover, the havoc these global problems wreak will inevitably corrupt people. For example, national leaders do violent things in reaction to terrorism, vainly hoping thereby to prevent further terrorism. It doesn't work. Israel's endless round of tit-for-tat violence is the most obvious and tragic example. Eventually the Israelis and the Palestinians will have to negotiate peace. The killing doesn't get them there. Similarly, at the global level wars and genocides will never solve the problems of how to achieve peace. Only structural agreements among groups of people—treaties and governments— will do that. The global problems haunting the world are not just matters of passing circumstance that will blow over, given enough time and a little luck. They are also not results of people failing to adhere to a particular religion, Christian, Muslim, or whatever. The more time passes without dealing with

27

global headaches as the structural problems they are, the more acute they become.

Trashing Our Values

In more specific terms than the brief sketch earlier in this chapter, how does U.S. foreign policy relate to American values? A few examples: Americans believe deeply in human rights, enshrined in the Bill of Rights as an integral part of our Constitution, yet the U.S. Senate has refused to ratify two of the most important human rights treaties of our time, the treaties on the rights of women and of children. Americans believe deeply in justice, but the Bush administration has launched a determined battle to destroy an epoch-making improvement in international justice, the International Criminal Court.

Americans want reasonable protection for the environment, on which we and all human beings depend for our lives, our health, and our economic well-being. We recognize that to destroy the earth's environment is to destroy the physical foundation of all prosperity and even life itself, and to rob our children and grandchildren of a life-giving heritage. Yet the pattern of our government's lone-wolf foreign policy includes rejection of a particularly vital treaty accepted by our allies and most of the other nations of the world, a treaty to head off one of the most dangerous environmental threats of our time, global warming. This rejected treaty is, of course, the Kyoto Protocols on global warming.

Americans want peace, but the pattern of our government's lone-ranger foreign policy includes starting an unnecessary war (euphemistically called a "war of choice"), refusing to pay U.S. dues to the United Nations for over a decade, and refusing to participate fully in almost all peacekeeping functions of the UN. This fact stands contrary to the popular myth that the U.S. military is inundated with peacekeeping missions. We do have one lone individual engaged in UN peacekeeping. We do some other peacekeeping, not for the UN but under NATO auspices in Bosnia and Kosovo, but that's about it. Our military is spread out all over the world, but we seldom do peacekeeping. Virtually all UN peacekeeping is done by other nations, not the U.S.

Even in Afghanistan, after the coalition of the U.S. and the Afghan Northern Alliance took it over from the Taliban, the U.S. has refused to do peacekeeping and nation-building work outside of the capital, Kabul. This refusal has caused serious detrimental effects on the stability of the country and its economic viability. It is fast returning to the warlords, the drug lords, and the poppy growers.

Despite our citizens' desire for peace and the widespread recognition that mutual arms reductions are a part of the road to peace, America's post-Cold War foreign policy includes abdication or violation of many of the great disarmament treaties of the past few decades, including the Nuclear Nonproliferation Treaty, the Comprehensive Test Ban Treaty, the Anti-Ballistic Missile Treaty, the Chemical Weapons Convention, the Biological Weapons Convention, and the treaty banning anti-personnel landmines. Our current leaders, judging from their actions and not their words, are determined to ignore or eliminate the disarmament efforts of the past, and in the process to risk accelerating the arms races that plagued the world during the Cold War. Rather than a "Let's establish more peaceful relations with our neighbors" initiative, the theory seems to be, "Let's exploit our huge advantage in military power and make sure everybody else lives in fear of us." Needless to say, this approach reduces trust and provides a motive for other countries to arm themselves and do everything they can, covertly of course, to weaken the U.S. It creates a lose-lose game in which everyone has to spend more on armaments and everyone is less secure from war.

Actions speak louder than words. The track record of post-Cold War American foreign policy as shown above, astonishingly places the U.S., in substantive action if not in rhetoric, against human rights, against international justice, against peacekeeping, against environmental protection, against global progress in disarmament, and in favor of initiating preventive wars in circumstances other than self-defense and without regard to the collective security apparatus of the UN—an absolute requirement of international law absent external aggression.

Henry Kissinger points out the following factual information: "America is engaged in a wide range of activities in the name of democracy and human rights. It publishes annual reports on the human rights record of every country in the world; it expresses public opinions on the democratic and human rights shortcomings of even permanent U.N. Security Council members; it applies Congressionally mandated sanctions; it has gone to war in Bosnia and Kosovo over human rights issues; it invaded Iraq in part to bring about regime change."[9]

However, a deeper look at this list from the point of view of global cooperation in human rights tells a less-than-totally upbeat story. The annual human rights report he refers to is an admirable effort, but it has some serious drawbacks. Rather than being done by an unbiased private sector or international organization, it is an American evaluation of other countries, as if the U.S. were impartial in its judgments and were in a morally superior position to judge others. In the report the shortcomings of our friends and allies are apt to be soft-pedaled, and those of our enemies and rivals are more likely to be sharply condemned. Our own human rights violations such as the detention of people without recourse to legal services in Guantanamo Bay are hardly likely to be given any attention at all. As a result, the report is an irritant to the international community. Our outrageous violations of human rights in the prisons of Iraq, notably Abu Ghraib, may make the continuance of this report impossible, a subject of extreme ridicule and revulsion.

The congressionally mandated sanctions are also irritants, and aside from the irritation have little effect except on American businesses, since the sanctioned countries simply move on to do business with other countries or if they must, to buy U.S. products through third parties. Unilateral economic sanctions generally don't work. Regarding Kissinger's mention of the Iraq war, it was indeed launched partly to bring about regime change, but also it was launched in clear violation of international law and in the teeth of overwhelmingly adverse global public opinion.

From the items on Kissinger's list of American human rights efforts, it is clear that only in Bosnia and Kosovo did the U.S. proceed in a way that was not tainted by moral posturing and obvious self-interest, and was appreciated as a part of a cooperative effort by the rest of the world. It should be acknowledged that the Kosovo intervention was enacted without a UN mandate, so technically it was illegal under NATO's and the UN's charters. However, the morality of the Kosovo intervention was widely accepted, in contrast to the intervention in Iraq. In the other instances, American leaders have taken an arrogant, go-it-alone approach and as a result have done the country, the cause of human rights, and the world little good in the process. In the same article, Kissinger acknowledges "widespread international criticism that charges us with hegemonic power and missionary crusading spirit." With this dubious list of positive accomplishments, intended by Kissinger to counter the criticism, it's no wonder.

This total pattern of our current leaders' behavior, as summarized in this book, defies interpretation as anything other than a systematic attack, driven by tribalistic feeling, the arrogance of power, and win-lose thinking, on American values as they apply to the world outside the U.S. This assault is directed toward multilateral treaties and toward the fragile and embryonic structures of international law and global order the U.S. and the rest of the world have worked to build for over half a century. Our leaders' across-the-

30

board resistance to global institutional cooperation and progress contrasts sharply with the preferences and values of the American public, as shown by numerous polls—scientifically designed to be unbiased—by multiple pollsters.[10] The contrast between what Americans believe and what our leaders do is so dramatic it represents a clear failure of representative democracy in the United States. There is simply no way to reconcile the values and beliefs of a majority of Americans with the overall pattern of the U.S. Government's international action since the end of the Cold War.

Moral Progress: Where Moral and Practical Converge

The bases of a concern for a strengthened global legal and political order are not merely moral; they are also deeply practical. They constitute a key arena where morality and practicality converge. Despite the jingoism of the "America first" crowd, the value of human life does not stop at the borders of the United States. All human life is valuable and interconnected. When American behavior on the international scene ignores this basic fact, the U.S. suffers adverse practical consequences in the long run. Referring to terrorism, philosopher Peter Singer writes, "For the rich nations not to take a global ethical viewpoint has long been seriously morally wrong. Now it is also, in the long term, a danger to their security."[11] I would add that serious moral wrongs always undermine a nation's security in the long run. Security is not just about armed guards in airports. Practicality and morality cannot be divorced, though they are sometimes in tension as pressures for expedient action clash with the long-run view.

September 11 demonstrated that the U.S. cannot forever thrive as one of two or three islands (along with Europe and the Pacific Rim) of security and prosperity in a chaotic and desperate world. America's disproportionate military and economic power will not last forever and even now cannot protect Americans from global threats such as terrorism, global monetary instability, and planet-wide environmental degradation. Coercive use of our disproportionate power works against our long-term interests by alienating our allies, intensifying the hostility of our enemies, and weakening the web of laws and institutions that is gradually moving the world toward a more democratic, stable and just order.

Setbacks there may be in this global moral and legal progress, and sometimes, to my dismay as a loyal American citizen, the setbacks are driven by U.S. policy. But moral progress, despite the setbacks, constitutes a strong trend spanning decades, even centuries. Two illustrations of this claim of a trend will suffice. There are many more.

One obvious example of moral progress is the history of slavery. Though there are still a few horrifying examples of it at the beginning of the 21st century, it is illegal everywhere and is a crime fought by most nation-states and by international institutions. Recent horrific evidence of international trafficking in women for sex slavery has demonstrated that slavery still exists, but it is under siege. By contrast, not so long ago in broad historic terms, it was a legally accepted institution enshrined in American laws and defended from church pulpits in the United States. Progress in overcoming it involved the devastating ordeal of a Civil War that claimed hundreds of thousands of American lives. This war was followed by decades of subsequent struggle against Jim Crow laws, segregation, and lynchings. But in the end, the moral wrongs of slavery and racism were widely recognized as wrongs and began to be rooted out of American life, laws, and institutions. There is a great deal of work yet to be done. Nevertheless, it would be strange indeed to view these changes as anything other than progress, and specifically, moral progress, not just a morally neutral political trend.

Another more global example of moral progress, one at the level of worldwide agreement on moral principles, is the development of the Universal Declaration of Human Rights (UDHR). Shortly after the United Nations was founded with strong U.S. leadership (this founding itself an example of the kind of progress I'm illustrating), Eleanor Roosevelt was appointed a U.S. Representative to that institution. She led the difficult political struggle to draft and eventually secure approval of the UDHR among UN member nations.

This noble declaration of principle has become the world's "Bill of Rights," a basic legal foundation for virtually all subsequent human rights treaties. It has also been incorporated by reference as a bill of rights into the constitutions of dozens of nations. Obviously not all these nations consistently practice the principles outlined in the UDHR. However, in each of these countries it is and will remain a standard reference point in legal action just as the Bill of Rights in the American Constitution is a key reference point for American lawsuits. Progress in implementing it is and will be gradual and intermittent, proceeding one lawsuit at a time, but such progress tends to be a one-way street toward improvement. It is a work not for the days and weeks but for the decades and centuries.

Furthermore, at the level of moral principle, the establishment of the Universal Declaration of Human Rights has once and for all refuted the philosophical concept of total cultural relativism in matters of ethics and morality. Its adoption has shown that some things are recognized as right and wrong in all cultures. There may be endless varieties of marital and family arrangements and sexual morays, infinite varieties of business practices, and so on, among different cultures. However, certain moral basics are universal, or at least are matters of strong and growing consensus.

Any philosopher or anthropologist who denies this fact and claims that right and wrong are entirely culturally relative is ignoring plain fact and 20th century history. What is more, the international moral and legal consensus on basic rights and wrongs advanced by the UDHR is growing steadily as international human rights law becomes further elaborated. Additional treaties further defining human rights and wrongs are constantly being drafted and agreed upon by the international community. This growing consensus and its legal implementation constitute one of the kinds of moral progress to which I refer throughout this book. Two of the latest are the treaties on the rights of women and children. As noted before, the U.S. stands alone among democracies in refusing to ratify them.

Connecting the Dots

Ironically, for years this anti-cooperative foreign policy pattern of America's leaders went largely unnoticed by the news media and hence the American public. No one who was reaching the public connected the dots and pointed out the pattern. However, after the run-up to the Iraq war, the pattern became too obvious to ignore. The U.S. could not get UN sanction for the war and found itself opposed by most countries. The U.S. was clearly isolated. So at last the pattern was observed and discussed in venues such as the in-depth interviews on the Charlie Rose TV show and the op-ed pages of the newspapers. However, these kinds of venues for in-depth consideration of issues hold the attention of only a small fraction of Americans. The run-up to the presidential election in November 2004 has further raised the visibility of these issues to some extent.

The Iraq war showed too clearly to be ignored that America's leaders believe, or act as if they believe, the country can take major actions that ignore international law and the consensus among other nations. The mounting number of nations whose leaders succumbed to bullying and "joined" the coalition supporting the war fooled only those who were desperate for evidence to support their preconceived notions. Stated a bit more bluntly, the attitude of American leaders in going into Iraq was "To heck with you, we'll do as we jolly well please. If you don't like it, you can take your marbles and go live on some other planet. Get out of our way. We're so powerful you can't stop us from doing whatever we want." It is, in short, the attitude and behavior of a bully.

This harsh formulation may not be the intended message, but it is certainly the message that comes across. It is the perspective of a spoiled child with too much power. It creates increasing political isolation for the U.S. in an increasingly interdependent world, and increasing resentment against the U.S. in all parts of the world, even among our closest allies. Resentment has consequences. It motivates terrorism, decreases our national security and generates roadblocks to our efforts to achieve our goals. It even has the potential to create a drag on the war on terrorism, which requires close cooperation with other nations.

The practical consequences of giving the U.S. a bad name in the eyes of the rest of the world go farther than creating resentment and diminished cooperation. Since these policies are deeply out of kilter with a growing worldwide consensus on values, to get its way the U.S. is forced to rely more and more on arm-twisting, bribing and bullying other nations to create reluctant acquiescence in overriding a deep-seated sense of right and wrong in their people and their leaders. In short, this pattern pushes the U.S. into a vicious circle of ugly and brutish behavior that demands that other countries violate their values.

A case in point is the failure of efforts by American leaders to induce our ally, Turkey, to provide a military base for the U.S. war in Iraq. Turkey has become a somewhat shaky democracy, partly at our insistence. Then, as the Iraq war approached, we turned around and insisted that its government support a war the Turkish people overwhelmingly opposed. As a result of public resistance, Turkey's parliament could not muster a majority for cooperation in the war despite heavy-handed American economic pressure and withdrawal of millions in American aid. After the war, Paul Wolfowitz, Deputy Secretary of Defense, railed at Turkey for this decision, saying that the Turkish military should have been more involved in the decision. In other words, after having been in the past pressured by the U.S. to become more democratic, Turkey should have reverted to authoritarian practices and acted like a military dictatorship to support the U.S. war effort. What's wrong with this picture? Not only our enemies, but also our traditional allies are becoming concerned, even alarmed, by the moral contradictions of our government's actions.

Two Views of the World

There are two contrasting visions of the world in its present state, and both are half-truths. One is reflected in the powerful trend of U.S. foreign policy toward dominance in a lawless, anarchic world. We must defend ourselves against even distant possible future threats; we don't always have time for other countries to get on board. Acting this way creates a self-fulfilling prophecy; the world becomes more lawless and anarchic. The alternative vision promotes cooperation, human rights, justice, and sustainable prosperity in an increasingly lawful and orderly world. This is a much slower and more difficult path. But the world's most powerful nation acting on this theory as often as possible promotes the further development of such a world. Because of its hugely disproportionate military and economic might, more than any other nation the U.S. has the power to influence which of these two kinds of worlds we will live in for the foreseeable future.

Of course coercion sometimes has to be used to roll back aggression, as in the first Gulf War (done under UN sanction to reverse Iraq's takeover of Kuwait, and therefore legal under international law), or to break up the home base of a terror network that had attacked the U.S., as we did in legitimate self-defense in Afghanistan. However, the U.S. can and should be looking for opportunities to build up international law, institutions, and cooperation rather than tearing them down. The coercive policies of "America the almighty" promote an anarchic world where our military and economic power place us in a position of overt dominance, and place the rest of the world in a *de facto* position of resentful and only partial submission.

At first thought, it seems strange to American citizens that U.S. foreign policy has been systematically tearing down much of the structure of international law and institutions we built up since the end of WWII and to some extent before that. The question "How is this happening in a democracy?" looms large in the minds of the people with whom I talk. Why doesn't our policy reflect the views and values of the American public? And what can we do to change it? I wrote this book driven by the conviction that it's time someone challenged the policies and did the necessary research and thinking to propose answers to these questions.

---

[1] London Review of Books (Vol. 24 No. 19) 3 October 2002
[2] Jessica Matthews, "Estranged Partners," *Foreign Policy* Nov./Dec. 2001
[3] Idem.

[4] Jimmy Carter, "The Troubling New Face of America," *The Washington Post*, Sept. 5, 2002.
[5] Stanley Hoffman, *Primacy or World Order: American Foreign Policy Since the Cold War*. N.Y., McGraw Hill Book Company, 1978.
[6] For the uninitiated, "multilateral" means treaties with many other countries, not just one other country. These agreements include human rights treaties, global arms control treaties and the charters of international organizations, among others.
[7] Joseph S. Nye, Jr., *The Paradox of American Power: Why the World's Only Superpower Can't Go It Alone*. N.Y., Oxford University Press, 2002.
[8] Zbigniew Brzezinski, *The Choice: Global Dominance or Global Leadership*, N.Y., Basic Books, 2004 p. 96.
[9] Henry Kissinger, "Intervention with a Vision" *The Washington Post,* April 11, 2004.
[10] The results of these polls are presented in some detail in the chapter, "The UN: Angel or Devil?"
[11] Peter Singer, *One World: The Ethics of Globalization*, Yale University Press, New Haven, Connecticut 2002, p. 13)

Chapter Two

THE STRUCTURES OF GREED AND TRIBALISM

Nothing can distort the true picture of conditions and events in this world more than to regard one's own country as the center of the universe, and to view all things solely in their relationship with this fixed point.

—Emery Reves

A majority of Americans are tolerant and principled and therefore prefer a cooperative, rather than a domineering and unprincipled foreign policy. So why don't their views and preferences prevail in a democracy? To answer this question requires delving into problems with the structure of the American political system, as well as some very uncomfortable truths about greed, the predominance of corporate business interests, and even bizarre distortions of religion in the U.S. We cannot hope to decipher the mystery of why our noble values and our government's current ignoble policies are at so odds without casting a harsh light on some of the darker corners of our cultural and national life. For some, this may make unpleasant reading.

Benjamin Barber's eloquent book, *Jihad vs. McWorld*, portrays a world in which ancient religious passions, values, and tribal loyalties which he calls "Jihad," (a much broader concept of the word than the usual narrow definition, "holy war") clash with the relentless materialism and standardization of global capitalism, to which he gives the shorthand label, "McWorld." In much of the world, especially the Muslim world, these forces are at least partially at odds with one another. Osama bin Laden engages in terrorism in Saudi Arabia, not only in the United States, because the Saudi royal family cooperates with "McWorld" in crucial matters such as selling Saudi oil to the United States, the country that is the financial backer of

Israel, and in the process compromises his extremist vision of Islam. In the U.S., the relationship between ultra-conservative religion and "McWorld" could hardly be more different.

Rather than contrast and conflict, in the U.S. we have an alliance of "McWorld" with "Jihad," of corporate power with extreme fundamentalist religion. Recognizing the reality of this strange alliance can carry us a good part of the way toward understanding why our foreign policy is so out of kilter with the values of most Americans and the rest of the world. Stated more fully and explicitly, at present the U.S. Government is heavily influenced, if not controlled, by an alliance of a *de facto* aristocracy of immense corporate wealth, power, and privilege ("McWorld") in combination with the tribalistic and rigidly legalistic religious outlook ("Jihad") of Christian fundamentalism. To get the picture, think of two examples: Vice President Dick Cheney's corporate background and loyalties and Attorney General Ashcroft's low-key but relentlessly consistent religious zealotry.

To grasp the depth of this alliance at the current center of American power, think of President George W. Bush's combination of the two: his family dynasty's oil wealth and political clout and his personal ultra-conservative religious views, often driving him to see only good and evil, black and white. He fails to see realistically a world where there are in reality endless shades of gray and a rainbow of other colors suggesting a diversity that is neither good nor evil. Conservative religion typically calls for punishment of evil rather than any resort to compassion or compromise. Hence war is more appealing than negotiation. A favorite Bush theme is that one must not "compromise with evil." However, we do of course compromise; we make friends with Uzbekistan and establish military bases there despite the country's appalling human rights record including such acts as boiling political prisoners alive.

Together these elements of President Bush's personal makeup, an entrenched and unthinking loyalty to a social class of wealth and power, plus an unthinking religious viewpoint that denies the real world's endless shades of gray, provide a snapshot of the dual phenomenon of religious tribalism or "Jihad" in full alliance with "McWorld," rolled up into one strategically central person. The combination goes a long way to explain why he had the backing—despite his personal limitations—that propelled him into the White House. However, this one person is smaller than the tip of the iceberg, he is the tip of the tip of the iceberg. The iceberg itself is a combination of corporate wealth throughout America and fundamentalist churches and other organizations that have become the centers of political energy and rhetoric required to keep the faithful in line with the political agenda.

The Pentagon of Power

Another, more coherent American power structure relevant to the "why" question is the sprawling economic and political powerhouse Dwight D. Eisenhower warned us about, the military-industrial complex. The U.S. military establishment with its $400 billion budget, its many far-reaching civilian arms—i.e., military contractors—and its dependent friends in the House and Senate, is by far the single most powerful political entity in the U.S. and therefore, the world. It has a clear focal point in the Secretary of Defense, and strong tentacles in Congress and in state governments. Its money, manpower, and political clout through defense contracts and bases in key states and congressional districts dwarf every other political force in the country. Civilian pork barrel spending is measured in the millions of dollars; military pork is counted in the billions. The Defense Department's budget is larger than the defense budgets of most of the world's other countries combined. And its budget is half the discretionary budget of the U.S., dwarfing other high priority concerns such as education, health care, and even homeland security.

By contrast with Defense, the State Department, established by the Constitution to manage U.S. foreign affairs, has a minute budget and no constituency among the American people. When the State Department and the Pentagon clash in developing foreign policy, the Pentagon, with its vastly superior resources and political clout, is likely to win. The struggle between the two titans, Secretary of State Colin Powell and Defense Secretary Donald Rumsfeld, over whether to launch a war against Iraq was an uneven contest, despite Secretary Powell's exceptional abilities.

I should digress for a moment to emphasize that professional military personnel are not the problem, or at most are a modest part of the problem. To demonize them would be to confuse the issue profoundly. The run-up to the Iraq war was not caused by any warlike tendency on the part of our professional military leaders. Their civilian political leaders did it all. The military leaders were reputed to be quietly reluctant. But there is little doubt that the disproportionate power and resources of the U.S. military and the tendency of civilian political appointees in the Pentagon to overuse this power contributed substantially, if not decisively, to the decision to attack Iraq despite its lack of connection with anti-American terrorism and 9/11 and despite the weakness of the evidence that Saddam had weapons of mass destruction.

The military professionals on active duty in the Pentagon could not publicly oppose the hawkish designs of their civilian overlords. However, a number of outstanding retired three- and four-star generals were free to speak and did so. Gulf War hero Norman Schwartzkopf, Marine General Anthony Zinni (former U.S. Commander in Chief for the Middle East), Brent Scowcroft, Wesley Clark (former Supreme Commander of NATO), and others did speak out against the Iraq war as a bad strategic decision. All were outside the administration and all were ignored. Events have demonstrated their wisdom.

On the subject of the professional military, it must be emphasized that our officers are outstandingly capable; our soldiers in uniform are hard-working and courageous; and a high level of professionalism pervades the military services. Their accomplishments and valor in Iraq should be celebrated at the same time we deplore the strategic decision-making that sent them there. Significantly, during the run-up to the Iraq war, Retired Army Chief of Staff General Eric Shinseki accurately estimated the number of troops that would be needed after the war to be in the hundreds of thousands. The civilian leaders of the Pentagon, Paul Wolfowitz and Secretary Rumsfeld, dismissed Shinseki's estimate as "way off the mark" and offered a low-ball estimate of about 40,000 troops. It turns out that the politicians' estimate was way off the mark and not surprisingly, the professional military estimate was more accurate. Currently 150,000 coalition troops are struggling to cope with the post-war insurgency and other challenges and clearly this number is not enough.

There is a painful irony in the relationship between the military and the civilians discussed above. The U.S. Constitution placed civilians in charge of the military to prevent it from gaining the upper hand in terms of power, with all of the adverse consequences that a dominant military can bring in its train. The first irony is that despite the constitutional precaution of making the military subordinate to civilians, the Pentagon is now so powerful it can "wag the dog" of the President and Congress. The double irony is that it was not the generals who led us into Iraq, but the civilian neoconservatives who oversee the military. They were more hawkish than the generals, and they dragged the country into war against the wishes of the State Department and a substantial plurality of the American public.

Whether the American military-industrial colossus should be considered a separate entity or a part of "McWorld" (the power of corporate wealth) is a question that need not be answered here. They are not the same, but they do extensively overlap. The main point is that these three broad forces—conservative religion, corporate wealth, and the military establishment—working together constitute a massive, almost irresistible power coalition within the American political and economic system. This is true even though together they do not constitute a majority of Americans. They do command a strongly cohesive plurality and they usually work together. As a result of this successful political alliance, American politics takes up the far right-wing of global politics and determines the posture of the U.S. as an isolated extremist on most of the issues discussed in this book.

These ideological and cultural groupings' joint control of the levers of national power, currently expressed through the Bush administration combined with control of Congress by a narrow majority of extreme conservatives, constitutes the main reason why American foreign policy does not reflect the opinions and values of a more religiously moderate middle-class majority of Americans. The economic and military conservatives and the religious/social conservatives have combined forces and effectively seized control of the country. What is striking is how extreme the conservatism is on both counts.

Together they possess two of the most vital keys to power. Money buys political advertisements, consultants, pollsters, travel and speeches, and religious passion provides the "boots on the ground," the troops in the electoral trenches, voting and working to get out the vote. Conservative church pulpits are a powerful force shaping public opinion, though for reasons of tax exemption, churches have to be careful to avoid overtly supporting specific candidates. The clergy can weigh in with passion on the issues (framed in religious terms, of course) and leave to their congregations the simple task of determining which candidates they are being implicitly encouraged to vote for.

Still, Why?

Why would being conservative, either economically or religiously, lead people to embrace a foreign policy opposed to consensus statements of moral principle on women's and children's rights, opposed to global institutions of justice such as the International Criminal Court, opposed to systematic global cooperation in protecting the environment, opposed to arms control treaties, and willing to start an unnecessary war? The answer is that it need not, but it does. Logic might suggest that conservatives would value law and order and would thus promote global law and order. Logic might also suggest that religious conservatives would espouse and advocate moral considerations in foreign policy such as preventing abuse of women and children and refraining from starting unnecessary wars. Certainly religious moderates, who are far less organized and active politically than the religious far right, do stand for these things. For example, all the major Protestant church organizations except the Southern Baptists went on record as opposing the war in Iraq.

But in politics, logic and sweet reason often don't win. The economic conservatives want less global regulation of commerce. With that "freedom" their companies can be as rapacious as need be to make more profits. Pollution, low wages and harsh working conditions become somebody else's problem; the profits are ours. Also, of course, a military empire spanning the globe is great for the immense U.S. armaments industry, and is useful in protecting the global dominance of American industry and assuring access to key resources such as oil. And of course a four-hundred billion dollar defense budget with forts and factories in key states and congressional districts is a strong incentive for ideological purity in Congress.

The overwhelming military superiority of the U.S. paradoxically drives a slightly paranoid sense of vulnerability about the International Criminal Court. According to the argument, the U.S. has special responsibilities for global security and is stationed all over the world, and thus is more vulnerable than other countries to frivolous lawsuits in the court. The Pentagon brass and their civilian leaders alike fear this possibility, apparently without reading the treaty establishing the court. But the court is designed with essentially airtight legal and procedural protections against this possibility. Further, the decisions establishing the court to date, such as the selection of judges with the highest professional qualifications, as required by the treaty, have been made with exemplary integrity. The consistent human rights abusers among the nations have not joined the court and most likely will not do so because if they did, they would be more vulnerable to serious action by the court. So there is no reason to fear their dominance but the irrational fear still persists.

The shocking abuse of American detainees in Iraqi prisons comes to mind as a possible reason for the U.S. military to be leery of the court, but these abuses arose well after hostility to the court had become entrenched. Further, the abuses will be dealt with in the U.S. military court system, thereby making them exempt from the jurisdiction of the International Criminal Court. A better explanation of the military's hostility toward the court is the generally dismissive attitude toward international law exhibited by Secretary Rumsfeld when he brushed aside the Geneva Conventions on prisoners of war as inapplicable in Iraq. The U.S. is so powerful it can declare itself above the law.

But why does conservative religion work to promote an unprincipled American foreign policy? One would think that religion would counsel people to protect the weak, to support justice, to promote responsible stewardship of the planet's resources, and to oppose war. Needless to say, the Bible weighs in constructively, even passionately, on many of these issues. They are the kinds of causes religions are designed to promote. The problem is that religious fundamentalism the world over is especially vulnerable to viruses such as tribalism and sexism. The anti-viral immune systems of reason and common sense are paralyzed. Metaphorical and symbolic passages in scriptures are taken 100% literally. Descriptions of dubious behavior are taken as normative, or at least acceptable. Traditions made by human beings are taken as divinely ordained. And in the process of all this, reason and common sense are forced to atrophy. The viruses of irrationality can thrive.

It isn't the liberals or the moderates among the world's billion Muslims who support anti-western terrorism or demand that women wear veils. And it isn't the liberals and moderates among Christians who advocate an "America first" foreign policy, rage against the UN, and oppose the treaties on women's and children's rights. In the view of ultra-conservative religion, we're going to heaven because our beliefs and only ours are true; other people are headed in the opposite direction and must be evil because their beliefs are different from ours and thus are false. Others must be embracing a lie; they must be tools of the devil. Psychologically, this is religious tribalism. It extends naturally into the realm of nationalistic tribalism.

Traditional human beliefs such as the "moral order" that makes the father the head of the household (and therefore the wife a subordinate who must take orders) become overriding considerations. Women's equality is not a part of the agenda. Although Jesus treated women as equals, sometimes to the surprise and dismay of his disciples, social viruses such as sexism can easily override such considerations.

The treaty on the rights of women (CEDAW) is deliberately neutral and silent on abortion, the hottest of hot-button political issues in conservative religious circles, but the treaty is still vilified by the religious right-wing as if it advocated abortion. Again, not abortion but the viruses of sexism and tribalism are the overriding considerations. After all, the treaty is a *global*

43

instrument supported by a supposedly very bad bunch, the feminists who *do* believe in the equality of women, many of whom do support "choice." Therefore, by association, the treaty must be evil.

Opposition to the UN and the consequent U.S. failure to pay its UN dues has a similar non-rational origin in religious tribalism. Through bizarre quirks of biblical misinterpretation, the richly suggestive and ambiguous prophecies in the book of Revelation are used to demonize the United Nations. These apocalyptic symbols were at one time used against the Catholic Church and the Soviet Union. Books were written and preachers thundered about how these evil institutions were evidently the Antichrist. However, eventually it became politically incorrect to apply the symbols to Catholicism and the Soviet Union inconveniently disappeared. Another Antichrist was needed. The UN was available as a convenient bogeyman. Just as in a fun-house mirror a slim person can appear fat or a short person tall, the UN can be seen through a fun-house-mirror of these apocalyptic prophesies as a hostile, powerful, and dangerous force in the world, rather than the cumbersome and weak but generally benign force it is. Irrational thinking such as this tilts the political playing field against the UN and in favor of go-it-alone action by the U.S.

On this critique of the convergence of wealth and religious conservatism, a few caveats are in order. It cannot be emphasized enough that there is nothing wrong with being rich, and there is most emphatically nothing wrong with being sincerely religious or deeply committed to Christianity. Being sincere and being rigidly literalistic and legalistic are not at all the same thing, though they are easily confused by fundamentalists. Socialism is not the answer to the problem I'm addressing here, and neither is atheism or agnosticism. Genuine religion, unpolluted by tribalism, sexism, racism, and narrow, doctrinal fanaticism, has long been one of the most positive forces for good in the world, and will no doubt continue to be. However, twisted into a motive for hatred, religious tribalism and fanaticism become one of the world's most malevolent forces, creating wars, terrorism and genocide.

The most significant political problem in the U.S. is that the interests and beliefs of the two overlapping American social minorities, the economic and religious ultra-conservatives, are far from those of the country as a whole. It should surprise no one that the interests of the rich tilt toward keeping their money in their own hands and that of their children. Making the world safe for ever-greater aggregations of wealth is naturally a priority. Robber baron global capitalism looks good from this perspective. Laws and regulations that protect the environment or protect poor and middle-class people look irresponsible and annoying because they get in the way of profits and increased market share. From this perspective, global poverty is not a problem; it is an opportunity to hire people at one-tenth labor cost of employees from developed nations. And if an oppressive government prohibits the formation of labor unions, so much the better.

In the desperate race of global corporate competition, the leaders want no speed bumps in the form of laws and regulations. If you are the president of the company, your interests are not those of the production-line workers who are about to be laid off to save the company money. Your interests are aligned with the staff analysts and money-managers who recommended layoffs. The ideological and personal viewpoint is the following: the invisible hand of the market will take care of those folks; meanwhile, let me use my two very visible hands to get at more money. This viewpoint overlooks the fact that the invisible hand of the market is Darwinian; it has no compunction about starving people who are left out of the financial inner circle. Democracy cannot live with this outcome. Therefore global corporations will prefer to deal with dictatorships (as they manifestly do) and there will always be a tension between democracy and uncontrolled laissez-faire capitalism, which is ruthlessly indifferent to human well-being.

Likewise with ultra-conservative religion. The interests of a passionate adherent of a minority religious point of view may be quite different from those of the majority when an issue of social policy arises that is relevant to religion. This situation is quite normal. Thank heaven for freedom of religion. However, the situation becomes problematic when a minority group exercises disproportionate power over political and social policy and tries to impose that power on the majority. The voice of the majority is then silenced or muffled in the policy-making process, and a key purpose of democracy is defeated.

The Iraq war can be seen as a kind of American Jihad in the narrow sense of a holy war. The metaphor of a holy war between good and evil inside the mind and heart of each individual is common to most, if not all, religions. Onward, Christian soldiers! Muslims have their inner Jihad. Hindus fight their inner battle on the plain of Kurukshetra (the body) between the Kurus of egotism and sense attachments and the Pandus of spiritual tendencies. When devotees of any religion project this inner battle onto the outer environment it can become a rationalization for launching wars and killing innocent people. Saddam was a profoundly evil person, as advertised or more so, and the world is better off without him. But starting a war of aggression, an American Jihad against his country, is hardly a noble deed, and it is certain to have unexpected tragic consequences in the long run. The chaos in Iraq in the aftermath of the war is ample evidence that American aggression is not the right answer to an external dictator's very real evil. Deeply religious Americans engaging in a noble battle against the evil in themselves would do well to keep the struggle internal, rather than projecting it into the international arena in a naïve hope of promoting compassion by violence and freedom by coercion.

The combination of corporate wealth and religious ultra-conservatism or tribalism currently in power in the U.S. is not a cabal nor a conspiracy, and it is not as sinister as it may sound. These are simply cultural forces that have (one hopes temporarily) converged and marshaled political power at a particular moment in U.S. history, very much to the detriment of the majority point of view and the stability of the world. This combination is a difficult-to-deny political reality in the U.S. at the beginning of the 21st century. Stated bluntly, perhaps crudely for clarity, these folks have in common a missionary zeal, a tribalistic belief that America, with its corporate wealth and its conservative religion, is the font of goodness in the world. The rest of the world should be remade in our image, by force if necessary, and of course this can be done also for our economic and political benefit. Self-admiring ideology and economic self-interest conveniently merge.

Americans constitute less than 5% of the world's population. About a quarter to a third of Americans hold the very conservative views explored briefly above. They hold the reins of political power at present. Holding 25% of the world's wealth and more than 50% of its military power, the U.S. does not hesitate to use this leverage in global policy negotiations and to go it alone against a global consensus. When combined, these numbers suggest that less than 2% of the world's people are now exercising a tremendously disproportionate share of the world's policy-making clout. They pull global policy-making processes such as treaty formulation in directions that are viewed as harmful by the rest of the world. Needless to say, the remainder of the world is apt to see this arrangement as an undemocratic right-wing American religious and financial oligarchy trying to run the world. The moment of open rebellion came when the UN Security Council refused to ratify the U.S.-led war on Iraq.

The Neoconservative Empire

An additional, highly elitist ideological strain deeply affecting current U.S. foreign policy is the neoconservative belief system held by op-ed writers such as Robert Kagen and senior government officials such as Vice President Richard Cheney, Deputy Secretary of Defense Paul Wolfowitz, and Richard Pearl, formerly a key civilian advisor to the Pentagon. The "neocons" as they are often called, concentrated organizationally in the American Enterprise Institute, trace their intellectual lineage to a number of sources, one of whom is the philosopher Leo Strauss, a German classical scholar who was shaken by the events in Germany before and during WWII. Seeing the weakness of the Weimar Republic as it succumbed to Hitler, he became an advocate of a strong and militant democracy that could withstand the profound evil he saw unfolding before him in the world.

Similarly, during his college years Paul Wolfowitz is said to have studied the history of the Roman Empire and become enamoured with the glamorous ideal of "national greatness" as embodied in ancient Rome. It would not be difficult to transfer this chauvinistic dream to the U.S. in the 20th and 21st centuries. But national greatness is a dangerous ideal in a tightly integrated world where the dominance of one country can only be a source of acute tensions and problems. Give and take and compromise are practical necessities in such a world. The brutality always needed to maintain an empire, a brutality comparable to that of the Roman Empire, can hardly be accepted by American citizens in the long run as they watch unfolding on their TV screens the death and misery created by their government. The humiliation and torture of prisoners at Abu Ghraib prison in Iraq may prove to be the turning point for Americans in the current episode of imperial self-indulgence.

Among nations, the U.S. is the "first among equals," but only in military and economic power. The U.S. no longer has any unique claim to moral stature. The western European nations are democracies now, with strongly entrenched human rights protections like those of the U.S. Moreover, it is arguable that during the past fifty years Europe has made more rapid progress in building human rights into its laws and institutions than has the U.S. On the international scene, for instance, Europe has established a transnational human rights court and has charged ahead in embracing human rights in treaties, while the U.S. has dragged its heels. It took 40 years for the U.S. Senate to ratify the Genocide Treaty, as if there were some doubt about whether genocide is acceptable.

Though it is dangerous to generalize about groups of people, it seems safe to say that the "neocons" give a new twist to jingoism or (more broadly) tribalism by advocating an aggressive, almost messianic view of American democracy. In this view, even attacking another country can be rationalized as "moral" if this violent act has a chance of forcing the attacked country and scaring its neighbors into eventually becoming democracies.

This "end justifies the means" approach overlooks the fact that imposing freedom by force, violence, and coercion is a transparently self-contradictory enterprise. The plausible-sounding theory is that in a dangerous world, it may be necessary to throw the first punch or fire the first shot to launch a preventive war. The moral and practical problem is that doing so makes the "first puncher" the aggressor and thus a new source of evil. And of course war is wildly unpredictable; the outcome may be far different from the intent. Rationalizing aggression promotes evil rather than ending it.

The radical new doctrine authorizing the U.S. to launch preventive wars and its "test case" application, the U.S. war on Iraq, are direct results of this thinking. Likewise, the buildup to a $400 billion dollar per year military budget, the systematic abrogation and dismantling of disarmament treaties, and the appalling renewal of research on tactical uses of nuclear weapons are also direct results. Operating this way is certain to have the effect of turning any country, even a democracy, into one of "the bad guys." It is not the solution to the problem of totalitarian states like Hitler's Germany or Saddam's Iraq; it is the creation of a new and serious evil. It is no accident that in the run-up to the Iraq war, public opinion outside the U.S. began to identify George W. Bush as the greatest threat to world peace, rather than Saddam Hussein.

Neoconservatives consider spreading the gospel of democracy and free markets the moral element in U.S. foreign policy. Since we have so much military power, force is a key element in this task. Stated baldly, from their perspective, it's O.K. to use violence and coercion as needed to maintain and extend our power and to bring the benefits of democracy and free markets to the rest of the world. Violence and coercion are used in a vain attempt to usher in democracy and freedom. In this view, global treaties and international organizations such as the UN are constraints on American freedom of action that the U.S. should not tolerate, since we know best how to run the world.

Can We Change the Picture?

To change this pattern, the progressive, religiously tolerant and egalitarian majority of the American public has a large task on its hands. How can this majority of American citizens change the disgraceful policies discussed above? Surprisingly, the answers to the "how" question are in some ways easier than the "why" question. Polls have shown that a majority of Americans strongly prefer more benign, progressive, and cooperative international policies than those our government has been implementing. We, the majority, have the vote. We can change the picture. But to assure the needed shift in votes we have to take collective action, not just individual action. Information, motivation, and finally mobilization are the missing links.

Getting organized is critical. Millions in the U.S. and all over the world marched in January and February 2003 against the war in Iraq. A new breakthrough in global citizen organization was evident in 660 cities throughout the world. Polls indicated that in most countries the demonstrators expressed the views of a majority of their country's population. The growing possibilities of mobilization became evident. The demonstrations did not win the day, but they may have been harbingers of future success. The web phenomenon, MoveOn.org, and its offshoots provided a key element in that mobilization and has continued to have immense political influence since then. Other domestic organizations such as the new nonprofit, Citizens for Global Solutions, focus more specifically on the problem of democratic global law and order versus American dominance and knee-jerk hostility to reasonable international laws and regulations. This subject will be taken up in more detail in the final chapter of this book.

Chapter Three

HUMAN WRONGS—OPPRESSION OF WOMEN

> As expressions of the world's conscience, the consensus decisions of international conferences are powerful instruments for promoting the right to equality.
>
> —UNFPA State of the World Population 2000 Report: Lives Together, Worlds Apart: Men and Women in a Time of Change[*]

At first thought, to an average American citizen, a chapter about a treaty on the rights of women in a book like this might seem off track, an instance of special pleading for a particular group of people. The argument might go as follows: If we're interested in global progress generally, or in the well being of all humanity, not just that of a particular group, why focus on a single segment, even a large one? Still more to the point, doesn't the U.S. do pretty well in its treatment of women? Certainly better than a lot of countries! So why should we concern ourselves with a treaty about women's rights? That's someone else's problem. The argument continues: we're the "good guys"; and some other countries are the "bad guys" in their treatment of women. (I've heard people use this kind of sexist language while making this argument without seeing the irony.) Other countries need the treaty; we don't. According to this point of view, we don't need to improve our record, and we certainly don't need other countries or a bunch of UN bureaucrats telling us how to improve!

This view can be summed up, with its moral foundation exposed, as the following: "Can't we Americans just stand aloof in our moral superiority and

---

[*] The U.S. is the only developed country in the world that has not passed this treaty.
—Loretta Ross on the Convention to End Discrimination against Women

go our own way?" The nose high in the air is all too evident. In the first place, although the record of U.S. treatment of women is good relative to quite a few other countries, there is substantial room for improvement. How substantial can be illustrated by a quick look at the scope of a few remaining problems.

A study by Dr. Gloria Bachmann estimates that in the U.S. as many as 38% of adult women were sexually abused as children. Less than half of such abuse cases are reported to authorities, so the actual number may be higher. A woman living in the U.S. has one chance in three of being raped, and 50% of all married women are battered at least once in their marriages.[1] According to another research study by Dr. Leah Dickstein, spousal abuse is the cause of one out of two suicide attempts among black women and one out of four suicide attempts among white women.[2] A study of gender bias in American schools carried out by the American Association of University Women confirmed an earlier study showing that boys are five times more likely than girls to receive the most attention from teachers, and eight times more likely to speak up in class.[3]

Of course, improved laws alone cannot change these statistics, though in some cases legal changes might help. These numbers do, however, suggest that the United States is less than a paradise in its treatment of women. I am not going to attempt to make a case for domestic improvements in this arena as a compelling reason to ratify a treaty. These improvements can be made without ratifying it. The point is to introduce some badly needed humility about the U.S. record on these matters before looking at the world as a whole.

The treaty I'm referring to is a major international convention graced with the catchy title, "Convention to End All Forms of Discrimination against Women" (CEDAW). (Please take a moment to focus on these initials; ungainly though they are, they will be used often in this chapter.) There are other less comprehensive and specific treaties on the rights of women, but this is the exceptionally important one I'm tackling in this book. The treaty entered into force internationally on September 3, 1981. As of March 20, 2000, it had165 States Parties, not including the U.S. (There are currently 191 member nations in the UN.) As noted above, the United States is the only developed nation that has not ratified or acceded to the treaty. Our company among the non-participants includes countries with the most backward human rights records in the world: Afghanistan (under the Taliban), Somalia, Sudan, Iran, North Korea, and Syria.

The main reason to ratify the treaty is that the United States is part of a larger world, and the misery or wellbeing of people all over the world affects us profoundly and pervasively. We cannot isolate ourselves in such a deeply integrated world, and should not try. Whether we support human rights treaties or not sends a powerful signal to the rest of the world about what we stand for and believe in, who we are, and what our values are. Something is seriously wrong when we stand alone among developed nations in refusing to ratify CEDAW. The message of this stance is that the U.S. does not care about or believe in the human rights of one half of humanity. This message contrasts with our history of human rights leadership and understandably makes the rest of the world wonder what has gone wrong with America. This message of U.S. indifference to human rights also stands in surprising and distressing contrast to the commitment of every other developed nation in the world. Not only are we failing to lead the world in this arena, we are neither cooperating, nor even following. We are silently but eloquently taking a stand *against* global moral and legal progress.

Our failure to ratify the women's rights treaty is itself a dramatic instance of a broader picture of recent U.S. failures to commit to international human rights efforts including the rights of children and the establishment of an International Criminal Court. These recent failures stand in stark contrast to the leadership the U.S. displayed in establishing its own Bill of Rights in its early history and initiating, drafting and supporting the Universal Declaration of Human Rights over 50 years ago in the UN. The U.S. has a long history of leadership in human rights, but recently it has earned a reputation as an obstacle to full global implementation of these same rights. The current U.S. failures in this arena unfortunately provide contradictory evidence to the oft-repeated claim that "we are the good guys." We once were, and we could be once again, if we begin to act like it again.

U.S. Action on the Treaty

The good news is that over 20 years ago the U.S. executive branch under President Carter advocated human rights as an integral part of U.S. foreign policy and participated actively in drafting CEDAW. President Carter signed the Rights of Women treaty on July 17, 1980.

Machiavellians, called "realists" in foreign policy circles, have ridiculed President Carter's strong stand for human rights. On the other hand, human rights activists, of course, admired his stand. Reviled or admired, the oft-invoked policy has stood the test of time and has (when implemented) increased the respect with which the U.S. is viewed by the rest of the world. Twenty years later, even conservatives raise human rights problems as one of the sets of issues that bear on international relations decision-making. For example, some conservatives objected to permanent normal trade relations with China on this basis.

President Carter transmitted the treaty to the Senate Foreign Relations Committee in November 1980 for ratification shortly before he left office. There it languished through the Reagan and Bush years without being supported by either of these Presidents. In the spring of 1993, soon after President Clinton's election, sixty-eight Senators (enough for the two-thirds majority needed to ratify the treaty) signed a letter to President Clinton asking him to take the necessary steps to ratify CEDAW. In June of 1993, then-Secretary of State Warren Christopher announced at the World Conference on Human Rights in Vienna that the Clinton administration would move on CEDAW and other human rights treaties. The prospects for ratification looked good. And for a moment, the U.S. looked better in the eyes of the rest of the world, and more consistent with its own explicitly stated values.

Legislative wheels grind slowly, and it was not until September 1994 that the Senate Foreign Relations Committee reported favorably to the Senate floor on CEDAW by a vote of 13 to 5 (with one abstention). Unfortunately, this occurred toward the end of the session. Several Senators anonymously put a hold on the Convention, thereby blocking it from moving to the Senate floor during the 103rd Congress. When the new and much more conservative Senate convened in January 1995, President Clinton resubmitted the Convention to the Senate Foreign Relations Committee, where it remained without action for the next eight years.

After this election, under the Senate seniority rules the U.S. Senate made Jesse Helms the Chair of the Foreign Relations Committee. Even his Republican colleagues were uncomfortable with his extreme views and behavior in such a key position, but no one was willing to take on both the ruthless Helms and the Senate seniority system. He was allowed to have his way with CEDAW after he became Chair. Senator Helms claimed that the treaty was so bad that even the Democrats didn't press for its ratification. However, the history of 68 Senators asking President Clinton to submit the treaty to the Senate for ratification refutes this statement. For years, Helms successfully blocked CEDAW from coming to the Senate floor by bottling it up in committee. Democratic Senators didn't bother to press for ratification because they knew they couldn't win against his strategic position, his intransigence against the treaty, and the opposition of the conservative majority and leadership of the Senate.

Does the treaty and the Senate's inaction on it matter? To get a feel for the issues at stake, and the kinds of treatment of women we are dealing with globally, let's turn our attention first to an episode in Afghanistan before the U.S. toppled the Taliban. Although the Taliban has been swept from the scene in the course of the war on terrorism (and good riddance!) the story illustrates how even national leaders who are actively and aggressively opposed to the principles of human rights and specifically women's rights may have no choice but to bow to the will of the international community and its moral and legal norms.

What's at Stake?

To make a long story very short, before the Taliban took over, Afghanistan was torn by civil war for decades. It was also a pawn in the Cold War and militarily controlled by the Soviet Union through a local dictator. The U.S.-supported opposition to Soviet rule inside Afghanistan combined with the toughness of the Afghan insurgents eventually made it too costly for the Soviets to maintain their hold on the country. They pulled out. In the absence of Soviet involvement and Cold War rivalry, the U.S. also pulled out, treating the Afghan rebels like the expendable pawns they were in the Cold War. Civil war continued after Russia and the U.S. withdrew. Strong resentment towards the U.S. developed as a result of our abandonment of the Afghan rebels.

After the Soviet and U.S. pullouts, the Afghan war dragged on inconclusively, devastating the country, which had a weak economy to begin with. Eventually a single group gained ascendancy —the fanatical religious, military and political force of Islamic fundamentalists called the Taliban. The Taliban had cohesion and courage, and many of the Afghan people supported them out of a desperate desire to replace chaos with some sort of order. They eventually took over about 90% of the country. One of their many glaring flaws was extreme views and practices regarding the role of women. All women—including doctors, lawyers, and teachers—were forced to stop working and stay at home. Girls were no longer allowed to attend school. Women could not be seen in public except when covered from head to foot, including a mesh over their eyes. Women without husbands, e.g., thousands of war widows, were simply out of luck. They couldn't work, they had no husband, and so they no means of support. Exacerbating the devastation of war, drought struck the country's economy. Eventually, a significant fraction of the population became dependent for food on international aid through the UN and other organizations such as CARE.

Fast forward to November 15, 1999. In reaction to the bombing of two U.S. embassies, the UN put into effect aviation and financial sanctions against Afghanistan's Taliban rulers for failing to surrender Osama bin Laden for trial on charges of plotting the bombing of the U.S. embassies. These sanctions further weakened an already crippled Afghan economy. However, the Taliban persisted in refusing to produce Osama bin Laden, whose attack on the U.S. made him a hero among Muslim radicals. The events that followed happened in a context of a severe drought and a war-wrecked economy in which food aid from the outside world was an essential component of survival for much of the population. The events unfolded in July and August 2000.

The crisis began with the Taliban issuing an edict banning employment of women, even by international aid agencies. The UN World Food Program (WFP) employed Afghan women at its bakeries, which fed about 270,000 Afghans each day in the face of the country's worst drought in 30 years. According to news reports, some 7,000 of the city's poorest women received subsidized bread for themselves and their families from the bakeries. Women with no male relatives to support them were left with begging and charity as their only means of support. Most families headed by widows were already surviving on bread and tea. The UN had established the bakeries specifically to assist the tens of thousands of women left widowed in Kabul as a result of twenty years of war. To give teeth to their edict, Taliban "religious" police visited some of the bakeries and threatened workers with beatings if they failed to close. UN officials said they would continue to pay wages to the bakers, although they could do nothing to help their thousands of customers. Other aid agencies had similar problems.

A couple of weeks later, the Taliban lifted the ban. This decision allowed 24 women-run bakeries to reopen. The news media reported the Taliban's reversal but didn't report the reason for it, and maybe they didn't know. However, a news report on another subject cast light on a probable motive. Just one day after the Taliban's decision to let the bakeries re-open, the media reported that the Taliban militia had appealed to the international community to grant it official recognition and a seat at the United Nations. The UN and most countries still recognized the old Afghan regime as the legitimate government of the country, thus depriving the Taliban of recognition of their legitimacy as the country's government. Only three countries at that time had recognized the Taliban diplomatically. "Afghanistan has completed all the criteria for official recognition," according to the Afghan Ambassador. "It controls more than 90% of the territory, including the capital of the country, all its international boundaries . . . and international airports." Still, ousted Afghan President Burhanuddin Rabbani, whose Northern Alliance forces controlled about 10% of the country, retained the support of the international community and controlled the country's seat in the UN General Assembly.

The timing of the lifting of the ban on women working in bakeries seems to suggest that behind-the-scenes negotiating may have taken place, or at least that the Taliban leaders were thinking about the international shock waves from the bakery incident in relation to the request to join the UN.

The Taliban wanted entry into the UN to validate their legitimacy as the ruling government of the country, to reduce its international isolation, and presumably eventually to try to get the economic sanctions lifted. They may have realized (or been told) that to gain the acceptance of the UN they had to display some minimal acceptance of UN norms and values on matters such as human rights. And of course, from the UN point of view, an international legal instrument such as CEDAW is a key to legitimizing negotiation pressure to improve human rights practices. The UN would have a weak or nonexistent foundation for arbitrary pressure on a country based on a vague feeling that people are being mistreated. It needs, and has in CEDAW, a widely accepted legal foundation, an explicit set of norms for such matters. Even though Afghanistan is not a signatory to the treaty, it has no choice but to deal with the reality of the norms embodied in the treaty and embedded in the institutions of the UN and the values of its other member nations.

(It is important to note here that the Koran doesn't lead to the kind of treatment of women displayed by the Taliban. This behavior pattern is a set of tribal customs that predate the Koran. This kind of treatment of women, though prevalent in some Muslim countries, is not in any way an essential part of the Muslim religion, which has millions of far more enlightened adherents.)

The Grim Picture Worldwide

While the behavior of the Taliban and its partial reversal was a dramatic case, the world is brimming with violations of basic human decency in the treatment of women. These have not magically vanished with the advent of a women's rights treaty, but CEDAW does constitute a powerful tool in creating constant pressure for improvement, as the Taliban bakery incident demonstrates. It shows that even a country that is not a party to the treaty must deal with the reality of this treaty and the internationally accepted norms it embodies.

The big-picture story of the worldwide mistreatment of women is told in devastating detail in a well-researched and documented report, the annual State of World Population 2000 Report, "Lives Together, Worlds Apart: Men and Women in a Time of Change" Published by the United Nations. The report paints a grim picture of the lives of women around the world who frequently endure discrimination and violence. Let me warn the reader that it may be painful to read the next few paragraphs. On the other hand, it can be too easy to glide over statistics without allowing oneself to realize what these things mean to real, breathing, individual human beings. If you are a woman, you can make these impersonal numbers more real by picturing yourself in these situations. If you are a man, you can glimpse their significance by picturing them as applying to the women you know and care about, including your wife or girlfriend, your mother, sister, or daughter. Too close to home? For the individual women affected, these grim realities are their lives.

According to the report, girls and women worldwide—across lines of income, class and culture—are subjected to physical, sexual and psychological abuse. Violence against women includes rape, genital mutilation and sexual assault; forced pregnancy, sterilization or abortion; forced use or non-use of contraceptives; "honor" crimes including "honor" killings; sexual trafficking; and dowry-related violence. One woman in four has been abused during pregnancy. Around the world, at least one in every three women has been beaten, coerced into sex, or abused in some other way, most often by someone she knows, including her husband or another male family member. (Consider that this conservative number, one woman in three, most likely includes numerous people you know, and constitutes one sixth of the world's population or one billion people. Stated another way, this number is four times the population of the U.S.)

Each year rape and domestic violence cost women worldwide the equivalent of millions of lost years of healthy life. Physical violence is nearly always accompanied by psychological abuse, which can be just as demeaning and degrading. Many cultures condone or at least tolerate a certain amount of violence against women, and their laws are written accordingly. As many as 5,000 women and girls are killed annually in so-called "honor" killings, many of them for the "dishonor" of having been raped. In other words, get rid of the problem by killing the victim. Again, in some countries if a woman has been "disgraced," this circumstance constitutes an excuse to escape criminal conviction for the family member who has killed her or a reason for a reduced sentence in criminal proceedings.

An estimated 4 million women and girls are bought and sold worldwide each year, either into marriage, prostitution or slavery. (To grasp the magnitude of this number, note that 4 million is equivalent to the entire population of two large American cities.) Although the greatest volume of trafficking occurs in Asia, Eastern European women are also increasingly vulnerable. It should be noted here that a recent national TV news report in the U.S. stated that 5,000 women annually are abducted and brought to the U.S. for forced prostitution or sweatshop work. When they escape from their abductors, they are treated as criminals by the U.S. legal system because of being illegal aliens. When sent back to their home countries, often they are mistreated and rejected or even killed because of having been prostitutes.

Limited access to healthcare among the poor has a greater relative impact on women than on men. In particular, poor women have an increased death rate due to pregnancy. A mother's death represents more than a personal tragedy; the economic and social costs include the impact on children's health and education, and on the father's ability to hold the family together.

Ninety-nine percent of the approximately 500,000 maternal deaths each year are in developing countries, where complications of pregnancy and childbirth take the life of about one out of every 48 women. It is not uncommon for women in Africa, when about to give birth, to bid their older children farewell. In the United Republic of Tanzania, mothers have a saying: "I am going to the sea to fetch a new baby, but the journey is long and dangerous and I may not return." In some settings, as many as 40 percent of women suffer from serious illness following a birth.

Infants and children also suffer as a result of poor maternal health. The same factors that cause mothers deaths and illness, including complications and the poor management of pregnancy and childbirth, contribute to an estimated eight million stillbirths and newborn deaths each year. Furthermore, tragically, when a mother dies, her children are also more likely to die. A study in Bangladesh found that if a woman dies after delivery, her newborn infant is almost certain to die.

Another study in Bangladesh found that children up to age ten whose mothers die are three to ten times more likely to die within two years than are children with living parents. In the United Republic of Tanzania, children whose mothers died were likely to have to leave school to take on household tasks.

The same comprehensive report also addresses education for women. An estimated two thirds of the 300 million children without access to education are girls, and two thirds of the 880 million illiterate adults are women. Perhaps because of this, economic returns on investment in women's education exceed those for men. On one hand, withholding education from women slows the social and economic development of a community or country. Conversely, studies repeatedly show that educating girls and women raises every index of economic and social development. Differences in fertility levels between regions are strongly related to differences in levels of health and women's education. A recent study attributed one third of the increase in male and female life expectancy between 1960 and 1990 to gains in the educational attainment of women.

While it is clear that education of women improves the lot of both women and men in a society, the problems of abuse and domestic violence may not be so "easily" solved. These problems cut across lines of class and culture, although they are not perfectly uniform across these lines. Domestic violence is not easily stamped out. However, laws can be changed to assure that women are not officially second-class citizens who can be beaten or killed by their husbands or families without legal consequences. These changes in law are a significant part of what CEDAW is all about.

Impact of CEDAW

What have all the grim realities for women discussed above to do with U.S. foreign policy? First, the Taliban story illustrates both the role of the UN and the role human rights treaties in the long, hard struggle to make life livable for much of the human population in the face of widespread human callousness, a callousness that may be driven by power struggles of leaders or merely by outmoded cultural traditions, but in any case makes a major contribution to human misery.

The Taliban incident illustrates how power can be marshaled for people. If humane treatment of people (like not forcing them into starvation) is to go beyond a warm, fuzzy impulse of the human heart and move into the realm of concrete, systematic action, it requires definite formulations, laws and treaties defining what is within the bounds of human rights and what is not. CEDAW is a key building block in that construct. The consequences are life-and-death matters to thousands, perhaps millions, of people. As the episode illustrates, international law matters, the UN matters, and human rights treaties matter.

Another set of events illustrates more direct action by the United Nations in implementing CEDAW. On March 6, 2001 the UN conducted a raid on Bosnian brothels, closing 38 of them and freeing 177 women from sexual slavery. The operation was carried out by Bosnian Serb, Croat, and Muslim police officers, and was observed by UN police monitors. Following the raid, UN officials began the process of interviewing the women to build a case against the brothel owners. Last year, according to the Washington Post article reporting this action, the UN assisted in the return of about 260 foreign women who had been forced into sexual slavery in Bosnia after being lured there with promises of well-paying jobs as waitresses and bartenders.

All this happened—the Taliban incident, the Bosnia incident, and many others—without ratification of CEDAW by the U.S. Senate. The good news is that events like the Taliban's reversal happen because much of the rest of the world does care enough to sign and ratify such treaties. Without widespread international support, human rights treaties like CEDAW could not be implemented.

When a tiny island country fails to pay its UN dues or ratify a treaty, not much harm is done. When the world's wealthiest and most powerful nation— "the world's only remaining superpower," and a leader among economically developed democracies no less—defaults on such basic human rights efforts, it tears at and damages the whole fabric of global cooperation. It also gives the U.S. a bad name with the rest of the world. It squanders the political capital of decades of accumulated goodwill the U.S. built up before this pattern emerged. At present, in a conversation with educated people in a foreign country, to claim that the U.S. is a leader in human rights is to invite scoffing laughter or outright rage.

Treaty Provisions; Senate Opposition

Why are some American political leaders, notably Senator Jesse Helms and the conservative leadership of the Senate from 1995 forward to at least the year 2003, against this treaty? What are its provisions? A quote at the beginning of the treaty summarizes its purpose. "The full and complete development of a country, the welfare of the world and the cause of peace require the maximum participation of women on equal terms with men in all fields." This statement isn't just poetry or high-minded principle. Its factual truth is supported, as noted above, by study after study that show that holding back education and opportunities to work from women retards the health and economic development of a country. Conversely, educating women and allowing them to work accelerates development. A country that suppresses the rights of women is not only harming half its citizens, it is also crippling its economy by refusing to use half its total brain power and human energy.

The treaty calls for participating countries to:

- incorporate equality of men and women in their legal systems
- abolish discriminatory laws and adopt laws prohibiting discrimination against women
- establish tribunals and other public institutions to protect women against discrimination
- ensure elimination of all acts of discrimination against women by persons, organizations or enterprises
- ensure women's equal access to, and equal opportunities in, education, health and employment as well as political and public life including the right to vote and to stand for election
- take measures, including legislation and temporary special measures, so that women can enjoy all their human rights and fundamental freedoms

In addition to the above broad points, CEDAW is the only human rights treaty that affirms the reproductive rights of women (neither including nor excluding abortion) and recognizes culture and tradition as influential forces shaping gender roles and family relations. It affirms women's rights to acquire change or retain their nationality and the nationality of their children. States Parties also agree to take measures against all forms of women trafficking and exploitation of women. Countries that choose to ratify CEDAW are legally bound (by their own choice) to put its provisions into practice. They are also committed to submit reports, at least every four years, on measures they have taken to comply with treaty obligations.

Two items here might be red flags for conservatives in the U.S. One is the reference to reproductive rights. The other is the seeming threat to national sovereignty in its talk about nations being legally bound to put its provisions into practice and report on progress. On this latter point, treaties in general, not just CEDAW, require nations that choose to ratify them to abide by their principles and provisions. That is the nature of a treaty. If we grant for the sake of discussion the arguments of opponents of the treaty that we in the U.S. already treat women relatively well, and therefore don't need any prompting by a treaty, presumably there would be nothing to report and the requirement would therefore be *pro forma* for the U.S. However, more realistically, to the extent that the U.S. may have deficiencies in its laws and practices regarding the treatment of women, the public attention these deficiencies could receive from such reporting might be beneficial, though of course highly irritating to promoters of extreme national sovereignty, who could be relied upon to attack the UN over such reporting rather than attacking and solving the American problem. Humble pie is not a favorite food of American leaders. This hyper-sensitivity to criticism of the U.S., whether justified or not, is clearly one impulse behind the less-than-constructive behavior of Senators like Jesse Helms.

What about reproductive rights? Essentially the treaty calls for shared child rearing by both parents. The ideal of shared child rearing obviously can't be achieved in all cases. This provision illustrates that the treaty, assertions by its enemies notwithstanding, is strongly pro-family. Typically, social conservatives in the U.S. consider child rearing by two parents to be ideal. They often inveigh against the adverse effects on children of single parent homes. In so doing, they are unwittingly agreeing with the treaty. It also calls for access to childcare that would allow a woman to combine family responsibilities with work and participation in public life. (It does not specify that the government must provide this, so presumably private arrangements such as are common in the U.S. would meet its provisions.) In addition, it mentions family planning, specifically stating that advice on family planning must be included in the education process and family codes must guarantee women's rights "to decide freely and responsibly on the number and spacing of their children and to have access to the information, education, and means to enable them to exercise these rights." In short, women's effective access to birth control is a provision of the treaty. To people who are unreservedly opposed to birth control under all circumstances on religious grounds, this provision of the treaty is bound to be unacceptable. The Vatican is one of the states that have not acceded to the treaty.

It should be emphasized that the treaty does not take a position on abortion for the obvious reason that it is too controversial to allow a consensus to emerge. An implication of this omission is that Roman Catholics and Protestants who find birth control acceptable but are opposed to abortion can support the treaty without a problem of conscience. *A point that cannot be emphasized enough is that access to birth control consistently results in fewer abortions. Conversely, limiting birth control results in more abortions.* There is no reason to doubt that full implementation of the treaty would thus lead to fewer abortions.

For those whose objections focus on sex education, it should be noted that "advice on family planning" need not entail explicit or detailed sex education. It could presumably mean as little as a few minutes of guidance to young women at some appropriate (late) stage in their schooling on how to get access to birth control locally if they wished to. Access obviously does not imply that a woman would have to use birth control if she didn't wish to for religious or any other reasons. More importantly, advice on family planning could, and probably should, include fact-based warnings about the hazards of irresponsible sex, pregnancies out of the context of marriage, sexually transmitted diseases, and the like, depending on the prevailing views in the local community. This advice could include thoughtfully expressed and factually well-documented warnings on the moral, emotional, and biological reasons to keep sex within the context of marriage and discourage it outside that context. There is research data on these matters; they do not require acceptance of this or that religious authority. This kind of information should probably be provided to students of both genders in schools early and often, with or without CEDAW as an incentive. Certainly the U.S. ratifying CEDAW would not in any way work against such enlightened educational policy.

In view of the problem of unwanted teen pregnancies, access to birth control might be considered a matter of common sense. Each unwanted pregnancy is evidence that moral rules and fear of pregnancy did not succeed in motivating abstinence. Still, in some quarters, this is understandably a volatile issue. It should be noted here that most women in the U.S. who want access to birth control already have it. To that extent, U.S. adherence to the treaty would not require significant change. An argument against the treaty based on access to birth control would thus be a red herring, unless religious conservatives were to make the untenable argument that access should be difficult or illegal.

Who Supports, Who Opposes CEDAW?

CEDAW has the support of numerous American organizations including Amnesty International, Human Rights Watch, American Bar Association, American Association of Retired Persons, American Jewish Committee, American Association of University Women, and the National Council of Churches of Christ in the USA. In contrast, most of the opposition to the ratification of CEDAW comes from a small number of conservative religious groups. However, the opposition is not only well organized and extremely vocal, but it has also received the support of a small number of powerful governmental figures, including Jesse Helms.

Rather than offering an insightful, justifiable rationale for opposing CEDAW, Helms did little more than feed the paranoia of the extremely conservative religious groups by emphasizing arguments that are baseless and founded purely on fear and intentionally misconstrued information. Helms criticized the intent of the treaty, stating that the "treaty is not about opportunities for women. It is about denigrating motherhood and undermining the family. The treaty is designed to impose, by international fiat, a radical definition of 'discrimination against women' that goes far beyond the protections already enshrined in the laws of the United States of America."[4]

Helms insisted that the intent of CEDAW is to promote an extreme feminist perspective that seeks to advance the liberal platforms on several controversial issues: "CEDAW ratification is about furthering an agenda which seeks to ensure abortion on demand, and which refuses to recognize any legitimate distinctions between men and women."[5] Helms' summary judgment on the treaty was that it "is a terrible treaty negotiated by radical feminists with the intent of enshrining their antifamily agenda into international law."[6] However, as we have already seen, and directly contrary to Helms' claims, the treaty is strenuously pro-family and is strictly neutral on abortion.

Representative Christopher Smith (R-NJ) has been a staunch supporter of the view that CEDAW would constitute a threat to the national sovereignty of the United States. According to Smith, "As a party to CEDAW, the US would subject itself to the jurisdiction or a UN committee that was established to enforce compliance with CEDAW."[7] The self-assured advice Helms gave to the supporters of CEDAW who are attempting to prevail over the likes of Helms and Smith and have CEDAW ratified is the following: "Dream on because it is not going to happen."[8]

Despite the failure to have CEDAW ratified in the federal government, a number of state and local governments have taken steps to implement its guidelines within their respective borders. The state legislatures of New York, Maine, Hawaii, South Dakota, North Carolina, Massachusetts, Vermont, Iowa, California, and New Hampshire have all approved CEDAW, as have the city governments of San Francisco, Los Angeles, Seattle, and Boston.[9] This fact illustrates that there is strong support within this country for the significant protections of women that CEDAW provides and that there are ways to endorse CEDAW even while extremely conservative members of Congress do everything they can to prevent it from being brought to the Senate for ratification.

The Treaty in Action: How it Works

No new treaty, bill, or constitution is self-implementing, and the deeper the change, the more protracted and difficult the political and legal battles for constructive change are likely to be. Male dominance or male superiority, and with it implicit female submission or inferiority, is deeply embedded in traditional cultures and laws all over the world. Replacing these patriarchal patterns with gender equity in law and in fact is a slow, hard, ongoing struggle that will take decades, if not centuries. It is not glamorous; it doesn't make headlines in U.S. newspapers. But in constitutional and legal battles all over the world, women are drawing on CEDAW as a resource or tool for legal reform in establishing gender equity. This fact may be uncomfortable for extreme traditionalists and male chauvinists, but in view of the widespread horrors documented earlier in this chapter, it can be recognized as genuine human progress. In the first two decades of its existence, CEDAW has proved itself useful in that struggle. It has proved especially powerful when a country is engaged in fundamental democratic reform of its constitution.

The following examples of legal reform are condensed from a booklet published by UNIFEM in 1998 entitled, *Bringing Equity Home: Implementing the Convention on the Elimination of All Forms of Discrimination Against Women*. The introduction to the booklet states, "What is apparent in each case is that CEDAW, as a document, did not in and of itself bring about these changes. Rather, it was the determined, cooperative, innovative, and strategic work of women's NGOs [non-government organizations]—and the stimulation of the political will of governments—that changed the conditions of women's lives. CEDAW provided them with a powerful, internationally recognised lever."

Constitutions

The principles of CEDAW have been incorporated into the constitutions of several nations, and as a result have taken central positions in the legal systems of those countries. Gradually, as case law evolves over the years,

65

more and more laws of these countries will be brought into alignment. And as new legislation is proposed, its constitutionality and thus its consistency with these principles will be explored, debated, and implemented. Here are a few examples.

Colombia: The Colombian Government ratified CEDAW in 1981. By the mid-1980s, it had become central to campaigns for women's human rights in Colombia. At the same time, Colombian citizens and leaders developed a new constitution they hoped would move the country out of the violent instability it had suffered. The President established working groups to create reform proposals for the new constitution.

Women's organizations advocated that CEDAW's principles be included in the constitution. Women formed a network of 70 organizations to support this effort. CEDAW was useful in influencing the content of the new constitution because its principles had the credibility and legal authority of mandates in an international human rights treaty that had already been ratified by the Colombian government. Using international human rights language proved effective, taking advantage of the fact that Colombia is constantly scrutinized by the international community for compliance with human rights principles. The network's efforts were successful. The Colombian constitution includes some of the most detailed and substantive guarantees of women's human rights in the world.

Brazil: Thanks to a national campaign by women using CEDAW as a starting point, Brazil's constitution, rewritten in 1988, now includes extensive guarantees of women's human rights. The Brazilian constitution now contains provisions on gender equality, gender-based violence, state responsibility for the prevention of domestic violence, the equality of rights within marriage, family planning, and equality in employment, all of which are similar to CEDAW provisions. As in Columbia, CEDAW provided internationally accepted standard language describing rights of women and thus increased women's negotiating strength.

South Africa: In South Africa's transition from apartheid to democracy in the early 1990s, a new constitution was a key component. As in Colombia and Brazil, a coalition of women's groups worked to include women's rights in the constitution. They called for comprehensive equality for women including guarantees of political, civil, economic, social, and cultural rights. A charter they developed included equality in all spheres: law, the economy, education, development and infrastructure, political and civic life, family life and partnerships, custom, culture and religion, health and the media. CEDAW provided a useful framework for specific rights.

As a result of their efforts, the South African constitution contains a number of important provisions on women's equality. In the "Founding Provisions," of the constitution, sexism is rejected as decisively as racism. The constitution's Bill of Rights prohibits discrimination on the basis of "race, gender, sex, pregnancy, marital status, ethnic or social origin, color, sexual orientation, age, disability, religion, conscience, belief, culture, language and birth."

The Courts

The 1998 booklet cited above, *Bringing Equity Home,* states succinctly the power of CEDAW in influencing court decisions about women's rights: "Some of the most interesting and significant decisions are produced when a court decides to combine a vague or inadequate constitutional guarantee of women's equality with the principles of gender equality articulated in CEDAW. . . . the protection afforded women's human rights becomes stronger and more meaningful than might even have been anticipated when the constitution was drafted."

The following items are court cases where CEDAW was useful in clarifying and amplifying the meaning of constitutional language about women's rights. They are condensed from Amnesty International's website, "Ratify the Women's Rights Treaty – Women's Rights are Human Rights: How Women in Other Countries are Using CEDAW."

Nepal: In Nepal, property law denied women equal property rights. CEDAW was used to promote the women's rights to inherit property, and also to raise the minimum age for marriage and require stiffer penalties for rape.

Japan: Japan ratified CEDAW in the early 1980s. It has been used in lawsuits to fight deeply entrenched traditions of unequal employment for women.

Tanzania: Tanzanian law prevented women from inheriting clan land from their fathers. The Tanzanian High Court cited CEDAW in a decision invalidating this law.

Australia: In Australia, the constitution limits the federal government's powers to legislate. Before Australia ratified CEDAW, courts determined that it could not legislate in the area of sexual harassment. Yet after Australia ratified CEDAW, the courts permitted a federal law prohibiting sexual harassment because the government's responsibilities for external affairs had expanded to include new international obligations to implement the treaty.

So Why Does U.S. Ratification Matter?

Granted that CEDAW has improved the human rights picture in other countries, why does it matter that the U.S. has not ratified this treaty? As noted earlier, over 165 countries have ratified CEDAW. This convention marks a milestone in worldwide recognition that women's rights are an important part of the totality of human rights. Women's rights are no less important than the more general rights documented in the Universal Declaration of Human Rights, which the U.S. led in developing fifty years ago. No one is surprised that nations that are notorious for human rights violations such as Iran and Sudan have not ratified CEDAW. It's not problematic that a few small nations such as Kiribati, Nauru, Palau, and Qatar have not ratified it. But in refusing to ratify this treaty (make no mistake, no one believes this is a case of accidental neglect) the United States Senate has placed the U.S. in a highly visible position as a non-supporter of basic human rights along side countries that are notorious for their abuses of human rights. With its persistence in this decision, the Senate leadership has explicitly demonstrated on behalf of the United States a lack of commitment to ending discrimination and violence against women, along with other severe human rights abuses.

If CEDAW were the only major human rights treaty the Senate refused to ratify, one could perhaps view it as an anomaly, an unusual reaction to a treaty presumed to have a few objectionable provisions. However, the Senate has a history of resistance to human rights treaties. Currently, the Senate is also refusing to ratify the Rights of the Child treaty, on which there is an even stronger international consensus. Refusal to ratify these two treaties are strong, firm steps on the way to giving the U.S. the ignoble crown of number one obstacle to global progress in human decency.

U.S. failure to ratify CEDAW is a major embarrassment internationally and a failure of the U.S. to live up to its most basic ideals and values. Ratification would help to correct this defect in our international posture and open new channels for this country to voice concerns about human rights violations globally. U.S. ratification would add a powerful moral and legal force to protect the human rights of women and girls all over the world. Polls show that we, the citizens of the United States, support this treaty when it is clearly and simply explained. We have the power to change the picture of the Senate's disgraceful intransigence by insisting with our votes, our letters to Senators, and our letters to newspaper editors that the Senators in our states must support ratification of this treaty.

---

[1] Christiane Northrop, *Women's Bodies, Women's Wisdom* New York: Bantam Books, 1998 pp. 4-5.

[2] Idem.

[3] Idem.

[4] As quoted in "Senate Discusses CEDAW on International Women's Day" which can be found on the UNA-USA website:
http://www.unausa.org/newindex.asp?place=http://www.unausa.org/policy/NewsActionAlerts/info/dc031400.asp

[5] As quoted in the "WFF statement on the United Nations Convention on the Elimination of All Forms of Discrimination Against Women," May 25, 2000 which can be located on the Women for Faith and Family's website: www.wf-f.org/CEDAW.html

[6] http://www.unausa.org/newindex.asp?place=http://www.unausa.org/policy/NewsActionAlerts/info/dc031400.asp

[7] www.wf-f.org/CEDAW.html

[8] http://www.unausa.org/newindex.asp?place=http://www.unausa.org/policy/NewsActionAlerts/info/dc031400.asp)

[9] "CEDAW: The Convention to Eliminate All Forms of Discrimination Against Women" found at the following website:
http://womensstudies.homestead.com/CEDAW.html

Chapter Four

HUMAN WRONGS – THE PLIGHT OF CHILDREN

A century that began with children having virtually no rights is ending with children having the most powerful legal instrument that not only recognizes but protects their human rights.

—Carol Bellamy, UNICEF
Executive Director

What are the stakes in international human rights efforts? Do they matter? Or are they, as some critics seem to think, just a bunch of "bleeding heart liberals" passing "feel good" treaties that make no difference to human well being? Consider, for starters, a study on the torture of children. A summary of it, quoted below, was included in the April 11, 2000 UN Wire, an internet wire service:

TORTURE: Millions Of Children May Be Victim, Group Says

The World Organization Against Torture, which advocates UN efforts to stop the practice of torture, said yesterday it has documented cases of child abuse and torture in more than 30 countries and fears that millions of children are victims every year.

The organization's director, Eric Sottas, said it is impossible to arrive at precise figures on the number of children tortured each year, but that the 2,169 cases his group has documented only scratch the surface. "I am afraid we are speaking in terms of millions and not tens of thousands per year," he said.

In a 327-page report entitled "The Hidden Crime," the organization says children "have increasingly become the target of oppressive regimes" and are subjected to kidnapping, rape, forced labor, execution, sexual abuse, beatings, murder, witnessing scenes of extreme violence against relatives, being denied food and drink, arbitrary arrest and detention.

The organization regards torture not only as cases in which government agents perpetrate violence, but when any adult is responsible. The report contains studies carried out between 1995 and 1998. Its release coincides with the annual session of the UN Human Rights Commission in Geneva[1].

These horrors illustrate the stakes, regardless of the uncertainties about the numbers in this article. In some of these situations, such as the civil war in Sierra Leone, rebel forces systematically committed atrocities against children, chopping off limbs of thousands and forcing others to kill their parents, then drugging them and using them as soldiers in combat. In wars like this the girls are often used as sex slaves. Of course, not all children in combat work for rebels. In other situations, rogue governments are violating the laws of their own country in carrying out such atrocities. When in the longer course of events rebels or rogue regimes can be brought to justice, these horrors can be dealt with by application of laws already in place. Courts then do not have to attempt the difficult and dubious legal maneuver of *ex post facto* trials for violation of laws that were not in place when the crimes occurred.

Almost nowhere in the world are such actions simply ignored or overlooked by the law. Thanks to international human rights efforts, and specifically the widespread ratification of the Rights of the Child Treaty, everywhere in the world these atrocities against children are illegal. Justice eventually prevails, but in some places, tragically, it is too late for thousands or tens of thousands of children. Appalling though it is, this situation is better than having no laws on the books and thus having no basis for justice at all, either as the atrocities are happening or after the fact. The Rights of the Child Treaty gives the UN and other international organizations vital leverage they need to bring economic, military, and political sanctions and other kinds of pressures to bear on the perpetrators of these ghastly crimes.

The U.S. Versus Justice

Strangely, in the context of the tremendous stakes illustrated here, the U.S. stands almost alone in the world as one of only two nations that have refused to ratify the Rights of the Child Treaty. This treaty, designed to prevent such extremes of child abuse as those described above, is a widely hailed landmark in international human rights and is one of the most widely accepted of all human rights treaties. Even such nations as Saudi Arabia, whose culturally ingrained oppression of women has led them to refuse to ratify the women's rights treaty (CEDAW), have ratified the Rights of the Child treaty. The only other nation in the world besides the U.S. that has not ratified it is Somalia. But Somalia has an excuse. It has no viable government, and therefore cannot ratify it.

Of course, as the torture and abuse of children demonstrates, this treaty has not yet succeeded in eliminating these atrocities. Implementing laws and treaties is a slow and painstaking process fraught with innumerable setbacks. But this process does gradually bring about constructive and lasting change. To fail to go through this long process is to capitulate to despair and to allow a permanent, unmitigated tragedy to fester and perhaps grow worse. Moving out of this kind of hopelessness and into the realm of organized effort, the treaty on the rights of children has created an all but universally accepted legal framework for dealing with such abuses. Consider the impact of the lack of such a framework. No reasonable person would advocate repeatedly coming along after there has been organized abuse of children and saying, those horrors should have been illegal, so we'll pass a law and make them illegal retroactively. Then we'll put the perpetrators on trial for violating laws that didn't exist at the time when they violated them." Trials for *ex post facto* crimes are prohibited in the U.S. Constitution and in the charter of the International Criminal Court; they cannot be made the norm at the international level.

In the courageous and genuinely noble venture of international cooperation in establishing this human rights treaty and others, the U.S., once a leader in human rights, is now the "odd-man-out" among the nations on human rights issues. We not only fail to lead; while other nations lead, we stand alone in refusing to follow. In some cases we actively oppose such treaties. Strangely, we of all countries stand *against* global progress in human rights. In this case, American citizens who more or less automatically support the wisdom of the U.S. government's decisions are pressed either to concede an exception or to make a case that the entire remainder of the world has gone mad. Our policy on this treaty in effect claims that we are in step and the rest of the world is out of step.

The President signs treaties; the Senate ratifies them. When ratified, treaties become an integral part of American law, carrying as much weight legally under the U.S. Constitution as any domestic law passed by the Congress and signed by the President. Why has the U.S. Senate taken the bizarre stance of refusing to ratify this treaty? Do our Senators think abuse and torture of children is O.K.? And what can American citizens do to change the picture? To arrive at the answers, first we need a quick overview of the treaty's content. You may wish to ask yourself as you read the following points, are these benign and reasonable guidelines or are they controversial and dubious?

The Treaty

For brevity, the following list of the treaty's key provisions had to be illustrative rather than exhaustive, but it does not conceal or omit any flaws or unreasonable provisions. Most of the language is taken verbatim from the text of the treaty. Following this brief summary I will explore the objections to the treaty by those who oppose it.

Very briefly, the treaty is about the survival and well being of children, free from abuse and exploitation. It is deeply and consistently family-friendly. It highlights and defends the family's role in children's lives. It refers to the family as the fundamental grouping of society and the natural environment for the growth and well being of its members, particularly children. States are obliged to respect parents' primary responsibility for providing care and guidance for their children and to provide parents with material assistance and support. States are also obliged to prevent children from being separated from their families unless the separation is judged necessary for the child's best interests. The treaty places great emphasis on family reunification in situations where children have been separated from their parents.

It guarantees children freedom of expression, within the normal constraints of law such as protection of the reputations of others, public order and health, etc. It protects children from all forms of physical or mental violence, injury or abuse, neglect or negligent treatment, maltreatment or exploitation—including sexual abuse—while in the care of parent(s), legal guardian(s) or any other person who has the care of the child. It provides for state support for care of children who have been deprived of their family environments. It calls for states to provide education for children.

It recognizes the right of the child to be protected from economic exploitation and from performing work that is hazardous or interferes with the child's education, or harms the child's health or physical, mental, spiritual, moral or social development. It provides that no child shall be subjected to torture or other cruel, inhuman or degrading treatment or punishment. It calls for states to protect children from being recruited into or forced into armed conflict. It provides for fair trials for children alleged to have committed crimes.

At this stage, I recommend that the reader stop and ask him or herself, what is there to disagree with in this? The refusal of the U.S. Senate to ratify this most benign and widely accepted of human rights treaties is, frankly, surprising and disturbing. It sends a message to the rest of the world that is heard loud and clear. It says to the rest of the world that we're not a team player, and we don't share your values, even about something as rock bottom basic as protecting children from abuse.

Yet as a nation we pride ourselves on caring for children and educating them. We have domestic laws against child abuse and child labor and requiring universal education. Few crimes arouse as much horror or public outcry among Americans as kidnapping, killing, or abusing children. We really do care. So why has our government refused to ratify this treaty in the face of otherwise unanimous world opinion?

The reasons are a mystery worth exploring. They shed light on other anomalies of U.S. foreign policy as well. There are at least four possible reasons: the Senate's continuing rejection of the treaty may be driven by (1) some unique (and possibly sinister) quirk in the view of children in American culture; (2) a very unrepresentative arrangement of power in the U.S. Senate, where treaties are reviewed for ratification; (3) a strong general prejudice in the Senate against all multilateral treaties; and/or (4) an important and objectionable element in the treaty that the U.S. alone has noticed or cared enough to react to, and yet is serious enough to be fatal to U.S. ratification. All four contain elements of the answer.

First, the cultural question. Do Americans see children differently? The short answer is that some Americans (a minority within a minority in the U.S. that nevertheless has extraordinary political power) do indeed see children and child rearing differently from most of the rest of the world, and from most other Americans. Not the whole of American culture, but a small and key part of it, is unusual. These folks are currently calling the shots of government policy regarding family values. One of the "shots" is persistence in refusing to allow ratification of the Rights of the Child Treaty.

Family Values

George Lakoff, in his remarkable book, *Moral Politics*, explores the role of family values in American political life. A cognitive linguist, Mr. Lakoff analyzes the unconscious metaphors that underlie and guide the political views of conservatives and liberals. He makes a persuasive case that "strict father morality" consisting primarily of rules and punishments for violating them constitutes the foundation of conservative family values and, by metaphorical extension, conservative political ideology in America. Similarly, "nurturant parent" morality that includes rules and firmness, but makes compassion and nurturing more important than the rules, governs liberal family values and political ideology. In both cases the theory on how to run a family and treat children serves as a metaphor for how the state should operate relative to its citizens. (Lakoff is careful to emphasize that political ideology and how people actually run their families may be quite inconsistent.)

The difference between the two sets of values and political metaphors is not absolute; it is a question of which has priority: rules and punishment, or compassion and nurturing. These priorities stem partly from contrasting underlying beliefs: that human nature is basically evil (requiring rules and punishment) or basically good (responding to love and nurturing). He explores this construct, far more nuanced and elaborated than it can be in this brief summary, in explaining the underlying thought patterns behind the liberal-conservative divide on a wide variety of domestic political issues.

In *Moral Politics* Lakoff applies his insights mainly to the domestic sphere rather than to foreign policy. However, on the Rights of the Child treaty, the relevance of his insights to the international arena is far too obvious to be ignored. Consider the following passage. Lakoff is quoting from a book, *How To Raise Children*, by a fundamentalist Christian author on childrearing:

Spanking should be administered firmly. It should be painful, and it should last until the child's will is broken. It should last until the child is crying, not tears of anger, but tears of a broken will. As long as he is stiff, grits his teeth, holds on to his own will, the spanking should continue." (Hyles, 99-100).[2]

In a later passage Lakoff quotes, Hyles adds interesting twists related both to the idea of unquestioning obedience and to the gender of the child:

Obedience is the most necessary ingredient to be required from the child. This is especially true for a girl, for she must be obedient all her life. The boy who is obedient to his mother and father will someday become the head of the home; not so for the girl. Whereas the boy is being trained to be a leader, the girl is being trained to be a follower. Hence, obedience is far more important to her, for she must someday transfer it from her parents to her husband. . . . This means she should never be allowed to argue at all. She should be submissive and obedient. She must obey immediately, without question, and without argument. The parents who require this have done a big favor for their future son-in-law.' (Hyles, 158)[3]

Could this worldview be clearer as a basis for hating and objecting to treaties on the rights of women and the rights of children? What rights? If instant, unquestioning obedience is what is required of a "good" child or wife, then "rights" are some sort of subversive fantasy. We have here in exaggerated but vivid form the underlying views that lead to the American religious far-right's strenuous objections to both treaties.

For other fundamentalist authors as well as Hyles, the demand for instant, unquestioning obedience from children seems to be unqualified. These writers offer more specifics on how the severe spankings Hyles advocates should be administered. As Lakoff notes, the "rod" in the Biblical quote, "spare the rod and spoil the child" is to be taken literally.

The rod is to be a thick wooden stick like a switch. Of course, the size of the rod should vary with the size of the child. . . . The use of the rod enables a controlled administration of pain to obtain submission and future obedience. . . . If the child repeatedly disobeys, then the chastisement has not been painful enough. (Fulgate 141 – 43)[4]

Another author in the same tradition suggests, "A number of rods [should be kept] throughout the house, in your car and in your purse [so that you] can apply loving correction immediately." (Tomczak, 117)[5] Evidently, frequent, severe beatings are expected to be necessary. Lakoff sums all this up with the following observations:

> We can now see a bit better what is meant when members of the conservative family values movement talk about 'discipline,' 'parental authority,' 'spanking,' and 'traditional family values.' 'Spanking' means hitting a child, starting in toddlerhood, with a belt, a paddle, or the branch of a tree.

> The conservative family values movement is pushing hard to stop the funding of social workers who investigate child abuse. They especially want evidence from bruises incurred during "spanking" not to count as evidence of child abuse....

> Gary L. Bauer's Family Research Council has been crusading against all efforts to ban the corporal punishment of children. It has been trying to get funds taken away from child protective services such as social workers investigating child abuse. Bauer sees such investigations as invasions of privacy by the 'therapeutic sector.'[6]

Another writer on the same subject, James Dobson, who is one of the more moderate of these writers, still advocates authority, unquestioning obedience, and swift, painful punishment as the main method of child rearing. The problem with this view, of course, besides the fact that it is cruel and produces bad results (violence-prone adults) according to the research, is that it contains no check on extremes of parental child abuse. What is being described in these passages is objectively a method of torture. (Not all spanking is so drastic. We'll deal with that in a moment.) One of the purposes of the Rights of the Child treaty is to introduce or reinforce checks on child abuse in legal systems throughout the world. Of course, such checks already exist in the U.S. But the Christian fundamentalist objection to the treaty would seem to be that the treaty would reinforce rather than undermine controls on child abuse in the U.S.

77

It should be noted from Lakoff's book that the key to the ideology here is that these extreme conservatives create a false dichotomy between harsh discipline and mushy over-indulgence. They deny the existence of any other alternative. They thus ignore a third way, a widely accepted child-rearing model that actually works, namely an approach in which love and nurturance are the first priority, but firmness, rules and discipline (not including harsh and frequent beatings) are integral parts of the total pattern. Lakoff comments:

I should say at the outset that virtually all of the mainstream experts on childrearing see the Strict Father model as being destructive to children. A nurturant approach is preferred. And most of the child development literature within the field of developmental psychology points in one direction: childrearing according to the Strict Father model harms children; a Nurturant Parent model is far superior.

In short, conservative family values, which are the basis for conservative morality and political thought, are not supported by either research in child development or the mainstream childrearing experts in the country.[7]

If the passages *by religious authors* that border on advocating child abuse quoted above don't leave the reader disturbed, I don't know what will. Strangely, this kind of treatment of children, borderline abusive even without the common element of a parent going overboard in anger, is not just a tragic social phenomenon, it is a child-rearing ideology espoused by American writers respected in a politically powerful segment of American society. It should be emphasized, gratefully, that not every fundamentalist Christian family treats its children this way. One can hope that few do. However, these writers and others with similar views of childrearing are the ideological leaders of this religious and political movement as regards family values. It is they and their ilk, not the decent ultra-conservative people, who impact the policy arena in the U.S.

The conservative family values agenda is, at present, being set primarily by fundamentalist Christians. This is not a situation that many people are aware of. Probably the most prominent figures in the fundamentalist Christian family values movement are Dr. James Dobson, who is president of Focus on the Family, based in Colorado Springs, and Gary Bauer, who runs the Family Research Council in Washington, D.C. These groups have been most explicit in developing a Strict Father approach to childrearing and have been extremely active in promoting their approach. Since the ideas in the Christian childrearing manuals are fully consistent with the Strict Father model of the family that lies behind conservative politics, it is not at all strange that such fundamentalist groups should be setting the national conservative agenda on family values.[8]

It should be noted that the individuals mentioned immediately above and their organizational affiliations may not still be in place by the time the reader reads this book. However, they were indicative at the time of Mr. Lakoff's writing. The point is that this view of child rearing prevails in this cultural and political group, and is aggressively promoted by their leaders in the public and political arenas. This segment of American culture, Christian fundamentalism, is clearly a minority numerically in the U.S. Yet, as of this writing in the year 2003, it has substantial influence in the Senate and the House of Representatives, and significant weight in the White House, and its ideology has a powerful sway in policy decisions.

Even before the Bush administration, through extreme conservative Senate leaders such as Jesse Helms, former chair of the Senate Foreign Relations Committee, Christian fundamentalists have for some time powerfully influenced U.S. foreign policy in the arena of human rights as applied to both women and children. Hence the treaty on the Rights of the Child and the Convention to End All Forms of Discrimination Against Women (CEDAW) have not been ratified by the U.S. Senate despite repeated attempts by concerned American citizens to move them forward. The more moderate majority of American citizens have allowed adherents of this extremist viewpoint, working in conjunction with corporate wealth, to take over the country politically and "call the shots" on family values and other values as well in American policy formulation.

In this political context it is not a surprise that a treaty on the right of children to be protected from abuse was not forwarded to the U.S. Senate by the White House, and why the former Chair of the Senate Foreign Relations

Committee, Jesse Helms, energetically opposed the Rights of the Child Treaty when he had the power to make a difference.

Proponents of the Convention on the Rights of the Child are numerous. More than 350 non-governmental organizations (NGOs) are persistently pushing to send the Convention to the Senate for ratification. These NGOs include Amnesty International, American Red Cross, U.N. Association of USA, National Education Association, National Council for Child's Rights, Children of the Earth, Planned Parenthood, U.S. Committee for the UN Children's Fund, National Council of Churches, Children's Defense Fund, American Academy of Pediatrics, American Bar Association, and many more. The counterweight to the proponents is a relatively small cluster of right wing groups that was firmly backed by Jesse Helms. This group includes the Christian Coalition, Concerned Women for America, John Birch Society, Family Research Council, National Center for Home Education, Focus on the Family, and the Rutherford Institute.[9]

While the proponents outnumber the opponent groups, it is the latter which have the political influence to pressure the Senate to avoid the possibility that the Convention will even be brought up for ratification. The opponents have also prompted a stronger coordinated response from their public than the supporters have been able to organize. Elaborating on the subject, Susan Kilbourne of the National Committee for the Rights of the Child stated, "These groups are well funded, organized and coordinated; and they are successfully motivating their members to contact the U.S. Senate to voice their objections to the Convention. Senate staffers have reported that their offices receive letters at the rate of 100 opposition letters for every letter in support of the Convention."[10] Addressing the Senate on February 25, 1995, Senator Bob Dole referred to this imbalance: "Mr. President, in the past several days, I have received thousands of calls from all over the country in opposition to this Convention. My office has not received one call for it."[11]

Jesse Helms never hesitated to let his opposition to the treaty be known to all. He was extremely outspoken regarding what he felt to be the danger the treaty posed to parental authority: "I am convinced that the treaty forces its way into the relationship of a parent and child, and should not be considered in federal legislation, let alone international treaties."[12] Expanding on his reasons for opposing the Convention, Helms stated, "The United Nations Convention on the Rights of the Child is incompatible with God-given rights and responsibilities of parents to raise their children," and that "the Convention has the potential to severely restrict states and the federal government in their efforts to protect children and to enhance family life."[13]

In June 1995, Helms joined 26 of his fellow Senators in co-sponsoring a resolution asking that President Clinton not put the treaty up for review in the Foreign Relations Committee (which Helms chaired.) Helms was in an incredibly powerful position in the U.S. government, as described by Jo Becker, Advocacy Coordinator for Children's Rights Projects at Human Rights Watch: "Helms is the gate-keeper to all international treaties, and he shares views with the religious right in this country. And Helms has more power than the (U.S.) President."[14] Of course, "more power" here refers to power over treaties, not power in the comprehensive sense. Due to Helms' influence as well as the continuation of his viewpoint among many Senators since his departure, the Convention has not yet been introduced to the Senate for ratification.

Rules, Penalties, and Spanking

Of course, there are two sides to the story about childrearing and the question of spanking. Everyone who has raised children (I myself helped raise four children in the difficult role of step-father) knows that child rearing is one of the most emotionally difficult and exasperating undertakings of a lifetime. Moral dilemmas abound, decisions are regularly challenged, and some rules are absolutely necessary. Penalties or sanctions are essential to enforce rules. Children are often volatile emotionally and have strong wills. They often rebel frontally or sneak around behind a parent's back to get their own way. Firm and consistent correction is necessary. Without rules and clear guidance, children are lost in a fog of confusion about the boundaries of acceptable behavior. And without appropriate discipline rules are meaningless and children may end up terribly spoiled and self-centered. For both the survival and sanity of the parents and the healthy development of the child, some basic rules must be explicit and must be obeyed. But rules also must also be reasonable and be understood by the child as protecting their longer-term well-being and the legitimate needs of others.

In other words, rules are natural corollaries of loving protection of the child and respect for the needs of others, not arbitrary whims to be enforced by the extreme violence of a domestic dictator. If a child doesn't understand the reasons for the rules, an essential element in his or her education is missing. This means that a child's questioning of the rules, far from evil, is valuable (even if partly motivated by rebelliousness) and the parent's honest explanations are educationally vital.

So what about spanking? Isn't it sometimes necessary? Some loving parents spank their children, usually as a severe penalty of last resort (normally with the hand, administered abruptly and firmly to the backside, one or several times). Some quite successful parents do not. Other penalties besides spanking can be effective. Millions of normal, healthy adults have been raised by loving parents with spanking (as described in this paragraph) as a penalty of last resort and without it. It has not proved essential in child-rearing. And sensibly and rarely used, it has not proved irredeemably destructive.

In order to deal with the problem of the rights of children in the United States and the U.S. failure to ratify the Rights of the Child Treaty, it is not necessary to arrive at an all-inclusive or doctrinaire answer to the question of whether a parent should or should not use spanking in this way in disciplining children. *The treaty does not prohibit spanking.* It does prohibit child abuse. The U.S. could ratify the treaty and parents could still spank their children as needed. It is simply a myth that the two are incompatible.

The extremes of cruelty advocated in some of the fundamentalist Christian child-rearing literature describe a far more destructive act than mere spanking, coupled with a blindly authoritarian mind-set. Children must not question, but must obey immediately and unthinkingly. (Viewed societally, this approach to childrearing is designed to create stunted growth in "thinking for oneself." This kind of training could facilitate living in a dictatorship or working in a military organization, or for that matter, any rigid hierarchy. However, it certainly is not conducive to the questioning and probing mindset needed for citizenship in a democracy.) This extreme harshness is not "normal" spanking; it is an early stage of child abuse. This kind of treatment produces withdrawn, fearful, resentful children. Research shows that as adults, they are more violence-prone than children raised more reasonably and lovingly.

Spanking In the Treaty

What does the treaty itself say about spanking? In a word, nothing. So far as I can tell in studying the treaty's full text, it does not address the subject. However, there are passages that could possibly be interpreted as obliquely relevant. Certainly there is much about parental authority. Parents with a bad conscience or a penchant for worry may be concerned about spanking being interpreted as "abuse." The answer is that the treaty does not address spanking but does, of course, address abuse. Here is one such passage:

82

Article 9

1. States Parties shall ensure that a child shall not be separated from his or her parents against their will, except when competent authorities subject to judicial review determine, in accordance with applicable law and procedures, that such separation is necessary for the best interests of the child. Such determination may be necessary in a particular case such as one involving *abuse or neglect* of the child by the parents, or one where the parents are living separately and a decision must be made as to the child's place of residence.

Another passage on abuse:

Article 37

States Parties shall ensure that:
(a) No child shall be subjected to torture or other cruel, inhuman or degrading…treatment or punishment. Neither capital punishment nor life imprisonment without possibility of release shall be imposed for offences committed by persons below eighteen years of age.

Spanking—done by normal, loving parents (my own, when I was a child, included)—hardly can be described as "torture or other cruel, inhuman, or degrading punishment." However, done as some abusive parents do it, the passage may apply. Parents who believe that these passages prohibit spanking are in effect admitting that the style of spanking they wish to use constitutes child abuse. If the shoe fits, wear it. As noted in other passages of the treaty, if extremely harsh spanking were to raise a question about abuse and became a legal issue, the treaty calls for the decision on where to draw the line to be made by competent legal authority based on evidence, not on a whim.

Other passages distantly related to spanking in the treaty imply that in extreme cases, and subject to relevant laws and court orders, a child could be removed from an abusive home environment:

83

Article 19

1. States Parties shall take all appropriate legislative, administrative, social and educational measures to protect the child from all forms of physical or mental violence, injury or abuse, neglect or negligent treatment, maltreatment or exploitation, including sexual abuse, while in the care of parent(s), guardian(s) or any other person who has the care of the child.

2. Such protective measures should, as appropriate, include effective procedures for the establishment of social programmes to provide necessary support for the child and for those who have the care of the child, as well as for other forms of prevention and for identification, reporting, referral, investigation, treatment and follow-up of instances of child maltreatment described heretofore, and, as appropriate, for judicial involvement.

Article 20:

1. A child temporarily or permanently deprived of his or her family environment, or in whose own best interests cannot be allowed to remain in that environment, shall be entitled to special protection and assistance provided by the State.

Another subject that may concern extreme religious authoritarians is freedom of speech for children. As we have seen in the passages by writers on fundamentalist family values, this concept is anathema. Children are to obey, and most definitely not to question. By contrast, here is the relevant passage from the treaty:

Article 13

1. The child shall have the right to freedom of expression; this right shall include freedom to seek, receive and impart information and ideas of all kinds, regardless of frontiers, either orally, in writing or in print, in the form of art, or through any other media of the child's choice.

2. The exercise of this right may be subject to certain restrictions, but these shall only be such as are provided by law and are necessary:
(a) For respect of the rights or reputations of others; or
(b) For the protection of national security or of public order, or of public health or morals.

A final passage that might give heartburn to a fundamentalist parent relates to freedom of religion:

Article 14

1. States Parties shall respect the right of the child to freedom of thought, conscience and religion.

2. States Parties shall respect the rights and duties of the parents and, when applicable, legal guardians, to provide direction to the child in the exercise of his or her right in a manner consistent with the evolving capacities of the child.

3. Freedom to manifest one's religion or beliefs may be subject only to such limitations as are prescribed by law and are necessary to protect public safety, order, health or morals, or the fundamental rights and freedoms of others.

At first thought, this may seem a startling provision. Obviously small children are not in a position to choose their own religion in contrast to those of their parents. As everyone knows who has raised children, small children usually accept whatever religious training their parents provide them. This reality is acknowledged above with its reference to the evolving capacities of the child. The rights and duties of the parents to provide direction to the child are also assured in the same passage. A difficult case for children's freedom of religion might be a young child of parents with an unusual religion in the social context, particularly if the child is required to wear distinguishing clothing that may provide an occasion for ridicule or taunting by other children. They and their parents have a difficult road, but the treaty will not help or hinder them.

Regardless of the treaty, when a child reaches an age at which the capacity for independent and critical thinking may come into play, presumably in the late teens, the parent had better have good answers for difficult questions. Certainly such a parent will find it is futile to attempt to force a set of religious beliefs on a teenager, either by verbal browbeating or by punishment. Nature has built into human beings an innate freedom of religion that oppression, even by a parent, cannot stamp out. A lip-service appearance of belief can be forced at great cost in terms of the relationship and the respect of the victim for the perpetrator of the oppression, but the reality of belief cannot be forced. In a sense, the treaty only acknowledges what is built into human nature. However, it is also saying that the state or community cannot impose a religion on a child either directly or, presumably, through the parents. It is interesting in this context that 189 member states of the UN, out of 191, have accepted this treaty.

In summation, as the passages above show, the treaty is far from unreasonable. It expresses a consensus view among reasonable people the world over. The opposition to the treaty in fundamentalist circles is based partly on an erroneous view of what constitutes effective child rearing and partly on misinformation and misinterpretation of the treaty. Stated bluntly, it is based on urban legends spread by fanatics, not on the plain meaning of the text.

Fundamentalism Versus Christianity

Before returning to the main subject of this chapter, the Rights of the Child Treaty, it is essential to digress briefly to ward off a potential misunderstanding. The adverse comments above about fundamentalist Christian childrearing ideology in the U.S. should not be understood as in any way a criticism of the Christian religion. Quite the contrary. Drawing from my own convictions, I have enormous respect for the Christian religion as one of the greatest sources of human well-being on the planet, alongside the other great religions of the world. When a particular group of Christians runs amok and does destructive things or takes destructive positions, in every case I have seen, they are unwittingly at odds with the core teachings of their own religion. Usually they are infected with one or both of two dangerous "viruses" that attack all religions—fanaticism and religious tribalism. The essence of these viruses: we have the only truth; everybody else is a tool of the devil. Fighting other ideas, even violently, is God's work; we must do it with all our might. Hence, in the extreme we get heretics burned at the stake.

Protestant fundamentalism, though a powerful cultural and political force in the U.S., is a small and atypical fraction of the totality of Christianity. The world contains about a billion Christians. That's about four times the population of the United States, and one-sixth of the world's population. Christians are spread out all over the world in scores of countries from Siberia to the Falkland Islands and include Catholics and Protestants, Baptists and Episcopalians, liberals and conservatives, Russian and Greek Orthodox, Coptics and Nestorians, and on and on. Christianity is a vast and diverse cultural phenomenon, as are the other great religions of the world. American protestant fundamentalists are only one of many groups of Christians, and have no legitimate claim to be more genuine, more "the real thing," than any other group of Christians.

The founder of the Christian religion famously said, "Suffer the little children to come unto me" (Luke 18:16). Compassion for all, including children, was for him a priority. More broadly speaking, his teachings and behavior clearly and consistently corrected the excessive, rule-bound legalism of the surrounding religion of his day. Another of his famous sayings, "The Sabbath was made for man, not man for the Sabbath," can in the totality of his teachings be seen as an illustration of a broader principle: the rules were made for man, not man for the rules. He consistently advocated that love, respect and compassion should be the primary guiding principles of human conduct, in contrast to the endlessly elaborated formal rules common in his day.

Borrowing Lakoff's phrasing, far from teaching the "strict father" morality of the Scribes and Pharisees of his day (whom Jesus strenuously criticized) or the authoritarian family values of the fundamentalist writers cited above, Jesus taught a "nurturant parent" morality. This shift in emphasis from law to love was a key element in the religious revolution he introduced. Whether one embraces Christianity or not, one should not imagine that the harsh, even cruel parenting practices advocated by the misguided zealots quoted above accurately represent the Christian point of view. They are an aberration. In fact, they are the opposite of what Christianity teaches. Fortunately, a great many fundamentalist families do not practice what their "family values" ideologues preach.

Does the Treaty Make a Difference?

The Rights of the Child Treaty is sometimes derided by its critics as ineffectual because it coexists in some countries that have ratified it with appalling abuses of children that go unchecked by the country's ratification of the treaty. In this respect it is similar to other treaties that are far-seeing in their intent and set a high standard as a goal, but are of course not self-implementing or instantly effective. Laws that posit basic principles and require extensive changes to actual practice in a society often take decades, if not centuries, to implement. The slow process of lawsuits, precedent-setting court decisions, legislative reforms and law implementation is not an overnight affair. Yet these actions are much more likely to be taken if a broad legal framework such as this treaty is present. They are much less likely to be taken if the legal framework is not present to move events in a positive direction. A country does not establish new implementing laws and regulations for a treaty it has not ratified. Defining certain principles and establishing certain behaviors as illegal are the first steps on a long journey. Without them the journey doesn't happen.

There is much to celebrate in the reality that all the world, except the U.S. and Somalia, has ratified the Rights of the Child Treaty. On November 10, 1999, the UN General assembly justly engaged in such a celebration:

The United Nations Children's Fund (UNICEF) said yesterday that despite disappointments and missed opportunities, the "world is a better place" because of the UN Convention on the Rights of the Child, the groundbreaking human rights treaty adopted by the UN General Assembly 10 years ago next week.

"There is no doubt in my mind that this convention has improved the lives of millions of children and made the world a better place," said UNICEF Executive Director Carol Bellamy. "It has stimulated legal reform in dozens of countries around the world, enjoined governments to take the health and well-being of children seriously and initiated a process of goal-setting that keeps everyone honest about global progress, or lack of it."

Acknowledging that "some might emphasize the ways in which the convention has fallen short" of its lofty aims, Bellamy argued that concrete achievements had confirmed the treaty's stature as "a fountainhead for the lasting improvement of children's lives."

Deputy Secretary-General Louise Frechette ... addressed the assembly, saying the convention has "inspired and guided the further strengthening of international standards on children's rights." But she expressed concern that the United States remains one of two countries that have not ratified it. Frechette: "To achieve truly universal ratification of the convention would be a fitting way to enter the new century, a century that will belong to the children of today."[15]

Unfortunately, and contrary to Frechette's hope, the world entered a new century and a new millennium without the U.S. ratifying the treaty and with the prospects for such ratification more remote than ever.

Our Unrepresentative Senate

If the Convention on the Rights of the Child were put to a vote of the American people and explained clearly, honestly and adequately, without the usual political spin and disinformation, there can be little doubt that it would be approved overwhelmingly, just as it has been by all the world's nations except the U.S. So why does the U.S. Senate refuse to ratify the treaty? Or more specifically, how does it happen that the Senate is controlled by extremist ideological forces that represent a minority of the American electorate?

The answer to this question appears to be an unfortunate convergence of structure and personalities in the Senate, in the larger context of a convergence of powerful minority political forces in the country. This latter convergence has already been explored: an ultra-conservative religious movement, mainly concentrated in rural, southern, and western states, has combined with economic conservatives backed by (or owning) immense corporate wealth. The latter wish to hang on to their money; the former wish to promote their dogma. Together these forces have gained a marginal hold on the Senate and the House, as well as decisive control of the White House in the person of President George W. Bush. This political coalition (conservative wealth and conservative religion) in the senate gave religious extremists such as Jesse Helms, the senior senator in the Senate Foreign

Relations Committee, the power to pursue an ideological agenda that is far out of alignment with the views of most Americans. Here are the details on how this works:

In American politics, money talks though TV advertisements. They are expensive, primarily a game for the rich. There is no control on the extent of "spin" in political advertising. Candidates, parties, and other interested organizations can exaggerate, distort, ignore facts and hype myths to their heart's content in advancing candidates who reflect their agendas. In this blinding blizzard of money-driven misinformation, during election season it becomes almost impossible for the average citizen to sort out what is truth and what is half-truth or outright falsehood. It is hardly surprising that some people throw up their hands and decide not to vote. Furthermore, people often respond emotionally to personalities (glamorized or demonized by the ads) rather than judging on the issues, about which they are often uninformed or deliberately misled. In this confusing fog of propaganda warfare, personality hype and character assassination, the side with a substantial funding advantage usually wins the election. It can hire the most talented spin-meisters and put out the most numerous ads. Every American knows this, but no one seems to be able to correct the problem. To date, admirable and well-intentioned efforts to correct it by campaign finance reform have been notably ineffective.

As a result, control of the U.S. Senate, blessed by the Constitution with two Senators each representing the tiny populations of states like Wyoming and the huge populations of states like New York and California, is a "crap shoot" in which the outcomes favor big money and states with small (i.e., rural and conservative) populations.

Another structural quirk (bestowed benignly in its intent by the Constitution) is that ratification of a treaty requires a two-thirds majority of the Senate. The Senate has been closely divided between the parties and between conservatives and liberals during most of the period to which this book pertains—the post-Cold War era (since 1989). Any issue that has a partisan stamp has no chance of acquiring a two-thirds majority, no matter which party is momentarily and marginally in control. Hence, to be ratified a treaty has to have little or no partisan or ideological opposition. As we have noted before, the Rights of the Child Treaty has active opposition from religious extremists with large numbers of constituents who are willing to write to their Senators. They devoutly believe the propaganda against the treaty perpetrated by their leaders. There is no corrective to even the most blatantly false or slanted claims about the treaty, which are many.

In addition to the randomness of control within the Senate, the seniority system used in that august body presents another problem. It selects the most senior member of the party that is momentarily in overall control to lead each of the powerful Senate committees. By this means one of the most bellicose, feared, and ideologically extreme members of the Senate, Jesse Helms, became the dictatorial Chair of the Senate Foreign Relations Committee and dominated key elements of American foreign policy during much of the tenure of President Bill Clinton.

Clinton took a benign and cooperative approach to foreign policy and genuinely believed in international human rights efforts. However, Helms exercised a *de facto* veto power over Clinton's policies. As an aggressive, go-it-alone unilateralist, Helms blocked ratification of treaties on human rights and numerous other subjects, blocked U.S. payment of UN dues (though under fierce pressure he eventually changed course on this), tirelessly whipped up Senate support for unilateral economic sanctions against other countries, and generally seemed to delight in jamming sticks into the eyes of countries he didn't like. He made a lot of enemies for the United States. When Helms rose to the immense power of the committee chairmanship, no small number of his fellow Senators were appalled by the prospect of his aggressively backward views controlling U.S. foreign policy. But in the face of his vindictive tactics and the power of the Senate's entrenched seniority system, no one dared to organize opposition to him. His fellow Senators rolled their eyes and shook their heads, but acquiesced.

Down With Treaties!

A discussion of the illustrative role of Senator Helms during the Clinton years brings us to a third reason the Rights of the Child Treaty has been rejected by the Senate. Helms and the other conservatives who have held sway in the Senate for much of the time since the end of the Cold War have demonstrated an overwhelming prejudice against multilateral treaties. That prejudice has been a key factor, perhaps the main factor, in the U.S. becoming a maverick (some use the harsher term "rogue") nation, radically out of step with the rest of the world.

To illustrate, the U.S. has either refused to sign or refused to ratify the Law of the Sea Treaty, the Ottawa Treaty banning landmines, the Rights of Women Treaty (CEDAW), the International Criminal Court Treaty, the Kyoto Protocols on Global Warming, the Comprehensive Nuclear Test Ban Treaty, the Convention on the Protection of Migrant Workers and their

Families, and the International Covenant on Economic, Social, and Cultural Rights, to name a few. The list goes on and on.

At first one might ask, don't most of these treaties reflect a liberal political view and thus naturally attract the wrath of conservatives?

A partial, but not quite complete, answer is "no." The Law of the Sea Treaty is deeply conservative and is loved and supported by conservative, pro-military boosters of the U.S. Navy, yet it was consistently rejected by the Senate during Helms' dominance of Senate foreign policy matters, and up to the time of this writing. At first it contained provisions that seemed to conservatives to limit the opportunities of the business community to exploit the mineral resources of the ocean. When these provisions were negotiated out of the treaty at the insistence of the U.S., the conservative rejection of it, led by Helms, continued without any visible reason, other than a prejudice against all such multilateral treaties.

To the question raised above, aren't these treaties mostly liberal, and therefore objectionable to conservatives, another partial answer is "yes." Many of these treaties are "liberal" if support for basic moral and legal principles such as human rights and justice are "liberal" causes. These treaties are "liberal" in the broad historical sense of the term "liberal democracy" that is the essence of American democracy. By this standard, Thomas Jefferson, a farmer who believed in limited government, was a "liberal." By this standard, the Bill of Rights of the American Constitution is a "liberal" document. However, I doubt that conservatives such as Helms and his ilk would want to be associated with the rejection of these American icons. In fact, the meanings of the terms "liberal" and "conservative" here are almost reversed. It is certainly considered "conservative" to cling to the Constitution and the Bill of Rights as foundational elements in American democracy. This is "conservative" in the noblest sense of conservation of all that is positive in the American system of government.

To illustrate what is meant by the term "liberal democracy," by contrast with what it is not, a democracy that lacks the protections of justice and human rights could by a legitimate vote put into power a majority that would oppress and torment and even systematically kill members of a minority. Without the "liberal" protections of human rights built into the constitution of a nation (or into a treaty it has ratified), there is no protection of minorities in a democracy.

There is a tremendous self-contradiction in American conservative ideology here. In the U.S. it is conservative (and obviously, to liberals and conservatives alike, a good thing) to cling to the traditions, laws, and institutions that assure human rights and justice at home. But it is also conservative to object strenuously to similar or essentially identical traditions, laws, and institutions at the international level. What is good for the domestic goose is bad for the international gander. The only explanation for this 180 degree reversal of basic principle at the boundaries of the good old USA is tribalism or jingoism. It cannot be defended logically.

The Right to Kill Children

Early in this chapter I began an exploration of a mystery, why the U.S. Senate has refused to even consider ratifying a treaty as obviously benign and constructive as the Rights of the Child Treaty. I listed four possible reasons: (1) some unique (and possibly sinister) quirk in the view of children in American culture; (2) a very unrepresentative arrangement of power in the U.S. Senate, where treaties are reviewed for ratification; (3) a strong general prejudice in the Senate against all multilateral treaties; and/or (4) an important and objectionable element in the treaty that only the U.S. has noticed or cared enough to react to, and yet is serious enough to be fatal to U.S. ratification. I have shown above that the first three reasons work powerfully in concert to prevent ratification. The fourth possible reason calls attention to an especially interesting but isolated issue. There is an element in the treaty that some extreme conservatives might object to. In effect it would prevent the U.S. Government from killing children. What's wrong with that? you may ask. Why would we want to kill children? It sounds like an outrage.

In a nutshell, the treaty prohibits the death penalty for children and defines children as persons under the age of 18. But in the U.S., 23 states permit the death penalty to be used for individuals who were under 18 at the time they committed the crime (age 16 is the minimum). Is this possibility just theoretical, or do we actually apply the death penalty to this group of teenagers? An article in the May 22, 2002 edition of *The Economist* notes that "since 1985, 18 child offenders have been executed—half of them in Texas—and another 84 were on death row in November 2001."[16]

Death penalty supporters don't want our freedom to kill teenagers for capital crimes rescinded. This is not one of the freedoms we are prone to brag about in arguing that "we are the good guys," but it is the law in almost half our states. And it appears to be especially popular in Texas, the state formerly governed by our 43rd president. Additionally, given that our Attorney General is an avid proponent of the death penalty, the treaty's constraint on the freedom to kill teenagers could be a powerful reason not to forward it to the Senate for ratification.

Bright Spots

Is the picture unremittingly bleak? The conservative family values political agenda that adamantly opposes ratification of the Rights of the Child Treaty has the effect of denying U.S. support to the world for a range of extremely valuable provisions of the treaty protecting children from abuse. Disgraceful though this stance may be in principle, obviously it should not be construed as support for such outright atrocities against children as torture or their forced use as soldiers or prostitutes.

It is a pleasure to report several strongly positive actions by the U.S. Government on children's rights and the humane treatment of children throughout the world. On July 20, 2000 a UN Wire special report announced UNICEF's praises for Clinton for signing two optional protocols to the UN Convention on the Rights of the Child. Two and a half years later, despite the Senate's continued rejection of the foundational Convention on the Rights of the Child, it unanimously embraced the two optional protocols to the treaty. They extend its meaning and impact. On December 23, 2002, the State Department's Office of the Spokesman announced these actions. One protocol concerned the use of children in armed conflict, the other, the sale of children, child pornography, and child prostitution.

The statement presents the fact that "over 300,000 girls and boys are used in government or rebel forces in over 30 armed conflicts in the world. They serve as soldiers, runners, guards, sex slaves and spies. An estimated one million children are currently trafficked for coerced sexual exploitation or labor. At the least, these children face interrupted or total suspension of education. Often, they live with fear, pain, and degradation—or don't survive at all." And later the same announcement affirms that "child victims of armed conflict and commercial sexual exploitation desperately need the world's attention. The United States advocates the widest possible acceptance and ratification of these historic protocols so that they speak for the entire world community."

In a highly positive practical footnote to this progress, a Washington Post news article on May 8, 2003 announced another positive step by the U.S. Government. Under the second Bush administration:

Labor Secretary Elaine E. Chao announced a $13 million initiative to help eliminate the use of children as soldiers in more than 30 countries and to help those who were enslaved. The forced recruitment and use of children is one of the worst forms of child labor, Chao said, opening a two-day conference on the issue. 'It is a moral outrage and must be stopped.' The initiative includes a $7 million global project by the International Labor Organization to help former child soldiers in Burundi, the Congo, the Congo Republic, Rwanda, Uganda, the Philippines, Sri Lanka and Columbia. An additional $3 million will be spent on education for such children in Uganda. Also, $3 million will go to help child soldiers in Afghanistan through UNICEF.

This financial support for efforts to rehabilitate child soldiers is admirable without any qualification. Kudos to Bush's Labor Secretary for supporting this effort. Whether $13-$16 million is enough money to make a substantial difference remains to be seen, but in any case, providing it is a move in the right direction. This is a clear instance when actions speak louder than words, and this time the actions are on the side of the angels.

This situation is somewhat reminiscent of the U.S. stance on landmines, where the U.S. has refused to sign the treaty banning landmines but also has provided funds to assist some countries in removing landmines from their territories. Taking both actions, supporting the treaty and assisting with demining, would be better. But financial assistance with demining is far better than doing neither.

Food For Education

Another truly outstanding action by the U.S. Government is the Global Food for Education Initiative. It provides meals for school children in poverty-stricken countries where both education and adequate child nutrition are spotty. The following passage from the web site of the U.S. Department of Agriculture Foreign Agricultural Service explains it:

Under the pilot Global Food for Education Initiative, USDA donated surplus U.S. agricultural commodities for use in school feeding and preschool nutrition programs in developing countries. These school feeding programs help assure that children attend and remain in school, improve childhood development and achievement, and thereby contribute to more self-reliant, productive societies. The initiative was announced in July 2000, building on ideas promoted by Ambassador George McGovern and former Senator Bob Dole.

The pilot initiative was implemented in fiscal years 2001 and 2002, with completion expected in fiscal year 2003. Under the pilot, USDA's Commodity Credit Corporation committed $300 million for U.S. commodities, transportation, and administrative expenses. ... The USDA-approved projects are being conducted through the United Nations World Food Program, private voluntary organizations, and eligible foreign governments.[17]

It is common in developing countries for girls to get the short end of the stick where both food and education are concerned. Of the estimated 300 million children in the world who are chronically hungry, the majority are girls. Often in developing countries they are valued less than boys and are shut out of schooling, especially when the system is under economic pressure. Not only is this reality appalling on its face, but also the economic growth and health of the entire society is stunted as a result, since half of the population is unable to contribute fully to the well-being of those around them. One of the special advantages of the Food for Education Program is that girls, as well as boys, will be eligible to go to school under the program and international agencies will monitor maintenance of their attendance numbers.

So What's Next?

The next steps for the American public and the United States as a nation among other nations in the world should be apparent to any reader at this point. The sensible, mainstream people who constitute the majority of Americans must organize and use the ballot box to take the country back from the ideological extremists, not only for the ratification of the Convention on the Rights of the Child, but for a host of other similar constructive actions. Not only the White House, but also the Senate will be key battle grounds in this effort to restore genuine moral integrity to

America's position in the world. The United States can then proudly re-join the rest of the human race on these issues. The final chapter of this book details how individuals can do more to contribute to this goal than the minimum, which of course is to vote. Mainstream Americans can return this country to the values it stands for if they organize and muster the political will to take action. The organizations already exist. All one has to do is join them, and possibly go further and become active in them.

---

[1] Associated Press/Long Island Newsday, 10 Apr
[2] George Lakoff, *Moral Politics*, The University of Chicago Press, 1996, p. 343.
[3] Ibid., p. 344.
[4] Ibid., pp. 344 &345.
[5] Idem.
[6] Ibid., p.348
[7] Ibid., pp. 339 & 340.
[8] Ibid., p. 339.
[9] "Death Penalty News: USA" 2-16-98, Available from http://venus.soci.niu.edu/~archives/ABOLISH/jan98/0307.html and "The UN Convention on the Rights of the Child: The Most Dangerous Attack on Parents' Rights in the History of the United States" by Christopher Klicka, 11-1-1999. Available from http://www.hslda.org/docs/nche/000000/00000020.asp
[10] As quoted on http://venus.soci.niu.edu/~archives/ABOLISH/jan98/0307.html
[11] As quoted in http://www.hslda.org/docs/nche/000000/00000020.asp
[12] As quoted in "Politics—US: Right-Wingers Block U.N. Children's Treaty, 2-15-98. Available from http://www.oneworld.org/ips2/feb98/usa4.html
[13] As quoted on Amnesty International's website. Available from http://www.amnestyusa.org/children/crn_faq.html
[14] http://www.oneworld.org/ips2/feb98/usa4.html
[15] This quote is taken from a November 10, 1999 report in the UN Wire, an internet news service on UN-related matters.
[16] "Oh, and Somalia too", The Economist, May 2, 2002. Available at http://www.economist.com/displaystory.cfm?story_id=S%27%29H%28%2DP%21%3B%25%23P%23L%0A
[17] http://www.fas.usda.gov/excredits/gffei.html

Chapter Five

ABOVE THE LAW

Seldom in the course of public discussion of a great national issue have so many great and good former officials been so misinformed about fundamental principles of international law.

> —Letter from 10 former presidents of the American Society of International Law, recommending acceptance of the International Criminal Court Treaty without changes in the text.[1]

"The hall erupted into applause that grew louder and louder, spilling over into rhythmic stomping and hooting that lasted a good ten minutes, the room becoming positively weightless with the mingled sense of exhaustion and achievement."[2] This was not a bunch of hooligans at a sports event; they were diplomats concluding a treaty negotiation. To put it mildly, diplomats are not usually so boisterous. The uproar was unprecedented. This was the moment, unique in human history, when hundreds of delegates and observers in Rome celebrated the birth of the International Criminal Court (ICC). This was an event everyone present knew would be remembered by future generations as a turning point in world history. Human rights experts have called it second only to establishing the UN as a landmark moment in establishing peace and justice in the world. For the first time, individuals, rather than nations, would be held accountable to international law for wholesale crimes against their fellow human beings, and there would be an institutional mechanism for holding them responsible.

The ICC is designed to bring to justice individual perpetrators of the most monstrous crimes against humanity, crimes such as the organized mass rapes in Bosnia and two main types of large-scale murder: war crimes and genocide. The vote for the Rome Treaty was 120 to 7, with 21 abstentions.

At this moment on July 17, 1988, the stage was set for the Court to be born. Commentators and legal scholars all over the world hailed the moment. Over the next few years, the treaty would be ratified by over 90 participating nations and the Court itself would come into existence. Conservatives dedicated to law and order, as well as liberals who believe in global human rights, had reason to celebrate. It was a victory for everyone who values human life and human well-being and prefers the orderly application of law over brute force, violence, and terror.

The ICC has jurisdiction only where domestic courts cannot or will not prosecute the offenders. Hence the ICC treaty is designed to plug a mile-wide hole in the world's system for establishing justice. It replaces with a permanent court the corrupt or nonexistent courts of failed states, the inefficient, after-the-fact courts such as the Nuremberg and Tokyo trials after WWII, and the ad hoc courts to try the war criminals of the former Yugoslavia and Rwanda. Most of the world's democracies celebrated, signed, and ratified the treaty. The world's genocidal and warmongering dictators like Saddam Hussein did not.

The vote by other nations to establish the ICC was a triumph of a core American value—the insistence on impartial justice for which the U.S. has stood since the establishment of its Constitution. To assure that justice was impartial, the U.S. Constitution made the Supreme Court independent of the Executive and Legislative Branches of the government. Similarly, the Rome Treaty made the ICC independent of the UN Security Council and General Assembly so its deliberations and decisions could not be politicized or controlled by a few votes or a single veto, whether from Russia, China, or the U.S. This move to make the ICC independent of politics was a particular triumph of the values championed by Americans.

Yet the United States voted against the treaty. It did so alongside such human rights luminaries as China, Libya, Yemen, Iraq, and Qatar. On that momentous day, values embraced by Americans triumphed globally but were trampled upon by American political leaders.

Ironically, one of the main reasons for U.S. opposition to the treaty was that the ICC was designed to be impartial and therefore was NOT subjected to the control of a political body, the UN Security Council, and thereby subject to an American veto. The U.S. Government wanted the Court to be subjected to political control, specifically, its own political control. However, most of the many democracies that supported the establishment of the Court, including some on the Security Council, wanted an impartial court, one with integrity and independence. They refused to yield to U.S. efforts to subordinate the Court to a political body. Ironically, they stood against the U.S. Government on behalf of values embraced by most Americans and by the framers of the U.S. Constitution. Given that the Court was not subject to the Security Council, the final obstacle for U.S. signature was the fact that the treaty did not single out Americans for exemption and thus did not explicitly set the U.S. above the law. Impartial justice was what American leaders did not want.

It is difficult to think of another moment when right and wrong were more clearly delineated, good and evil more dramatically highlighted, than when the ICC was established. Why on earth (literally) at this of all moments in history did the U.S. stand with "the bad guys," the mass murderers and human rights abusers among the nations, and oppose "the good guys," the democracies and upholders of justice and human rights? The world was stunned.

You might expect that the historic establishment of the Court and the shocking initial decision by the U.S. to vote against it would have been headline news in the U.S., publicized and challenged in the American press. Certainly it should have been, but the press had something more important to talk about. At the time it was obsessed with a certain young woman named Monica and the sordid details of her relationship with the President. There was no column space or airtime for "less important" matters. NBC and CBS did not mention the event, and there was nary a mention of it in *Time* or *Newsweek*. Sex in the White House was exciting; the future of justice in the world and U.S. opposition to it was not.

The timing of the "Monica scandal" may have had an unexpected side effect on the President. His overzealous prosecution by Special Prosecutor Kenneth Starr may have actually been a factor in Clinton's initial failure to approve the signing of the treaty. His prosecution (or more accurately, persecution) by Kenneth Starr may have made the groundless fears of the Court's enemies about prosecution of U.S. citizens for war crimes (a very unlikely event, given the way the Court is set up) more plausible to a beleaguered president. Is the Court well-protected against political abuse? The answer is explored below.

Nixing Political Abuse

During the years of negotiations leading to the Rome Treaty, military law experts from the Pentagon, with the diplomatic muscle of the U.S. Government behind them, successfully inserted into the treaty elaborate protections against abuse of the Court for political purposes. Thanks to these American efforts (something to cheer about in American foreign policy), the treaty contains the most thorough set of protections from political abuse ever concentrated in one document. Far from being the Swiss cheese of dangerous loopholes its spooked-out critics vaguely imply, the design of the treaty is a well-crafted bulwark against abuse. The bulwark was made in America. As shown below, these efforts render absurd the exaggerated fears of the opponents of the Court.

A brief summary such as this chapter cannot list all the protections against political abuse included in the Rome Treaty, but the following items are illustrative. They include a few of the most important ones. To make life easy for the majority of readers who are presumably not attorneys, I've phrased these safeguards in layman's language rather than technical legal jargon. Here are a few key protections:

- The Court can only try crimes committed after the Court is established; earlier crimes are not covered.
- The principle of complementarity: a nation with a competent judicial system is expected to investigate and prosecute its own cases; if it is willing and able to do so with integrity, the ICC then has no jurisdiction and can take no action.
- A three-judge Pre-Trial Chamber decides whether an alleged crime is within the jurisdiction of the Court (including applying the principle of complementarity).
- States may appeal to an Appeals Chamber if they disagree with a decision of the Pre-Trial Chamber.
- Crimes are defined narrowly and in detail to minimize doubt about what constitutes a crime for the purposes of the Court and to assure that only the most serious crimes are considered.
- When the Court finds ambiguity in the definition of a crime, the definition shall be interpreted in favour of the person being investigated, prosecuted or convicted.
- Intent to commit criminal behavior is an essential element in determining whether a crime has been committed, so for example, accidental deaths and injuries of civilians in a war are not considered crimes.
- References to previously established international law such as the Geneva Conventions build bridges for consistency and clarify

101

relationships between the Rome Treaty and other well-established international laws.

- High and explicit professional qualification standards for judges and staff of the Court and rigorous processes for their selection prevent appointment of political hacks.

Theoretically, a series of extremely corrupt implementing decisions could have undermined some of these protections. As of this writing, the implementing decisions establishing the Court have been made with the highest integrity. Even the harshest critics of the Court are silent on these decisions, not daring to claim that they lack integrity. The die has been cast.

All of the ICC's 18 judges come from countries closely allied with the United States. The special prosecutor, Luis Moreno Ocampo, illustrates the caliber of Court appointees. He is an Argentine national who was most recently the Robert F. Kennedy Visiting Professor of Latin American Studies at Harvard Law School. When he was appointed, human rights advocates noted that it's hardly likely that such a man would engage in unwarranted or politically motivated prosecutions of American citizens.

The accountability of the Court to international institutions is a key issue. The treaty sets up the ICC to be guided and controlled by an Assembly of States Parties, the countries that have signed and ratified the treaty. The overwhelming majority of these countries are democracies and allies of the U.S. Far from being "unaccountable" as the Court's foremost critics— Senator Jesse Helms and others of his ilk—loudly proclaimed, the Court has a structure that is in fact fully accountable to this appropriate representative body. The ICC is the same in this respect as other international organizations as diverse and widely accepted as the World Health Organization and the Food and Agriculture Organization.

The powers of the Assembly of States Parties over the Court are quite extensive. They include establishing an independent oversight mechanism for inspection, evaluation, and investigation of the Court; electing judges, prosecutors, and other Court officials; and determining the Court's budget. The Assembly will be able to vote to dismiss judges, prosecutors, and other Court officials. There is little chance the Court could run amok while subject to the oversight of some 90 democratic countries.

Paradoxically, the U.S., by opting out of the treaty, shoots itself in the foot. It has no say in the Court's Assembly of States Parties, so the Court is not accountable to the U.S. By "sulking outside the tent" the U.S. has created the only lack of accountability our most chauvinistic politicians care about, accountability to us.

Might the Assembly of States Parties be infiltrated and corrupted by dictators, human rights abusers and war criminals? In a word, no. Dictators of nations that kill and torture masses of their own citizens and have in the past committed war crimes with impunity wish to minimize or eliminate the jurisdiction of the Court over any future crimes they may commit within their own countries. Violence-prone dictators, to protect themselves, thus have a powerful incentive to not become a party to the treaty. Most of them have stayed away and can be relied upon to continue to stay away in their own strong "best interest." They can thus have no say in the Court's operations and no power to corrupt the Court.

Unfortunately, this limitation on the jurisdiction of the court does mean that dictators of countries that are not states parties to the treaty are able to continue human rights abuses within their own countries with impunity. However, they are subject to the court's powers if they commit violations such as war crimes or crimes against humanity (e.g., orchestrated mass rapes) outside their own countries.

Since human rights-abusing dictators have an incentive to avoid joining the Court, the danger of its political abuse is further diminished. In view of these incentives, the warning by the Court's critics (mostly extremist-conservative American leaders) that it may be controlled by abusers of its power is either dishonest or a paranoid fantasy. The combination of policy and procedural protections built into the treaty, the Court's accountability to the Assembly of States Parties, and the alignment of national interests surrounding it make this a fear that cannot materialize.

Some American critics of the Court have claimed that it is unconstitutional and lacks the legal protections provided to all American citizens. This argument would be devastating if it were true, but in fact it is completely false. The Clinton administration requested that the Justice Department review the treaty and assess its constitutionality. The Justice Department cleared it as being consistent with the Constitution. This outcome is hardly surprising, given the following facts: Representatives of the United States were extensively involved in negotiating the Rome Treaty establishing the ICC. The ICC was Made in the USA. A military lawyer from the U.S. Department of Defense led the negotiations concerning the crimes that the Court will be able to try. The first phase of negotiations was completed in 1998 with the adoption of the Rome Treaty, also known as the Rome Statute. The second phase, completed in June of 2000 at a meeting of the Preparatory Commission, achieved the adoption of text on the Elements of Crimes and the Rules of Procedure and Evidence. The U.S. proposed most of these protections against abuse and affirmed its full acceptance of these documents by joining the consensus on their adoption on December 31, 2000.

The following protections of individual rights under the U.S. Constitution are also present in the Rome Statute and its amendments. They were included by the American legal experts mentioned above.[3]

- Presumption of Innocence
- Speedy and Public Trial
- Assistance of Counsel
- Right to Remain Silent
- Privilege Against Self-Incrimination
- Right to Written Statement of Charges
- Right to Examine or Have Examined Adverse Witnesses
- Right to Compulsory Process to Obtain Witnesses
- Prohibition against Ex Post Facto Crimes
- Protection against Double Jeopardy
- Freedom from Warrantless Arrest and Searches
- Right to be Present at Trial
- Exclusion of Illegally Obtained Evidence
- Prohibition against Trials in Absentia
- Only the right to a trial by jury is missing from the Rome Statute because of the impracticality of impaneling a jury to try, for example, Slobodan Milosevic (Bosnian war crimes, 1990-1995 and Kosovo genocide, 1999) or Pol Pot (Cambodian genocide, 1979). Also:
- Far fewer due process protections are guaranteed to American citizens accused of crimes abroad. They are subject to trial in foreign justice systems, many of which do not provide for a jury trial or other valued due process protections.
- The United States has signed a number of extradition treaties that specifically allow Americans to be tried abroad in foreign courts without jury trials.

*Even in the United States, American servicemembers are not guaranteed a jury trial under the Courts-Martial system."[4]

Are the due process protections for the accused as good as they sound? On this subject the most impressive group of experts on the relevant international law that one could possibly find, ten current and former presidents of the American Society of International Law, wrote a letter on "Misconceptions about the Proposed International Criminal Court" to the House Committee on International Relations. In this letter they called these protections "at least as comprehensive as the American Bill of Rights—in certain cases even more detailed and specific."[5]

Why a Permanent Global Court?

Why is an international court needed? Why not just let national courts prosecute the criminals? The answer is simplicity itself. These kinds of crimes are typically committed or encouraged and protected by dictators of undemocratic states or by rival factions of collapsed states. In neither case can a fair trial be conducted. In a dictatorship, the judiciary is far from independent and is virtually always corrupted by fear and coercion. A fair trial is therefore impossible. For example, genocide is a crime that is usually perpetrated by the government of a country. Obviously the government that launched the genocide is not going to put itself on trial.

In a failed state where factions are struggling for control, there is often no functioning government. Atrocities may abound on both sides, but there is no court system to put the criminals on trial, and often there are no accepted laws to use in judging the case. A trial, fair or not, cannot happen.

In both cases, then, an impartial international criminal court is the only hope for justice. Almost by definition, the problem is the failure of the nation state to protect its citizens and to abide by international law, so the national government cannot solve the problem. The government's behavior, or its absence or weakness, is a critical element of the problem.

Perhaps the most powerful single protection against abuse of the International Criminal Court stems from the principle of complementarity. The ICC exists to complement the laws of nation states, not to replace or override them. If a state does have a competent judiciary that is able and willing to conduct a fair trial, the ICC simply has no jurisdiction. It cannot try the case. In view of these provisions, clearly U.S. citizens are not in jeopardy.

Rather than establish a permanent court, why not go on with *ad hoc* courts as before? Why does the world need a permanent court? The need stems from a few basic facts. The crimes are frequent, and dictatorships or rebel factions are often the perpetrators of the crimes. They are typically not capable of conducting a fair and unbiased trial, or any trial at all. In these cases an international tribunal is the only possible source of justice. And the frequency of such crimes throughout the world makes continued use of *ad hoc* international tribunals, one after another, an administrative absurdity. A permanent international court is the only way to solve these problems.

Fears and Worries

The objections of the U.S. Government and its behavior during the preparatory negotiations on the Court were driven not primarily by the preferences of the State Department or the Clinton White House, but by the Pentagon and the Senate Foreign Relations Committee chaired by Jesse Helms. Helms had announced that the treaty would be dead on arrival at the Senate if it lacked an absolute exemption for Americans from prosecution. The rhetoric suggested that it all boiled down to extreme fear of one extremely unlikely possibility: that a U.S. citizen might be put on trial by the Court. Though highly improbable, this outcome is theoretically possible.

The next question: why such fear and revulsion? Would it be the end of the world if an American were accused before the Court and steps were taken by the Court to investigate whether prosecution was appropriate? Obviously if this were to happen, the U.S. would immediately launch its own investigation of the alleged crime, thereby removing it from the jurisdiction of the ICC. The big problem from the Pentagon's point of view: the possibility of an investigation triggered by the ICC might mean the destruction of a soldier's—or more likely an officer's—career, whether or not he or she was guilty.

One wonders whether acute sensitivity to an unlikely danger to the career of an as-yet unknown soldier was the real reason for resistance to the Court. The evidence suggests that Jesse Helms, at least, had more tribalistic and ideological concerns stemming from his view of American national sovereignty and the jurisdiction of the Court over individuals. The applicability of the Court's decisions to individuals is precedent-setting international law, which in the past typically governed only relations among nations and left out individuals. By contrast with the ICC, the already existing International Court of Justice (ICJ), better known as the "World

Court," only adjudicates disputes among nations. It has no jurisdiction over individuals.

The ICC's jurisdiction over individuals is a remarkable legal advance. In the past, when the leader of a nation committed crimes (e.g., Saddam) the international community could only deal with the leader by sanctioning a whole nation, harming millions of its citizens. With the ICC, it becomes possible to single out individuals for international legal action. However, this change could be viewed as encroaching on the sovereignty of the nation-state, which heretofore had had an exclusive monopoly on applying laws to individuals.

As a concern of the Pentagon, fears about the impact on careers of high-level officers may have made some perverse sense. Senior officers, not soldiers in the trenches, are the ones who have command responsibilities that could theoretically trigger an accusation before the Court. The definitions of crimes for which the Court is responsible set the bar high. They are narrower in the Rome Statute than they are in international law generally. To meet the definitions, alleged crimes would have to be not the isolated, albeit brutal, incident like the My Lai massacre in Vietnam, but even more horrific atrocities affecting large numbers of people and driven by deliberate policy and systematic action. These are the stuff of senior officers' orders, but are also extremely unlikely because of the entrenched American policy and practice of teaching the laws of war to officers and following these laws operationally.

Another worry of opponents of the Court is its mention of aggression as a potential category of crimes under its jurisdiction. Due to the extreme difficulty of defining the term in a way that was politically acceptable to all parties, the treaty negotiators in Rome could not agree on a definition. Aggression, though mentioned in the treaty, is therefore excluded as a crime under the statute until such time as it is defined by an amendment. Any amendment requires a two-thirds majority. Also, amendments cannot be introduced for seven years. So don't hold your breath. It is important to add that military action taken without a Security Council mandate is not treated as a crime in the treaty, so, for example, the U.S. action against Iraq without Security Council sanction would not be covered even if the U.S. were a party to the treaty.

The Colossus and the Court

Due primarily to resistance to the International Criminal Court from the Senate and the Defense Department, the U.S. not only refused to sign the treaty but also continued strenuous negotiations for an absolute exemption for U.S. troops from the jurisdiction of the Court. The U.S. must be above the law. Fortunately for the impartial application of justice and the rule of law, other nations firmly, even angrily, rejected the exemption demanded by the U.S. as a violation of the fundamental principles of justice on which the Court was founded.

Lawrence Weschler, an astute observer of the tumultuous negotiations at the Rome conference, notes that the position of the U.S. during the treaty negotiations in Rome was "truly paradoxical."[6] Secretary of State Madeleine Albright's ambassador-at-large for war crimes issues, David Scheffer, led the forty-person U.S. delegation to Rome. According to Weschler, during a conversation in a rooftop cafeteria Scheffer "became quite emotional, describing a trip he had taken to Rwanda … accompanying Secretary Albright: the horrors he had witnessed, the terrible testimonies he had heard. He grew silent for a moment, gazing out toward the Coliseum, before continuing: 'I have this recurrent dream in which I walk into a small hut. The place is a bloody mess, terrible carnage, victims barely hanging on, and I stagger out, shouting 'get a doctor! Get a doctor!' and I become more and more enraged because no one's reacting fast enough.' He went on, passionately invoking the importance of what was going on down below us and insisting on the necessity of its successful outcome."[7]

But Scheffer's deep concern for the success of the treaty negotiations did not prevail. Weschler describes Scheffer's face as "ashen" when, under directions from superiors in Washington, he had no choice but to cast the historic U.S. vote against the Court at the end of the Rome conference. He and the State Department could not prevail over the combined forces of the Pentagon and Senator Jesse Helms, then Chair of the Senate Foreign Relations Committee. Helms had succeeded in creating an anti-ICC "groupthink" phenomenon in his committee. Weschler describes it vividly. Less than a week after casting the U.S. vote against the Court, David Scheffer was called to appear before Helms' committee. Speaking of Scheffer, Weschler says:

If, by the end there in Rome, he was being treated as a sort of pariah or leper, now back in Washington he was being unanimously praised as a kind of returning hero. Positions that had provoked nary a chord of resonance in the Rome Conference hall were almost drowned in a rising chorus of defiant triumphalism on Capitol Hill.

Senators Helms, Rod Grahams, Joseph Biden, and Dianne Feinstein each addressed Scheffer in turn, congratulating him on the fortitude of his resolve and pledging their undying contempt for that monstrosity spawned in Rome. Not one of them focused on Bosnia or Rwanda or Pol Pot or Idi Amin or the Holocaust or Nuremberg.... They all seemed utterly and almost uniquely transfixed by the treaty's exposure implications for American troops, vowing to protect them and fight it.[8]

The names of Senators in the paragraph above demonstrate that Helms' fear-mongering and disinformation campaign against the Court had misled some exceptionally able people who were ordinarily capable of independent thinking. Weschler quotes Senator Helms from this meeting:

"I've been accused by advocates of this court of engaging in eighteenth-century thinking....Well, I find that to be a complement. It was the eighteenth century that gave us our Constitution and the fundamental protections of our Bill of Rights. I'll gladly stand with James Madison and the rest of our founding fathers over that collection of ne'er-do-wells in Rome any day."

At some level, of course, Helms was way off the mark in his choice of antecedents. James Madison, for one thing, was a Federalist – with Alexander Hamilton, the principle author of *The Federalist Papers* – and as such, ranged himself passionately against the nativist states-righters of his day and in favor of a wider conception of governance.[9]

It should be noted here that Helms' straight-out prejudice, the gross display of jingoism revealed in his mention of "that collection of ne'er-do-wells in Rome" will have an ironic ring when the longer run of world history accords those "ne'er-do-wells in Rome" a stature similar to that of America's founding fathers. The human longing for justice cannot be denied forever, even by one of the most backward-looking leaders of a maverick hyperpower. In the more distant future, the founders of the ICC are virtually certain to be viewed with admiration as the founders of a new global system of justice. Hence, in the decades and centuries ahead, Helms is bound to take his rightful place beside the eighteenth century obstructers of progress, those who opposed the U.S. Constitution and tried to stop the visionaries such as James Madison and Alexander Hamilton who played key roles in bringing it into being. The opponents of these great men eventually were defeated as the Constitution took shape, and most of them are now forgotten except by small numbers of scholars.

The argument of Helms and company was that the huge military presence of the U.S. throughout the world made the U.S. an exception because it was uniquely vulnerable to politically motivated accusations of war crimes. Strangely, the Pentagon retained this fear despite the successes of its own negotiators in including in the treaty the most complete set of protections against the political abuse of power by a court anywhere in the world. The Pentagon remained wary despite the absolute power it had to negate the jurisdiction of the Court by conducting its own good-faith investigation of any allegations against American soldiers or military leaders. Paradoxically, the greater the military power and presence of the U.S. all over the world, the greater its perceived vulnerability to this small risk.

The irrationality of this position suggests a different real, underlying cause: a subliminal fear of the gradual evolution of international law that would limit the wild west freedom of the world's only superpower to do whatever it pleases whenever it pleases in an anarchic world. The U.S. Defense Department is the spear-point of that power, the power to kill people and destroy property. Raw power or brute force in the midst of chaos is more exciting and more useful in maintaining the role of the military and the dominance of the U.S. than is the boredom and predictability of life under the rule of law. Preserving security in an anarchic world requires military power. Building the rule of law makes it less necessary. The European nations understand this. As their mutual cooperation and institutional interlinking has increased, their military budgets have decreased. The Pentagon has an incentive to prevent parallel events in the U.S. To be fair to the U.S., during the Cold War the U.S. military played a key role in protecting Europe from the threat of Soviet expansionism and permitted Europe to get by with a smaller military capability than it would otherwise have needed. Now that the Cold War has passed into history, the huge U.S. presence in Europe is no longer needed, and neither is a large indigenous military capability on the part of Europe.

I should emphasize here that I am not accusing the leaders of our military establishment of consciously and deliberately maintaining and promoting international anarchy. I'm sure they sincerely believe they are protecting the U.S. and maintaining the rule of law. However, the overwhelming weight of modern psychology tells us that people are often driven by unconscious motives. Maintaining and increasing one's power is one of the most predictable of human motives, whether conscious or unconscious. Worldwide, improvement in the rule of law is well served by the International Criminal Court. However, this institution does not enhance the power of the Pentagon. In the long run, it will reduce the need for that power. Judging from the behavior of the U.S. military, the ICC is felt, emotionally but certainly not rationally, to be a threat.

Understandably, other countries do not see why the U.S. should be above the law, and see in the vast military presence of the U.S. a need to assure that the U.S. is not automatically exempt from the jurisdiction of the Court.

Justice Prevails – For a Moment

Despite the initial decision to vote against the Court at the Rome Conference, a window of time was still available for the U.S. to sign the Rome Treaty. The treaty allowed a country's executive to sign it until December 31, 2000. After that date it would be necessary for a country to both sign and ratify the treaty at the same time. This is a virtual impossibility in the American system, which requires the President to sign a treaty and then forward it to the Senate for ratification. Once it is forwarded, the Senate often takes years to act.

Two and a half years after the July 1988 Rome Conference, during the final two months of the year 2000, the deadline for Clinton to sign the treaty approached. Human rights and global justice groups launched a huge letter-writing campaign in support of the Court. Heather Hamilton, a leading activist on behalf of the Court, wrote: "The Washington Working Group on the ICC (WICC), coordinated by WFA [the World Federalist Association] helped generate sign-on letters to President Clinton, including letters from 28 Congress persons, 18 Senators, and over 60 non-government organizations and prominent individuals."[10] WFA also coordinated 1,600 letters from individual citizens to Clinton in support of the Court.

111

John Washburn, another leading American activist supporting the treaty, wrote the following description of the cliffhanger approach to Clinton's final decision:

Just hours before the final, rigid midnight deadline on the evening of Sunday, December 31...UN doors remained open ... as anxious government representatives waited for final instructions from their capitols. ... David Scheffer, U.S. Special Ambassador for War Crimes and head of the American delegation through five years of ICC negotiations, showed great satisfaction through his weariness as he signed on behalf of his country. Hastily informed representatives of nongovernmental organizations stood by as the flash of official photographers flared.[11]

Knowing there was stiff opposition to the Court in a conservative-dominated Senate, Clinton did not play Don Quixote and forward the treaty for ratification. Still, under international law, his signature committed the U.S. to take no actions in opposition to the Court. All over the world proponents of the Court and of justice and human rights heaved a sigh of relief. However, political conservatives in the U.S. were outraged by the decision. Right-wing op-ed pieces screamed, "Un-sign that Treaty!" Ultra-conservative politicians such as Jesse Helms thundered their disapproval. Misinformation and outright lies about the Court abounded. Despite its clear structure of accountability and strong protections against abuse, it was labeled a "rogue court" and vilified as unaccountable. The love of law and order that is a core conservative virtue and that should have led to conservative support for the Court had given way to rampant American jingoism.

Despite the frenzied attacks on the Court from extreme conservatives in the U.S., in the rest of the world ratifications rolled in from a variety of countries, and it became clear that the Court was popular with the world's democracies. It would become a reality even sooner than expected. In the U.S., President Bush assumed his position in the White House after a controversial election. From this point on, the battle against the ICC became a cause of the White House as well. The President of the United States weighed in against the Court.

A Citizen's Voice

For the treaty to go into effect, 60 ratifications were required. Despite passionate U.S. opposition to the ICC from the Bush administration and the U.S. Congress, including strenuous bullying of other countries in an attempt to dissuade them from ratifying the treaty, by July 2000 it was ratified by 66 nations. The ICC came into existence amid fanfare and celebrations among proponents of justice all over the world. July 1, 2002 became a day to celebrate. At the first meeting of the Court's Assembly of States Parties on September 3-10, 2002, the Assembly recognized an umbrella organization of citizens organizations, the Coalition for the International Criminal Court (CICC) for its work in bringing the Court into existence. The CICC is a vast global network of thousands of citizens' organizations that created the political pressure within their countries to bring the ICC to fruition against all obstacles.

The lead organization of this coalition, the World Federalist Movement (WFM), served as the Secretariat and organizer of the CICC. Its Executive Director, Bill Pace, had by that time served as the Convenor of the coalition for eight years. Lucy Webster, the WFM Council's Vice-Chair, spoke for WFM at the Assembly. Her remarks that day acknowledged both the bright side and the dark side of the situation:

WFM believes that the primary hope for preventing a repetition in the 21st Century [of the violence, war and destruction of the 20th Century] rests not on militaries and war, but on fundamental strengthening of the rule of law in international affairs. International justice is an essential pillar of the rule of law.... The adoption of the Rome Statute represents ... one of the greatest advancements of democracy in international affairs." On the role of the U.S., she commented:

For the world's most powerful state to oppose this treaty is very ominous. For this state to use its veto in the Security Council to seek immunity from the ICC; to pit peacekeeping against international justice; to endanger victims and nations worldwide; to undermine the [UN] Charter and the legitimacy of the Security Council is almost unbelievable. The Assembly and the new ICC must have the courage to stand against these threats to the basic principles of international law.[12]

An American citizen had to acknowledge that the behavior of her own country was an "almost unbelievable" attack on international law. The story below outlines the reality to which she referred.

Going Back On Our Word

On May 6, 2002, shortly before the ICC treaty came into effect, President Bush shocked the world by withdrawing the U.S. signature. Leaders of all nations have in the past honored the major multilateral treaty commitments made by previous executives of their own countries. Bush's action was unprecedented in the history of multilateral treaty negotiations. Further, the timing of Bush's "unsigning" of the treaty was a clear slap in the face to all the countries, mostly U.S. allies, that had worked to establish the treaty, ratified it, and were preparing to celebrate the first steps in its implementation. Foremost among these were Germany and South Africa, two countries that had suffered terribly from genocidal treatments of their own people in recent memory. From the beginning they had been among the most active supporters of the establishment of the Court. They knew in terms of real human pain and tragedy what the crimes covered by the Court mean to the people of a nation.

This act of Bush in unsigning the ICC treaty demonstrated not only a disturbing lack of U.S. commitment to justice at the international level as represented by the Court, but even more deeply and gravely, a contempt for the value of U.S. commitment to the web of international law that is the bedrock of global cooperation among nations. Bush's unsigning of the treaty announced to the world for the first time that the signature of a President of the U.S. on a treaty with scores of other nations is not worth the paper it's written on. It can be overturned on a whim a few months later by another president. The unsigning also said in effect that a new and even more extreme era of arbitrary and capricious international obstructionism could be expected from the world's only superpower. The U.S. would be, even more than before, a bull in the international china shop. No other country has so decisively negated its own credibility for future multilateral negotiations.

Protection Racket – The "Hague Invasion Act"

In reaction to President Clinton's signing of the Rome Treaty at the end of the year 2000 and long before Bush's unsigning of it, Senator Jesse Helms

(R-NC), supported by Senator Tom DeLay (R-TX) and Representative Henry Hyde (R-IL), had gone on a rampage of hostile legislative action. Helms launched the American Service Members Protection Act (ASPA), a benign-sounding bill with some of the most destructive features, in terms of the U.S. relationship with other countries and with international law, ever put together in a piece of legislation. Using coercive tactics, the bill tries to dictate to other countries that they must not ratify the ICC treaty, or if they do, they must exempt American soldiers from extradition to the Court. If they take a stand for impartial justice and don't agree to exempt American soldiers, they will be hit hard by withdrawal of U.S. economic or military aid.

The law was designed to cut funding for any U.S. government activities involving the Court; end military aid to other countries that have ratified the Rome Treaty (including Switzerland, Argentina, and New Zealand); and authorize the use of force to free any American held by the Court. This latter feature inspired the bill's derisive informal label, the "Hague Invasion Act." Though Senator Helms is long gone from the Senate as of the writing of this book, the legacy of this legislation lingers like a foul stench, gravely poisoning U.S. relationships with other countries.

For years Helms had trouble getting the bill passed, but eventually, on August 2, 2002, he succeeded. A press release from Human Rights Watch noted that,

A new law supposedly protecting U.S. servicemembers from the International Criminal Court shows that the Bush administration will stop at nothing in its campaign against the Court....'The states that have ratified this treaty are trying to strengthen the rule of law,' said Richard Dicker, Director of the International Justice Program at Human Rights Watch. 'The Bush administration is trying to punish them for that..... Many of the ICC's biggest supporters are fragile democracies and countries emerging from human rights crises, such as Sierra Leone, Argentina, Fiji.'

Making War on the Court

The 21st Century seems to represent a new era in warfare. After September 11, 2000 the U.S. declared war on an ill-defined non-state entity, terrorism. This war was partly metaphorical and partly literal. It entailed strategies and tactics and cooperative arrangements such as sharing

115

intelligence with other countries to a degree not seen before. Wars against countries were not passé, as the wars in Afghanistan and later Iraq demonstrated, but they ceased to be the only type of war. 9/11 demonstrated that terrorism and particularly al Qaeda were politically appealing targets of a war, however unconventional, and the American public enthusiastically went along.

Since then, the U.S. has waged an undeclared but fairly open war on another non-state entity, the International Criminal Court. This appears to be the first time in history the U.S. Government has waged war on an institution of international law supported by its own people (according to polls) and by the overwhelming majority of its allies. The anarchists in the "battle of Seattle" broke windows in opposition to the World Trade Organization, but it is rather less conventional for the U.S. Government to run an organized campaign to undermine an institution that promotes the rule of law. Of course, the war against the Court is a metaphorical "war", but it is nonetheless determined, organized, and extremely destructive, leaving legal and political havoc in its path. Here's a quick summary of the action immediately preceding and following the unsigning of the treaty:

"In May 2002, the U.S. first threatened to destabilize UN peacekeeping operations by promising to veto the UN mission in East Timor unless its military personnel were granted immunity from the ICC."[13] This effort was essentially blackmail, in effect saying, "We'll trash this important peacekeeping effort if the military personnel don't get immunity from prosecution by the ICC." Other nations resisted. They felt that the Security Council did not have the authority to grant such immunity, thereby overriding a treaty established in a totally different legal venue. After a strenuous political battle, the U.S. had to back down and the peacekeeping operation in East Timor was renewed without the immunity provision. It's important to note that this move was purely a blow aimed at the Court, not at protecting American troops, since the peacekeepers in East Timor were Australian, not American. Clearly the attack was ideological, not self-protective. Having failed in May, the Bush administration tried again in July. This time they succeeded. "On July 12, 2002, the U.S. obtained a one-year renewable exemption [from the ICC's jurisdiction] for UN peacekeepers in the context of the Security Council debate on the UN mission in Bosnia-Herzegovina."[14]

As events progressed, the Bush Administration systematically implemented the most noxious elements of the American Servicemembers Protection Act. The most outrageous provision of the act created dilemmas in which small countries had to decide between holding to legal and moral principle on one hand and kowtowing to the U.S. on the other. Bush attempted to impose Bilateral Impunity Agreements (BIAs) on other nations. These agreements between the U.S. and other countries prohibited them from surrendering to the ICC any U.S. citizens including government officials, military personnel, and contractors. The agreements do not oblige the U.S. to conduct an investigation even if they are accused of the serious kinds of wrongdoing the Court is concerned with. In other words, the BIAs completely circumvent the intent of the International Criminal Court by assuring impunity of Americans for alleged crimes, whereas the court is designed to end impunity for such crimes.

> In capitals around the world, U.S. government representatives are seeking bilateral immunity, or so-called "Article 98," agreements in an effort to shield U.S. citizens from prosecution by the newly created International Criminal Court. Dubbed "impunity agreements" by leading legal experts, these bilateral agreements, if signed, would provide that neither party to the accord would bring the other's current or former government officials, military or other personnel (regardless of whether or not they are nationals of the state concerned) before the jurisdiction of the Court.

> Many legal, government and NGO representatives argue that the U.S. is misusing Article 98 of the Rome Statute.... Legal experts furthermore contend that if countries that have ratified the Rome Statute enter into such agreements, they would breach their obligations under international law.[15]

> The U.S. government is using coercive tactics to obtain immunity from the jurisdiction of the ICC for its nationals. U.S. officials have publicly threatened economic sanctions, such as the termination of military assistance, if countries do not sign the agreement. In several instances, there have been media reports of the U.S. providing large financial packages to countries at the time of their signature of bilateral immunity agreements.[16]

> Despite the intense pressure for signature of these agreements, a number of important U.S. allies and regional bodies have rejected them.

Argentina, Canada, New Zealand, Sweden, Norway, South Africa, Trinidad and Tobago, Slovenia and Croatia, plus all 15 members of the European Union, are among countries that have refused the U.S. request. The EU Presidency last week welcomed a declaration by the 10 EU accession countries, and other associated states and European Free Trade Association (EFTA) countries, in which they affirmed the EU Common Position rejecting the U.S. bilateral immunity deals, and resolved that their national policies would adhere to that position. The EU has stated that the bilateral treaties proffered by the U.S. violate Article 98 of the Rome Statute.

"The Bush administration has renounced sixty years of U.S. support for international law and justice," said William Pace, convenor of the NGO Coalition for the ICC. "The only politically motivated 'prosecutions' are by the U.S. against the ICC."

"What we're seeing is that the Bush administration has been signing these immunity deals with the world's poorest countries, many of which cannot stand up to a threat of the loss of aid," said Heather Hamilton, director of programs at the World Federalist Association. "We've also seen that the U.S. government is exceeding the terms set out in ASPA [The American Servicemembers Protection Act] by concluding these agreements with countries that are not formal supporters of the ICC," she added.[17]

A number of countries have reportedly received large sums of U.S. financial assistance upon signature of the bilateral immunity agreements. In the case of Sierra Leone, upon signature of a bilateral immunity agreement it was announced that the U.S. would invest $25 million in the Sierra Rutile mines. In other instances, pressure for signature of a bilateral immunity agreement has included threats such as restricted accession to NATO, as has been reported in some of the Balkan states.[18]

The Bush administration's threats against nations that refused to sign the bilateral immunity agreements were not idle. The UN Wire reported the following story from the New York Times:

At the beginning of April 2003 the Bush administration carried out its threats to cut off military assistance to 35 countries that refused to sign impunity agreements with the U.S. and against the ICC. The aid to be cut off was for training programs and funding for weapons and equipment. A total of $47.6 million in aid and $613,000 in military education programs were to be cut. The New York Times reported that many of the nations cut off, such as Colombia and Ecuador, were considered vital to the Bush administration's foreign policy agenda. Some of the countries impacted, such as Croatia, were preparing to join NATO and relied on U.S. military aid to modernize their forces.[19]

Colombian scholar and journalist Maria Cristina Caballero is a fellow at Harvard University's Center for Public Leadership at the John F. Kennedy School of Government. She wrote the following in the July 22, 2003 International Herald Tribune:

The situation is most shocking in Colombia. President Alvaro Uribe was the only Latin American president to support the U.S.-led war against Iraq. He has also followed U.S. guidelines to spray coca crops in an effort to stop the flow of cocaine into the United States.

Yet Uribe's allegiance meant nothing when he didn't sign the U.S. immunity agreement. Now about $135 million in U.S. military aid is at stake. The Bush administration has withheld the first $5 million and threatens to suspend the full package. The first installment was destined for a Colombian Army unit protecting an oil pipeline operated by Occidental Petroleum, a U.S. company.

Later in the same article Caballero adds,

Carlos Vallejo, president of the Ecuadorian parliament's National Defense Committee, called the U.S. decision a "moral offense" and warned that if military aid was suspended, it must include the withdrawal of U.S. troops from the Manta Base in Ecuador used by the United States to control drug trafficking.

It is time for Washington to reconsider its war against a court that serves to defend human rights around the world. It is time for the Bush administration to start focusing on the pressing issues confronting the Americas - terrorism and drug-trafficking, serious economic and social problems and crises of governance - and stop nonsensical sanctions against countries that have taken a stand for human rights.

It should be obvious to the most casual observer that the behaviors of the U.S. Government described above constitute bribing and bullying large numbers of other democracies. This is not behavior designed to enhance the attractiveness of American values, and it is certainly not leadership. It is the abusive behavior of a petty tyrant. Though it has been little noticed by the American public, this bullying of other countries over the International Criminal Court has had a significant impact on respect for the United States abroad, especially because of the context of the war against Iraq, which was launched in blithe disregard for the overwhelming public opinion of the rest of the world. The leaders and the people of other countries are beginning to see the U.S. Government, as led by the Bush administration, not only as arrogant and insensitive, but even as downright dangerous.

The reaction of the world to Iraq and the war against the ICC was well-illustrated by President Bush's visit to Africa in July, 2003. When he earmarked $15 billion to fight AIDS in Africa, a dramatic increase in U.S. funding, and later visited the beleaguered continent, one might have expected him to be cheered in the streets by roaring crowds of well-wishers. But the severe damage he had done to public opinion by the Iraq war and the ICC bullying could not be repaired overnight, even by such a colossal increase in aid for such a critical problem. He got a cold reception. African crowds demonstrated against him and diplomats subjected him to snubs. In South Africa, Nelson Mandela publicly criticized him and arranged to be out of the country when he arrived. "Even in Senegal, a West African country not noted for anti-Americanism" an article in the Washington Post notes, "as the Bush motorcade traveled into the capital, Dakar, from the airport on Tuesday, hundreds of people lined the streets—but they stood still, staring, not cheering."[20] In customarily warm and hospitable Africa, as a "greeting" for an American president bringing financial aid, this is an extraordinarily icy reception, a devastating rebuke.

Invincible Ignorance?

The sad, disgraceful story of the U.S. opposition to the International Criminal Court, the greatest advance in international justice since the establishment of the UN, is far from over. The opposition to the Court is based on ignorance of the plain meaning of the treaty by American political leaders who should know better, but have been led to believe erroneous assertions and to fear dangers that do not exist. Like a bald eagle flying straight into a brick wall, they are taking a course that cannot be sustained against the realities of world events. They are also causing devastating and possibly irreparable harm to the respect other countries hold for the U.S. and its values.

As new war crimes, genocides, and crimes against humanity are committed, the need for a court to put their perpetrators on trial will become vividly apparent, as happened before in Nuremberg and Tokyo, Rwanda, Bosnia, Sierra Leone, and Cambodia. As I write, similar horrors are unfolding in the Democratic Republic of the Congo. But now there is a difference. There will be no more *ad hoc* courts. Now there is a permanent court to accomplish the purpose. American leaders will have to choose between swallowing their pride and working with the International Criminal Court—which was signed by an impressive 139 nations—or standing on the sidelines, unable to contribute to the course of events, or perhaps allowing justice to be aborted. I suspect that public opinion will drive them toward cooperation with the Court. A longing for justice is built into human nature; in a democracy it cannot long be denied.

The U.S. will not be able to escape ridiculous contradictions as it tries to implement justice in other arenas but oppose it in the International Criminal Court. A recent press release, presented in full below, exposes vividly the absurdity of the Bush anti-ICC position in practice. Essentially the U.S. penalizes Serbia for refusing to agree to U.S. demands for immunity for our own citizens, then penalizes Serbia again for extending immunity from an international court to its citizens. Our citizens get immunity; yours don't. If you don't agree, we penalize you coming and going. Here's the press release.

121

PRESS RELEASE
Harpinder Athwal
202 546 3950 ext 112
hathwal@globalsolutions.org <mailto:hathwal@wfa.org>

April 1, 2004
IMMEDIATE RELEASE

Heather Hamilton
202 546 3950 ext 107

IRONY REACHES NEW HEIGHTS
Serbia Aid Cuts Send
Contradictory Messages

WASHINGTON, D.C. - Nine months after cutting half a million dollars in military aid to Serbia because it refused to sign an agreement to shield U.S. citizens from an international war crimes tribunal, American officials announced yesterday that they are suspending more aid because Serbia is not handing over its own citizens to the International Criminal Tribunal for Yugoslavia (ICTY).

Nearly $26 million aid cut was announced yesterday after Secretary of State, Colin Powell certified that Serbia was not adequately cooperating with the ICTY by arresting and transferring indicted Serbians. Last July, the U.S. had cut assistance to Serbia because they refused to sign a bilateral immunity agreement (BIA) with the U.S. that would shield all U.S. citizens, government employees and contractors charged with war crimes or other grave atrocities from transfer to the permanent International Criminal Court (ICC).

"It's commendable that the U.S. is putting pressure on Serbia to hand over indictees to the ICTY," said Heather B. Hamilton, Vice President for Programs of Citizens for Global Solutions, "but how can the U.S. expect to send consistent messages on the need to bring war criminals to justice when it's simultaneously penalizing countries who refuse to grant immunity to U.S. citizens from the International Criminal Court? The irony is astounding."

122

The U.S. has suspended military aid to over 20 allies that have refused to sign a BIA with the U.S. While the U.S. contends that these bilateral immunity agreements are permitted under Article 98 of the ICC charter, most of the 92 ICC member states say that they go too far, and concluding such an agreement would be in violation of their obligations under the treaty.

Notes to Editors:
While this may seem like an April Fool's spoof, we are sad to say that it is not.

Resources on the U.S. government's campaign for bilateral immunity agreements, including a table of countries that have lost assistance, text of the agreements, legal analysis and more is available at <http://www.globalsolutions.org/programs/law_justice/icc/bias/bias_hom e.html>

Perhaps America's leaders will change with the times. Or it may be that their paranoia and willful ignorance on the subject of the ICC is invincible, their prejudices and fears unchangeable. In that case, one hopes the American people will have the sense to replace them with minds more susceptible to reason. It is too early to tell. But it is not too early for American citizens of good will and common sense to take action to bring about change by joining organizations that work for constructive movement on these issues, by writing to Congress and the White House, and by voting for candidates who work to establish and implement a more benign and sensible foreign policy when the opportunity arises.

---

[1] Letter headed, "Misconceptions about the Proposed International Criminal Court " forwarded to Henry Hyde, Chairman of the House Committee on International Relations on February 21, 2001 by Monroe Leigh of Steptoe and Johnson, LLP, Attorneys at Law. 1330 Connecticut Avenue, NW, Washington, DC 20036.
[2] *The United States and the International Criminal Court: National Security and International Law*, Sarah B. Sewall and Carl Kaysen, eds., Rowman and Littlefield Publishers, Inc, 2000, p. 108.
[3] This list was derived from the USA for ICC web site, but the information presented is no longer active.)

[4] Idem.

[5] Letter headed, "Misconceptions about the Proposed International Criminal Court " forwarded to Henry Hyde, Chairman of the House Committee on International Relations on February 21, 2001 by Monroe Leigh of Steptoe and Johnson, LLP, Attorneys at Law. 1330 Connecticut Avenue, NW, Washington, DC 20036. Note that this is Ibid the epigraph at beginning of the chapter.

[6] Sewall and Kaysen, *The U.S. and The ICC*, Rowman and Littlefield, 2000, p. 91.

[7] Idem.

[8] Ibid., p. 110.

[9] Ibid., p.111.

[10] Heather B. Hamilton, The World Federalist, Winter 2001, p.1.

[11] John L. Washburn, U.S. Signs on to International Criminal Court, The Interdependent, Volume 26, Number 4, Winter, 2001.

[12] "International Criminal Court to Open Its Doors for Business" The World Federalist News, #44, Fall, 2002

[13] http://www.iccnow.org/documents/otherissuesimpunityagreem.html

[14] Idem.

[15] Idem.

[16] Idem.

[17] Press release from the Coalition for the International Criminal Court, "U.S. Threatens to Cut Military Assistance to Nations Supporting the International Criminal Court Law: Pressures Non-U.S. Allies to Sign ICC Immunity Pacts," New York, June 30, 2003

[18] Idem.

[19] Elizabeth Becker, U.S. Cuts Military Aid To 35 Countries Over Int'l Court, New York Times, April 2, 2003 as quoted in UN Wire

[20] Dana Milbank and Emily Wax, "Critical of U.S. Policies, Africans Are Giving Bush Chilly Reception," *The Washington Post*, July 10, 2003.

Chapter Six

A NICOTINE CLIFF-HANGER

The research, published in the Sept. 13 issue of the medical journal The Lancet, shows that global tobacco deaths were about 4.8 million in 2000, with about 2.4 million each in developing and industrialized nations. The study shows that for men, the shift has already occurred. About 2 million men died in developing nations in 2000 from smoking-related illnesses compared with 1.8 million male deaths in industrialized nations.[1]

—Alvin Powell, Harvard News Office

The United States told the World Health Organization this week that it is unlikely to sign the first treaty to curtail tobacco use worldwide unless the 171 nations that hammered out its language agree to a clause that would allow governments to opt out of any provision they find objectionable." ... "Foreign diplomats say that the demand is an attempt to water down the treaty to benefit tobacco companies or to unravel the agreement entirely. The draft of the treaty ... was overwhelmingly approved at a Geneva conference in March. Since then, only the United States and the Dominican Republic have objected, WHO officials said.[2]

My first reaction to this grim news was, here we go again. The U.S. Government was insisting that 171 other countries reverse course on a dime after three years of difficult negotiations and come around to the American point of view, pronto, or the U.S. would trash the whole effort. Based on its past negotiating record, there was every reason to believe that the U.S. negotiators were not bluffing and the U.S. would indeed pull out at the end. At this stage, the situation appeared to be not a cliff-hanger, but an inevitable train wreck. Unfortunately, the behavior pattern was consistent with U.S. post-cold-war negotiating tactics on a number of other treaties.

We have seen before the same American stance of "accept our crippling changes to the treaty or we'll pull out." This kind of gross insensitivity to the views of other countries and to the integrity of the negotiating process breeds deep anger and resentment towards the U.S. Typically the changes demanded are not made and the U.S. does indeed pull out. The U.S. has displayed a similar negotiating pattern in the last-stage negotiations on the International Criminal Court treaty and other treaties as well, including treaties on the rights of women and children, on global warming, on landmines, on the law of the sea, on torture, and even on a treaty against cloning.

The claim by foreign diplomats that the Bush Administration officials were trying to water down the tobacco treaty or destroy it had considerable merit. During the negotiations, the U.S. "not only opposed the taxes, the labels, and even the minimum age of 18 for sales to minors. It went into high and highly dubious dudgeon at the carefully circumscribed ban on advertising and marketing, on the grounds that it limited the 'free speech' of corporations."[3] News articles reported that the Bush Administration worked to weaken every treaty provision.

What's a Few Million Deaths?

In the case of the anti-tobacco treaty, the possibility of any country on a whim opting out of any provision is a critical impediment to the effectiveness of the treaty. Key provisions place global restrictions on tobacco advertising. These provisions have a large potential impact on American tobacco companies. These companies are compensating for expensive lawsuits and decreasing domestic consumption by advertising and selling abroad and thus increasing their profits from overseas cigarette sales. U.S. tobacco companies have the financial and production clout to pressure other countries to opt out of key treaty provisions. As a result they could flood the world with advertisements and tobacco products. "Smoking is on the decline here [in the U.S.], but it's on the rise from Eastern Europe to Asia. Philip Morris now makes more money abroad than at home."[4]

Domestically, as things stand, about 400,000 Americans per year die prematurely from tobacco use—from heart disease, lung cancer, emphysema, and other diseases that typically follow from tobacco use. (This number includes a correction for the fact that a certain predictable percentage of people would die of these diseases without using tobacco. They are not included.) That number, 400,000 people dead, is the equivalent of 133 World Trade Center catastrophes per year in terms of loss of American lives. And it does not include the impact of the emotional devastation and trauma to friends and relatives, the physical misery of the dying, or the billions of dollars in medical care costs incurred by hundreds of thousands of people on the way to their deaths. Osama, eat your heart out. We don't need you to kill us; we have an industry to seduce far more people into greater devastation with slower and more painful results. Further, we can make a tidy profit for the tobacco industry and various support industries and get hefty campaign contributions for our politicians in the process. However, since more and more Americans are opting out of this tragedy and are filing lawsuits against tobacco companies, why not export this boon to the rest of the world? Maybe they will be less fussy about dying.

Globally, "tobacco is now killing 4.9 million people per year. At this rate, the WHO figures the premature death toll will reach 10 million a year within a generation – with 70 percent of the deaths in developing countries. And unlike AIDS or SARS, this disease doesn't come from a virus, but from an industry. An industry that contributed about $6.4 million to the 2002 campaign chests of Republicans."[5] Do these deaths matter to the tobacco industry? Apparently they do. "Just two years ago, Philip Morris, which sells 80 percent of the smokes to the Czech Republic, commissioned a study showing that cigarettes shortened lives by an average of 4.3 years. It bragged [seriously] that the tobacco deaths actually saved the Czech government $30 million a year in pensions, housing and health care for the elderly."[6] This admirable cost savings could be replicated all over the world if we just took all restrictions off tobacco, or more simply and cheaply we could just kill people when they reach a certain inconvenient age. Of course, there's something to be said for a do-it-yourself approach.

Was it true that the treaty provisions restricting advertising were in fact the target of the U.S. inclination to opt out of "objectionable" provisions? "William Pierce, spokesman for the Department of Health and Human Services, said the primary concern of U.S. negotiators is that parts of the treaty could prove to be unconstitutional by interfering, for instance, with tobacco companies' free speech rights. In addition, he said, the treaty calls on the Congress to approve policy changes it might not accept – such as changing the size of warning labels."[7] In other words, though we already restrict tobacco advertising in the U.S., doing so in other countries would violate the free speech provisions of the U.S. Constitution. And the inconvenience of our companies having to revise the labels on the packages weighs more heavily than saving thousands of lives. After all, they are only the lives of foreigners.

Tribalism and Greed

The "thinking" behind this obstructionism is classic. It exemplifies a powerful convergence of two psychological forces. They are tribalism (their lives are less valuable than ours), and greed (their lives are less important than our profits). The tribalist assumption that other lives are less valuable than American lives is unconscious of course. No one would state this explicitly— probably not even a tobacco company executive. (Though one must admit, saving the Czech government money by selling Czech citizens a product that kills them is hard to beat.) To articulate explicitly that foreign lives are less valuable than American lives would fly in the face of the central tenet of America's secular faith, that all are created equal and are endowed with certain inalienable rights, among which are life, liberty, and the pursuit of happiness. This most famous line from the Declaration of Independence does not specify only American lives. The enlightenment philosophy on which it is based makes no distinctions of nationality. It is a universalist belief system.

However, the assumption that foreign lives are less valuable than American lives is an inescapable foundation of the original tobacco policy the U.S. worked to negotiate in Geneva. Logically, this view has to underlie the belief that it's O.K. to discourage tobacco sales in the U.S. to save American lives and at the same time protect those sales even though they destroy the lives of people in other countries. (Remember, "we're the good guys"; maybe that's why our lives are more valuable.) The role of greed is obvious: tobacco manufacture and sales is all about making money even if the product, when used as directed, kills people.

Is the position stated above shrill or extreme? If you're inclined to think so, consider this: the negotiations showed that the Bush Administration "thinks that tobacco companies should be able to market overseas in ways that are prohibited here [in the U.S.] — with everything from free samples to sponsorship of youth events."[8] In other words, it's not O.K. to do it in the U.S., but it is O.K. to do it in other countries. Advertising to young people in youth events is especially important because it's critical to get people addicted to tobacco while they're young and impressionable. Millions of young people are needed as replacements for older customers who are dying prematurely from tobacco use. It takes a lot of new recruits to replace 4.9 million deaths per year among the older regular customers.

Three years of patient negotiating and difficult compromise produced the agreement among 171 nations, minus the U.S. and the Dominican Republic. This was a costly process in time and effort, one in which every nation made sacrifices to reach agreement. On the U.S. end-game demand that 171 nations suddenly reverse course and agree to let nations opt out of any provisions they dislike, Belgian negotiator Luk Joossens said, "I think it is impossible to reach a consensus, and this could easily be the end of the entire tobacco convention. If you open one article, it will encourage other nations to open articles they don't like. And if the reservations are included, then crucial aspects of the entire effort will be weakened. There is a lot of anger in so many countries about this American action."[9] Decent people don't negotiate like this, and the U.S. Government shouldn't either.

This situation highlights a crippling structural problem with the way international law is created. Unlike a nation's parliament or the U.S. Congress, where a majority vote gets a law passed that applies to everybody, treaty negotiating is a consensus process. Everyone must agree, but if one country opts out, it is not subject to the treaty. If that country is a small island nation, its withdrawal may not matter much. However, if that country is the U.S., and it has the lion's share of the action the treaty addresses, its decision to opt out is likely to be problematic or fatal for the whole effort. In the case of the tobacco treaty, the U.S. does have a substantial share of the global tobacco industry the treaty is attempting to regulate.

It is tempting to take an imaginative moment to wonder if the future—probably the far future—might include a better way to form agreements among nations. The European Union provides a hint of the possibility, but clearly the difficulties and complexities are staggering. The European Union contains no maverick hyperpower such as the U.S. If it did, the kind of systematic cooperation (despite huge difficulties) and convergence of mutual interests that are emerging before our eyes in Europe could not happen. As the stresses and strains in the expansion of the European Union show, large power discrepancies between nations are among the most problematic influences in formulating power-sharing rules. Still, the fact that the European Union is moving toward a power-sharing system within which England, France, Germany, and Italy can operate under the same roof with Latvia, Lithuania, and Estonia is encouraging.

129

The Costs of Obstructionism

Returning to the tobacco treaty, for the U.S., opting out or persisting in demanding a crippling amendment would have created adverse consequences besides triggering yet another instance of anger toward the U.S. on the part of the rest of the world. News reports commented that the U.S. has a positive stake in the treaty: it wishes to control cigarette smuggling and is concerned about the link between this type of crime and terrorist groups. To be able to participate in ongoing meetings that refine and implement the parts of the treaty that deal with these issues, the U.S. would have to sign the treaty.

Although going after cigarette smugglers and related terrorism was one advantage to the U.S. in joining the treaty, it appeared that the tobacco lobby and the industry's profits were a more powerful concern than crime and terrorism. The concession demanded by the U.S. was all but certain to be rejected by other nations. Anti-tobacco activists said of this demand, "This looks like an American effort to blow up the treaty, or to neutralize it for the benefit of Philip Morris and other cigarette makers." Matthew Meyers, president of the Campaign for Tobacco-Free Kids, said that if reservations are allowed, smaller nations are concerned that tobacco companies will pressure them to opt out of specific provisions of the treaty such as the advertising ban.[10]

There are moments when even partisan politics serve a useful purpose—in this case, exposing hypocrisy. In a letter to President Bush, Senate Democratic leader Tom Daschle and House Democratic leader Nancy Pelosi praised him for his "public statements that tobacco use is the greatest health issue facing the nation, but then [they] said the delegation to Geneva negotiated in a different spirit. 'In contrast to these public statements, your Administration went to great lengths to weaken many important provisions of the treaty,' they wrote. 'In addition to advancing weak language, the U.S. delegation also inappropriately pressured other nations to adopt the U.S. positions.'"[11]

Again, there is no real inconsistency in the Bush Administration's original stance if you accept the proposition that human lives in other countries are less valuable than lives in America. Bush said that tobacco use is "the greatest health issue *facing the nation*." He never said anything about its being one of the greatest health issues in the world, which it is. Concern for the rest of the world was apparently not a factor. His negotiating stance on the treaty was geared to protecting, not human lives, but American tobacco *sales* outside the nation. That's a different matter.

If tribalism and greed were not the real controlling factors in this situation, the U.S. would be negotiating for the same restraints internationally that we have in the U.S., both for consistency in principle and for simplicity in the practice of administering tobacco laws and regulations.

Of course, political realists would say, the U.S. Government is not negotiating in a vacuum, it is under heavy pressure from the tobacco companies. Precisely. When the government caves in to the pressure, it inherits and implements the tobacco industry's greed and tribalism. With these negotiations the U.S. Government once again appeared to be tearing up the fabric of international cooperation to support the selfish interests of a narrow but powerful constituency. These interests are so selfish they knowingly destroy the lives of millions of people. This is an evil so monstrous it can easily be considered on a par with that of Saddam Hussein. Obviously the American political system managed to muster the political will to create the existing tobacco laws in the U.S. If it failed to negotiate consistently with those laws in the international arena, then clearly the arrow of political will was pointed in a different direction. A double standard was at work.

A Surprise Reversal

Sometimes U.S. foreign policy provides sensible people with cause for celebration. On May 18, 2003, newspapers reported a surprise reversal. The head of the U.S. delegation, Secretary of Health and Human Services Tommy G. Thompson, informally announced U.S. support for the treaty. He said he would formally announce the U.S. position when he addressed the assembly. "I'm going to support it, much to the surprise of many around the world. I'm not going to make any changes. We have no reservations. The delegation here, headed by me, is in support of the tobacco treaty."[12]

"'We are thrilled about the new U.S. position,' said Derek Yach, the WHO official who led the tobacco negotiations. 'The U.S. delegation has told us they will not be obstructionist in any way.'"[13]

Adding a hint of remaining suspense, "Thompson said that while the President is 'quite supportive' of the treaty, he did not know whether the President would sign it or send it to the Senate for ratification. 'I don't make that decision.'"[14]

According to one article reporting the reversal, the U.S. has long been a leader in international tobacco control and has funded global anti-smoking programs. However, the U.S. is also home to some of the world's largest tobacco companies. Anti-tobacco advocates claim that these companies have influenced U.S. policy. Philip Morris has been a generous donor to Bush.[15] A counter-consideration in favor of improved tobacco control might be one of Bush's core constituencies: conservative Christians who, (outside the tobacco-growing South) are strongly opposed to tobacco use. Here is cause for celebration of a constructive influence from that sector, assuming it was brought to bear. Further, as noted before, the U.S. government is vitally interested in reducing cigarette smuggling and would have cut itself out of talks on that subject if it had rejected the treaty.

However these various considerations may have weighed in the decision, George W. Bush deserves kudos for his last-minute reversal allowing HHS Secretary Tommy G. Thompson to support the treaty without reservations. This was the right decision in a clear-cut case of right and wrong. A news article on the adoption of the treaty said, "The World Health Organization yesterday adopted a sweeping anti-tobacco treaty in an unprecedented global effort to regulate a product it says kills half of its regular users. Ending four years of turbulent negotiations, WHO's policy-making annual assembly unanimously adopted the accord amid thunderous applause."[16] Well-deserved and hard-earned applause!

Initially, one important caveat was unavoidable in celebrating this victory of right over might, of life over death and greed. The same article summed it up by adding later, "The United States, however, said it has made no decision about signing the pact, illustrating the challenge of putting it into practice. Health and Human Services Secretary Tommy G. Thompson said the Bush administration was 'reviewing the text of the convention.' 'The United States is not making a commitment to sign or ratify,' said Judith Wilkenfeld of the Campaign for Tobacco-Free Kids. 'They recognized that the rest of the world wanted to go forward but didn't say they would join the rest of the world in ratification. It's an incredible missed opportunity.'"[17]

Although the administration did miss the opportunity to formally and finally sign the treaty at the convention, Bush had painted himself into a positive corner. The dramatic reversal of his opposition on the treaty from resistance to support without reservations left little political room for yet another dramatic reversal. Politically, President Bush had narrowed his politically viable options to signing the treaty or delaying signing and waffling on sending the treaty to the Senate for ratification. If he wished he could have held up action indefinitely by saying that there were still problems with details that need to be ironed out later. Much to his credit, rather than take this low road he approved HHS Secretary Tommy

Thompson's formally signing the treaty on behalf of the U.S. On May 10, 2004 he signed the treaty, and the U.S. became the 108th nation to take this step. As of that date, although 108 nations had signed the treaty, only nine had ratified it. Forty ratifications are required for it to take effect. There seems to be little doubt that the required ratifications will be forthcoming.

These events represented a rare and fortunate moment in which the two key components of the Bush administration's political base, corporate wealth and conservative or fundamentalist Christianity, were in conflict. The conflict is probably what created the benign flip-flop, whether it expressed itself externally in the political arena or only in the recesses of George W. Bush's mind. The world has reason to celebrate the fundamentalists' win. Despite the remaining uncertainty about ratification by the Senate, their influence this time came in on the side of the angels.

---

[1] http://www.news.harvard.edu/gazette/2003/09.18/26-tobacco.html

[2] Marc Kaufman, "U.S. Seeks to Alter Anti-Tobacco Treaty," *The Washington Post*, April 30, 2003.

[3] Ellen Goodman, "Smoking: America's Gift to the World," *The Washington Post*, May 3, 2003.

[4] Idem.

[5] Idem.

[6] Idem.

[7] Kaufman, Op. Cit.

[8] Goodman, Op. Cit.

[9] Kaufman, Op. Cit.

[10] Kaufman, Op. Cit.

[11] Kaufman, Op. Cit.

[12] Bob Stein and Marc Kaufman, "U.S. Backs Pact Curbing Tobacco Use Worldwide: Move Is Surprise Reversal," The Washington Post, May 19, 2003.

[13] Idem.

[14] Idem.

[15] Idem.

[16] "Anti-Tobacco Treaty Adopted," The Washington Post, May 22, 2003.

[17] Idem.

Chapter Seven

FIDDLING WHILE EARTH BURNS

I think these guys are bought and paid by Big Oil in America, and they are going to do nothing that will in any way go against the demands and interests of the big oil companies.

—Thomas L. Friedman on the Bush White House[1]

As I began drafting this chapter in August 2003, thousands of people were dying in Europe from the worst heat wave there in recorded history. Estimates ran as high as eighteen thousand deaths in France alone, and thousands of deaths were reported in other European countries as well. Hospitals were overwhelmed. Bed space had run out. Morgues were overflowing with corpses, many of them unidentified. This horror is not merely a regional aberration or one-year oddity. A string of years from 1988 forward have set new heat records in the U.S., Europe, and worldwide.

According to scientists at a 2003 World Climate Change Conference in Moscow, a similar but even more devastating human toll affects mostly children in developing nations threatened by diseases and health concerns such as malaria, diarrhea and malnutrition.

According to the scientists, from the World Health Organization and the London School of Hygiene and Tropical Medicine, warmer temperatures can extend the range of mosquitoes that spread malaria to more regions and cause floods that contaminate water supplies and wash away crops. 'We estimate that climate change may already be causing in the region of 160,000 deaths ... a year,' said Andrew Haines, from the London school. 'The disease burden caused by climate change could almost double by 2020.'[2]

Meanwhile the snows of Kilimanjaro and every other mountain on the planet are melting at unprecedented rates. Mountain glaciers are turning into rivers and the glittering white tops of the high mountains are turning brown. Mountain glaciers are one of the plant's key fresh water storage systems. They melt during the summer and rebuild in winter. When they disappear, rivers will dry up for parts of each year and millions of people who depend on the steady flow of rivers may die.

The polar icecaps too are melting at dramatic speeds. In the south, huge chunks of Antarctica are falling into the ocean, floating away and melting. Especially disturbing was the collapse of one gargantuan ice shelf a thousand feet thick and roughly the size of Rhode Island. As regards the northern polar region, on December 9, 2002 the UN Wire reported, "Satellite images indicate Greenland's ice cap melted across a record 265,000 square miles, an area roughly the size of Texas. Oceanographers have observed changes in salinity and temperature below the ice, suggesting potential changes in the ocean's circulation and possibly dramatic effects on the ocean's largest currents. Such melting in the past has led to century-long droughts and sea level increases of a magnitude that could doom today's low-lying cities." Farewell, New York and New Orleans.

The melting ice caps are feeding a measurable rise in the level of the oceans, flooding coastal areas and encroaching on wetlands and farmlands in areas as disparate as Florida and Bangladesh. The warming of the oceans is causing bleaching and ultimately death for coral reefs all over the world. These reefs are among the most valuable foundations of the food chain in the oceans. They are unique sources of biodiversity. On land, animal species, sensitively adapted to certain temperature ranges, are moving toward the poles for survival. Unfortunately, plant species are not so mobile. Many are expected to become extinct.

Increasing heat energy in the atmosphere is fueling unusual numbers of violent storms, droughts and floods, and they in turn are devastating human habitations and costing insurance companies billions of dollars in lost revenues, where people are lucky enough to have insurance. Unlike the carbon-based energy producing and consuming industries, the insurance industry is concerned about global warming. In poverty-stricken countries where insurance is scarce, there is little recourse from storm devastation except for the survivors to absorb the losses and struggle to rebuild their shattered homes and lives, or migrate elsewhere.

In North America, droughts and increasing heat have set off a chain reaction of events that could hardly have been anticipated in advance. Consider the following excerpt from an article on climate change by two environmental experts:

In July [2003], the U.N. World Meteorological Organization affirmed that warming of the atmosphere and deep ocean currents is intensifying droughts, along with heat waves and floods, worldwide. The prolonged droughts in the U.S. West are a part of this phenomenon and directly attributable to anomalous sea surface temperatures in the Pacific Ocean.

As the earth's surfaces warm, evaporation is drying out forests and soils, increasing susceptibility to fire. Last summer, more than 7.3 million acres of U.S. forests burned during an intense drought. This year, there have been more than 800 separate fires in British Columbia; Oregon has seen fires lay waste to pristine areas; and wildfires have sent haze billowing from Arizona to Montana.

Most alarmingly, as an intergovernmental panel concluded in 2001, earth's biological systems are already responding to climate change. The current epidemic of bark beetles adds a new dimension to the risk of fires. In just the past few years, bark beetles have damaged forests in Arizona, New Mexico, southern California, Wyoming, Oregon, Alaska and British Columbia. In British Columbia, nearly 22 million acres of lodge-pole pine have become infested—enough timber to supply the U.S. housing market for two years.

The article goes on to explain the reason for the beetles' sudden increase in activity:

Warming is increasing the reproduction, abundance, and geographic range of the beetles, destabilizing the age-old, hard-won truce between insects and vegetation. Since 1994, mild winters in Wyoming have helped the beetle larvae survive the season. Usually 80 percent die, but the mortality rate has dropped to less than 10 percent. In Alaska, spruce-bark beetles are sneaking in an extra generation a year due to warming,

136

and have denuded 4 million acres in the Kenai Peninsula in the past five years.[3]

So global warming is not only causing droughts in North America, but is also causing unexpected biological chain reactions that are wreaking more havoc than drought alone would cause.

The droughts have meant that the forests are burning. So the Bush administration has been touting an innovative plan to prevent forest fires. The idea is to allow the logging industry to thin forests, taking away some trees and leaving others, in the belief that this action will make the forests less vulnerable to fires, even when they are dried out. The reality, however, is a little different from the political rhetoric. Under this program, "the extensive logging and clear-cutting that would be allowed...is a practice that damages soils, increases sedimentation, reduces water-holding capacity, and dries up rivers and streams—all increasing susceptibility to pests and fires."[4] But of course the logging industry gets its goodies, which is the real point.

Forests are far from the only living things threatened by global warming. In January 2003 scientists reported that "nearly 40 million Africans at risk of starvation may be among the first human victims of climate change worldwide."[5] A scientist who studies the effects of climate change on food supplies for populations, Cynthia Rosenzweig, comments, "It's an amazing thing for a scientist: The things we've been predicting for years are starting to happen now. It's already having real effects on vulnerable people. And the predictions get even worse."[6] (Note that the 40 million figure here is the number of people threatened, in contrast to the estimated 160,000 children per year already affected according to the Moscow conference cited above.)

Researchers reported in May 2003 that "climate change caused by global warming could result in losses of up to 10 million tons of corn, potentially affecting 140 million people in developing countries."[7] The report further notes that a substantial proportion of the up to 40 million poor livestock keepers in Latin America and the up to 130 million in sub-Saharan Africa depend on corn for survival.[8]

The global picture briefly portrayed above, including melting polar ice caps, rising ocean levels, devastating heat waves, droughts, floods, and violent storms, sounds like a science fiction horror story, or perhaps an alarmist "Chicken Little" claim that the sky is falling. But all these things are actually happening. One can read about them in the daily newspapers or the weekly newsmagazines, or watch them happen on TV. They are not made up or exaggerated.

Consider the following report, accidentally and ironically published on the birthday of the nation that is the world's greatest polluter. It is important to realize that the organization that produced the analysis, the World Meteorological Organization, is a staid and cautious scientific organization, not an advocacy outfit like Greenpeace. It is roughly the international counterpart of the U.S. Weather Service. It reports the facts without making policy judgments.

July 4, 2003 UN Wire: WMO Cites "Record Extreme"
Weather Events Worldwide

The continuing rise of temperatures worldwide could lead to an increase in the number and severity of "extreme" weather phenomena, which are already setting records, the World Meteorological Organization warned yesterday.

The WMO cited "record extreme events" such as a European heat wave last month during which Switzerland recorded its highest temperatures in at least 250 years, a record 562 tornadoes in May in the United States, a heat wave in India that left 1,400 people dead and Sri Lankan floods and landslides caused by heavy rains.

"These record extreme events (high temperatures, low temperatures and high rainfall amounts and droughts) all go into calculating the monthly and annual averages which, for temperatures, have been gradually increasing over the past 100 years. New record extreme events occur every year somewhere in the globe, but in recent years, the number of such extremes have been increasing," the WMO said.

The organization added that the temperature increase during the last century was 0.6 degrees Celsius, about 0.15 degrees higher than previous estimates; that new analyses indicate the temperature rise in the Northern Hemisphere over the last century was probably the greatest of any century in 1,000 years; that the 1990s were probably the warmest decade and 1998 probably the warmest year in 1,000 years; that global temperature increases since 1976 have been about three times the 100-

year average; and that global average land and sea surface temperatures in May were the second-highest since 1880, when record-keeping began.[9]

Reports such as these illustrate that global warming is happening rapidly and it is destructive. One doesn't have to be a climatologist to know that an overwhelming majority of experts in the climate sciences are asserting with confidence the reality of global warming and its destructive effects. This is a consensus view based on an immense mass of scientific data. The many uncertainties are not about the overview, what is happening in the aggregate. They are mainly about regional specifics, what will happen in particular places. Part of the danger from global warming stems from the unpredictability of these regional effects. Reducing or at least better understanding these uncertainties by further research and preparing for them is a vital long-term undertaking, but not as vital as dealing promptly and decisively with the global problem.

Causing the Problem

At one time the air-polluting industries fought pressures to change by denying the existence of global warming. Having lost that battle decisively, they are now claiming that it's not clear that the effect is man-made. They have a partial point. Man-made production of greenhouse gasses is not the only source. However, there is abundant evidence that human activity is causing a dramatic increase, and the problem of global warming would be much less severe or possibly nonexistent without it. Human production of greenhouse gasses is the part of the problem we human beings can deal with, the part where we have a choice, and there is no doubt that it is significant, and probably decisive.

There is virtually no doubt that carbon dioxide is being produced faster by human and automotive activity, industrial manufacturing, etc., than natural mechanisms can absorb it. The concentration of carbon dioxide in the atmosphere is increasing with astonishing speed. Scientific studies of Antarctic ice cores at Cape Roberts give us a snapshot of earth's climatic past. These studies "tell of major climatic events dating back to the very birth of the ice sheet.... They have already confirmed computerized models of climate patterns dating back 33 million years. But the cores also confirm that carbon dioxide levels, always closely linked to climate change, *are now increasing a thousand times faster than anything previously recorded.* [Italics mine.] Team Leader Peter Barrett is convinced our climate is set to heat beyond anything experienced since long before humans evolved."[10] In other words, since at least the past 160,000 years.

According to the website ClimateArk.org, scientific studies of ice core measurements (air bubbles trapped in ice) reveal that atmospheric carbon dioxide began at about 280 parts per million by volume (ppmv) before the industrial era and have increased to about 367 ppmv at present. This rapid increase in carbon dioxide concentrations has been happening since the beginning of industrialization. The increase has closely followed the increase in carbon dioxide emissions from fossil fuels.[11] Rudimentary math tells us that this increase in carbon dioxide in the earth's atmosphere is an astonishingly large 31%. Stated another way, there is almost one-third more carbon dioxide in the earth's atmosphere now than there was before the industrial revolution. When human beings began burning coal and oil industrially they started rapidly returning to the atmosphere carbon that had been lying dormant on or under the surface of the earth for millions of years. There is no reason to doubt the major contribution of humanity to this problem.

Consider the following excerpts from a report submitted by Joe Fiorill in the December 5, 2002 UN Wire: CLIMATE CHANGE: "U.S. Pushes Research As U.N. Stresses What Is Known."

WASHINGTON – As U.S. President George W. Bush's administration today wraps up a controversial three-day meeting to plan further research on climate change, U.N. officials have been stressing what is already known about the phenomenon while largely avoiding direct criticism of U.S. policy.

World Bank chief scientist Robert Watson, Pachauri's predecessor at the IPCC [the Intergovernmental Panel on Climate Change], told UN Wire yesterday that the purely scientific nature of the two organizations may explain why the administration invited them, rather than an agency such as the U.N. Environment Program, to the meeting. Pachauri [the current head of the IPCC] said repeatedly that his panel is "policy-neutral," and Obasi, according to Watson and others, rarely speaks out on policy. But both agency heads spent much of their time at the podium highlighting not uncertainties but certainties about global warming. Drawing on his panel's third and most recent global climate change assessment, Pachauri said most warming over the last 50 years has been human-induced, carbon dioxide emissions in this century will be the dominant factor in climate change, and important means of mitigating climate change exist. [Italics mine] He also cited work by the Union of Concerned Scientists on the effects of climate change on the United States in particular, which include deadly heat waves, water shortages, endangerment of natural resources and wildlife, human health problems and economic losses.

Obasi said that 'the existence of . . . uncertainties does not also imply that there is total lack of knowledge on the subject.'

When the Bush administration emphasizes the uncertainties on climate change and denies the man-made nature of the threat, it is using arguments by the highly polluting energy industries, arguments that have been thoroughly discredited, and denying well established scientific fact.

What Will It Take to Change?

Greenhouse gasses (water vapor, carbon dioxide, ozone, methane, nitrous oxide and the chlorofluorocarbons or CFCs) trap the heat energy that constantly rains down on the earth from the sun and contributes to the warming of the atmosphere. Some of this phenomenon is a good thing, sustaining life, but an overdose may be deadly. Any responsible effort to solve the huge problem of global warming or even mitigate it will require immediate and substantial global movement toward production of smaller quantities of greenhouse gasses by every means possible including conservation (improved energy efficiency) and vigorous pursuit of clean energy sources, both by exploiting those that are available such as wind and solar power, and by developing new technologies.

The most common and pervasive of the greenhouse gasses is carbon dioxide, which is already naturally present in the earth's atmosphere but is also produced by burning carbon-based fuels such as coal, oil, and gasoline. While other greenhouse gasses can be chemically "scrubbed" out of smokestack effluents, carbon dioxide and heat energy are the most basic products of the combustion process. Burn carbon-based fuels, you get carbon dioxide. Or carbon monoxide, which is worse. There is no escaping it except by not burning those kinds of fuels. Hence conservation and alternative

141

energy sources are the main answers in the final analysis. Another partial answer is development of carbon "sinks" or absorbers. Carbon dioxide is absorbed by forests and by the oceans, but these sinks have their limits. Especially when the forests are cut down in the name of preventing forest fires. Carbon sinks do not lend themselves to expansion, except possibly by planting additional forests. And as noted above, human activity is producing carbon dioxide far faster than natural sinks can absorb it.

The most immediately available positive action to curb carbon dioxide production is conservation. The great news about conservation is that it produces additional benefits besides cutting greenhouse gas emissions. It saves consumers money and also prolongs the life of the limited supply of the planet's petroleum. Conservation creates win-win dynamics. It can be achieved readily by such means as promulgating standards requiring more energy-efficient cars, promoting hybrid cars and requiring or promoting more energy-efficient buildings and appliances.

If we are to produce fewer greenhouse gasses, certain industries would be inconvenienced and would have to make challenging adjustments (even— horrors!—to spend money on research and development and to innovate). Balancing this, other industries that produce clean energy could be encouraged by realistic means such as collaborative research and tax incentives. These changes would both cost money and save money. There are always developmental costs associated with change, but these also create improved efficiencies and profitable spin-offs. These latter are certain to happen but hard to predict in detail, so conveniently, only the costs have been counted by the industries opposed to change and the politicians who are boosted into office by their campaign contributions.

To fail to do anything to address the problem would be the height of irresponsibility. It would be to inflict on our children and grandchildren, if not on ourselves, a much larger, more expensive, and quite possibly uncontrollable problem. Scientists know from studying the history of climate change in rock and ice that there are tipping points where change is sudden and drastic. Such changes could in turn have massive disruptive effects on human agriculture everywhere in the world, devastating huge populations. As noted above about Africa, these changes are already beginning to happen. We do not know with total finality when or where other, similar changes will kick in, but the speed with which destructive change is now occurring is unprecedented historically.

We do know that the U.S. produces one-fourth of all greenhouse gasses produced throughout the world. We are the world's largest producer of these gasses. If we do nothing, this generation of American leaders may be remembered by future generations the world over as imitators of the Emperor Nero on a global scale, leaders who fiddled while the planet burned. It would take political courage to act, to stand up to the fossil fuel, smokestack, and automotive industries and press for constructive change. That kind of courage is notably lacking. In fact, the exact opposite is true. The problem is not merely lack of courage to confront these industries, but an active collaboration between the offending industries and the Bush administration to suppress information and effective action on the problem. First, we need to look at the role of the industry in denying the increasingly obvious.

Muddying the Waters

There has been no lack of public argument against global warming, challenging the increasingly clear evidence for its presence and its human origins. Public awareness of global warming began during the blistering summer of 1988, when 96 deaths across the U.S. were attributed to a heat wave. A NASA scientist named James Hansen testified about global warming to the U.S. Congress. His dire predictions made headlines around the world. He was a real scientist, not a crackpot, and his findings and warnings were widely considered credible. Since that time thousands of scientists have studied the huge, complex jigsaw puzzle of global climate change. Most of their findings have reinforced Hansen's observations and predictions.

However, it is the nature and the mission of scientists to be skeptical, to challenge arguments and lines of reasoning and to formulate alternative hypotheses. Especially in the early days, global warming faced a few skeptics. They focused, as any good scientist should, on the weaknesses, gaps, and seeming inconsistencies in the data supporting the thesis that the earth's atmosphere was warming. But this was not an esoteric argument among specialists that could stay safely inside the scientific community.

Leaders of the coal and oil industries were alarmed by the cost and competition implications for their industries. Like the tobacco industry when faced with the devastating public health impacts caused by its product, these industries opted to fight the scientific evidence for the sake of their profits rather than adapt and change in response to new information. In 1989 they formed the Global Climate Coalition to present a different story more favorable to industry, and to frame the discussion as a debate about scientific claims that were supposedly not firm, but debatable. Initially they launched a

143

campaign called the Information Council for the Environment (ICE). They understood advertising, and they selected their audience: "The targets of ICE, according to documents obtained by the Washington-based environmental group Ozone Action, were 'older, less-educated males from larger households who are not typically active information seekers' and 'younger, lower-income women.'"[12] The efforts of ICE met with little success, but they constituted the first step in a sorry, if predictable, chain of events.

The oil and coal companies launched a decade-long campaign to persuade the public and the politicians that global warming was a controversial, uncertain idea and that there was no cause for alarm. In short, they chose to fight science with public relations. But to do that, they needed a few tame scientists on their side for credibility.

In the year 2003, 2,500 scientists contributed to the IPCC findings that global warming is both real and dangerous. Such a large number of climate scientists suggests that a few articulate skeptics should not have been hard to find, especially during the decade of the 1990s when the state of the art in climate science was less developed and the uncertainties about global warming were greater. The industry searched for and found the needed skeptics and provided them with funding and speaking venues. They became the darlings of the oil and coal industries and its *de facto* spokespersons to the public on the subject of global warming. After all, who has more credibility on a scientific subject than a scientist?

Some of the best-known names in this tiny band of well-funded and celebrated skeptics are Patrick Michaels, Richard Lindzen, Robert Balling, Jr., Sallie Baliunas and S. Fred Singer. It should be stressed in fairness that all of these people are respected and accomplished scientists, but it also should be emphasized that all have accepted industry funding and have moved out of the usual circles of careful and exacting scientific debate and into the public arena, speaking persuasively to audiences of business people and politicians. In other words, they speak to audiences who have little basis on which to compare their arguments and data with those of the overwhelming majority of the other climate scientists. In the venues in which they speak, no one has the knowledge or credentials to challenge them.

Of course, they have an absolute right to dissent and to speak to the public. And they are no doubt convinced of the truth of their arguments; no one is accusing them of deliberately distorting their scientific findings to accommodate industry funding. What has happened is that a few persuasive and well-credentialed mavericks with extreme and unusual views, people who apparently are swayed by their own limited findings but are overlooking the totality of the data, have been given celebrity status by an industry desperate to confuse an increasingly clear and dire picture.

All scientists are skeptical; that's the nature of science. They're always trying to figure out 'Is this right?' and making certain they are correct," said Michael MacCracken, a lead scientist in the U.S. Global Change Research Program. "My sense is that a number of critics, who like to call themselves skeptics, are being quite selective of the information. I prefer to call them 'contrarians,' because they often don't look at the balance of the evidence. They actually are trying to require perfection in the explanations."[13]

Often speaking alone, without what in scientific circles would be the inevitable challenge from a foe, they visit business groups, conservative political events and members of Congress. And they dazzle. 'Most of them would be laughed out of a science conference if they tried to pull some of this stuff with us,' said Jerry Mahlman of Princeton University, who has devoted his career to understanding climate change. 'But out there, nobody is onto them.'[14]

One scientist, apparently the one member of the highly visible dissenters on global warming who has not accepted industry funding, made a splash in 1995 with findings that seemingly weakened the case for global warming. John Christy analyzes satellite data used to monitor temperatures in the upper atmosphere. He announced readings that suggested that the atmosphere had been cooling during the past 20 years. His findings seemed to contradict most of the other available data. However, the peer review process of science raised questions. Another scientific team corrected Christy, calling attention to a failure to correct for "atmospheric drag" in his data. With the correction, the data seemed so say that the earth is warming. However, Christy countered that when he made the correction, his data still showed the earth to be cooling.[15]

Christy's findings applied to the upper atmosphere. The lower atmosphere is apparently a different story. Since the debate discussed above, J. Christy and R.T. McNider have reported in the scientific journal, *Nature*, that "satellite observations of temperature trends in the lower atmosphere indicate a warming rate of about 0.1° C per decade since January 1979." The scientific article reporting the findings concludes, "the satellite observations of Christy and McNider are within the range expected from increased greenhouse gas levels for this period."[16]

The technical intricacies of the scientific discussions on global warming are endless. Fortunately for non-scientist readers, they are far beyond the scope of this book and the author's expertise. But one thing remains clear. The scientific consensus that global warming is real and substantially man-made has become stronger, to the point of being all but undisputed by credentialed scientists.

Nevertheless, the coal and oil industries have continued to fight the battle. "Industry-funded efforts have grown more sophisticated. The Greening Earth Society, with the coal trade group Western Fuels identified in fine print as its principal funder, touts global warming as a good thing. 'Its 'Greening of Planet Earth' videos, encased in white plastic adorned by a photo of a wide-eyed chimpanzee perched among super-green jungle foliage, were shipped last year [1998] to every member of Congress. The scientific advisers to its climate newsletter—Balling, Michaels and Baliunas—provide the fodder by casting doubt on current mainstream global climate science.'"[17]

The Greening Earth Society has all the earmarks of a fake NGO, that is, an organization that appears to be grassroots or citizen-driven, but is in actuality a tool of an industry. It keeps a low profile about its true funding sources. Further, it goes to some lengths to appear environment-friendly, while actually making two inconsistent arguments, namely that global warming is really not happening and also that it's good for the planet. As demonstrated by the information presented at the beginning of this chapter, both arguments are transparently false, as well as mutually contradictory. Although the IPCC with its 2,500 scientists has assimilated and explained Christy's data on the upper atmosphere and moved on, the Greening Earth Society argues that the debate continues. Evidently it does; the society, a creature of the industry, continues it, but without scientific merit.

The realities are impossible to deny. Human activity is still pouring carbon dioxide into the atmosphere at a rate far faster than carbon sinks can absorb it; the ice is still melting at the poles and on the mountains; the oceans are still warming and rising; coral reefs are still dying; people are still dying from unprecedented heat waves; and ever-increasing numbers of record-breaking storms and droughts are still ravaging human populations. The coal and oil industries cannot hide these realities behind a smoke screen of dubious statistics and denial.

Suppressing the Facts

The Bush administration has apparently bought the discredited arguments of the global warming skeptics, or has simply been bought by the carbon-fuel and automotive industries. Consider the following bit of very recent history regarding Bush administration suppression of information on global warming.

U.S. President George W. Bush's administration issued demands for revisions that led the U.S. Environmental Protection Agency to remove from an upcoming report a detailed analysis of the risks posed by global warming, the New York Times reported yesterday. The administration reportedly demanded the agency emphasize what Bush calls uncertainties surrounding climate change science.

The administration's changes were so extensive, according to an April 29 internal Environmental Protection Agency memorandum, that the report "no longer accurately represent[ed] scientific consensus on climate change," and the agency decided to scrap the section in question.[18]

In other words, the science didn't fit with the preconceptions of the politicians in the White House, so the science had to go. The section in question was indeed scrapped from the report, and one of the most important pollution problems the world faces was thus ignored in a supposedly comprehensive report by the Environmental Protection Administration. According to the same news report, "After reviewing a draft of the report, the Bush administration reportedly ordered the removal of references to the negative effect rising global temperatures are having on human health and the ecosystem, as well as seeking to modify language to indicate alleged confusion concerning climate change."[19]

When the EPA and the White House could not agree on the matter, eventually the section on global warming was deleted from the report in its entirety. There is cause for strong concern when the highest level of the U.S. Government denies and suppresses the publication of scientific facts and judgements on an issue that urgently affects the long-term well-being of the U.S. and the whole world.

Would the additional expense of dealing sensibly with air pollution in general and global warming in particular be a drag on the U.S. economy? A study by the Office of Management and Budget (OMB) casts an interesting light on the question. The study concludes:

> Environmental regulations are well worth the costs they impose on industry and consumers, resulting in significant public health improvements and other benefits to society...

> The report ... concludes that *the health and social benefits of enforcing tough new clean air regulations during the past decade were five to seven times greater in economic terms than were the costs of complying with the rules.* (Italics mine.) The value of reductions in hospitalization and emergency room visits, premature deaths and lost workdays from improved air quality were estimated at between $120 billion and $193 billion from October 1992 to September 2002.

> By comparison, industry, states and municipalities spent an estimated $23 billion to $26 billion to retrofit plants and facilities and make other changes to comply with new clean-air standards...[20]

It is important to acknowledge at this stage that although the pollutants of concern in the OMB study cited above are serious and immediate threats to human health, they do not include the more difficult long-term problem, carbon dioxide. However, Bush administration decisions to weaken anti-pollution rules and the adverse economic impact of these decisions exposed by the OMB study shows all too clearly where the Bush administration's loyalties lie. They are with the industry, even if the short-term cost is tens of thousands of American lives and billions of dollars and the longer-term cost is endangerment of millions of lives all over the planet.

Government of, by, and for the Industry

Would it be too cynical to believe that the lobbying and campaign contributions of the major energy-producing and polluting industries had an impact on the Bush administration's decisions? One item of evidence is the oft-noted fact that almost the entire Bush team is recruited from the top tiers of the oil industry, starting with Vice President Dick Cheney. But this could be dismissed as the logical fallacy, argument *ad hominem*. A person or group's background doesn't always tell you why they behave in a certain way. People do sometimes transcend their past. (Though groups of people seldom do.)

An indicator of the role of campaign contributions is suggested by the data on who is making the contributions. A full year before the November 2004 elections, the Bush campaign had already raised $49.5 million in the third quarter, an all-time historic record. "The record receipts—more than triple the top Democrat's fundraising for the quarter—were driven in large part by just 285 men and women, who collected $38.5 million or more."[21] This group included 100 "Rangers" who raised at least $200,000 each and 185 "Pioneers" who raised at least $100,000 apiece. "The power and energy industries, which the Bush administration has supported repeatedly with both legislative and regulatory initiatives over the objections of environmental groups, have produced at least 14 Rangers and Pioneers."[22]

An even better body of evidence on the extent to which the Bush team is in bed with the carbon-based energy industry comes from a General Accounting Office (GAO) report on the Bush administration energy plan. "The White House collaborated heavily with corporations in developing President Bush's energy policy but repeatedly refused to give congressional investigators details of the meetings, according to a federal report issued yesterday."[23] It said "Energy Secretary Spencer Abrams privately discussed the formulation of Bush's policy 'with chief executive officers of petroleum, electricity, nuclear, coal, chemical, and natural gas companies, among others.' An energy task force, led by Vice President Cheney, relied for outside advice primarily on 'petroleum, coal, nuclear, natural gas, electricity industry representatives and lobbyists' while seeking limited input from academic experts, environmentalists and policy groups,' the GAO said."[24] The report also noted that none of the meetings were open to the public. In short, the industry and its lobbyists wrote the policy, and did so in secret.

Now of course, any responsible approach to the nation's energy problems would and should include discussions and input from the energy industries mentioned. No problem here. What is significant is first, the highly unusual refusal to share information about these meetings with the GAO. It is difficult to escape the inference that there was something to hide. "An unusually caustic GAO news release complained of the office's 'persistent denial of access' to task force records."[25] Further, "David M. Walker, comptroller general of the United States and head of the GAO, said in an interview that the standoff over the task force documents called into question

149

the existence of 'a reasonable degree of transparency and an appropriate degree of accountability in government.'"[26]

The other disturbing element in this report is the limited input from academic experts, environmentalists and policy groups. The report shows unmistakably that the whole process of information gathering for the Cheney/Bush energy task force was strongly skewed toward the industry perspective (and presumably profits) and was not balanced and concerned with independent viewpoints and the public good. The report also mentions that the task force was subject to tight political control from the top and relied little on nonpolitical expertise in the government. The Interior Department, which manages federal lands on which oil and gas exploration would occur, was not given a lead role in the preparation of any of the report's chapters.

In summary, the Bush-Cheney energy policy was researched and prepared in secret under tight political control and reflected only the perspective of the established energy industries. It locked out professional expertise on energy within the government and the private sector and allowed for no input from the public. There seems to be no evidence that the rapidly growing and now quite large industry concerned with clean energy production and consumption was consulted. There are not only companies and jobs behind the factories with smokestacks that belch pollution; there are also companies and jobs that make the scrubbers that clean up the pollution and companies that build hybrid cars and the windmills for wind power and the cells for solar power. The views of the large and growing clean technology industries were evidently not requested.

It is almost impossible to imagine that the product of this extremely biased process would be anything other than a plan for the profits and expansion of the existing, highly polluting energy industries, without any opportunity to consider conservation options or alternative energy sources and without the slightest regard for the well-being of the American public or the world at large.

The power of the carbon-based or fossil fuel-based energy industry to shape American public policy in ways harmful to the long-term well-being of the human race and the planet did not begin with the Bush administration, of course. It may have reached a culmination or high point with President George W. Bush, but it started much earlier.

Not Saving the World at Rio

At a major environmental summit in Rio de Janeiro in 1992, informally called the Earth Summit, the world's nations hammered out a variety of complex agreements on protection of the environment. (The full title of the conference was the UN Convention on Environment and Development, or UNCED.) By the time of this conference, many of the world's scientists, economists, and political leaders had come to realize that destruction of the earth's air, land, and water was a one-way road to disaster. It had become clear that environmental degradation was leading to the destruction of the foundations on which all successful economic activity, as well as the biological survival and well-being of human life itself, depended. The concept of sustainable economic development, that is, economic development that did not destroy the environmental foundations on which it stood, was coming to be widely recognized across the world as a critical necessity for the human race.

One of the agreements the nations of the world struggled to negotiate at Rio was a plan to restrain the production of greenhouse gasses. In 1990, two years before the Rio summit, the problem had been explored by the Intergovernmental Panel on Climate Change (IPCC), an international network of two thousand leading climate scientists. They had arrived at the jolting conclusion that *a 60% to 80% reduction in carbon dioxide emissions would be necessary to stabilize atmospheric concentrations of greenhouse gases.* In other words, human activity was producing these gasses several times faster than the earth's natural systems could absorb and dispose of them. This sobering finding established the background of the negotiations on the earth's atmosphere at Rio.

However, the U.S. Government had a very different agenda from stabilizing atmospheric concentrations of greenhouse gasses. Its leaders had the companies that contribute the most to air pollution standing foursquare behind them and had representatives physically present behind the scenes of the Rio conference. The U.S., with these companies providing the essential arguments and propaganda, single-handedly destroyed the global consensus that was forming at Rio on greenhouse gasses. The diplomatically worded UN report of the negotiating effort (the gracefully named "UN Intergovernmental Negotiating Committee for a Framework Convention on Climate Change") asked a natural question: "If the Intergovernmental Panel on Climate Change, an international network of leading scientists, concluded that a 60% to 80% reduction in CO_2 emissions would be necessary to

151

stabilise atmospheric concentrations of greenhouse gases, why does the treaty not go beyond stabilising developed country emissions in the year 2000 at 1990 levels?" (About a 10% cut.)

The answer the report gave, in a nutshell, was that "negotiators sought a broad consensus. The result is a general treaty that sets an overall 'framework' within which all governments can work together." Elsewhere in this report we find, *"During the negotiations, the U.S.A. was alone among developed countries in objecting to a clear treaty commitment by such countries to cut back greenhouse gas emissions to 1990 levels by the year 2000."* (Italics mine.) In other words, the U.S. stood alone in its ultimately successful effort to further weaken an agreement that was already critically weak in addressing the problem of global warming. The U.S. was able to do this because the negotiators were struggling to reach a consensus, rather than operating by vote and leaving the U.S. outside the consensus as the sole negative vote.

This weakened agreement emerged only after the U.S. repeatedly brought the negotiations to the brink of collapse by insisting inflexibly on its own point of view, including a refusal to allow the agreement to set specific numerical targets. The situation became critical, almost destroying the success of the Earth Summit, and the U.S. received a great deal of domestic and international criticism over it. Nevertheless, our leaders persisted. The eventual solution was two-pronged. The Europeans decided a weak treaty with the U.S. was better than a strong one without, and capitulated to the U.S. on timetables and numerical targets. They also agreed to a delay in the resolution of key differences pending further negotiations.

The final result was a non-binding agreement to reduce greenhouse gas emissions to 1990 levels by the year 2000. The agreement, the UN Framework Convention on Climate Change, also established a framework for further negotiations. In effect, it postponed resolution. After a great deal of interim negotiating, these further negotiations were intended to reach completion five years later in December 1997 in Kyoto, Japan. The purpose of these negotiations was to develop more specific protocols implementing the Rio agreement. Hence the expression, "Kyoto Protocols."

By the end of the Rio Earth Summit, it was clear that the European Community was in the lead, most other countries except the U.S. were following Europe, and the U.S. was an outsider, a spoiler whose main role was to block consensus. Nevertheless, President Bush (senior) claimed that the U.S. was leading the pack. As with most of the global issues dealt with in this book, the U.S. was a self-proclaimed leader without followers. The U.S.

supposedly led, but the rest of the world was headed in the other direction. Bush further annoyed everyone by stating that "The American way of life is not up for negotiation." ("A Greener Bush" *The Economist*, February 15, 2003.) In other words, Americans' current lifestyle preferences are more important than the future of the planet, including the future of our own children and grandchildren. Myopia and narrow self-interest have never been formulas for leadership.

The situation would soon change, but only temporarily. In November 1992, five months after Rio, Bill Clinton defeated George H. W. Bush in his bid for a second term as President. On April 21, 1993 President Clinton announced the official U.S. position, declaring: "I reaffirm my personal, and announce our nation's, commitment to reducing our greenhouse gas emissions to their 1990 level by the year 2000. I am instructing my administration to produce a cost-effective plan by August that can continue the trend of reduced emissions."[27] This commitment, though only a promise, proved to be the high water mark of U.S. cooperation with the world on global warming.

Al Gore, Clinton's Vice President, was a convinced environmentalist, having written a best-selling book, *Earth in the Balance*, on the subject. Al Gore was genuinely concerned about the dangers of global warming. He took the Clinton administration's policy lead on the subject. Eleven months after Clinton's election, Gore's policy team released a new U.S. policy, the Climate Change Action Plan. It committed the U.S. to reducing carbon emission levels to 1990 levels by the year 2000. This was the same goal the rest of the world had advocated at Rio. Now strongly supported by the U.S., the Rio treaty soon came into force with the requisite number of ratifications.

A mere 13 months after Al Gore's release of the Climate Change Action Plan, Newt Gingrich stormed into the U.S. Congress leading the most extreme group of conservatives within recent memory. A high percentage of his protégés had not set foot outside the United States and they seemed proud of their radically provincial outlook. To them "big government" and environmental concerns were enemies to be diminished, if not eliminated. The political climate in the U.S., at least at the leadership level, had shifted substantially.

As the U.S. Government was swinging to the right, in Europe the Green Party was gaining strength and the European Union was evolving. These European developments both reacted to and intensified a growing European resentment of American global dominance and, among other issues, a frequently observed American backwardness on environmental matters. "In a sense, environmentalism, and particularly climate change policy, became an expression of European nationalism and a declaration of European independence" from the United States.[28] In short, the U.S. and Europe were poised to head in opposite directions on environmental problems.

Not Saving the World at Kyoto

On the way to Kyoto there was a first Conference of the Parties in Berlin in 1995 and a second in Geneva in 1996. The third and supposedly final negotiation was held in Kyoto, Japan in 1997. Before the first of these conferences in Berlin, the Larsen Ice Shelf in Antarctica, a thousand-foot thick shelf of ice the size of Rhode Island, collapsed. Needless to say, this extraordinary event made headlines worldwide. Leading up to that moment, New Orleans had experienced five consecutive years of winters without frost and was overrun with termites, mosquitoes, and cockroaches. Spain was surviving its fourth year of record drought. Summer heat melted the asphalt on the runways of one of Moscow's airports. The global warming problem was clearly not going away.

The Intergovernmental Panel on Climate Change now had 2,500 scientists participating in its studies. In 1995 it issued a second report demonstrating that its computer models could predict the past as well as the future. In other words, the model's predictions were testing out to be aligned with reality. The IPCC findings strengthened the disturbing 1990 conclusions mentioned above and asserted that the balance of evidence pointed to human influence in global climate change. It predicted continually rising sea levels, more violent storms and more droughts.

At the second Conference of the Parties in Geneva, Under Secretary of State Tim Wirth, reporting to President Clinton, took the lead, drafting a policy statement called the Geneva Declaration that reversed the former position of the U.S. and even went so far as to support legally binding targets for overall production of greenhouse gasses. Suddenly the U.S. was "on the side of the angels" on global warming. Not all countries welcomed this change. Though the U.S. was for the moment aligned with Europe, other countries, specifically the Australians, New Zealanders, Russians, Canadians, and Japanese were not so sure. Further, the developing countries wanted to be excluded; they saw their inclusion as likely to stymie their economic development. And of course the U.S. carbon-based energy industry strenuously objected. So much so, in fact, that it established the Global

Climate Coalition to fight an impending agreement at Kyoto that was assumed to be adverse to its interests.

The Global Climate Coalition argued that the Geneva Declaration, if implemented, would reduce American economic growth and cost jobs. The coalition further argued that even if the Geneva Declaration were implemented it would not have the desired effect since the emissions from the developing countries, which were not subject to all of the restrictions, would cancel the effects of American restraint and further, these countries would become more of a magnet for American industry moving abroad.

Environmentalists countered that the cost of doing nothing would be catastrophic. However, this argument didn't carry much weight with the ultra-conservative U.S. Congress. Considering the gravity of the issue, the attitude of the Congress seemed a bit frivolous, as the following anecdote illustrates. Congressman Dana Rohrabacher (R.) of California, an avid surfer, chaired the House Subcommittee on Energy and the Environment. "When told that scientists project a 3-foot rise in sea levels that will drown up to 60 percent of U.S. wetlands and inundate an area the size of Connecticut over the next century, Rohrabacher responded 'I'm tempted to ask what this will do to the shape of the waves and rideabilty of the surf. But I will not do that. I will wait until later, when we get off the record.'"[29]

The Global Climate Coalition and its well-heeled political action committee carried the day with overwhelming success. The U.S. Senate passed by 95 to 0 a resolution as a kind of sendoff guideline to the U.S. negotiation team headed for Kyoto. It stated that the Senate would not ratify a treaty that would harm the U.S. economy or that would exclude developing countries from constraints on pollutants. Viewed with history in mind and stripped of fine euphemisms, this resolution amounted to a morally outrageous claim: we've already trashed the global commons, i.e., the atmosphere, in the course of developing our economy. We've got our goodies and we're going to keep them, so there's no room left for the poor to do more of the same. They will have to continue to do without. We will continue to pollute and to profit from it; they will not be allowed to. There's no room for their pollution alongside ours. Of course, a fairly simple solution would be an organized process of technology transfer and financial assistance that would allow the poorer countries to afford and use advanced technologies that would minimize pollution from their new power plants. However, this solution would require thinking globally rather than thinking selfishly and parochially.

At Kyoto, the American team was forced by domestic political realities to oppose Europe once again and drive a hard bargain. After tough negotiations, brinkmanship and near collapse, a deal was struck. The American team managed to weaken the agreement by securing inclusion of greenhouse gasses that were easy to reduce or eliminate, and got approval of carbon sinks, i.e., forests, as a way of reducing the demands for emissions reductions on U.S. industries. (The U.S. reforesting in the northwest provides, in the form of new trees, a carbon absorber or "sink" that reduces its net emissions of carbon dioxide.) However, the definition of how to account for carbon sinks was postponed for later negotiations. This postponement created problems later. The U.S. tried and failed to get inclusion of emissions trading, a system by which countries that had less need than others to reduce their emissions to reach established goals could trade this credit with other countries that were unable to reach their goals. On targets and timing, the U.S. and Europe agreed to specifics: emissions reductions below 1990 levels of 6% for Japan, 7% for the U.S. and 8% for Europe, to be achieved between 2008 and 2012. The developing countries were off the hook. The Protocol was to take effect when ratified by at least 55 countries that represented 55% of the emissions of greenhouse gasses.

The fact that the developing countries were not required to participate in the agreement, though they were encouraged to, meant that the U.S. Senate would not ratify the protocol. However, the White House signed the agreement, and there was some possibility of forward progress on that basis. Further negotiating sessions were needed to wrap up the details. And of course in such follow-up sessions, formerly established deals can be reopened. A key detail-oriented session was held at The Hague in November 2000.

Simultaneous with this session, the race for the U.S. Presidency had proved to be essentially a tie and was being fought out in the U.S. courts. U.S. negotiators knew this session might be the last chance for an agreement by an administration concerned with environmental issues. They needed generous accounting on forest sinks and at least some emissions trading. "On the other hand, the European negotiators genuinely feared concluding a cynical agreement would be vitiated by loopholes. Any fakery by the developed countries, they thought, would kill their hopes of getting a commitment from the developing countries."[30] In the end the effort collapsed, and a deal was not achieved. And the George W. Bush team won the court fight over who would be President.

What happened next was extremely unfortunate for U.S. leadership and the respect it was accorded in the world, but paradoxically, it may have saved the negotiations. The new President could have simply allowed the situation to drift and the treaty would probably have died a natural death through neglect and the inability of the rest of the international community to come to agreement. Europe still had significant disagreements with Japan, Canada, Australia, and Russia. Left alone, the treaty probably would have died, not with a bang but a fizzle.

However, Bush was firmly aligned politically with the energy industry and had little concern for the environment. His oil-rich family and Texas oil contacts and their financial support were key elements in his accession to the Presidency. His Vice President and others in his inner circle were oil industry heavyweights, and his new energy plan for the country reflected these realities. Among other items that were anathema to environmentalists, his plan included drilling for oil in Alaska's Arctic National Wildlife Area, increasing funding for coal technology, and easing environmental regulations on coal and oil refineries. Although he was not able to get the Alaska drilling through Congress due to passionate lobbying by environmental groups, he did eventually loosen regulations on the dirtiest air polluters of heavy industry, as noted earlier in this chapter.

Presumably to play to his domestic audience of go-it-alone unilateralists in foreign policy and business-oriented members of Congress, Bush seemed to delight in alienating and offending America's European allies. Whatever his motives, rather than remaining silent as he could have done, he slapped the Europeans in the face with an announcement that as far as he was concerned, the Kyoto Protocol was dead.

Not only did this announcement create a global uproar, but it energized the Europeans to move forward vigorously without the United States. They proceeded to negotiate generous forest sink agreements with Russia and Canada. They accommodated Japan and Australia with increased emissions trading. And by these means they got a deal without U.S. involvement. Europe's assumption of the mantle of environmental leadership was complete.

At the beginning of August 2001, the Senate Foreign Relations Committee unanimously approved a resolution supporting further bargaining over Kyoto, either with new proposals or by proposing a new binding treaty. This resolution constituted a surprising change for the Committee, which had previously fought the negotiations. Senators ranging from John F. Kerry (D-Mass.) to Jesse Helms (R-N.C.) supported the resolution. Even Senator

Chuck Hagel (R. Neb.), who had been a strong critic of Kyoto, said that the Senate never intended to withdraw from negotiations on some sort of agreement.[31] However, consistent with previous Senate positions, the resolution did require that any future agreement protect U.S. economic interests and include developing countries. The resolution did call on the administration to create by the upcoming meeting in November an alternative plan that would keep the U.S. in the negotiating process over Kyoto or a binding alternative.

Secretary of State Colin Powell and White House spokesman Scott McClellan claimed that the President shared the Senate's goal and would have a proposal ready for upcoming negotiations in November in Morocco. Later Condoleeza Rice and EPA Administrator Christie Todd Whitman denied that the administration had such plans.

Why these political flirtations with a position that had previously been unacceptable to the Senate and the Bush administration? One possible explanation could be that even some of the country's largest utilities were pressing for clarity on the matter. "Executives from . . . American Electric Power Co., the Cinergy Corp. of Ohio and the Wisconsin Electric Power Co., argue that the regulation of carbon dioxide is inevitable and that they want some certainty in the coming decade as they invest billions of dollars in plant expansion."[32] The Bush administration was said to be drafting a plan for U.S. caps on other pollutants, but not carbon dioxide. The problem for industry was that they might invest large sums in upgrading plants to reduce other pollutants and later be forced to spend additional large sums to meet new carbon dioxide restrictions. They needed an answer.

In the end, the Bush administration did not come up with an alternative to Kyoto. Ironically, the revision to the Kyoto Protocols other countries finally agreed to in November, 2001 in Marrakech, just one year after the efforts at The Hague had failed, contained everything the U.S. had fought for under the Clinton administration. But the U.S. was not on board. At Marrakech the U.S. could have gotten a deal that was both affordable and a modest step in the right direction. It would have at least moved toward leveling, if not reducing, the greenhouse gasses being pumped into the atmosphere. In the process, the U.S. would have recovered some of the respect of the rest of the world it squandered when George W. Bush gratuitously punched it in the eye over Kyoto. But Bush was in charge, and the U.S. did not sign. In the process of these negotiations, the U.S. had earned a negative three-fold reputation—for being anti-environmental, for being arrogant and uncooperative, and for failing to follow through on a commitment to come up with alternative proposals.

The virtual certainty that the U.S. would not sign or ratify the Kyoto Protocols, at least while Bush was in office, created a strong possibility that the agreement might never go into effect. To take effect it must be ratified by countries that produce a total of at least 55% of the world's production of greenhouse gasses. Either the U.S., which produces 25%, or Russia, which produces 17%, could push the number over the 55% mark, but neither was on board. No other country or combination of countries was in the running to do this. In 2003 President Putin's top economics advisor, Andrei Illarionov, launched a highly visible campaign against Kyoto. For a time it appeared that the Kyoto treaty was dead. But in May 2004 events breathed new life into the treaty. As a part of a deal with the European Union to get Russia accepted into the World Trade Organization, President Putin had to agree to Europe's demand that Russia get on board with Kyoto.[33] If the deal holds and Putin's negotiations with other WTO members succeed, Russia will join both WTO and Kyoto and the Kyoto Protocols will at last go into effect. Unfortunately, the U.S. will still be standing outside the tent and making little or no effort to reduce its greenhouse gasses.

A Hydrogen Smoke Screen

After Bush's tactless rejection of the Kyoto Protocols, EPA chief Christie Todd Whitman, "possibly putting on a brave public relations face—assured the press that the United States was going to 'do its own thing' to curb greenhouse emissions. That spring, Bush reversed a campaign promise to force heavy industry to clean its emissions, offering instead a voluntary arrangement that environmentalists derided as useless."[34]

In April 2003 the Bush administration's energy secretary, Spencer Abraham, made an announcement that sounded promising. Touting a "World Partnership for Clean Energy," he proposed an international effort to develop hydrogen as an energy source for vehicles, thus limiting dependence on carbon-based fossil fuels. As noted earlier in this chapter, when hydrogen burns, it combines with oxygen to form water, leaving no pollutants behind. Abraham argued that the U.S. and Europe, working together, can speed the day when hydrogen-burning cars are available on the market. He committed the U.S. to spend about $1.7 billion over five years and said that the European Union would spend about $2 billion for research on hydrogen and other renewable energy sources.[35]

One of the catches is that success, by no means guaranteed, of course, would mean competitively-priced vehicles on the market by 2020, 17 years away. At the swift pace at which global warming is taking place, this delay would be a disaster. One wonders, where is the mention of hybrid cars that use a combination of gasoline-powered internal combustion engines and electrical power? These cars produce significantly less pollution and use less gasoline per mile than their conventional, non-hybrid counterparts, and are available now. The proposal studiously overlooks the obvious in favor of a doubtful future and an unconscionable delay.

Another major drawback of the hydrogen fuel cell project is that hydrogen is not available just anywhere in nature. It is available naturally in parts of Europe, but apparently far less so in the U.S. The alternative to finding natural sources is to burn fossil fuels to generate electricity which is then used to separate hydrogen from the oxygen in water. This is not a solution, it is merely a more roundabout and less efficient way to get energy out of carbon-based fossil fuels, with all the pollution they entail. Further, to implement this "solution" a huge system would be necessary to generate hydrogen, deliver heavy and cumbersome tanks of it to tens of thousands of outlets (formerly gas stations), and totally re-tool the automobile industry to build cars containing fuel cells. These drastic and expensive changes are not likely to happen. The whole idea is thus seen by most analysts as a not-very artful dodge. As a solution it is far in the future, uncertain of outcome, and has virtually no impact on the present situation except to create the illusion of concern and action.

Considering the available but neglected current technologies such as hybrid cars, it is not difficult to understand the environmentalists' reaction to Abraham's proposed "World Partnership for Clean Energy." They rolled their eyes and pointed out the obvious, that it can hardly be viewed as anything but a delaying tactic. It is a non-solution to a huge and urgent problem.

Is There a Future?

Eight months before Marrakech, in March 2001, the IPCC had issued a third report. The science behind it reflected further refinements of the accuracy of the atmospheric models. The new report confirmed and reinforced the direst findings of the previous two reports. It included even stronger evidence of human activity as a contributing cause in global warming. It solved the seeming discrepancy in earlier evidence noted above, documenting a difference between increasing temperatures in the lower atmosphere and little change in the upper atmosphere. It also documented rising ocean temperatures. It predicted a larger temperature increase during the next century than has occurred during the past ten thousand years. The basis of these predictions, of course, had to be an assumption of continuation of human activity on the same course. A change in human activity, which is almost certain to occur, would change the picture for better or for worse.

In view of this report and the solid science behind it, the folly and the danger of the Bush administration's denial and suppression of the evidence on global warming and its decision to allow increased pollution from the dirtiest factories, is staggering. So what is required; what can be done?

Given the current absence of dramatic new inventions for cleanly producing huge quantities of energy, the main short-term solution is conservation, as noted earlier. Though this alternative lacks glamour, numerous studies have shown that conservation can produce quite substantial savings in fossil fuel energy consumption and hence the pollution that goes along with it. A combination of moderate, sensible regulation plus tax incentives could produce dramatic conservation results.

The needed conservation measures are well within the capabilities of the U.S. economy by a variety of readily available means, and would save the public money as well as reducing greenhouse gasses. One of the available ways to conserve, as mentioned before, would be to promote hybrid cars and especially to require substantial but achievable improvements in the fuel efficiency of gas-guzzling SUVs. Hybrid cars use a combination of internal combustion engines and electric power. They constitute an already-available technology that can cut in half the gas consumption of a car. Some foreign-made hybrid cars are already on the market. There is no reason American car manufacturers could not make these cars as well, if they had the proper incentives. The change to hybrids creates savings in fuel costs for the consumer as well as a marked reduction in output of carbon dioxide and other pollutants. Gradually replacing the gas-guzzling current SUVs with hybrid SUVs would produce even more dramatic savings of both fuel consumption and pollution. Of course, developing hybrid cars initially costs manufacturers and hence increases costs for consumers. Either start-up tax incentives or regulations that change the cost-benefit equations could ease this problem.

Setting aside for a moment the advantages of the new hybrid car technology, merely strengthening standards for efficiency can make a major difference. The aftermath of the crisis in gasoline availability in the early

1970's illustrated the potential of conservation. During the 12 years following 1973, cars in the U.S. doubled their fuel efficiency as a result of the Corporate Auto Fleet Efficiency (CAFE) standards established at that time. "These standards have saved Americans some $400 billion, even as our cars have grown more powerful, more reliable, and safer."[36] This period of dramatic efficiency improvement ended because increased availability of gasoline led to diminished political pressure for improvement. Although it was happening, global warming did not become politically visible until 1988. Furthermore, the dramatic growth in SUVs, which were classified as light trucks and thus were exempt from fuel efficiency standards, reversed the trend toward improved efficiency.

"The Environmental Protection Agency estimates that even a one mile per gallon increase in CAFE standards would save six billion gallons of gasoline, $9 billion in consumer fuel expenditures, and 15 million tons of global warming gasses each year and would reduce the trade deficit by up to $6.3 billion."[37] A single mile per gallon is far less than the increases that are needed and feasible. Far more substantial savings in costs and greenhouse gas production are well within the realm of possibility with further tightening of these standards. Why have such changes not been made? The only answer available is the political power of the oil and automotive industries to block progress, and a lack of political will coming from the public. As the period of improvement from 1973 to 1985 demonstrates, the main requirement to produce change is enough citizens' will to override the self-interested lobbying of the oil and automotive industries. Regime change in Washington would also make a major difference.

Automotive use of carbon-based fuels is not the only area where conservation could make a substantial difference, both in savings to the public and in greenhouse gasses. For example, the Bush administration recently rolled back an efficiency standard for central air conditioners that was already signed into law by President Clinton. An analysis by the Alliance to Save Energy points out that if the Bush administration had supported this stricter standard instead of the reduced level, the need at the national level for an additional 43 electricity-generating power plants could have been avoided.[38] Was the higher standard too stringent for the air conditioning manufacturers to meet? America's second-largest air conditioner manufacturer, Goodman, had already met the higher standard.[39]

Other conservation measures could also have a major effect. They include "programs to reduce energy use in new buildings such as building energy codes, tax credits, and public benefit programs [that] would avoid [the need to construct] 170 power plants."[40] Further, "programs to improve existing buildings, by targeting residential air conditioners, commercial lighting, and commercial cooling, can trim demand projections by another 210 power plants."[41]

According to Vice President Dick Cheney's famous statement in Toronto, "Conservation may be a sign of personal virtue, but it is not a sufficient basis for a sound, comprehensive energy policy." His mention of personal virtue implies that individuals recycling their trash or turning down the thermostat are not going to solve the problem. He's right about that. But the important opportunity his statement ignores is the absolutely vital role of sensible government regulation to promote energy efficiency. Reasonable regulations to require improved energy efficiency are not the whole story, but they are an essential ingredient in a comprehensive policy. Leaving them out overlooks the obvious and aggravates the problem of out-of-control energy consumption.

Besides conservation, another key ingredient in a comprehensive policy is renewable energy sources such as solar, wind, and geothermal power. They are clean and productive sources of energy that are readily available. But they're neglected in favor of highly polluting oil and coal. Already 10% of California's energy is provided by these sources and advances in technology are increasing their potential to contribute to the mix of sources that will be required to create a livable future on the planet. Most of the rest of the country is behind California in the use of these power sources, but would gain by playing catch-up. Even in California, their further growth has been politically stymied by heavy lobbying of the state legislature by the oil and coal industries.

Sensible government action to promote these sources of clean energy could both minimize pollution and reduce the nation's reliance on a key source of energy, oil, that makes us dependent on other countries, runs up our trade deficit, and in the end is certain to run dry.

While it is clear that conservation offers the only short-to-middle term solution to over-production of greenhouse gasses, it is equally clear that the only long-term solution is creating as-yet-undiscovered new technologies and far more aggressively developing and exploiting existing technologies. These courses of action will have to be pursued vigorously, with both private-sector innovation and strong and flexible government backing. Both the short- and long-term solutions require political leadership that is willing to acknowledge the problem and tackle it with energy and vision.

With all these as-yet unutilized means to reduce greenhouse gasses, analysts have pointed out that there is still a possibility for the U.S. to recover some measure of the respect it lost in the international community by committing itself to the Marrakech revision of the Kyoto Protocol. But as we have seen, the Bush administration has fully demonstrated the depth of its entanglement with the oil and coal industries and its hostility to anything that is objectionable to those industries. Clearly the policy is to ignore global warming and forge ahead with whatever is perceived to be in the short-term interests of the fossil fuel energy industries and the automotive industry no matter how harmful the long-term impacts on the country and the world. Grassroots political pressure will not change this picture; at this stage it is clear that only regime change in Washington DC can create the necessary policy changes.

---

[1] "Timesman Tears Bush Limb from Limb" *The Washington Post*, 9/24/02.

[2] "Global Warming Said Responsible For 160,000 Deaths Per Year," *UN Wire,* October 1, 2003.

[3] Paul R. Epstein and Gary M. Tabor, "Climate Change Is Really Bugging Our Forests" The Washington Post Outlook, September 7, 2003.

[4] Idem.

[5] "Africa: Failed Harvests Fulfill Predictions On Climate Change," UN Wire, January 7, 2003

[6] Idem.

[7] The report, developed by the Consultative Group on International Agricultural Research and published in "Global Environmental Change," is quoted by Carrie Lee in UN Wire: "Climate Change: Corn Production Could Drop By 10 Percent, Study Says"

[8] Idem.

[9] World Meteorological Organization release, July 2, 2003 as quoted in "WMO Cites 'Record Extreme' Weather Events Worldwide," *UN Wire*, July 4, 2003.

[10] Allen Braddock, "Antarctica: The End of the Earth, Episode 1: Katabatic" Videotape published by Thirteen WNET/Educational Broadcasting, 1999.

[11] "Introduction to climate change: Vital Climate Graphics: Global Atmospheric Concentration of CO2" from ClimateArk.org, a web site devoted to providing information and web links on climate change to the public.

[12] Kitta MacPherson , "Warming trend has doubters. Industry loves and pays them" *Star Ledger* (New Jersey) 08/01/99

[13] Idem.

[14] Idem.

[15] Idem.

[16] http://archive.greenpeace.org/climate/database/records/zgpz0303.

[17] MacPherson op. cit.

[18] "Bush Accused Of Censoring Climate Information," *UN Wire*, June 20, 2003.

[19] Idem.

[20] Eric Pianin, "Study Finds Net Gain From Pollution Rules" The Washington Post, Sept. 27, 2003.

[21] Thomas B. Edsall and Sarah Cohen, "Bush Campaign Raises a Record $49.5 Million" *The Washington Post*, October 15, 2003

[22] Idem.

[23] Mike Allen, GAO Cites Corporate Shaping of Energy Plan," *The Washington Post*, August 26, 2003.

[24] Idem.

[25] Idem.

[26] Idem.

[27] United Nations Intergovernmental Negotiating Committee for a Framework Convention on Climate Change (INC/FCCC) press release: "The Climate Change Treaty - One Year after Rio" Geneva, June 1993.

[28] Clyde Prestowitz, *Rogue Nation*, Basic Books, 2003, p. 129.

[29] Gelbspan, Ross, The Heat Is On: The Climate Crisis, the Cover-up, the Prescription," Boston: Perseus Publishing, 1998, p. 4 as quoted by Clyde Prestowitz in *Rogue Nation: American Unilateralism and the Failure of Good Intentions* Basic Books, 2003, p. 132 &133.

[30] Prestowitz, op. cit., p. 139.

[31] Eric Pianin, "Bush Urged to Negotiate Global Warming Treaty" The Washington Post, 8/2/03

[32] Idem.

[33] Peter Baker, "Russia Backs Kyoto to Get on Path to Join WTO*" The Washington Post*, May 22, 2004.

[34] U.S.: "EPA Chief, Who Challenged Bush Over Kyoto Protocol, Resigns" Traci Hukill, *UN Wire*, May 22, 2003.

[35] "Hydrogen: U.S. Proposes World Partnership For Clean Energy" *UN Wire*, April 29, 2003

[36] T.F. Valone, Bush-Cheney Energy Study: Analysis of the National Energy Policy, Alternative Energy Institute, August, 2002 p. 16.

[37] Idem.

[38] Alliance to Save Energy Fact Sheet (www.ase.org/media/factsheets/facts1300.htm)

[39] T.F. Valone op. cit. p. 15

[40] Alliance to Save Energy op. cit.

[41] Idem.

Chapter Eight

VIOLENCE AND COERCION OR LEADERSHIP?

For 45 years of the Cold War we were in an arms race with the Soviet Union. Now it appears we're in an arms race with ourselves.

—Admiral Eugene Carroll, Jr., U.S. Navy (Ret.)

A liberal world free from tyranny and terror may—and hopefully will—come, but it will not come soon, nor will it come as an act of American will. Governance based on consent rather than force, amity between peoples, and the rule of reason and law cannot be meaningfully imposed or long sustained at gunpoint.

—Edward Rhodes

At the beginning of any discussion of military power, it is important to step back and remind ourselves of certain basic realities. In the storms of political rhetoric and slanted news we are all subjected to, nice words and euphemisms habitually substitute for less pleasant words to mask the uglier realities. Our politicians, journalists and scholars speak blandly, even glibly, about using force when they in fact mean killing and injuring people and destroying property. We talk about "collateral damage" when we mean dead and wounded civilians, often women and children.

Nevertheless, using violence is sometimes a terrible necessity, as a last resort in self-defense or in the defense of others. This chapter is not written from the perspective of a pacifist. Let me emphasize the following: war in self-defense is morally and legally acceptable, and may in some situations be

166

even be morally required. However, our euphemisms can all too easily numb us into forgetting that it is morally reprehensible for an individual or a nation to kill and maim people and destroy property for less compelling reasons than attempting to protect human life from still greater destruction. Further, glib talk about self-defense against remote threats will not do. Historically, moral and legal thinkers, philosophers and international legal experts have agreed: Only a response to an actual attack or an imminent threat of attack are sufficient dangers to justify initiating a violent attack upon others. In the latter half of the twentieth century, one more legitimate cause for such action has been added—action for collective security under the legal authority of the UN Security Council. Those who scorn this source of legal authority are flying in the face of laws established by the United States and supported by every other nation on the planet by virtue of their membership in the United Nations.

Iraq: A Threat or a Temptation?

This chapter is not primarily about the Iraq war; it is primarily about the enormous, historically unprecedented military superiority of the United States in relation to the rest of the world, and its consequences for the U.S. and for the world. Since U.S. military spending consumes over half of all discretionary spending in the U.S. budget, its far-reaching impacts are domestic as well as global. However, a discussion of the Iraq war at this juncture is inescapable because it towers above other concerns in the years 2003 and 2004 and probably will for some time after that. Further, America's global military preeminence was one of the key causal elements in the decision to launch the war. The Iraq war is "Exhibit A" of the kinds of problems that flow from over-reliance on military force (i.e., resorting to violence or the threat of violence) in American foreign policy.

America's immense military power provided the ability and created the temptation to deal violently with the apparent security problem presented by Saddam. There was an alternative: Before the attack on Iraq, containment worked with Saddam and it worked well for a half century against a far more dangerous enemy, the USSR. While fully appreciating the horrors of Saddam's killings of hundreds of thousands of Iraqi people and in no way diminishing these horrors, Americans need to be clear and unequivocal on the reality that the U.S. military killed thousands of Iraqi people in the process of taking over the country, and did so in a "war of choice" (a euphemism for aggression) in clear violation of international law* and without anything remotely approaching an imminent threat from Saddam Hussein. Even the advocates of the war seldom tried to claim that Saddam posed an imminent threat. They posited a long-term threat. Even that long-term threat was supported by highly doubtful evidence that turned out to be totally wrong.

A problem seldom discussed by politicians and the news media is the temptation to use our overwhelming military force even when it is not appropriate to the situation. Even if it is not quite the right tool, or not remotely the right tool, we have it. Moreover, in the aftermath of 9/11, we are angry and afraid, so we are trigger-happy. American leaders in effect held a gun on the rest of the world; after 9/11 they blustered and used it. Iraq was a perfect target, seemingly threatening, but in reality weak. By contrast, North Korea could annihilate South Korea's capital in an afternoon. North Korea was and is threatening—far more dangerous than Iraq—but it is not weak enough to be a good target. It seems safe to say that we will not attack North Korea.

Was Iraq really a terrorist threat, as advertised, or merely a temptation— a new bogeyman to go after when Bush was embarrassed by the U.S. military's inability to capture bin Laden? The FBI and the CIA have discredited the faint traces of evidence that Saddam was involved with Al Qaeda, though Vice President Cheney continues against all evidence to assert a link. Following the war, President Bush was eventually forced by interviewers on television into a sheepish admission that there was no evidence of a link between Saddam and 9/11. Was there a link between Saddam, weapons of mass destruction, and al Qaeda? Several months after the war, Colin Powell admitted there was not. But he had other more

---

* The U.S. Constitution makes treaties the law of the land, equal in weight to any law passed by the Congress and signed by the President. The UN Charter is a treaty signed and ratified by the U.S. Government. The UN Charter allows member nations to launch war only under one or more of three circumstances: having been attacked, being subject to imminent threat of attack, or under UN Security Council authorization. There is no doubt whatsoever that none of these situations pertained to the U.S. attack on Iraq. The oft-cited UNSC 1441, passed unanimously by the Security Council, was sold based on a clear understanding that it was not to be used as a trigger for war. When the U.S. and England went back to the Security Council to request explicit authorization for war, they were unable to garner the needed votes and abandoned the effort. There never was an authorization for war under international law.

interesting things to say, and at a much earlier time. Early in his tenure as Secretary of State and well before the drumbeat of hostile rhetoric from the Bush administration preparing Americans for the war against Iraq, Powell—equipped with abundant access to intelligence reports and analyses—had asserted flatly that Iraq was not a threat. He went on record on a State Department website with the statement that *"Iraq posed no threat to its neighbors, and possessed no 'significant capability' in weapons of mass destruction."*[1]

What a contrast to Powell's later persuasive (but later shown to be erroneous) speech to the UN and the world about the danger Iraq posed. He couldn't have been right both times. In the aftermath of the Iraq war, it is clear that he was right the first time, before loyally taking his marching orders from an ill-advised Commander in Chief.

Where did the bad advice come from? Viewed in terms of American institutions of governance, the picture is disturbing. Putting it starkly, President Bush placed responsibility for the analysis leading to the biggest foreign policy decision of his presidency—whether to go to war with Iraq—in the hands of the Pentagon's civilian political leaders rather than those of the State Department. Deputy Secretary of Defense and the chief architect and advocate of the war, Paul Wolfowitz, working in conjunction with Secretary Rumsfeld and Vice President Cheney, won the argument. Clearly the Defense Department had more influence in the matter than did the State Department. The people wielding the gun were in charge of the all-important policy to use the gun. The people who were experts on international relations and could better foresee the consequences of using the gun were marginalized. Although Powell was getting little traction in slowing down the rush to war, under his leadership the State Department developed contingency plans for the postwar period. They knew that establishing the peace would be far harder than winning the war. The Pentagon ignored the State Department's postwar planning, and partly as a result, the postwar period was chaotic and unplanned, a disaster far worse than it had to be.

Here's a reminder of a well-known but easily forgotten fact: Regarding Saddam's alleged weapons of mass destruction, even before the war the UN inspection team had searched 100 Iraqi sites the CIA thought were the most suspicious and found no trace of them. As the launch date of the war approached, the evidence that American intelligence was simply wrong about this threat was impressive and growing. One hundred supposedly promising sites and zero findings is not a trivial record of failure. This information seemed to have the paradoxical effect of giving President Bush a greater sense of urgency for attacking Iraq. It appeared that he wanted to hurry up and launch the war before the rationale for it evaporated completely. Militarily and politically he had already invested so much he had gone beyond the point of no return. While the rest of the world virtually begged for more time for the inspectors to do their work, he went ahead with the war.

Even more decisively after the war, the picture on the ground utterly failed to substantiate the claim that Saddam was a threat: "Among the closely held internal judgements of the Iraq Survey Group, overseen by David Kay as special representative of CIA Director George C. Tenet, are that Iraq's nuclear weapons scientists did no significant arms-related work after 1991."[2] Later, as he resigned from his job as chief weapons inspector, David Kay reported that he had found no significant WMD capability in Iraq. Does this after-the-fact judgement reflect adversely on the front-end judgements about Saddam's capabilities? Maybe Bush and company can be excused for missing the truth ahead of time. After all, they didn't have the advantage of hindsight and the detailed analysis of David Kay and his team.

However, "according to records made available to *The Washington Post* and interviews with arms investigators from the United States, Britain, and Australia, it did not require a comprehensive survey to find the central assertions of the Bush administration's prewar case to be insubstantial or untrue."[3] In other words, putting it more bluntly, it was evident before the war that Saddam was not a threat. But was it evident only to insiders such as intelligence analysts with access to classified information?

As I conducted research before the war in the process of writing this book, I had no access whatsoever to classified information. I had to rely on documents in the public record. In these sources I encountered abundant, solidly factual evidence that the Bush administration's central assertions about Saddam's weapons of mass destruction and al Qaeda connections were false. All one had to do—and all I did—was to read the newspapers. Experts who knew better than to believe in the threat were speaking out and presenting the evidence; news analysts were digging up and publishing the evidence, but the politicians and many of the op-ed writers were ignoring it, as was the President.

Devastating facts refuting the Bush administration's claims were headlined in news articles and analyses in widely read sources such as the *Washington Post*, *The New York Times*, and *Newsweek*. I'm not speaking here of arguments in liberal editorials and op-ed pieces, but clear-headed, well-researched analyses of the facts of the situation. (I've presented much of this evidence in the chapter, "An Unnecessary War" in this book. I wrote the chapter before the war.) Strangely, despite the plain facts refuting the arguments for war published in the major newspapers, editorials in some of these same newspapers, including the supposedly liberal *Washington Post*, supported the war. In the case of the *Washington Post*, the hard evidence refuting the need for the war was clearly presented in news articles despite an explicit editorial policy favoring the war.

Evidently the country's opinion leaders, including editorial writers, were mesmerized by the nation's widespread post-9/11 fear, by President Bush's post-9/11 popularity, by his bellicose political rhetoric, and—underlying it all—by the certainty of America's overwhelming military might. There was never any doubt that we could win this war militarily. There was also never any doubt that bringing about a stable peace afterward would be incredibly difficult. However, the arguments for the war were emotion-based, not fact-based. The mindset was as follows: "Saddam is a threat, period. We must take him out." A nationwide jingoistic "groupthink" seized a large percentage of the opinion leaders in the news media. More disturbingly, major stories about public opposition to the war (e.g., tens of thousands marching against the war on the Mall in Washington DC and in other cities throughout the country) were often not reported.

It followed from the abundant evidence available even before the war that Saddam was not a real threat, and hence that the war was not a real security requirement. Rather it was a temptation stemming from excess military capacity and a strong impulse to use that capacity to get rid of an evil dictator, even by means that trampled on international law. So the problem is the reverse of the way it is often presented. The problem in a larger time perspective is not primarily a lack of sufficient military power to follow up on the war and establish the peace in Iraq and move on to other happy hunting grounds (Syria? Iran? North Korea?), but rather an excess of military power that contributed to an unnecessary war in the first place. Overwhelming military power fueled the arrogance of the President and his civilian advisors in the Pentagon and the Vice President's office. Their access to coercive power and impulse to use it was the driving force behind the war and it empowered them to sell the war to the Congress and the public. Without that excessive power, U.S. officials could not have been tempted to commit such a gross exercise of imperial overreach. The U.S. and the world will suffer the consequences of that overreach for a long time to come.

Anyone who stated these objections to the war was subjected to near-hysterical accusations of being unpatriotic. Patriotism was suddenly equated with going along with your country's leaders even if they trampled one of the most fundamental principles on which the country was built, the rule of law. But as four-star general Wesley Clark, hardly a pacifist or opponent of military power, has pointed out, "Democracy demands dialogue. It demands discussion and disagreement and dissent. And there is nothing—nothing—more patriotic than speaking out, questioning authority and holding your leaders accountable, whether in a time of peace or a time of war."[4] The America I grew up in and admire envisions itself as a leader among nations in human rights, freedom, and justice, not as a bully. Patriotic Americans need to speak out against the corrupting effect on our leaders of the all-but-unlimited power to commit violence that is bestowed by our overwhelming military supremacy, a supremacy so great that its effects are injurious both domestically and globally.

To a patriotic American, there can be no more important goal than keeping this country on the side of moral and legal integrity, including using violence only for genuine self-defense, that is, response to attack or imminent threat of attack, or for collective security in defense of ourselves and others under the well-established legal authority of the UN Security Council. A person who genuinely shares the central American value of preserving human life cannot also be on the side of building a global empire by causing and threatening death and destruction to others for American global advantage. With the evolution of an American empire of coercion and military force, we may be gaining control of the whole world but losing our own soul as a nation. We are certainly losing the admiration and trust the rest the world has accorded the U.S. when it acted on the values upon which it was founded.

In the fear and anger following 9/11, suddenly it became acceptable (indeed, it became formally announced government policy) to kill and injure people (in other countries, of course) on the chance that some of them might attempt the same against us at some undetermined time in the future. The same politicians and media pundits who supported the war would not have dreamed of cooperating with a family member or friend in bypassing the police and killing a dangerous, violent neighbor who might be a threat at some time in the future. They would have seen immediately that to do so would be to rationalize murder. But the morally identical reality of the preventive war they condoned and actively supported was obscured by the impersonal scale on which it was done and the seemingly noble purpose of ending the rule of an evil dictator and ending an assumed long-term security threat to the U.S. Essentially they were rationalizing a vigilante action, and moving the world toward anarchy rather than away from it.

Of course, regarding the U.S., it is an article of faith that "we are the good guys," which makes whatever we do O.K. Our motives are pure. The good-evil dichotomy promulgated by the Bush administration suggests we're more than pure; we're the heroes and saviors of the world in a cosmic struggle with the forces of evil. By his rhetoric claiming that others must choose to be either with us or against us and we must destroy the evildoers and oppose the axis of evil, Bush creates an artificially clear dichotomy that contrasts with a real world containing endless gradations of gray. In doing this, he conjures an apocalyptic religious vision. If the world is a struggle between good and evil, then the "good guys" must never relent and must always use maximum force to be absolutely sure of victory. They must never succumb to doubts as to the absoluteness of their own goodness, lest they falter in the task of overcoming evil. This quasi-religious vision is a dramatically different vision of the world from the morally ambiguous reality of the past in which American foreign policy has threaded its way through endless complexities and moral shades of gray and has often struggled to select the lesser of several evils, balancing moral issues such as human rights with economic issues important to American national interests.

Apocalypse Now

Robert Jay Lifton, a distinguished psychiatrist at Yale and later at Harvard, has spent a lifetime studying the effects of deep and devastating trauma on groups of people such as genocide survivors and survivors of Hiroshima and Nagasaki. He has also studied the psychology of apocalyptic cults such as Aum Shinrikyo, the Japanese cult that released sarin gas in Tokyo subway trains on March 20, 1995. Lifton has some thought-provoking insights into the effects of the trauma of 9/11 on Americans and American political leaders and their foreign policy attitudes. In his book, *The Superpower Syndrome*, he explores the evidence that the "Christian fundamentalist mindset blends with and intensifies our military fundamentalism. Together they give rise to a contemporary American version of apocalyptic violence. The events of 9/11 did not create this combination but did enlarge it exponentially."[5]

Lifton notes the relevance of George Bush's division of the world into good and evil, his identification of certain countries as the "axis of evil" and his goal of ridding the world of evil. Though it is very different from the

173

apocalyptic vision and violence of the Islamist radicals who perpetrate terrorism, it plays into their hands in a kind of partnership or dance of death in which each side demonizes the other and sees itself and its killing as heroic enactors of God's master plan. Since neither side has any realistic chance of winning a final victory, the struggle is eternal as well as cosmic in its significance.

In one revealing statement, he [Bush] declared, 'At some point, we may be the only ones left. That's okay with me. We are Americans.' In such declarations, he has all but claimed that Americans are the globe's anointed ones and that the sacred mission of purifying the world is ours alone.

The amorphousness of the war on terrorism carries with it a paranoid edge, the suspicion that terrorists and their supporters are everywhere and must be preemptively attacked lest they emerge and attack us. Since such war is limitless and infinite…it inevitably becomes associated with a degree of megalomania as well. As the planet's greatest military power replaces a complex world with its own imagined stripped-down us-versus-them version of it, our distorted national self *becomes* the world.

Despite the Bush administration's constant invocation of the theme of 'security,' the war on terrorism has created the very opposite—a sense of fear and insecurity among Americans, which is then mobilized in support of further aggressive plans in the extension of the larger 'war.' What results is a vicious circle that engenders what we seek to destroy …creating ever more terrorists and, sooner or later, more terrorist attacks.[6]

Lifton's observations address broadly the war on terrorism, but they also help explain more specifically the irrationality of the Iraq war. It was from the start a war in search of a rationale. It began behind the scenes with a sense that the first Gulf War was a missed opportunity to topple Saddam and that the oversight needed to be corrected. More importantly, it was influenced by a strong neoconservative sense that America has a mission in the world and the military power to shape history and fulfill its manifest destiny as a transformer of the world.

174

In preparing the public and Congress for the attack on Iraq, these arrogant and quasi-religious thought streams were suppressed for political purposes. The public was presented with a sanitized claim, a threat from Saddam's supposed weapons of mass destruction and alliance with al Qaeda. These were at first the only reasons put forward for the projected war. Both proved to be false claims. (After the war its chief architect, Deputy Defense Secretary Paul Wolfowitz, called this the bureaucratic rationale, the one that everyone could agree on. Could anything be more typical of a government at its worst?)

As the war approached and these chimera, Saddam's weapons of mass destruction and his alleged connections with 9/11 and with al Qaeda began to disappear, they were replaced by a rationale much more like the apocalyptic one Lifton describes—a noble but bloody crusade of freedom, democracy, and free-market capitalism against the forces of oppression and dictatorship throughout the Middle East. In this ridiculously overoptimistic vision, Iraq would become a shining example of democracy that would inspire the rest of the Middle East. (If this works, why doesn't Turkey, a majority-Muslim democracy, inspire them?) America's violent takeover of Iraq was a prelude to a better world. A bloodbath leads to purification. This is classic apocalyptic thinking. An explanation of how this transformation of the rest of the Middle East was to come about without similarly violent overthrows of other governments was conveniently omitted. Regrettably, the postwar reality is not proving to be so splendid. It continues to be a bloodbath, and Iraq appears to be headed for civil war when the American military lid comes off the pressure cooker. The rest of the Middle East, e.g., the Saudi and Egyptian governments, do not seem to be rushing pell-mell toward democracy.

The bottom line is that the American people were seduced by fear, anger, and the availability of our overwhelming military power into going along with war for reasons other than genuine self-defense or defense of the lives of others. As noted earlier, the Bush administration's radical September 2002 National Security Strategy, stripped of euphemisms, is the following: if you suspect that your neighbor might try to kill you at some time in the future, it's O.K. to kill him now. In the private sector, criminals and paranoid schizophrenics act this way; rational, law-abiding citizens do not. They keep a wary eye on dangerous people, but they don't take the law into their own hands and murder them. The same goes for law-abiding nations.

Though preventive attacks in the absence of an imminent threat have often been practiced in the dismal annals of past warfare over thousands of years, this essentially criminal practice has never been recognized as reasonable or morally acceptable by respected philosophers, religious teachers, or legal scholars. Referring to these traditions and streams of thought, the churches of America and the world all but unanimously said "no" to the war in Iraq. The only exceptions were some of the fundamentalist churches that take literally the apocalyptic symbols in the Book of Revelation. A policy that says, "kill them first on the off-chance that in the future they might try to kill you" is a formula for endless brutality and endless war. It is a reversion to the international anarchy that bequeathed to us World War I and World War II, a dismal past we began to leave behind when the world, following American leaders, established the United Nations. Acting on his new/old radical policy, President Bush brushed aside sixty years of global progress, bumpy and incomplete though it was, dismissed the UN as irrelevant, and launched the war without an imminent threat to the U.S. and without the assent of the Security Council. Welcome to the nineteenth century. Warning: There may be world wars ahead.

Leadership Versus Bullying: Back to Basics

Among individual people and among nations, we all know well that leadership and bullying are not the same thing. A leader inspires people to work together toward mutual goals they share, toward a vision of a better future. People follow a genuine leader voluntarily and often enthusiastically. A leader does not have to violate the freedom of followers; they exercise their freedom by getting behind the leader in pursuing mutually beneficial goals. A bully's power is the opposite of a leader's. He uses a credible threat of harm against others to inspire fear and to force reluctant, temporary cooperation toward a goal that may be far from attractive to his unfortunate "followers" or more accurately, victims. Whereas leaders use cooperation, mutual trust, mutual interests, moral suasion, and teamwork as their tools and motivators, bullies use coercion, violence or the threat of violence, and fear. Bullies usually come to a bad end because nature has a built-in backlash against such behavior: the resentment of the victims and the likely failure of ventures that are sabotaged and not supported by the majority of followers.

Of course, not every person in authority operates exclusively one way or the other. Some use leadership as portrayed above to attract one set of followers, and at the same time or later, bully and coerce unsympathetic or non-cooperative outsiders, usually a minority inside a country, an opposing political party, or a weaker external group. It "helps" if the voluntary followers see opponents as different and therefore unworthy, i.e., members of a different political party, race, nationality, religion, ethnicity, or whatever. It must be self-evident at this stage that military power has a key role in these maneuvers to establish and maintain power by brute force or fear, especially with external groups or internal dissidents.

As with individual leaders, so with nations. Within a nation, enthusiastic cooperation from within a framework of democratic institutions to achieve common goals is always more effective than sullen acquiescence to the goals of a dictator or an oligarchy. These lessons we have learned internally in the U.S., but we have turned them upside down in our relations with our neighbors. We praise democracy but we still try to bully other countries into submission. Is "bully" too strong a word? For an example other than the Iraq war, which is rife with examples of bullying, consider our coercive treatment of other nations in our undeclared war on the International Criminal Court. We have threatened to cut off financial aid to 35 smaller and weaker countries that have refused to sign impunity agreements exempting our citizens from the jurisdiction of the court. The reason for their refusal is a matter of principle; these countries joined the court not because anyone has coerced them to sign the treaty establishing it, but because they believe justice applies to all, not just to the weak with an exemption for the strong. We are trying to coerce them into giving way on a matter of principle by threatening withdrawal of our aid. They are the weak, and we are the strong, and we are demanding that they agree to impunity for us. This is one pattern of classic bullying behavior.

Killing: What's It For?

There are three basic uses for killing people or destroying property: defense of others, self-defense, and bullying or coercion. The latter we call terrorism or dictatorship when we don't like the people who are doing it or their cause. If we do like their cause our politicians call them freedom fighters. Defense of others may be the most admirable motive for force, though it has serious moral and legal risks and is the least used, especially by the U.S. Government. One genocide after another has passed by in the past century with little protest and no intervention by the U.S. or the rest of the international community. However, in conflicts that may spread, the UN Security Council has repeatedly called for peacekeeping missions in various parts of the world (with American concurrence; we have the veto), but, with the exception of the Balkans, the U.S. has for the most part avoided getting

177

involved in peacekeeping, except to provide logistics. The myth that we are involved in peacekeeping all over the world is not borne out by the facts. We are militarily present all over the world, but for the most part we have avoided peacekeeping roles.

The second reason for violence mentioned above, self-defense, is of course justified if the violence is kept to the minimum necessary for self-protection. I strongly agree with the mainstream view that self-defense is essential, and in the present dismal state of relations between nations, it is a sufficient justification for a nation to establish and maintain military power that is at least reasonably proportional to external threats. In a world of international anarchy and violence, a nation needs enough military power not only to fend off attack, but to defeat an aggressor convincingly enough to prevent future aggression. However, if each nation independently strives for this goal, the result is an endless arms race. Arms races foment fear and distrust and usually end in war. Hence the value of arms control treaties, or better yet, the gradual replacement of brute force with lawful, institutionalized cooperation, thereby eliminating the temptation to war. The European Union is now doing this among its member states with great difficulty; it's no easy road. This is not fuzzy-minded idealism. It happened in the United States when the colonies united and eventually established a constitution, and subsequently built one of the greatest nations in the history of the world. It is happening in Europe, and a major war between European nations is now unthinkable. It is an eminently practical course of action.

Just over sixty years ago World War II devastated the world. The difference now is the willingness of European nations to give up small increments of nationalistic independence to gain a level of cooperation and trust between nations that virtually abolishes war while promoting prosperity. In Europe, since the terrible trauma of World War II, jingoism is out and cooperation is in. The contrast of Europe past and present seems to be lost on conservative American leaders who sing the antiquated and dangerous siren song of national sovereignty above all other values. National sovereignty *über alles*. The Europeans understand the consequences of goose-stepping along to this song. They have proved that people and nations can agree to change their world.

In the United States, the ultra-conservative emphasis on national sovereignty (fancy language for tribalism) above other more basic values has specific and dangerous consequences. One of these consequences is that U.S. foreign policy is moving decisively away from arms control treaties. Conservative American policy leaders (with the notable exception of Colin

Powell) seem to abhor the idea, applied to the international level, of lawful, institutionalized cooperation of the type this country was built on internally, and that Europe is now cultivating.

How Much is Too Much?

It is easy (because comforting) to neglect the next logical step after self-defense and defense of others in considering the need for military power's capability for violence. Military power that goes far beyond the necessity for self defense is almost certainly either designed for intimidation or is a waste of resources. Politically, such waste can be caused by inertia such as failing to scale down after requirements such as the Cold War, or by pork barrel. Furthermore, any effort to maintain wildly excessive military power and simultaneously to deny that it's a waste of resources naturally creates a temptation to use it for bullying, or to invent a bogus threat or create a real one sufficient to rationalize maintaining the excess.

Since September 11, 2001 and the wars in Afghanistan and Iraq it has become taboo, if not suicidal to one's credibility, to question the need for the current size and capability of the U.S. military establishment. Most of the talk and action by the Washington pundits and the politicians is about increasing it. In a world of severe threats and requirements such as those we face, in the light of the strain on U.S. military personnel Iraq represents, how can one question America's need for an extremely powerful military? The answer, of course, is one cannot. The need for a powerful U.S. military is genuine and obvious.

But a larger question is, do we have a powerful military, as needed, or much more than that? How much is enough military power for the U.S.? Is there such a thing as too much? It seems likely that most Americans, if asked how much is enough (and I among them), would agree that the United States is justified in maintaining the most powerful military in the world. The U.S. is the wealthiest single country in the world (we are less than 5% of the world's population but have 25% of the world's wealth) and we are one of the larger nations geographically. Because of our wealth we are better able to afford a powerful military establishment than other countries, and we have the most at risk. It also seems safe to say that most Americans realize that we do in fact have the world's most powerful military. Who would question it? I believe most Americans would also agree, if asked, that the U.S. should only use its military power defensively, and that starting wars to dominate and control other countries is flatly immoral and is not the American way of

179

doing things. Outside of a small circle of extremely powerful neoconservatives, there is little appetite for empire in the American stomach. We would rather just mind our own business and make money.

To get a feel for how much is enough military power, we need to hark back to the end of the Cold War, when the Soviet Union ceased to exist and fell apart into one giant, Russia, and a gaggle of far smaller countries. Russia turned haltingly and stumblingly toward capitalism and toward the west, particularly the U.S., for aid. Frank exchanges of military information replaced deep secrecy and suspicion. A new day really had dawned. The probability of a nuclear exchange, everybody's worst nightmare, gradually receded to near non-existence, as did the possibility of a dash across Europe by Russia's conventional forces. Under pressure from other priorities, the U.S. gradually and cautiously began to scale back its super-colossal military establishment. Some conservatives railed about the dangers, but the inescapable truth was that there were no longer real dangers that required the military mega-monster we had created.

Nevertheless, despite the cutbacks since the end of the Cold War, any rational look at U.S. military power in relation to that of the rest of the world leads directly and swiftly to the conclusion that the U.S. has grotesquely more—many times more—military power than it needs to fend off any existing or foreseeable conventional threat. Yet we are extremely vulnerable to unconventional threats such as suicidal thugs with box cutters. Clearly there is an imbalance in capability and commensurate spending that cries out to be corrected.

The surprise for most Americans might be the colossal magnitude of the discrepancy in military spending versus domestic spending and the still greater discrepancy in spending and capability between the U.S. and any potential rival. Starting with external comparisons, we spend more than *six times* as much per year on our military than does the second-biggest military spender, Russia. Further, it is no secret that Russia's decaying military with its underpaid troops and antiquated equipment, despite its spending requirements, is far less than one-sixth as powerful as that of the U.S. Its one trump card is its nuclear weapons and intercontinental ballistic missiles, which despite their deterioration are probably still capable of annihilating the U.S. or any other part of the world in a matter of minutes. The U.S. conventional superiority, no matter how large or small, does not affect this. Fortunately, the totally changed post-Cold War international atmosphere does change the threat implications completely.

180

Looking beyond Russia, the $399 billion U.S. military budget for 2004, *not including* an additional $150 billion in extra requirements for the Iraq war, is larger than the military budgets of the other top 20 military big spenders *combined*. These top twenty include, among others, Russia, China, Japan, the United Kingdom, France, Germany, Saudi Arabia, Italy, India, South Korea, Brazil, Taiwan, and Israel. These military "giants," placed side-by-side with the U.S. in military spending and clout, are reduced to Lilliputian dimensions. Their defense spending ranges from Russia's one-sixth of that of the U.S. to one thirty-eighth. Even more important is the fact that these tiny big spenders are not hostile to the U.S. Not one of the list of the top thirteen above is anywhere near hostile enough to represent a threat, even if they had the power to mount a threat.

It's worth noting from these numbers that the proposed *increase* in U.S. military spending in a single year as a result of the Iraq war exceeds the entire Russian military budget for a year, $65 billion, and also exceeds the combined military budgets of the 27 countries ranked after the top twenty. In other words, when we include the cost of the Iraq war in the count, we are outspending the top 47 big military spenders combined.[7] Our military reach is global; we have divided the world into sectors, regional commands with generals sometimes referred to in the press as American "proconsuls" in charge of coordinating the various branches of the U.S. military – Army, Navy, Marines, and Air Force – in each major sector of the globe. No other country in world history has had the military power to do anything like this. Would-be world conquerors such as Alexander the Great, Napoleon, and Hitler, to name a few, dreamed of such a global reach but never came close to achieving it. In the light of these dramatic facts, the word "superpower" as applied to the U.S. is not an exaggeration, it is an understatement. The English language has no word extreme enough to sum up the reality. Even "hyperpower" falls short of the mark. For some time we have been an elephant spooked by mice and trying to get stronger to defend itself.

Since before the Iraq war we maintained a military establishment larger and, due to advanced technology, many times more powerful than the combined power of the 47 other biggest military spenders, who are we afraid of? What threat are we defending ourselves against? Why do we maintain and even expand this immense level of preparation for war? Perhaps we're secretly preparing to fend off an attack from extraterrestrials. There are no signs that the forty-seven next-biggest military "powers" are planning to gang up on us. Most of them are our friends and allies (though we often seem to be doing our best to alienate them). Moreover, given their diverse interests, cultures, and locations, there is no way they could muster the political will to coordinate militarily against us. To even mention the possibility is to call attention to its absurdity.

Another way of looking at the adequacy of U.S. military power is to focus on the countries that have poor relations with the U.S. or are outright hostile to us. These are Iran, North Korea, Syria, Cuba, Sudan, and Libya. Their combined military spending is roughly $19 billion, in contrast to the $399 billion budgeted by the U.S., excluding funds for Iraq. In other words, we spend about 21 times as much as all six of these least-friendly countries combined. The two biggest spenders, Iran and North Korea, each have military budgets of about $5 billion. The U.S. spends roughly 80 times as much on its military as either of them. Again, these spending numbers are far from exact indicators of relative military power. The power gap is much greater considering that our military is far better trained and equipped. In reality we are hundreds of times more powerful than they are.[8]

Naturally the super-colossal U.S. military budget has far-reaching domestic implications. U.S. military spending constitutes about half of all discretionary spending in the U.S. budget, and completely overshadows (and crowds out) vital spending for the future of the country on essentials such as education and health care. This level of military expenditure seems especially strange in a world in which nations that are powerful militarily are not hostile to the U.S., and those that are hostile are among the weakest. In the context of the U.S. Government's discretionary military spending (ballpark $400 billion, or half of the total), consider that other discretionary spending in fiscal year 2003 included $52 billion for education, (about one-sixteenth of the discretionary spending total) and $44 billion for health, or about one-eighteenth of total discretionary spending. We spend $33 billion on justice, or about one-twenty-fourth of all discretionary spending. Similar to that of justice is the budget for natural resources and the environment, $29 billion.[9]

The problem is not merely a matter of money. As a result of extreme overspending on the military, many of the most highly productive scientific and engineering brains of the nation are drawn away from potentially more constructive purposes and directed toward military threats that simply do not exist unless we create them as we did in Iraq.

Meanwhile spending on real defenses against terrorism is a relatively small investment. As the Center for Defense Information puts it, "Military spending ... dwarfs spending on other areas of national security and foreign policy. The entire spending for the Department of State and other foreign affairs agencies amounted to a mere $8 billion in 2003, less than 2 percent of the military total. Economic development aid, which Bush has acknowledged is a useful tool in countering terrorism, totaled less than $9 billion. The discretionary budget for all homeland security programs excluding the Defense Department was only $32 billion."[10]

The U.S. is poorly equipped to fight terrorism, but remains well set up to fight the Soviet Union, although it no longer exists. The end of the Cold War left the colossal U.S. military establishment dazed and confused. Suddenly the noble and essential purpose for its existence was gone. Self-defense on the scale for which we were prepared was no longer an issue, and bullying hadn't yet gained much political cachet. Besides, most Americans don't like bullies and don't really want their country to be a bully.

Dazed and Confused

William Greider captured the problem in his book, *Fortress America*, written in 1997, eight years after the conventionally accepted date of the end of the Cold War. At just one location, Fort Hood, Texas, he speaks of what he saw on a visit, including "something like 2,400 tanks, Bradleys and other kinds of tracked vehicles—plus more than 11,500 trucks, tankers, Humvees, and other, heavier vehicles on wheels.... The Fort Hood motor pool stretches along North Avenue for six and a half miles."[11] He goes on to sum up the post-Cold War (but pre-Iraq) dilemma of the U.S. military as illustrated by too much equipment:

The parking lots of armor reflect, crudely, the great national dilemma we are evading. America is experiencing a deep confusion of purpose at this moment of history, holding onto a past that is defunct, but unable to imagine a different future. The Cold War is over, but not really, not yet.

Too many tanks with nowhere to send them. Too many bombers and fighter planes, too many ships and rockets. Too many men and women in uniform. Our troops are the best in the world, splendidly trained and capable, brilliantly equipped with dazzling weaponry. But what exactly are they to do, now that a general peace is upon us? We don't know the answer. We don't even want to talk about it.[12]

The Pentagon has been dumping old tanks like an army-navy surplus store conducting frantic "going out of business" sales. Giving them away to friendly nations. Selling them at deep discounts. Offering them free to local museums. It dumped one hundred old Sherman M-60s into Mobile Bay off the Alabama coast to form artificial reefs for fish in the Gulf of Mexico. Several hundred more are being sunk along other coastlines for the same purpose.[13]

The services appear to be giving away still useful equipment in order to justify procurement of the new weaponry…. Much of the equipment now declared 'excess' is quite serviceable. In fact, a lot of it was purchased or reconditioned in the Reagan arms build-up of the 1980s.[14]

In this desperate situation, it's not surprising that creativity took over. Inventing an imaginary threat was tried first. A prize for invention goes to the Pentagon military planners who developed the two-war scenario, necessitating that the U.S. have a military capable of conducting two regional wars at the same time. For a while this invention, unlikely but not entirely implausible, served to prop up some semblance of a rationale for maintaining the huge U.S. military machine.

The Gulf War, Kosovo, and the war in Afghanistan provided brief but real requirements for at least a significant fraction of the immense capability of the U.S. military. However, they were over quickly and left a continuing problem: what next? Are we going to run out of such opportunities to use our massive capability?

The grand prize for creativity in a second category, creating a threat where none existed, goes to the neoconservative senior civilians in the Pentagon who advocated the second war with Iraq. They worked on cultivating a second Iraq war from 1991 forward, but gained little traction with George Bush Senior. However, one has to give them credit for trying. During the Clinton years they were out of power. However, after Clinton, with a new and aggressive President in the White House who was less notable for prudence than his father was, and with the fears and angers generated by 9/11 putting wind in their sails, the neoconservatives found their moment. Of course, an enemy supposedly equipped with weapons of mass destruction and supposedly linked to al Qaeda was an invaluable step in the process. Belief in Saddam's WMDs and his connections with al Qaeda, bolstered by a few shaky threads of evidence and a lot of fear, were assets essential to persuading the President to initiate and Congress to authorize war.

In addition to invention, an essential element was bullying or threatening, which is always a helpful step in creating a real enemy or the appearance of an enemy. A dangerous enemy is helpful if one is to maintain an immense military capability. Otherwise, what's it for? And bullying Saddam seemed morally impeccable, since this enemy, though no real threat, appeared threatening and was certainly an appallingly evil and vicious dictator. No invention was needed on that score. Saddam was the perfect bogeyman, and thus a perfect target.

Six months and more after the end of major combat operations in the war, its rationale is discredited and its cost in lives and dollars is steadily rising with no end in sight. However, one aspect of dealing with Saddam did in reality require a credible threat of war—a rare legitimate use of it—the need to coerce Saddam into agreeing to intrusive and effective UN inspections for weapons of mass destruction. This requirement illustrates the usefulness of a powerful U.S. military. But for the Bush administration the inspections were only means to an end. Evidently President Bush expected Saddam to balk at the inspections and thus to provide the perfect rationale for war. From the beginning Bush's rhetoric left no doubt that his single, one-track goal was to topple Saddam. Bush made it crystal clear that war could be averted only if Saddam stepped down, an event so improbable it could safely be dismissed as hypothetical. But Saddam had a surprise up his sleeve. He did not step down of course, but also he did not interfere with the UN inspectors as they checked the first hundred sites identified by the CIA. When they found no weapons of mass destruction, the rationale for the plan to attack Saddam was in serious jeopardy.

The UN Security Council balked at authorizing the war, a hint that the rationale, always weak, was getting weaker. Credibility for the rationale was eroding, and the weather in Iraq was changing for the worse. An impatient President Bush launched the war, and a use for that huge American military capacity was at last found. The first Gulf War, the Kosovo campaign, and the war in Afghanistan, of course, had offered legitimate uses for U.S. military prowess, even to some extent vindicating the need for it, but they were over awfully quickly. The war on terrorism, with the exception of the initial mopping up of Afghanistan, didn't really require our huge military arsenal; it was primarily an intelligence war. Iraq II was another story. It seemed a vindication of the need. The only problem: it was an unnecessary war based on false premises.

185

The Empire of Arrogance

Neoconservative writers have argued that we should use our unprecedented military superiority as the core of our foreign policy and maintain a de facto American empire around the world—an empire of raw power but not of territorial expansion, an empire that cannot possibly be challenged by any other nation. The purpose of this ambitious agenda is a crusade to bring secular democracy and free markets (i.e., create purchasers of our goods) to the whole world. Setting aside for a moment the tremendously important moral and legal problems with achieving these goals by violence and coercion, these academics overlook the practical fact that the power to kill people and destroy property is a blunt instrument, far too crude for most purposes of international deal-making. It is useful only for threatening and coercing a handful of extremely hostile and dangerous nation-states. In the post-Cold War world, these countries are far outnumbered by friendly and neutral states and by both friendly and unfriendly non-state actors. The latter are far less constrained by aircraft carriers and fighter jets than by advanced intelligence methods.

Making our overwhelming military power the centerpiece of our foreign policy is simply not workable. The diplomats who actually carry out the majority of international relations work such as foreign service officers in the State Department seldom agitate for bigger military expenditures to back their efforts. They know greater military power won't help them. Are we going to negotiate with other countries over trade deals backed by threat of military force? To do so would precipitate shock and rage and bring about an abrupt halt to negotiations. Certain minimum levels of civility, trust and mutual interest are the foundations of such negotiations. Of course, this fact is a no-brainer, but it illustrates how far out of kilter with reality the neoconservative vision is and how radically limited military force is as a means for achieving American international objectives. As Henry Kissinger put it in the statement also quoted on the frontispiece of this book,

The United States must resist basing foreign policy on hegemonic power. Many of the problems affecting world order are not susceptible to solution by military means. History shows that sooner or later every powerful country calls into being countervailing forces. And at that point—and I would insist even now—the United States will not be able to sort out every international problem alone without exhausting itself physically and psychologically. . . . The ultimate challenge for U.S. foreign policy is to turn dominant power into a sense of shared responsibility."[15]

As concrete embodiments of that critically needed sense of shared responsibility, multilateral institutions like the UN, NATO, and the European Union are the stabilizing factors, not the U.S. military alone. For the overwhelming majority of international negotiation and deal-making, military force is at best irrelevant and at worst counterproductive. Foreign policy is mainly about cooperation, not coercion. It is not surprising, then, that Colin Powell, as Secretary of State, was the one key Bush advisor who firmly and steadily opposed the war in Iraq as long as possible before getting on board. His position on the war was not only a result of his cautious and balanced personality and his experiences in Vietnam, but also of his duties as a diplomat.

It is no accident that it was a patriotic and politically conservative negotiator of trade deals for Ronald Reagan, Clyde Prestowitz, who wrote a hard-hitting critique of U.S. foreign policy entitled *Rogue Nation: American Unilateralism and the Failure of Good Intentions*. As a negotiator of trade deals, he knew the value of working with at least a minimal base of mutual understanding and trust. He summarized the central thesis of his book with the following observations:

What troubles me, and has inspired my title, is that increasingly large numbers of people abroad, including many longtime friends of America, are beginning to see us, if not exactly like Saddam or other brutes, certainly as, in the words of Webster's dictionary, "no longer . . . belonging, not controllable or answerable, and with an unpredictable disposition." [The definition of the word "rogue."] In fact, today's [Monday, February 24, 2003]Washington Post carries a front page story saying that many people in the world consider President George W. Bush a greater threat to world peace than Saddam. Nor is this a recent development resulting from the debate over what to do about Iraq. Listen to the Guardian of London: "America, the 'indispensable nation' begins to resemble the ultimate rogue state. Instead of leading the community of nations, Bush's America seems increasingly bent on confronting it. Instead of a shining city on a hill . . . comes a nationalistic jingle: we do

187

what we want . . . and if you don't like it, well, tough." That passage was not written yesterday, but in the spring of 2001 at the time of the U.S. rejection of the Kyoto treaty to control global warming.[16]

The arrogance that drives neoconservative American political leaders to stiff-arm the rest of the world and run up unprecedented levels of resentment against the U.S. with no thought of the consequences rests primarily on our overwhelming military superiority. Power corrupts. Nobody dares attack us, so we can do as we please, including attacking others, no matter how offensive or threatening our behavior is to the rest of the world.

Of course, someone did try, successfully, to attack us on 9/11 despite our overwhelming military power, and our response was more of the same—to rely still more on a kind of military force that is incapable of stopping terrorists. After two wars and two nations' governments have been toppled (I grant that Afghanistan was done in self-defense and was necessary), we are no safer than we were before. The U.S. is still, as of this writing, on code orange—high alert for terrorism—and Osama bin Laden is still very much alive, and al Qaeda continues to operate. Denied its geographic headquarters in Afghanistan, al Qaeda is more diffuse and harder to find and destroy than before. All our vast conventional and nuclear military power has not changed this troubling reality. Not aircraft carriers and fighter jets, but relentless intelligence work in cooperation with other countries is the only way to root out terrorists by force. Furthermore, benign and constructive relationships with the rest of the world are the only way to pave the road for cooperation and to reduce the number of people who hate the U.S. enough to become recruits for anti-American terrorism.

Coercion as Policy

Brute force and coercion generate fierce resentments that undermine everything else we try to do. Under George W. Bush the neoconservatives have led the way in using coercion, but their efforts aren't new. Well before their dominance, Senator Jesse Helms used the coercive power of his position as Chair of the Senate Foreign Relations Committee to strive to make coercion the heart of U.S. foreign policy. His approach was to use unilateral economic sanctions to try to force other countries to do our bidding. As often as not, American business interests were hurt more than the intended target countries, whose businesses and governments could readily get the goods and services they wanted elsewhere. What Helms did accomplish was to ratchet up resentment against the U.S. in other countries.

Using coercion, whether economic or military, as a preferred tool is inherently untenable. In 2003-2004, during and after the Iraq war, the U.S. has hit an all-time low in terms of respect and regard from other countries. Fortunately, most people overseas blame Bush rather than the U.S. as a whole for their dismay and disgust with the current arrogant and high-handed U.S. foreign policy. But if this policy pattern goes on long enough, the excuses will cease, and it will be America, not merely George W. Bush, who is seen as the rogue. Our one-sided support for Israel has helped to assure that this transformation is already well under way, if not completed, in the Islamic world. Our policies have created an almost unlimited ocean of potential recruits for terrorist attacks. Out of the billion plus Muslims in the world, if only one in a thousand is radical enough to become a terrorist who will risk or sacrifice his life to attack the U.S., that makes a million potential recruits for anti-U.S. terrorism. Alienating and trampling on the rest of the world is not the answer to our problems.

Threats, Vulnerabilities, and Temptations

There is no question that the threat of terrorism from al Qaeda and probably other sources is real and implacable. It will not go away in response to skillful diplomacy. But the only effective response to this threat is an intelligence campaign conducted in cooperation with the intelligence agencies of other countries, plus improved security at home. The lead agencies for carrying out this "war" are the CIA and the FBI, supplemented by more pedestrian domestic agencies such as the U.S. Customs Service and the Federal Aviation Administration. The Defense Department cannot lead these kinds of efforts. It has an important role, but it is not the primary actor. If we think it is, we are getting trapped in our metaphor, the "war" on terrorism. The relevance of additional warships and fighter planes to the terrorist threat is doubtful.

The terrorist bombing of the battleship Cole in the Yemeni harbor of Aden suggests that our highly visible military presence around the world both provokes fear and anger and makes us sitting ducks. Our ships and planes are marvelous targets of opportunity for terrorists, as are our troops in Iraq. Now that we're there, our soldiers are proving to be a target-rich environment for terrorists, whether they are Islamic extremists from other countries or homegrown Iraqis tying to throw off a foreign military occupation. In Iraq and elsewhere, our military power and presence often make us more vulnerable to terrorists, not less so. We are proliferating the vulnerabilities we are trying to overcome.

Wagging the Civilian Dog

The highly visible international wars fought recently by the U.S., including the first Gulf War and the wars in Afghanistan and Iraq have created the impression that international wars are commonplace. Fortunately, this is not true. The world's best news is that in the post-World War II and post-Cold War world stitched together by the U.S., Europe, and the international community generally, wars between nations are increasingly rare. Although international wars are the most dangerous, most wars are now civil wars. (The notable exception is Africa, where national boundaries are all but nonexistent in reality and hence wars are often regional. They often create major humanitarian horrors, but seldom directly threaten major U.S. interests or those of the rest of the world.) Civil wars do spill across even well-defined boundaries into other countries and threaten wider war, and thus often involve neighboring nations in an effort to defuse them through negotiations. The ability to bring military power to bear as NATO did in Kosovo is vital, and validates the need for a reasonable sufficiency of military power. However, the extreme disproportion of U.S. military power has little relevance to most internal conflicts in other countries, and even to the spillovers.

Ironically, the presence of this overwhelming power leads to repeated calls from the international community for U.S. involvement in humanitarian interventions all over the globe. The plea is simple in principle: This needs to be done and you have the power, so why don't you do it? Or at least lead a coalition in doing it? The U.S. seldom complies, thus looking stingy, callous, or over-cautious, and leaving the rest of the world to wonder what all that military power is for. The answer—the war in Iraq—was not a good solution; it is proving to be a vindication of the critics who say the power is excessive.

The Pentagon's overwhelming power also creates a problem that is, if possible, more dangerous than those. Domestically, it creates a situation in which the Pentagon can and does take over U.S. foreign policy whenever it wishes, even against the will of the American people. The seeming balance-of-power counterweights of the President and the Congress often fail to control, or are complicit in, the military's dominance of foreign policy. On the landmine treaty, the International Criminal Court treaty, the

Comprehensive Nuclear Test Ban Treaty (CTBT), the war in Iraq, and a host of other foreign policy issues, the Pentagon has muscled out not only the State Department as the legitimate, designated policy maker, but far more importantly and gravely, the American people. Civilian control of the U.S. military is becoming more myth than reality. The realities of power are the other way around. The military tail wags the civilian dog.

Treaty Aversion: Who's Really in Charge?

It's important to recognize that the advocates of the Iraq war were the civilians in the Pentagon, not the military professionals. The professionals saw the dangers and problems. They didn't want the war, but they couldn't speak out against the Commander in Chief. So their surrogates, outstanding retired generals like Anthony Zinni, Wesley Clark, Norman Schwartzkopf, and Brent Scowcroft to speak for them. It was Paul Wolfowitz, a key civilian architect of the Iraq war, who estimated that the U.S. could hold Iraq after the war with 40,000 troops, and it was General Shinseki, the military professional, who estimated that 200,000 would be necessary. Wolfowitz dismissed the general as far off the mark, but Shinseki was right. By most accounts, 130,000 troops have not been enough. Probably 200,000 would not have been either; the success of the Iraqi guerilla fighters does not depend on the U.S. army being below a certain size threshold. But there is no question that the Wolfowitz estimate of 40,000 would have been less than one-fifth of what was needed.

One thing is clear from the role relationships between the military professionals and the civilian politicos in the Pentagon and the White House: it was the tempting and corrupting power of the military tool in the hands of civilian leaders, not the tool itself, that contributed to the war—an arrogant blunder of colossal proportion. The ring of power does corrupt its wearer, even when he is a soft-spoken academic like Paul Wolfowitz.

But there are other areas where the Pentagon has demonstrated the power to override the preferences not only of the State Department, but also of the American public. Arms control treaties are typically popular with the majority of Americans for reasons of common sense and human decency. Preparations for war have never been known to prevent war and have often created the mistrust and fear that are contributing causes of war. Mutually reducing arms is a clear though bumpy and uncertain path to increasing trust and reducing international tension. Even unilateral moves to reduce arms, though risky, have sometimes have been successful. In other cases such as the treaty to ban landmines, the purpose of arms reduction is primarily humanitarian rather than a reduction of tensions and arms races between countries. In the case of landmines, the U.S. military establishment stood on one side of the issue, the public on the other. The military won. So much for democracy and civilian control. Here's the story in a nutshell.

Clinging to Landmines, A Prickly Precedent

"It burrows into the ground and sits, sometimes for years, waiting for an innocent child at play, a mother seeking the child, young men playing football, or farmers plowing new fields. Always it waits for someone who is unaware. Then, when the unsuspecting are at last in just the right spot, it explodes without warning, eviscerating the victim's bodies or tearing off arms and legs."[17] Every year this scene is repeated thousands of times. Landmines annually kill and injure about 26,000 people in seventy countries where an estimated 110 million landmines have been left behind after past conflicts.[18]

In World War II, minefields were marked and mapped so they could be avoided by friendly troops and could be cleared later. However, in the 1960s the U.S. used scatterable landmines indiscriminately dropped by the thousands from airplanes during the Vietnam War in an effort to control and channel the movement of enemy troops. It became impossible to document where the mines were landing in any kind of usable detail, and as a result U.S. troops sometimes ended up moving through their own minefields. "It is estimated that nearly one-third of all U.S. casualties during the war were caused by friendly landmines."[19]

During the 1980s, a number of humanitarian organizations worked independently to deal with problems caused by leftover antipersonnel landmines. They cleared mines in Afghanistan so farming would once again be possible, cared for landmine victims in refugee camps, and developed a prosthetics clinic for those who had lost limbs. In 1991-1992 a number of these organizations came together to create the International Campaign to Ban Landmines (ICBL). With Jody Williams, now a Nobel Peace Prize winner because of her efforts, as their leader and the internet as a powerful new tool, they created a coalition of over 1,300 non-government organizations (NGOs) to pressure governments all over the world to ban landmines. They even managed to get through to the U.S. Congress. The high watermark of U.S. Government support for these efforts came early with the passage of a law calling for a one-year moratorium on the export of landmines by the U.S. Impressed with the U.S. move and pushed by their own citizens, leaders of other countries jumped on the anti-landmine bandwagon.

President Clinton expressed support for the cause, announcing the plan to discontinue future use of "dumb" mines, (those that go off at any time, even far in the future) except in Korea. However, his announcement gave the U.S. leeway to continue to use "smart" mines that self-destruct after a set time interval. Use of smart mines would continue until an international agreement could be reached banning all antipersonnel mines.[20] These caveats were early hints of the desire of the Pentagon to retain the use of landmines in a new form.

Clinton's statements seemingly supporting the landmine ban along with enthusiasm from other countries (pressured by their humanitarian activists) combined to create a green light for the energetic and progressive Canadian Foreign Minister, Lloyd Axworthy. He established a process to break out of cumbersome UN negotiations and create a fast track, the Ottawa Conference of 1996, to bring together governments that favored a total landmine ban. But as Canada and other countries charged forward, the U.S. began to backtrack under the influence of the Pentagon. In October 1996, fifty participating governments, twenty-four observer states, and participants from the NGO community and the UN met in Ottawa to discuss strategy. Axworthy announced a planned meeting in December 1997, to complete a treaty banning antipersonnel landmines of all types. This was too fast and too far for the United States.

As the Ottawa process moved forward, the U.S. position—driven by Defense Department concerns—called for a return to the slower UN negotiation process and insisted on exceptions for the U.S. These exceptions were that the U.S. be free to continue to use antipersonnel mines in the Demilitarized Zone (DMZ) between the two Koreas, to continue using antipersonnel mines in conjunction with antitank mines, and to continue to use "smart" mines that would self-destruct after a predetermined time period. In short, the U.S. military called the shots of U.S. foreign relations and demanded a slower negotiation process and a number of exceptions, some of them sharply at odds with the consensus among countries supporting the treaty. Taking this position was a disaster for the U.S. from a public relations point of view. Vehement criticism erupted in the world's press and in Congress. Clinton backed off and agreed to stay with the Ottawa process, but continued to seek exceptions for the U.S. The rest of the world did not see any legitimacy in the U.S. demands for exceptions, and thus did not grant them.

Amid fanfare and global elation among people who care deeply about human well being, 122 nations signed the Mine Ban Treaty in Ottawa in September 1997. However, the U.S. stood out by its refusal to do so. Again the U.S. took a great deal of heat from the press worldwide for its backward-looking approach to the issue. The Clinton administration announced that the U.S. intended to develop alternative systems, with the aims of discontinuing landmine use outside Korea in 2003, and signing the Mine Ban Treaty by 2006. (This latter commitment is clearly wishful thinking; it was hardly likely that Clinton's projection of events in 2006 would be considered binding by whoever is the President of the U.S. at that time, especially if it turns out to be George W. Bush.) As of November 2003, six years after the original signatures in Ottawa, the 1997 Mine Ban Treaty has 141 States Parties and an additional 9 signatories (countries that have signed but not ratified).[21] The United States is not one of these countries, nor is there any hint that it will be in the future, at least as long as the U.S. Defense Department and a militaristic President call the shots.

The U.S. position on the landmine treaty has a familiar look. Once again, as with the treaties on the rights of women, the rights of children, the International Criminal Court, the Kyoto Protocols on Global Warming, the Antiballistic Missile Treaty, the Comprehensive Nuclear Test Ban Treaty, the Biological Weapons Convention, a protocol to strengthen the 1987 Convention Against Torture, and the Law of the Sea Treaty—to mention a few—we have the spectacle of the U.S. standing alone against a global consensus on a matter of high and widely recognized legal, moral and humanitarian importance. Meanwhile, other nations, Canada in this case, are taking the lead. Once again, the nation often proudly called the "leader of the free world" by unthinking American journalists long after the end of the Cold War, is not only failing to lead, but is refusing to cooperate in a positive venture. The U.S. Government again pulls apart from a constructive global trend, in effect declaring itself, for highly dubious reasons, to be an over-muscled maverick—the exact opposite of a team player or a constructive force in the world.

However, to give the U.S. Government its due, it is important to recognize and celebrate the positive side of the picture. The U.S. Government is spending millions of dollars on landmine removal projects all over the world. It accelerated this spending in the aftermath of the devastating backlash of criticism triggered by its refusal to sign on to the

Mine Ban Treaty. However, removing mines doesn't constrain the U.S. military from planting them or dropping them in droves from planes somewhere else in the future. At the same time, we can be both humanitarians and yet reserve the right and power to do devastating harm later. The two-faced god Janus is the only worthy symbol of this convenient dichotomy.

Additional good news, besides the demining efforts, is that while the U.S. reserves the right to manufacture and presumably to seed new landmines, it is not in fact doing so as of this writing. As with a number of other matters of principle, curiously, sometimes the practice of the U.S. Government is better than its stand against principle. This peculiar posture could almost be considered hypocrisy in reverse. Just say "no" to moral and humanitarian principle, but act benignly (some of the time) in practice. Unfortunately, the instances of "no" are shots heard round the world, and the contrasting actions are often neither visible nor consistent. There should be no doubt in anyone's mind that the U.S. military under its current leadership would scatter landmines by the millions if they thought there was some marginal gain to be achieved by doing so. These are the same people who are resurrecting the Frankenstein horror of tactical nuclear weapons and calling them "usable" nuclear weapons.

Yet more good news: it is a pleasure to report that late in his first term Bush has taken a small step in the right direction. In early 2004 he pledged to ban all landmines that are not timed to self-destruct. Though he will neither scrap landmines altogether nor sign the Treaty to ban landmines, he deserves commendation for this constructive action. In the long run this decision, though it maintains U.S. isolation from the rest of the international community on landmines, may yet save lives.[22]

Is the pro-landmine position of the Pentagon essential to national security? Challenging its need to keep these weapons was a statement by eight retired senior military officers including former commanders in Korea and a former superintendent of West Point. At the time of the debate over the treaty they jointly argued that antipersonnel landmines are obsolete weapons that harm U.S. forces more than they help them. More specifically, they stated that if combat were to occur in Korea, the landmines in the DMZ would be more likely to interfere with the movements of U.S. and South Korean troops than those of North Korea. They also pointed out that the landmines in Korea's DMZ would not be affected by U.S. signing the treaty if it were to do so because the mines are under the jurisdiction of South Korea, not the U.S.[23]

At first glance this latter point about South Korea having jurisdiction over the mines seems merely technical, but actually it is especially telling. In treaties, as in all matters of law, jurisdiction is critical to the meaning and applicability of the law. The military law experts who developed the U.S. position on landmines in the DMZ cannot have been ignorant of the basic point that the U.S. does not have jurisdiction over the mines. The centrality of a patently bogus argument in the U.S. position against signing the treaty strongly suggests that the military must have had different motives than the stated ones for opposing it.

The most likely unstated motive is fear of the precedent it might set for civilian political forces to succeed in banning a particular deadly and dubiously useful category of weapons: "Despite intense scrutiny, the U.S. defense establishment refused to allow the public to drive its policies. The military establishment sensed that it would be the beginning of endless interference. They stuck to this policy even though landmines were described by many retired military men as being of questionable usefulness."[24]

In short, the Pentagon was not clinging to a weapon it badly needed; it was clinging to a weapon it didn't need and would be better off without. It was doing so in order to prevent civilians from having a say in the matter. A dangerous precedent (from the Pentagon's point of view) of civilian control of the military was averted. As noted earlier, civilian control of the military in the U.S.—a key principle in the constitutional governance of the country and its preservation as a democracy—is not the reality, despite structural and constitutional safeguards.

Nuclear Proliferation: Soft on Nukes

One of the gravest problems the world faces for the foreseeable future is the proliferation of nuclear weapons. Not only are millions of lives and untold human suffering at risk, but in its most extreme form, the problem could be a life-or-death issue for human civilization. The horror of nuclear weapons—after the world saw the cruelty and devastation they wreaked on Hiroshima and Nagasaki—led to a widespread sense among the world's more civilized people that these weapons ought to be taboo, that their spread among nations and their further use would be catastrophic and was morally intolerable. Harry Truman, who had given the orders to use them in the struggle with Japan, refused to use them again when the U.S. military advocated doing so against China during the Korean War. Despite the terrible American losses of that war, Truman held steady in his determination not to resort to nuclear weapons. But the 45-year face-off between two nuclear superpowers, the U.S. and the USSR, prevented these doomsday weapons from being abolished from the human scene and promoted their further development.

As more nations now acquire the capability to build nuclear weapons, even crude ones, the danger of their actual use in wars that might otherwise be minor regional skirmishes rises exponentially. Pakistan and India, two long-standing enemies that are often at loggerheads and even shooting wars over disputed territory in Kashmir, have nuclear weapons and may eventually use them. Unstable and volatile North Korea has them and threatens the entire surrounding region. Israel has them, and this fact creates pressure on the surrounding Arab nations to try to acquire them. Despite the end of the Cold War, the U.S. and Russia have them on hair-trigger alert and accidents do happen. In the context of this spreading danger, one would think that rational American leaders would take a worldwide lead in efforts to eliminate the threat of all nuclear weapons and would use American weapons only as incentives to others in reducing all such weapons, including its own, to eventual nonexistence.

The Nuclear Nonproliferation Treaty (NPT) was just such an effort. In 1970, a time when leaders were apparently more lucid than they are now about the dangers, the treaty committed states parties that possessed nuclear weapons to negotiate their elimination. The nuclear powers that agreed to the treaty and thus to negotiating the elimination of their arsenals were Britain, China, France, Russia, and the United States. (Three of the four countries that stayed outside the treaty still have nuclear weapons: India, Israel, and Pakistan. Cuba is the fourth country outside the treaty.)

Non-nuclear countries, to be induced to sign the treaty and thus to forego development of nuclear weapons, insisted that the nuclear powers agree to end the nuclear arms race, agree that they would not use nuclear weapons against non-nuclear states, and negotiate the elimination of such weapons at an early date. With the exception of North Korea, the non-nuclear states that are parties to the treaty have kept their end of the bargain. The nuclear states, including the U.S., have not.

The extent to which the U.S. Government is in violation of its commitments under the treaty is stark. The Bush administration's Nuclear Posture Review (NPR) asserts the U.S. "right to continue over the long haul not only to possess but to further develop an already extensive nuclear weapons capability" despite its commitments for disarmament under the NPT.[25] An additional clear violation of the treaty, again a stated policy in the

Bush administration's NPR, is the decision to make a list of countries that may be targeted with nuclear weapons.[26] This decision is not a minor technicality, but a shocking and major abandonment of principles long held in the international community as well as explicitly stated in the Nuclear Nonproliferation Treaty.

Tough negotiations for an indefinite extension of the Nuclear Nonproliferation Treaty were held in 1995. Concerned that the treaty locked them into a disadvantageous position, the nations that had exercised restraint and had not developed nuclear weapons struggled to drive a hard bargain with those that already had them. The negotiations were contentious. Advocates of an indefinite extension of the treaty (replacing periodic renegotiations or extensions) were forced to make a major concession: a commitment to complete negotiations on the Comprehensive Test Ban Treaty (CTBT) by 1996. The following two paragraphs from the excellent study of broken security treaty obligations, *Rule of Power or Rule of Law?*, tell the story of what happened next:

In 1996 the International Court of Justice unanimously held that Article VI obligates states to "bring to a conclusion negotiations leading to nuclear disarmament in all its aspects." In the 2000 NPT Review Conference, all states agreed upon a menu of 13 disarmament steps, including an "unequivocal undertaking" to "accomplish the total elimination" of nuclear arsenals pursuant to Article VI, ratification of the CTBT, U.S.-Russian reductions of strategic arms, application of the principle of irreversibility to disarmament measures, further reduction of the operational status of nuclear weapons, and a diminishing role for nuclear weapons in security policies.[27]

Rule of Power or Rule of Law? goes on to document the American follow-up to these admirable commitments in the Nuclear Nonproliferation Treaty:

The U.S. Senate rejected the CTBT in 1999. As set forth in the U.S. 2002 Nuclear Posture Review (NPR) reduction of deployed strategic arms will be *reversible*, not irreversible, because they will be accompanied by the maintenance of a large "responsive force" of warheads capable of being redeployed in days, weeks, or months. The May, 2002 U.S.-Russian agreement limiting "strategic nuclear warheads" on each side to no more than 2200 by the year 2012 does not provide for destruction or dismantlement of reduced delivery systems and warheads. It is therefore consistent with the U.S. plan for a "responsive force" and contrary to the NPT principle of irreversible disarmament. There are no announced plans to employ dealerting measures to reduce the operational status of the large deployed strategic forces that will remain after reductions. The NPR expands options for use of nuclear weapons against non-nuclear weapon states including preemptive attacks against biological or chemical weapon capabilities and in response to "surprising military developments," and to this end provides for development of warheads including earth penetrators. This widening use of options is contrary to the pledge of a diminishing role for nuclear weapons in security policies, the declaration of non-use of nuclear weapons against non-nuclear weapons states parties, and the obligation to negotiate cessation of the arms race at an early date. The [Bush administration's] NPR also contains plans for the maintenance and modernization of nuclear warheads and missiles and bombers for the next half-century. Above all, the lack of compliance with Article VI lies in the manifest failure to make disarmament the driving force in national planning and policy with respect to nuclear weapons.[28]

In other words, the non-nuclear states were misled when they agreed in 1996 to continue to refrain from developing nuclear weapons on condition that the nuclear powers move to join them and create a non-nuclear world. No such movement took place, and President Bush has moved aggressively in the opposite direction. There was in 1996 at least the possibility of a future world without the shadow of annihilation or extreme catastrophe by nuclear weapons. But hawkish Senators and later a hawkish President made it clear that the U.S. was not as good as its word and was instead going to take a stand for brute force rather than cooperation and diplomacy. The U.S. Government ignored its treaty commitments and solidified itself as the preeminent nuclear power of the world, sustaining its capacity to annihilate any nation that stepped out of line. As a result, the world is a much more dangerous place.

Naturally this strategic decision by the U.S. creates a precedent that makes it more likely that other countries will develop or try to develop nuclear weapons and will eventually use them. As of this writing, North Korea is the most vivid example of this impulse. It has nuclear weapons and is busily and openly making more. Ironically, North Korea's nuclear deterrent is a part of what is protecting its despotic regime against the kind of attack the U.S. launched against Iraq. We attacked Iraq on the dubious supposition that they might be developing nuclear weapons (they weren't) and we don't attack North Korea even though they admit they do have nuclear weapons and are building more. The lesson to other small nations is clear. On the other hand, Libya, worn down economically by sanctions and perhaps frightened by the U.S. action in Iraq, has decided to give up on nuclear weapons. Which way other countries, notably Iran, will go is undetermined, but the North Korean approach may be tempting.

There is no question that in the long run, the U.S. maintaining and enhancing its nuclear arsenal promotes the proliferation of these doomsday weapons, and this makes the world a more dangerous place for Americans and everyone else. Nevertheless, in the short run they seem to give the U.S. an edge in the risky and reprehensible power game of threats and coercion. The economic and conventional military power of the U.S. is so great it needs no such edge. The policy should be determined movement toward elimination of nuclear weapons from the face of the planet, in keeping with our commitments under the Nuclear Nonproliferation Treaty.

Ballistic Missiles, Carriers of Doom

During the Cold War an uneasy balance of lethal power was an ugly fact of life between the United States and the Soviet Union. The balance was the key. Called Mutually Assured Destruction (MAD), it was considered an essential ingredient in preventing war between the two superpowers. With MAD, war was recognized as a lose-lose game. What one side started, the other side would finish, and both would be utterly destroyed. However, by the 1970s the remote possibility existed that one of the Cold War antagonists could surprise the other with a massive strike using ballistic missiles with multiple, independently targeted warheads and wipe out most of the other power's nuclear armaments. The catch was that in all probability the other side could still launch a devastating retaliatory strike with just a few surviving nuclear-tipped missiles. If one side or the other could develop effective anti-ballistic missiles, such a diminished retaliatory strike could be neutralized and a nuclear war "won" by one side or the other.

To prevent this theoretical possibility and promote strategic stability, the United States and the Soviet Union negotiated the Anti-Ballistic Missile (ABM) Treaty and agreed to it in 1972. The treaty limited future development of defensive missiles that could shoot down incoming ballistic missiles. The purpose was to maintain a balance between the U.S. and the USSR and thereby prevent surprise attacks. This treaty was one of the keys to strategic stability between the two superpowers over the next twenty years. However, during the 1990s, American conservatives and some voices in the Pentagon became restive under the restraints of the treaty and wanted to negotiate changes. Given the growing scientific and technological lead of the U.S. over Russia, these proposed changes were not welcomed in Moscow. Any move to unshackle the nuclear Prometheus was understandably seen by Russia as a threat.

The power ratio had shifted decisively to the U.S. and the Cold War was believed to be over. So on the surface, at least, much less was at stake than during the Cold War. Still, each country had nuclear weapons targeting the other on hair-trigger alert. There was a possibility of a change toward nationalistic leadership in Russia leading to a renewal of the Cold War, or even mutual annihilation by an accidental launch.

In 2001, the new President, George W. Bush, displayed impatience with treaty restraints on U.S. actions generally and evidently saw no need for this particular treaty at all. After all, the U.S. was the only remaining superpower, so it could do as it pleased. The Cold War was over, and a diminished Russia would have to swallow hard and accept anything we dished out. After trying unsuccessfully to negotiate changes to the Anti-Ballistic Missile treaty with Russia's new president, Vladimir Putin, Bush announced a unilateral U.S. withdrawal from the treaty. This slap in the face to Putin was hardly calculated to build trust, but evidently Bush did not care. Putin had little choice but to accept it. Historically, this was a watershed event: "The first formal unilateral withdrawal of a major power from a nuclear arms control treaty after it has been put into effect. The U.S. action is especially troubling in the context of its decision to make a list of countries that may be targeted with nuclear weapons in its Nuclear Posture Review."[29] The stance was clear and the intent was imbalance—we can threaten them (whoever "they" might be) but they will be less able to threaten us.

In tandem with his final unilateral withdrawal from the ABM Treaty, Bush took a related coercive step in dealing with the U.S. Congress to force the funding of his Star Wars initiative: "The administration warned it would veto the 2003 defense spending bill unless Congress restores the $814 million cut from the missile defense program by the Senate Armed Services Committee. Defense Secretary Donald H. Rumsfeld wrote to the committee warning that he would recommend that Bush veto the $393 billion spending bill if the full Senate, which takes up the measure soon, does not restore the funding. Bush seeks $8.7 billion next year for missile defenses. The Democratic-controlled committee objected to plans by the administration to increase the secrecy of the testing program."[30]

The Congressional objections to secrecy were motivated by an understandable concern. The testing program had already showed that this multi-billion dollar system did not work well, if at all. The billions to be spent might very well be wasted. The program looked to opponents like a huge boondoggle for the benefit of military contractors, with dubious benefits to national security. If embarrassing test failures such as those that had visibly happened could be concealed by increased secrecy, an unrealistically positive picture of the system could be sold to the public and the Congress as a basis for further expenditures.

One of the rationales for the abandonment of the ABM Treaty was to permit the U.S. to put pressure on nations that developed weapons of mass destruction contrary to their nonproliferation treaty commitments. But the effect was the opposite; it provided an example and an incentive for them to follow our lead and pull out of these same treaty commitments. Not surprisingly, the double standard—we don't have to stay within treaty commitments but you do—failed to work. North Korea followed the U.S. example by withdrawing from the Nuclear Nonproliferation Treaty and openly working to develop a more capable nuclear arsenal.

North Korea has also been developing multi-stage ballistic missiles, while the anti-missile technology of the U.S. is in a crude stage that is far from effective or reliable and far from being ready for deployment. As noted above, tests have not been reassuring in showing reliability in hitting incoming missile warheads. Consider the monstrous technical challenge of reliably hitting a target following a curved trajectory at close to 18,000 miles per hour with another object traveling another curved trajectory at a similar speed (often compared to hitting a bullet with another bullet). Anti-missile technology may never be effective. Furthermore, a ballistic missile can be rigged to release decoys that confuse an oncoming defensive missile's targeting system, and thus neutralize even a high degree of accuracy.

To summarize, partly as a result of the Bush administration's abandonment of the Anti-ballistic Missile Treaty, North Korea is a greater threat, the U.S. and North Korea's neighbors are presently defenseless

202

against its increased nuclear arsenal, the Nuclear Nonproliferation Treaty has been seriously weakened worldwide, and the long-standing strategic stability provided by the ABM Treaty has been destroyed in favor of a precarious American dominance. Further, in explicit reaction to the U.S. withdrawal from the ABM Treaty, Russia announced its withdrawal from its commitments under the START 2 arms reduction treaty. This treaty had not yet gone into effect, but Russia had shown signs of support for it before the unilateral U.S. withdrawal from the ABM Treaty.

There is an important but somewhat ambiguous silver lining around this cloud. President Bush proposed and Russia's President Putin reluctantly agreed on May 13, 2002 to a brief arms reduction treaty that goes well beyond START 2, calling for U.S. and Russian nuclear arsenals to be cut down from the present range of 5,000 to 6,000 warheads to a new range of 1,700 to 2,200. This change is scheduled to take place gradually over ten years and to be completed by 2012. This treaty leaves in place enough warheads to annihilate both countries, but it is considered symbolically significant and is well below the cuts in the START 2 treaty, which would have reduced arsenals to a range of 3,000 to 3,500 warheads. However, the risk of an accidental trigger for a nuclear exchange appears to be undiminished. If the two countries finish implementing the new treaty in 2012, and if there is then a nuclear exchange, the rubble won't bounce quite so often. Of course, radioactivity and economic devastation would kill the few people who survived the explosions. This is the nature of "progress" when we continue to play the nuclear terror game rather than gradually and systematically getting rid of all nuclear weapons as we agreed to do.

In negotiating this treaty, the ideal Russia strove for was to destroy warheads that were taken out of service in keeping with the intent of the Nuclear Nonproliferation Treaty. However, at President Bush's insistence, the new treaty does not call for the destruction of warheads. Moreover, it does not prevent the U.S. building a missile defense system, and after the ten-year reduction period it allows either side to return to any level it wishes. During the ten-year period either side may pull out of the treaty within 90 days. In other words, the treaty is as fragile as a drop of water poised to roll off a lotus leaf. It depends entirely on the good will, honesty, and strategic steadiness of purpose of both parties. Strategic steadiness of purpose relative to the commitments of previous administrations has been notably lacking in the U.S. since the Bush administration took power. Let's hope that future administrations are not so cavalier about abandoning prior American treaty commitments. And let's hope that the Russians behavior is far better than Bush has been on this important matter.

Russian leaders still object to the U.S. plans to store hundreds of warheads rather than dismantle them, but they could not dissuade Bush from retaining the option of storing warheads. The treaty also does not prevent the U.S. from developing a new type of nuclear weapon, the low-yield bunker buster, and maintaining and refurbishing its existing nuclear arsenal. These actions, as noted above, are direct violations of the Nuclear Nonproliferation Treaty and keep the Frankenstein monster of potential nuclear holocaust looming over humanity.

In short, the new treaty changes little except as an important indicator of a new spirit of trust and cooperation (one wonders how lasting or fleeting) between the two powers. On the weaknesses of the new treaty, Sam Nunn, former Senate Armed Services Committee Chairman, commented, "There are no mileposts for performance. There is nothing really to verify except good faith. If things start going sour between the two countries and we get into a period of intensive distrust, this document will be looked back on as having no legal enforcement mechanism, no performance mechanism and not much of an accomplishment at all."[31]

In negotiating the new treaty, "Putin wanted an agreement that covered 'verification and control.' He had just finished another meeting with Bush where he got nowhere in trying to preserve the Anti-Ballistic Missile Treaty's limits on defense tests, a cornerstone of superpower nuclear policy for 30 years."[32] The Russians began the negotiations on the new treaty with an ambitious agenda. "The Russians wanted both sides to eliminate missiles, long-range bombers and submarines. They reasoned that if launchers were taken out of service, then the warheads would follow.... But the Bush administration wanted to focus on deployed warheads. That meant counting each atomic warhead on a submarine, in a missile silo or on a bomber base."[33]

At the end of the negotiations, Joseph Cirincione, an expert on nuclear proliferation at the Carnegie Endowment for International Peace, commented, "This treaty represents an opportunity lost. The Russians were putting their nuclear weapons on a platter for us, and we couldn't take yes for an answer."[34] Another comment came from Daryl G. Kimball, Executive Director of the Arms Control Association, who said, "The administration erred by not renouncing the redeployment of warheads from service." "These reductions are important and a useful first step," he said, "but they fall far short of what the U.S. and Russia could have achieved by making these cuts more permanent and more verifiable. The United States has resisted doing so in the interest of maintaining maximum flexibility well into the future."[35] So we have our nuclear superiority and flexibility, and as a result the danger of a global nuclear catastrophe continues largely unabated.

Double Standards and Bad Faith:
Inspecting Weapons of Mass Destruction

Due to a small but strategically placed group of ultra-conservative politicians hijacking the treaty ratification process, the history of negotiations on the Chemical Weapons Convention (CWC) and the Biological and Toxins Weapons Convention (BWC) provide some especially bizarre cases of the U.S. Government's self-contradiction in the pursuit of national security through arms control treaties. In the past, to its credit, the U.S. has been staunchly opposed to chemical and biological weapons and has even acted unilaterally to discontinue developing and stockpiling these kinds of weapons. Until the year 2001, efforts to control these truly terrible weapons have been a serious concern of Democratic and Republican administrations alike. "Attempts to control these weapons date to the Geneva Protocol of 1925, adopted as a reaction to large-scale use of poison gas in World War I."[36] During the Cold War, efforts to negotiate restrictions on these weapons progressed slowly, and eventually, in 1969, President Richard Nixon unilaterally renounced biological warfare and declared a no-first-strike policy for chemical weapons. (We might term this courageous action "benign unilateralism" in contrast to the present approach of going it alone in a way that makes the world more dangerous.) Additional moves in this same direction included a 1985 Congressional mandate to destroy U.S. stockpiles of certain types of chemical weapons.

In the aftermath of the Persian Gulf War in May 1991, President Bush Senior declared that the United States would forswear using chemical weapons for any reason, including retaliation, once the UN talks had concluded a Chemical Weapons Convention (CWC). These negotiations did conclude in January 1993 with a very straightforward and tough treaty that called for destruction of chemical weapon stockpiles, a ban on further manufacture, and creation of an inspection and verification body.[37]

The CWC's inspection regime was particularly strong. Not only were states parties required to declare any chemical weapons facilities and stockpiles and allow routine inspections and challenge inspections, but they were required to allow routine and challenge inspections of dual-use chemicals and production facilities that might be used in ways counter to the treaty.[38]

In characteristic fashion, the Senate delayed ratification for four years, from the time of the U.S. signing of the CWC in 1993 until April 1997. The causes of the delay and the follow-on events form a disturbing story. Seldom has there been a more dramatic example of U.S. foreign policy being hijacked by a small number of extremists in the U.S. Senate, despite overwhelming support from all other directions. The extreme right-wing Senators moved successfully to destroy the effectiveness of the treaty and undermine or reverse the commitments the U.S. had already made to the other states parties during years of arduous negotiations. Two paragraphs from the executive summary of the book, *Rule of Power or Rule of Law?*, tell the story.

The United States played a significant role in negotiating the CWC, advocating a treaty broad in scope and with a thorough verification and inspection regime. The CWC was supported by three presidential administrations, Democratic and Republican. The treaty enjoyed public support, and endorsement from the intelligence community, the Department of Defense and the chemical industry. Despite the widespread support, several influential Senators, including Jesse Helms, then Chair of the Senate Foreign Relations Committee, threatened to prevent ratification of the CWC unless U.S. commercial and national security interests were better safeguarded. After lengthy negotiations the treaty was ratified, but Congress imposed limitations on how the United States implements its terms.

Several of the restrictions imposed by Congress amount to a refusal to comply with the terms of the treaty relating to inspections. Under CWC Article VI, states parties are required to subject specified toxic chemicals and facilities to verification measures (inspections and declarations) as provided by the Verification Annex. Pursuant to the implementing legislation, however, the President has the right to refuse inspection of any U.S. facility upon determining that the inspection may "pose a threat to the national security interests." Another restriction narrows the number of facilities that are subject to inspection and declaration provisions. Also the United States refuses to allow samples to be "transferred for analysis to any laboratory outside the territory of the United States" though the Verification Annex permits, if necessary, "transfer [of] samples for analysis off-site at laboratories."[39]

In addition to "sharply limit[ing] the number of U.S. facilities subject to declaration and routine inspection...the United States also refused to pay its share of the cost of the convention and neglected to provide adequate financing to help destroy Russia's vast stockpiles."[40]

In other words, we agree to the treaty, but we opt out of key elements of its implementation and we won't help others implement it. It is difficult to imagine a more self-defeating policy. Not only was this blatant hypocrisy and bad faith negotiating, but it also inhibited implementation by other countries (notably Russia) and invited them to create similar dodges to the most important verification provisions of the treaty. The U.S. has every reason to want other countries to accept the verification procedures, but we created an example of the will and the means to opt out. Following our lead, India has prohibited samples being taken out of the country, and Russia has moved in the same direction.[41] The treaty was seriously weakened.

To be fair, a small group of Senators is not the only villain in the saga of gutted opportunities to limit biological and chemical weapons. The Executive Branch carried out another instance of U.S. self-reversal or self-contradiction on the subject during the years 2000-2002. The same ideology of American preeminence regardless of security concerns was behind it, as were some of the same people.

Over thirty years ago, in 1972 the UN sponsored the Biological and Toxins Weapons Convention (BWC). It committed states parties "'never in any circumstances to develop, produce, stockpile or otherwise acquire or retain' biological agents or toxins for military purposes."[42] The U.S. ratified this treaty in 1975 and it has been in effect ever since. However, it lacks mechanisms for inspection and enforcement. Two specific concerns triggered efforts to develop a verification regime. In the 1990s Russia's president, Boris Yeltsin, revealed that the now-defunct Soviet Union had carried out an illegal anthrax program. And after the Gulf War, concerns were strong about possible biological weapons in Iraq, given Saddam's record of using weapons of mass destruction in its war with Iran and on his own people. A UN committee was established to develop a new legally binding verification regime for the treaty. The U.S. supported the effort and at first called the plan "a major step forward."[43]

In January 2001, a new President stepped into the White House who was almost as averse to multilateral treaties as Jesse Helms, and a new era in U.S. foreign policy began. Meanwhile, the U.S. conducted simulations of the new protocol's proposed verification system on its own chemical and biological installations. The results of the simulations were not promising in terms of providing the needed verification. From my perspective as a person lacking detailed evidence and lacking specific expertise on these kinds of facilities, the test methods used, etc., it is impossible to judge whether these results were valid and whether they were treated fairly by a political establishment hostile to these kinds of treaties. But whatever the real reasons, technical or political or both, in July 2001 the U.S. told the committee that it was discontinuing negotiations based on concerns about national security and about putting confidential business information at risk. In an administration noted for favoring the business community, the concerns about exposure of confidential business information may have been the greater concern, but again, without an in-depth, independent study it is impossible to make a definitive judgment. One thing is clear; the international community was surprised and dismayed by the abrupt U.S. turn-around and appeared to question the good faith behind the new position.

Subsequent events suggest that the real reasons for the Bush administration's decision to cut off support for the new protocol were based on political ideology rather than any technical inadequacy of the verification methods. Undersecretary of State Bolton, an extraordinarily radical Jesse Helms protégé, is perhaps the most hawkish and hostile of all Bush appointees toward arms control treaties. During nomination hearings Helms once praised Bolton as the man he would most like to have with him in the battle of Armageddon. As a result, Bolton acquired the nickname the "Armageddon candidate" by his many detractors, meaning that based on his hawkish record, he was the nominee most likely to bring the final battle about. Placed in control of U.S. arms control negotiations, he has boldly moved to scuttle or weaken every arms control treaty he has been able to influence.

Bolton represented the U.S. at a Biological Weapons Convention committee meeting in November 2001 and made several suggestions for strengthening the BWC that he claimed had never been considered. In fact, however, all but one of them were contained in the Protocol the United States had just rejected. None of that deterred Bolton, who proposed on the last day of the conference that the committee simply be disbanded. A few months later, the United States insisted on having the head of the Chemical Weapons Convention inspection unit fired on grounds, we said, of financial mismanagement. But no one believed that. As Lord Rea of Britain pointed out, much of the financial difficulty was the result of U.S. refusal to pay its dues. The real reason, many believed, was that the inspections director was planning unannounced inspections in the United States.[44]

Several pieces of the puzzle fit together. Bolton's patently bogus argument that the U.S. was concerned about strengthening the protocol when it fact it had already been strengthened in the ways he proposed, the U.S. refusal to pay its dues and scapegoating of the head of the inspection unit for alleged fiscal mismanagement, and the surprise motion at the end of the committee meeting to disband the committee all suggest strongly an administration determined to scuttle the protocol, not to strengthen it in order to make it workable and effective. The international community was justly appalled at the behavior of Undersecretary Bolton and by implication, the Bush administration and the U.S. Government. It was clear that in the immensely important area of controlling biological weapons, the U.S. would rather have a toothless, essentially meaningless treaty than one that could bring about inspections of the U.S. itself. Either the U.S. Government has something to hide, or national pride is out of control. Stated in terms of principles, we placed a misguided concept of national sovereignty above both national and global security. As a result, the world is a more dangerous place for the U.S. and everyone else. Thanks to Bolton's efforts, any country can secretly develop biological weapons with no fear of being exposed by inspections or sanctioned in response.

Dirty Bombs, the Terrorist's Dream Weapon

Nuclear weapons that create nuclear fission or fusion explosions (A-bombs and H-bombs) are expensive, require advanced technology including highly refined uranium or plutonium, and are relatively difficult to conceal when under development. It is therefore highly unlikely that non-state terrorists such as al Qaeda will be able to create them for some decades, if ever. It is also highly unlikely that any dictator, by definition a megalomaniac, will go to the huge expense and take the substantial risks of developing such weapons and then give them to terrorists. Dictators are the ultimate "control freaks"; the last thing any such person would do would be to give away control of the crown jewels of his coercive power to an unpredictable non-state actor. To think otherwise is, frankly, to dream up paranoid fantasies or to try to induce them in others, as the Bush administration did with the American public in promoting the war in Iraq.

After 1991 Saddam had no nuclear weapons (they were destroyed in conjunction with the UN inspections at the time) and due to the UN sanctions, he lacked the resources to develop them. If he'd had them he certainly would not have given control of them to a hostile power like al Qaeda. (Osama bin Laden is a religious fanatic; Saddam ran a secular socialist dictatorship and revered Joseph Stalin more than Muhammad. They were ideologically poles apart, and there was never any credible evidence of a connection between them.) Yet the Bush administration tried to convince the American public that Saddam was developing nuclear weapons and might very well give them to bin Laden or other terrorists. The world has enough real dangers; we don't need to create them out of whole cloth with our imaginations. Nor do we benefit from succumbing to the machinations of politicians who promote such irrational fears.

However, there is a real possibility, even a high likelihood, that terrorists will be able to create or buy "dirty bombs" that use a conventional chemical explosion to scatter radioactive materials far and wide, creating immense problems including numerous casualties and rendering parts of cities uninhabitable or their water supplies undrinkable.

How real is this threat? Would dirty (nuclear) bombs be hard for terrorists to obtain? Would they kill large numbers of people? A recent Pentagon-funded study by the Center for Technology and National Security Policy of the National Defense University provides disturbing answers to these kinds of questions. The study looked at radiological accidents that have already happened for information on what could happen as a result of a deliberate large-scale release of radiation. The study said, "A well-executed 'dirty bomb' attack on a U.S. city could expose hundreds of people to potentially lethal radiation."[45] According to the study, there could be "massive financial losses—perhaps greater than those caused by the Sept. 11,

2001 attacks—if a large dirty bomb were set off in the heart of New York City or Washington."[46] The study goes on to say, "The threat of radiological attack on the United States is real, and terrorists have a broad palette of [radiological] isotopes to choose from."[47] The problem is not only fatalities, sickness and economic damage, but also the long-lasting contamination radiation leaves behind. Cleanup could take years, and could require completely dismantling and disposing of large buildings and other structures if they were contaminated.

The terrorists who executed such an attack might never be found, but if they were, a few people in jail would be small compensation for the immense damage to the U.S. such an attack would cause. September 11 taught us that there is a far higher probability of such an attack than, say, a ballistic missile attack from North Korea. The latter would result in instant retaliatory annihilation of the country and its leader, not a consequence Kim Jong Il and his military establishment are likely to find acceptable. However, suicide is an acceptable, even desirable consequence of action for a fanatical terrorist, and it might not even be required to assure success.

Another disturbing truth is that dirty bomb warheads for surface-to-surface rockets are quite likely for sale on the international black market and have already disappeared from formal controls. How did this horror come about? In Moldova, a former Soviet republic freed by collapse of the Soviet Union, things have gotten out of control. A huge weapons cache there is being sold off bit by bit on the international weapons black market. One of the weapons formerly in that cache is of special interest. Excerpts from a report on the subject follow:

In the ethnic conflicts that surrounded the collapse of the Soviet Union, fighters in several countries seized upon an unlikely new weapon: a small, thin rocket known as the Alazan.... The Alazan rockets were packed with explosives and lobbed into cities. Military records show that at least 38 Alazan warheads were modified to carry radioactive material, effectively creating the world's first surface-to-surface dirty bomb.

The radioactive warheads are not known to have been used. But now, according to experts and officials, they have disappeared.... They are for sale, according to U.S. and Moldovan officials and weapons experts.[48]

In other words, terrorists may not even have to improvise a rocket with a dirty bomb as a warhead, they may be able to buy it "off the shelf." They also do not need a rocket as a delivery system; many other approaches might be effective. A suitcase or car bomb full of radioactive material could create a devastating mess, wreaking havoc on several square blocks of a major city and its inhabitants. Anti-missile technology is entirely irrelevant to such a danger, which is much more likely than an incoming ballistic missile.

While American leaders obsessed about Saddam Hussein, beat the war drums for his ouster, and finally launched an expensive and destructive war against him although he was not much of a threat, we overlooked or failed to deal with a real threat—illegal arms sales in Moldova and elsewhere.

In fairness, it should be not only mentioned but emphasized that behind the scenes the U.S. intelligence community and military have been strenuously, even heroically struggling to track down and contain the threat of loose nuclear weapons getting onto the black market. Most of this effort, as far as can be ascertained from the public record, has been focused on gaining control of poorly secured nuclear fission bombs. It is not clear whether these efforts also encompass, with appropriate emphasis, dirty bombs that can be detonated by conventional means. But there also may have been clandestine, unreported and unsuccessful efforts to deal with such problems as the Moldovan arms sales. It may be that in the short run these potential stories for future nonfiction spy thrillers must be kept secret even after they are accomplished and thus cannot be used to make domestic political hay and boost the President's poll numbers in the present tense. Apparently though, they have not been allocated the billions of dollars that have been spent in toppling Saddam and in developing anti-missile defense systems. One wonders about the priorities.

Fear, Domination, or Pork?

After 9/11, fear drove the actions of the public and the politicians. Rationality went out the window, if it ever had been present. An example of the irrationality that prevailed at the time is the pathetic and somewhat comical post-9/11 surge in individual purchases of guns. Whatever one may think of the merits of large numbers of citizens owning guns, the logical connection between this behavior and terrorism is a wild stretch. In a conversation, an acquaintance of mine pointed out to me that the new post-9/11 concerns are a justification for people rushing out to buy guns. This, he thought, was in turn a justification for opposing any controls on gun purchasing and ownership. My response was, if a terrorist were to fly a plane toward your house, would you be safer if you got out your gun and blazed away at it? Would the people in the World Trade Center have been safer if they'd been carrying guns? Could they have seen those huge commercial jet liners coming before they hit the buildings and deflected them by shooting at them? In short, what does 9/11 have to do with personal ownership of guns? The only connection is that fear produces irrational behavior. People felt threatened and angry so they rushed out and bought guns. After doing so they may or may not have felt safer, but they certainly weren't better protected from airplane hijackers and terrorism or from the economic consequences of the 9/11 catastrophe.

Similarly irrational was the explosion in defense spending after 9/11 that was unrelated to fighting terrorism. A major boost in spending on intelligence work (intelligently spent) would certainly have been warranted. However, unrelated military pork barrel suddenly had a field day. Somehow a multibillion dollar system for anti-missile defenses against intercontinental ballistic missiles received a political boost—as if such a system would protect us from suicidal fanatics with box cutters. The military budget, already bloated beyond all reason (see "Dazed and Confused" and "How Much Is Too Much" above), began swelling like a balloon, and no political leader had the courage to challenge it.

The war on terrorism (or rather, if it were properly focused, the war on al Qaeda,) was a belated and necessary response to September 11 and other al Qaeda terrorist attacks. Though calling it a war is a stretch and a metaphor, a major (and thoroughly multinational) campaign against al Qaeda should have been launched after the bombings of the U.S. embassies in Africa, if not before. Attacked once again, we paid insufficient heed to the warning of the bombing of the battleship Cole in the Yemeni harbor at Aden. In response to these red-flag calls to action, the Clinton administration was asleep at the switch. Pinprick bombings of doubtful targets in Sudan were an inadequate response. They didn't scratch the surface of what needed to be done. Maybe the embassy bombings didn't waken the American sleeping giant because few Americans were killed, and the deaths were in a place far from the "homeland." Mostly local people were killed. The bombing of the Cole hit mainly Americans, but again the ship was remote from the "homeland" and the target was military. There were critical op-ed pieces, of course, but there was no public outcry at the minimalist response mounted by the Clinton administration.

The war on terrorism is primarily a clandestine intelligence struggle, not a military exercise of massive and highly visible force to be fought with fighter planes, aircraft carriers, nuclear weapons and anti-missile weapons. An absolute prerequisite for success is a high level of cooperation between American intelligence services and those of other countries. In this context, anything that significantly alienates friendly and more-or-less neutral nations is a blow to the success of the enterprise. The Iraq war was just such a blow, deeply alienating longstanding allies in Europe and even more deeply alienating Muslim countries. It worked against the war on terror coming and going. It motivated terrorists by making them feel that Muslims were the target; it damaged trust and cooperation with allies; and it drained away critical and scarce resources such as the limited numbers of Arabic-speakers who could be used in the real war on terrorism by eavesdropping on terrorists and questioning captives. Far from being a part of the war on terror, it was a distraction that weakened it.

This judgment—that the Iraq war was a sideshow, not a genuine part of the war on terrorism—is not merely a political opinion; it is also a carefully analyzed strategic military judgment backed up by an impressive study of military strategy published by the Strategic Studies Institute of the Army War College.[49] The study summarizes the war against Iraq, from a military point of view, as "a detour from, not an integral component of, the war on terrorism; in fact, Operation Iraqi Freedom and its continuing aftermath may have expanded the terrorist threat by establishing a large new American target set in an Arab heartland. The unexpectedly large costs incurred by Operation Iraqi Freedom and its continuing aftermath probably will not affect the funding of the relatively cheap counterterrorist campaign against al Qaeda. But those costs most assuredly impede funding of woefully underfunded homeland security requirements."[50] In other words, we are no more secure, and quite probably less so, as a result of the war in Iraq.

The war was and continues to be an extraordinary and unprecedented event that has changed the whole equation of the U.S. defense posture. Before Iraq, we had too many uniformed troops, now suddenly we have too few. We had too much of many kinds of equipment, now we have too little. After the Cold War and before Iraq the continued mammoth disproportion between U.S. military spending and that of any other country suggested paranoia, the behavior of a guy who is not threatened by his neighbors but still keeps bombs and guns by the thousands in his basement. After the war, it looks more like an expression of a latent desire (now more fully expressed) to bully the rest of the world. Most Americans don't condone bullying, but

214

there is abundant evidence that the U.S. Government, especially under the second Bush administration, practices it with a vengeance. However, neither reason—paranoia or intent to dominate—is a fully satisfying explanation for our bizarrely huge military expenditures. There is an additional explanation.

Pigs at the Trough, or Pentagon Pork

A revealing but disturbing explanation for stratospheric U.S. military spending is to view the military budget as at least partly high-tech pork barrel. This is hardly a new insight, but it has often been ignored or suppressed in the name of flag-waving chauvinism or fear-mongering bluster. Seen from a moral perspective, if not a legal one, use of the military budget for multi-billion dollar pork barrel, by far the largest dollar category of this practice, is corruption. Key politicians use the military budget to pick the pockets of all Americans to fill the pockets of their constituents, who then respond by voting to keep them in power. The hapless victims are the taxpayers in other districts or states who are told that this is essential for national defense and this noble enterprise is vital for their safety.

Defense contractors in Congressperson X's district or Senator Y's state mean jobs—often high tech jobs—in that district or state. It is no accident that major military forts and defense contractors are concentrated in the districts and states of Representatives and Senators on the relevant appropriations committees. They make sure their districts get the goodies, even if laws and regulations have to be stretched beyond their elastic limits, and the rest of the taxpayers foot the bill. Is this view too cynical? Or is it boringly obvious? It should be seen as neither, but rather as a reality and a source of concern, if not outrage. A news report published in October 2003, one of many similar stories down through the years, illustrates the answer. The headline is "Rules Circumvented on Huge Boeing Defense Contract."

The Boeing Co.'s campaign to win federal backing for a lucrative new military airplane contract was in trouble in October 2002. The Head of the Office of Management and Budget had just told the Air Force and Congress that the acquisition plan—which *featured the most costly government lease in U.S. history—was not urgent, and would squander billions of dollars.*

Then White House Chief of Staff, Andrew H. Card Jr., acting at what officials say was the direction of President Bush, told the Air Force and OMB to resolve their differences. *Bush had been lobbied hard by House Speaker J. Dennis Hastert (R.-Ill.) and Rep. Norman D. Dicks, (D.-Wash.) whose districts are in states that include, respectively, Boeing's headquarters and a key production facility.*[51]

The article goes on to point out, "With Card's intervention, obstacles to the deal eventually fell away." It continues, "Vehement objections raised by OMB and Pentagon budget analysts—that the planes were too expensive and leasing would set a bad precedent—were muted or withdrawn." This intervention in the procurement process "was but one fruit of a two-year lobbying campaign, mounted jointly by the Air Force and Boeing, that has brought the $21 billion to $25 billion deal within one congressional hurdle of being passed."[52] The article goes on to mention that dozens of interviews and thousands of documents showed that "Boeing circumvented the usual route of Pentagon acquisitions—and with it, many of the rules and regulations enacted over the past three decades to forestall defense contracting abuses."[53]

Apparently the media outcry about the deal led to reconsideration. Eventually the Congress worked out a revision that required the Air Force to split the acquisition into two contracts. The change was expected to save taxpayers $5 billion.[54]

This is hardly a unique incident. Down through the years, news articles about deals in which the Pentagon and contractors cooperated in taking the American taxpayer for a ride are fairly common. These deals have cropped up like poisonous toadstools, again and again. Reforms such as the Department of Defense's acquisition regulations were put in place to prevent such corruption, but it continues wherever politicians are willing to put self-interest above the well being of the nation. It seems we have found one of the key reasons why the U.S. defense establishment is so oversized and over-funded. Not national defense, but joint efforts to raid the national treasury between private sector contractors, senior Pentagon brass, and politicians looking out for their districts (i.e., the votes that get them re-elected) at the expense of the rest of the country, are the real reasons. Fear from 9/11 provides a golden opportunity to bamboozle the public and the news media into failing to ask questions. Anyone who asks questions can be labeled unpatriotic.

After the Cold War there was no legitimate defensive need for a military establishment of the size and power the U.S. retained, despite serious downsizing. A military six times the size of our nearest potential rival's, a rival that had become cautiously friendly and very dependent? What nation-state would even think of attacking us frontally, even if our military power were half what it had become even after the Cold War? In this context it is hardly surprising that the asymmetrical warfare of terrorism became the greatest threat to the U.S. It was the only possible response by those who wished to do us harm, and many orders of magnitude cheaper than conventional military power. The best way to fight terrorism in the short run is effective intelligence in cooperation with other countries, and in the long run it is not to build more aircraft carriers and fighter jets, but to behave so as to diminish the incentives of others to attack us. Endlessly expanding our military capacity may have the opposite effect.

The Global Policeman

There is one rationale for the U.S. to maintain such a colossal military establishment after the Cold War removed the need for it. That rationale is for the U.S. to serve as a policeman or enforcer of an international order substantially built by the U.S. with the cooperation of the rest of the international community. Michael Hirsh makes a case for this role for the American military in his book, *At War With Ourselves: Why America Is Squandering Its Chance to Build a Better World*. Hirsh argues that during the Cold War the U.S. led the world in building an international system of laws and institutions, and on the back of that we nurtured the growth of an international system of trade, manufacturing and commerce, all of which, he says, is protected and stabilized by American military might.[55]

In other words, the U.S. has led in the creation, partly intentionally and partly accidentally, of a loosely structured global economic and political system, the "international community." (Conservative writers often ritually and vehemently deny its self-evident existence. But as they fly from place to place outside the U.S., they rely on it for their survival every minute of the day in such routine matters as international air traffic control. There are innumerable similar manifestations of the supposedly non-existent international community.) Hirsh argues that using our huge military establishment, we have in effect made ourselves the world's policeman, protecting not just our own borders, but the entire international system.

217

Such a role might be a good thing for the world as long as the policeman uses coercive power legally and with restraint, for the benefit of all. But does an 800-pound gorilla have an incentive to behave legally and with restraint? If he doesn't, who will stop him? The Iraq war showed that when he chose to abandon restraint, no one could stop him. The reality is that the U.S. uses its military and economic power to strong-arm other countries into going along with its own interests, and only incidentally those of the international community as a whole. This self-interested use of brute force, especially coming from the Bush administration's vantage point of indifference if not hostility to international law and institutions such as the UN, transforms the U.S. military into the world's bully, not the world's policeman.

In short, the American global police force is not a police force at all, because it is at present controlled by leaders who blithely ignore international law and institutions or openly oppose them. Given the values of American citizens, our military could and should support the international community, and it would if the leaders of the U.S. were committed to the rule of law at the international level. But clearly at present they are not. I should emphasize that Michael Hirsh's book mentioned above is concerned with this very problem. As the title makes clear, it is far from arguing that U.S. foreign policy is headed in the right direction. Building a better world is exactly what we are not doing.

Nightmare In a Nutshell

If we pull the pieces of this analysis together into a few paragraphs, we get a compressed picture of an arena in which American public policy has gone mad. We spend over half of our nation's discretionary budget to expand and refine our capacity for violence, for killing, maiming, and destroying property. That capacity, we are solemnly assured, is for self-defense, even though there is no enemy in the world within light-years of being able to generate the magnitude of threat for which we are prepared. The enemies who do constitute a serious threat—terrorists—are not deterred by these gargantuan expenditures.

The immense magnitude of our military superiority has tempted us to launch a war that has alienated our allies and intensified the hatred of our enemies. We have used this power to attack and occupy another country that turns out to be a minor threat or no threat at all, but is now a sinkhole for scores of billions of dollars and hundreds of American lives. The occupation has become an occasion for shame and disgrace for the U.S. in the human rights arena. We face a probable outcome in which our leader's dream of establishing a stable and democratic country is not likely to succeed and the region we hoped to stabilize, the Middle East, is less stable.

From a defensive point of view, the aftermath of the unnecessary Iraq war, the necessity to occupy and attempt to govern the country despite strong resistance, has severely strained the U.S. military's capabilities, especially as regards manpower, and tied it down so that it is no longer available for other major military actions should they be needed. China seems emboldened in its threats against Taiwan, and North Korea appears emboldened in its development of nuclear weapons. Neither has much to fear from a preoccupied and overstrained United States. Even opponents of the Iraq war seldom stress the strategic weakness it has created for the U.S. This consequence of the war is, in a way, the darkest "secret" of supporters of the war who also believe in overwhelming American military superiority as a primary source of national security. The war has tied the American military giant to Iraq with bonds of steel and has drastically curtailed its flexibility to operate elsewhere if needed. As a result, in yet another way Americans are less safe as a result of pursuing it. Osama bin Laden, if he is thinking strategically, must be pleased.

We react with righteous indignation and coercive blustering when we suspect that other nations are trying to develop nuclear weapons, but we violate our own solemn treaty obligations by maintaining and further developing our own nuclear weapons. Our colossal military expenditures leave a few scraps, small fractions of what we spend on the military budget, for crucial domestic priorities such as education and health care. Elaborate cultivation of military force, far beyond necessity, and its uninhibited use has not served us well on any front and has definitely has not made us safer.

---

[1] Richard Wolffe, "A Man With a Mission" *Newsweek*, October 27, 2003, p. 33.

[2] Barton Gellman, "Search in Iraq Fails to Find Nuclear Threat," *The Washington Post*, October 26, 2003.

[3] Idem.

[4] Harold Meyerson, "Gen. Clark, Picking His Battles," *The Washington Post*, 10/22/2003

[5] Robert Jay Lifton, *The Superpower Syndrome: America's Apocalyptic Confrontation with the World,* New York, Thunders Mouth Press/Nation books, 2003, p. 117.

[6] Ibid., pp.115 & 116.

[7] These military budget numbers are drawn from a table in the web site of the Center for Defense Information (CDI), www.cdi.org/budget/2004/world-military-spending.cfm updated March 19, 2003. The table was prepared by Christopher

Hellman, CDI Senior Analyst, based on information from the International Institute for Strategic Studies, Department of Defense.

[8] Marcus Corbin and Olga Levitsky, "Vital Statistics: The U.S. Military" *The Defense Monitor*, Vol. XXXII, Number 5, 2003, p.4, figure 4.

[9] Ibid., p. 6, figure 6.) In short, our military spending dwarfs our spending on these other priorities. As it rapidly balloons, they are further squeezed.

[10] Ibid., pp. 5 & 7

[11] William Greider, *Fortress America*, Public Affairs, N.Y. 1998, p. 9.

[12] Idem.

[13] Ibid., p.p. 11 & 12.

[14] Lora Lumpe and Paul F. Pineo in a 1997 study by the Federation of American Scientists, as quoted in Greider, op. cit. p. 12.

[15] Henry Kissinger, "A Dangerous Divergence," *The Washington Post* 12/10/02.

[16] Prestowitz, Clyde. *Rogue Nation: American Unilateralism and the Failure of Good Intentions.* New York: Basic Books, 2003, pp. 1-2

[17] Prestowitz, op. cit.

[18] Bob Fehribach, "Using Landmines Offers No Benefit to U.S. Military." *Lansing State Journal.* January 14, 2003 as quoted in Prestowitz, op. cit.

[19] "The Problem of Landmine History." Canadian Landmine Foundation. www.canadianlandmine.org/landmineProb.History.cfm. as quoted by Prestowitz, op. cit.

[20] Dunne, Nancy. "Clinton to work for an end to land mines." *Financial Times*, May 17, 1996 as quoted in Prestowitz, op. cit.

[21] Landmine Monitor Fact Sheet Prepared by Handicap International Belgium, 11 November 2003 (http://www.icbl.org/lm/factsheets/eapc_2003.html)

[22] http://www.cnn.com/2004/US/02/27/bush.landmines.ap/index.html

[23] Prestowitz, op. cit

[24] Cecilia Fuentes, "The Ottawa Convention: A U.S./Canadian Leadership and Policy Comparison", an unpublished paper written in 1998. The Fuentes paper cites as its source Roberts, Shawn and Williams, Jody, *After the Guns Fall Silent: The Enduring Legacy of Landmines*, Vietnam Veterans of America Foundation, 1995, p.5

[25] *Rule of Power or Rule of Law?: An Assessment of U.S. Policies and Actions Regarding Security Related Treaties,* edited by Nicole Deller, Arjun Makhijani, and John Burroughs, The Apex Press, New York, 2003, p.XXI

[26] Ibid., p. XXIII.

[27] Ibid., p. XVIII.

[28] Ibid., pp. XVIII and XIX.

[29] Ibid., pp. XXII and XXIII.

[30] Dana Milbank, "U.S. Withdraws From Missile Treaty" *The Washington Post*, June 14, 2002

[31] Peter Slevin, "Ambitious Nuclear Arms Pact Faces a Senate Examination," *The Washington Post*, July 17, 2002.

[32] Idem.

[33] Ibid.

[34] Dana Milbank and Sharon La Franiere, "U.S., Russia Agree to Arms Pact," *The Washington Post*, May 14, 2004.

[35] Idem.

[36] Prestowitz, op. cit. p. 154.

[37] Idem.

[38] *Rule of Power or Rule of Law*, op. cit. p. xxiv.

[39] *Rule of Power or Rule of Law*, op. cit. p. xxv.

[40] Prestowitz, op. cit., p. 155.

[41] Idem.

[42] Ibid., pp. 155-156.

[43] Idem.

[44] Ibid., p. 156.

[45] Joby Warrick, "Study Raises Projection For 'Dirty Bomb' Toll," *The Washington Post*, January 13, 2004.

[46] Idem.

[47] Idem.

[48] Joby Warrick, "Dirty Bomb Warheads Disappear," *The Washington Post*, Dec. 7, 2003

[49] Dr. Jeffrey Record, "Bounding the Global War on Terrorism," U.S. Army War College, Strategic Studies Institute, December 2003, at http://www.carlisle.army.mil/ssi/pubs/2003/bounding/bounding.htm.

[50] Ibid., p. 49.

[51] R. Jeffrey Smith and Renae Merle, "Rules Circumvented on Huge Boeing Defense Contract" *The Washington Post*, October 27, 2003.

[52] Idem.

[53] Idem.

[54] Renae Merle, "Senate Approves Tanker Compromise," *The Washington Post*, November 13, 2003.

[55] Michael Hirsh, *At War With Ourselves: Why America Is Squandering Its Chance to Build a Better World,* Oxford University Press, Oxford, 2003.

Chapter Nine

THE UNITED NATIONS — ANGEL OR DEVIL?

U.N. Peacekeeping has maintained order in such diverse places as Namibia, El Salvador, Cambodia, eastern Slavonia, Mozambique, and Cyprus. The traditional U.N. mission is a confidence-building exercise, conducted in strict neutrality between parties that seek international help in preserving or implementing peace.

—Madeleine K. Albright,
Foreign Policy, 9&10/03

The U.N. Security Council unanimously adopted a resolution Wednesday that will compel governments to make it a crime to transfer nuclear, biological and chemical weapon materials to terrorists and black-market arms dealers.

—Colum Lynch, *The Washington Post* 4/29/04

More than two-thirds of Americans, when asked their opinions, support the United Nations and U.S. payment of UN dues. But a vocal and passionate minority fear and demonize the UN. Through their organized effort, their impassioned letter writing, and through strategically placed political leaders such as former Senator Jesse Helms and other extreme conservatives, they succeeded in keeping the U.S. from paying most of its dues to the UN for the better part of two decades. When the U.S. occasionally did pay it did so late, partially, and with strings attached. Some of the "strings" were constructive, demanding better fiscal discipline from the UN, but when the UN complied with the U.S. demands, the funds owed were still not forthcoming.

In signing and ratifying the UN Charter at its founding and also in later negotiations, the U.S. agreed to a system that distributes the cost of supporting the UN among member nations based on their wealth. From the days of the founding of the UN it was obvious that it would not make sense nor even be possible to charge the world's most poverty-stricken countries the same dues charged to the wealthiest nations. The U.S., as the world's wealthiest nation, naturally has had to carry its proportionate share of the cost. No country is better equipped to do so. As the European nations and Japan have gained in wealth, the U.S. share of UN dues has declined substantially, but still not enough for our most conservative politicians.

The U.S. refusal to pay was a serious matter, a decision by a great and prosperous nation to go back on its word before the whole world and incidentally to force other countries, many of them less prosperous, to carry the brunt of supporting the UN financially. The decision provoked serious, highly visible crises in the management of the UN's finances and caused intense anger among other member nations against the U.S. This anger was fully legitimate. Cross-cultural studies have shown that a deeply ingrained moral sensitivity in human beings everywhere is the requirement that each member of a community carry his or her share of the load of work and resources supporting the community. A habitual violator of this norm, a freeloader, quickly becomes a scorned pariah.

During this period, the U.S. was both the wealthiest country in the world—better able to pay than any other—and also a non-paying freeloader that still, rather than fading into the background as its freeloader status would have suggested, shamelessly tried to dominate every debate and discussion. It was as if the only millionaire in a small town crippled the town's government by refusing to pay his taxes and at the same time tried to dominate the town council. Resentment was acute. It reached the point where the U.S. could not propose a resolution without risking automatic opposition by other nations. American resolutions were submitted through surrogates like England to have a chance. How did we get into this grim position?

The UN Phobia

According to several polls, about 20% of Americans oppose the UN so strenuously they advocate U.S. withdrawal. A significant number are highly vocal and passionate. Many of them absolutely despise and demonize the UN and have the energy to do something about it. A substantial number of them wield two political tools effectively—they are organized and they write to their Representatives and Senators and to editors of newspapers. As a result they create for Congress and the press a powerful illusion of being far more numerous than they are. By contrast, among the majority supporting the UN, the bulk of people are not nearly so passionate, and consequently are far less visible politically. Among their numbers, the intensity factor is missing. The result has been an upside-down perception within Congress and the press of what the American public thinks of the UN. This misperception leads politicians to timidity about principled support for the UN.

American citizens constitute less than 5% of the world's population (about 280 million out of 6 billion), and yet have 25% of the world's wealth. The refusal of the U.S. to pay its proportional share, 25% of UN dues crippled the UN financially and undermined peacekeeping and humanitarian efforts all over the world. The UN Charter, a treaty the U.S. signed and the Senate ratified, requires payment of these dues, but the responsibility to keep our word as a nation did not sway the U.S. Congress. The most frequently used rationale for our non-payment was the claim that the UN was a bloated, inefficient bureaucracy. There was some truth in the claim. Eventually pressure to pay resulted in the Congress setting benchmarks for improved efficiency and management reforms in the UN. Partly in response to these demands from the U.S., the UN instituted management reforms (fully meeting U.S. demands), maintained a no-growth budget for years, and cut its staff by over 1,000 employees.

After the UN had clearly met U.S. demands for reform, the U.S. Congress still refused to pay the required back dues and produced yet another list of demands. At the peak of its fiscal crisis, to keep afloat financially without the U.S. contributions the UN had to borrow money from its peacekeeping accounts, which meant that it could not pay back other countries money it owed them for peacekeeping efforts under explicit financial agreements. This failure to pay undermined further efforts to get nations to contribute troops and supplies for peacekeeping. Through the non-payment of our UN dues, the U.S. was de facto forcing our allies and other countries, including many that were poor, to float zero-interest loans to the U.S. through the UN.

During the period of U.S. non-payment of dues, conservative American leaders routinely complained that the U.S. had to pay too much to the UN and could not afford such an extravagance. The amount of money involved ran to the hundreds of millions of dollars, eventually rising to $1.6 billion. These figures sounded enormous to the general public. However, the reality was quite different. For a perspective on what was at stake financially in the

U.S. refusal to pay its dues during the period, and to get a feel for how accurately the Congress was representing the views of the American people in cutting off U.S. payment of UN dues, it would be useful to take a quick snapshot of what was going on in 1996, near the peak of the budgetary problems between the U.S. and the UN.

Consider the results of polls on the subject at the time. The following paragraph is from the website of the Program on International Policy Attitudes (PIPA), a university-based organization that studies American views on international relations. PIPA found that most Americans, far from being concerned about the cost of the UN, wished to see it expanded, even though they believed it to be much more costly than it was.

Support for an expansive UN exists even though most Americans appear to grossly overestimate the magnitude of UN activities. This can be inferred from the public's exaggerated notion of the UN budget. In September 1996, PIPA asked respondents for their impressions of the size of the UN budget, offering four other government budgets for comparison: those of Wyoming ($2 billion), Alabama ($10 billion), Texas ($40 billion), and the US federal government ($1600 billion). Forty-eight percent thought the UN's budget was closest to that of Texas, and 28% thought it was closest to that of the US government (closest to Alabama, 13%; closest to Wyoming, 7%). When the budgets for the UN, for UN peacekeeping operations, and all UN agencies (supported by states' voluntary contributions) are rolled together, the total is less than $10 billion. In short, 75% believed that the UN budget was four or more times its actual size. Yet this (mis)perception of the UN as already being much larger than it is does not dissuade the public from wanting to see a stronger UN.[1]

To update these numbers from eight years ago to the year 2004, the U.S. contributions to the overall UN system budget, including peacekeeping and independent agencies is now approximately $3 billion. By contrast, the U.S. Federal budget is $2.4 trillion. In other words, the U.S. budget is currently about 800 times the size of the U.S. contribution to the UN.

One of the factors that led some congressional leaders to withhold UN dues was an attempt to coerce UN agencies that were concerned with family planning to forego discussing abortion with their clients. Polls showed that the public was divided about funding international family planning, but that a large majority of Americans opposed attaching to UN dues legislation an amendment with such restrictions. Again, the politicians were not representing the true views of the American public.[2]

In reaction to the refusal of the U.S. to pay its dues, other countries could and did make life uncomfortable for the U.S. in a variety of ways. A typical instance was the loss of the U.S. seat on the UN Human Rights Commission in May 2001. Diplomats said that the vote was a sign of international irritation over the Bush administration's stands on global warming, missile defense, and AIDS medication. And of course, these annoyances pale in comparison with the pervasive background irritation that resulted from the U.S. long-standing failure to pay its UN dues. This pattern of refusal to carry our share of the load was proving to be extraordinarily poor diplomacy. Eventually one of America's greatest diplomats weighed in, and made a difference.

The *New York Times* reported a breakthrough in the depressing saga of UN dues on February 7, 2001:[3]

Richard C. Holbrooke, who served as the Clinton administration's United Nations ambassador, brokered a deal to reduce American dues for the first time in more than 28 years. In a game of brinkmanship, Congress withheld a portion of the United States' dues to the United Nations for more than a decade, arguing that the American people were paying too much for peacekeeping missions and that the United Nations was mismanaging its money.

The standoff complicated diplomatic relationships and drew criticism from other nations, which labeled the United States an arrogant, deadbeat superpower. Senator Jesse Helms, the chairman of the Foreign Relations Committee, who spearheaded the crusade to reform the United Nations, said he was sufficiently satisfied with the United Nations to free the bulk of the $926 million owed in arrears. The Bush administration, which has yet to appoint a new ambassador to the United Nations, also supports the bill. The legislation now goes to the House, where passage is expected.

Amid the swirl of numbers about what was being spent and saved, Senator Jesse Helms, then the Chair of the Senate Foreign Relations

Committee, triumphantly claimed the reduction in U.S. dues would save $170 million a year that the United Nations would have cost taxpayers. He did not mention that in this diplomatic triumph, the U.S. incurred the intense anger and scorn of 188 other member nations of the UN for over a decade and had finally achieved a savings of one one-hundredth of one percent (0.01% or one ten-thousandth) of the U.S. federal budget. This sum amounts to about seventy cents per American citizen per year. At that point I wondered, should we celebrate this great achievement by breaking open a seventy-cent can of soda? It would cost more to break out champagne than we saved by causing intense irritation for over a decade to all the other countries in the world. By any reasonable estimate, the cost-benefit ratio of this "victory" was thousands to one against the U.S.

Despite arduous negotiations and the agreements described above, much of the money was not actually delivered to the UN. The obstructionism of the U.S. Congress continued on various pretexts until September 11, 2001. Then, as President Bush and Secretary of State Colin Powell struggled to put together a coalition of nations to fight terrorism, the recalcitrance of Congress buckled and the U.S. Government paid a large fraction, though still not all, of its back dues. At that point the price of congressional non-cooperation had become too great and too obvious, and a change was clearly necessary. When we desperately wanted something from the rest of the world through the UN, we had to cough up. But not before.

Why?

Why has the U.S. so often refused to pay its dues to the UN, and why have American politicians so often gone along with or deliberately intensified the demonizing of the UN by a small minority of American citizens? Is there something dangerously, desperately wrong with the UN? And if there is something so wrong, why do most Americans favor the UN, while still acknowledging its flaws? Much of the rest of this chapter answers these questions with a look at the UN—good and bad—at the U.S., and at the American attitudes—both sensible and bizarre—that influence the rocky relationship between them.

More important than the past U.S.-UN relationship is the future of the UN and its inconsistently successful efforts to create a more peaceful and just world. Does the UN have the potential to evolve into a global force that is tyrannical, sinister and dangerous, or a global influence that is democratic, effective and constructive—an influence that actually facilitates solving

227

global problems? Will the U.S. use its extraordinary power to steer the UN toward the latter course, rather than opposing and obstructing it at every turn? These questions are closely linked to the largest of all questions: Can the world we are building be made sustainable? Is there hope for the civilization we have created or is it doomed to go down into ruin and chaos?

The answer to this latter question is not a foregone conclusion. The fact that there are genuine global problems that need urgent and decisive attention and global solutions is illustrated by the tangible presence of the following influences: the potential and actual spread of AIDS, SARS, bird flu, ebola and other natural diseases; the proliferation of weapons of mass destruction (including nuclear weapons and biological weapons that may be genetically engineered); the unpredictable effects of severe environmental degradation; and the instability of the current house-of-cards global economy with its wildly erratic monetary flows, rendered more fragile by terrorism.

None of these problems can be solved by nations operating individually. All require highly organized cooperation. The human race has choices, and the United States, with its extraordinary power, has particularly critical choices affecting the future of the world. The U.S., in constructive alignment with the United Nations, has a chance to steer the world toward survival. If the U.S. remains at odds with the UN, the world will continue to be gridlocked and critical global problems will not be addressed.

How It All Started

By the end of World War II the United States and the world were desperate to see an end to war. The most important concern in the minds of presidents and politicians, scholars and millions of ordinary people was how to prevent a recurrence. There was no doubt about it, world wars had to stop. The world had been all the way to hell for a second time in less than fifty years and was just beginning to stumble back. The loss of life and economic devastation were mind-numbing—absolutely beyond comprehension. Everyone had been harmed if not devastated by the war. More horrifying yet, the intolerable pain, death and loss from these wars were nothing by comparison with what the future held if the next global war included a nuclear exchange. Permitting another round of such devastation—or much greater devastation—was unthinkable. Prevention was imperative.

In this context, two American Presidents, Franklin D. Roosevelt and Harry Truman, led other world leaders in establishing a global organization designed and intended, in the language of the UN Charter, to save succeeding generations from the scourge of war. In addition to this goal and deeply related to it, the UN Charter affirmed human rights, justice, respect for treaties and other sources of international law, and the use of international mechanisms for the economic and social advancement of all peoples. All of these were recognized both as good things in themselves and also as means to the end of preventing further wars.

The UN Charter rang with a nobility of purpose reminiscent of the U.S. Constitution, the Declaration of Independence and some of Abraham Lincoln's greatest speeches. And of course, being a human institution, the UN itself was and is radically imperfect, a fragile patchwork of uneasy compromises. Still, it represented immense hope and promise and received overwhelming support from the American public and American political leaders. Unlike its predecessor, the League of Nations, which was strangled in its crib by isolationists in the U.S. Congress, the UN was hugely popular and was overwhelmingly approved. It was seen as the last, best hope of a world that was still reeling from the catastrophic devastation of a global nuclear war. Hiroshima and Nagasaki were fresh in people's minds.

Although the UN was established to save succeeding generations from the scourge of war, since its establishment innumerable wars have been fought. Some have been regional and many have been civil wars within the borders of individual countries. At first thought, these wars might seem to indicate failure by the UN. However, the single most important fact of the second half of the twentieth century is that despite some narrow escapes, there has not been another devastating world war engulfing all continents and most nations and killing millions of people.

No one claims that the UN is the sole reason World War III was averted, but it would also be foolish to argue that it was not a factor in preventing that war to end all wars—and maybe all human civilization. Despite the unnerving possibility of a regional nuclear exchange, e.g., between India and Pakistan, almost sixty years after the establishment of the UN the ultimate nightmare of a global nuclear exchange now seems remote. (Of course, there are writers who argue that the Cold War was World War III. But one only has to think briefly about what the world would have gone through and would now be like if the Cold War had turned into a real hot war to realize that they are speaking metaphorically and in so doing obscuring the most important facts.)

The most dangerous single crisis in the second half of the 20th Century was the confrontation between the U.S. and the Soviet Union over Soviet missiles in Cuba. A nuclear exchange between the U.S. and the Soviet Union appeared to be a likely outcome. Key moments in that crisis were played out at the United Nations on TV before the eyes of the world. Down through history, negotiations at the brink of war had been carried out behind closed doors, if they happened at all. Of course, behind-the-scenes diplomacy was conducted as the Cuban missile crisis unfolded, and those negotiations were vital factors in preventing war. But the UN offered something additional that was new, a universally accepted place for public debate and discussion. The UN had no power of arbitration, no power to coerce either side, but it did provide a venue for debate and a well-recognized, explicit moral norm of rejecting war and negotiating peace as a way to settle disputes. Rhetorical missiles flew, but nuclear-tipped ballistic missiles did not. The world was saved.

Naturally, the UN has changed over time, moving in new directions unforeseen at its establishment. A key change is the growth of the UN General Assembly (UNGA) from its original 51 member nations to 191 members, almost every nation on the planet. Many of these are former colonies of the European powers and many are small, poor, and relatively powerless. Most did not exist on June 26, 1945 when the original nations signed the UN Charter in San Francisco. By virtue of their numbers, these new nations—when most of them agree—have a powerful say in the affairs of the General Assembly. While the votes of the UNGA have no enforcement mechanism or binding power under international law, they still represent an important indicator of global opinion.

The sheer numbers of countries in the UN General Assembly and the divergence of their viewpoints and interests from those of the world's lone superpower make them impossible for the U.S. to control. Their collective independence from American influence often makes American leaders uncomfortable. The U.S., despite its immense military and economic power relative to the rest of the world, often finds itself standing alone and casting the only "no" vote or one of the few dissenting votes in the UNGA. American leaders and journalists love to think of the U.S. as the great leader among the nations. They endlessly repeat the claim that the President of the United States is the "leader of the free world." But the reality is that in the UNGA, the U.S. is not a leader, but typically the odd-man-out. In the world's most comprehensive body of nations, the U.S. is neither a leader nor a follower, but rather a superpowered maverick, a kind of rogue elephant in the international china shop.

A study of U.S. voting patterns in the UNGA is illuminating. Steven Hollaway, in the journal *Global Governance*, reports his study showing that the U.S. says "no" to mainstream votes in the General Assembly far more often than other nations. "After the end of the cold war and the supposed creation of a new world order – the U.S. representative to the Forty-seventh General Assembly was moved to vote 'nay' on 61 percent of the final resolutions adopted by a majority of the membership." Subtracting out votes that were intended to protect our beleaguered ally, Israel, we still were far and away the biggest nay-sayer of all UN member nations on solid statistical grounds.[4]

Later in the same article Hollaway quotes an editorial in the staid English magazine the *Economist*, which he accurately cites as "a British magazine not usually noted as a bastion of radicalism or anti-U.S. sentiment." He quotes the following passage: "The United States has a sorry record of shilly-shallying, or plain obstruction, in the development of international law. Instead of leading, America has ratified many human-rights treaties only after most other countries have already done so." The article goes on to note the 40 years it took the U.S. to ratify the Genocide Convention, 28 years for the Convention Against Racial Discrimination, and 26 for the International Covenant on Civil and Political Rights— "the most important treaty of all."[5] The article goes on to discuss the ongoing failure of the U.S. to ratify the treaties on the rights of women and children.

America's overwhelming power has not translated into legitimacy in the UN and elsewhere partly because its genuinely noble values have so often been contradicted by its actions. The problem is not a public relations problem; it is a policy substance problem. In the view of the rest of the world, American might has not made right. The Vietnam War and the second war with Iraq are among the most dramatic examples of American power misused; both debacles had the effect of alienating much of the rest of the world. And of course, the unbalanced U.S. support for Israel, without regard for the well-being of the Palestinians, has alienated the Muslim and Arab worlds—about a billion of the six billion people on the planet—and left a bad taste in the mouths of numerous other countries including our European allies.

For much of the world outside the U.S., that is, for about 95% of the world's population, the UN's policy positions on global issues have more perceived legitimacy than the policies of the U.S. This is hardly surprising since the UN is a more accurate barometer of world opinion than the actions of the U.S. Furthermore, the United States has primarily its own interests at heart and not necessarily those of the rest of the world, whereas the UN represents a pooling of the interests of large numbers of nations.

However, inside the U.S., the arrow of perceived legitimacy is sometimes reversed, especially when a spasm of tribalism infects the country. After September 11, an American President could look tough and draw applause from a conservative audience by denouncing the UN as irrelevant if it didn't do America's bidding, as if the U.S. were the UN's boss, or by asserting that the U.S. doesn't need a permission slip to go to war. When the French and other Security Council members had the audacity to oppose the U.S. in launching a dubious war, it was time for flag-waving American jingoists to pour French wines into the gutter and rename French fries "freedom fries." Freedom to start unnecessary wars, that is.

The contradiction at the level of principle is that conservative U.S. leaders, in "dissing" the UN and asserting their right to trample on international law and attack others as they please (because those being attacked are evil, of course), are acting out a desire (one hopes unconsciously or only semi-consciously) to be the elite of a *de facto* global oligarchy, a nation of 5% of the world's population that controls by military and economic power the other 95% while hypocritically promoting democracy. It is difficult to take the democracy part too seriously. The rest of the world isn't buying it.

America's leaders do indeed want other countries to be or become democracies, but they will abandon that preference in a heartbeat when U.S. economic interests are at stake. When the U.S. props up malevolent dictators (as we did for a while even with Saddam and have done with many others) for political convenience or access to oil, the impression of hypocrisy is clinched. The rest of the world sees that the rhetoric about democracy is for domestic consumption; the real goal is American power.

Ironically, the recent jingoistic American excesses of contempt for the UN, as exemplified by Bush's declaration of its irrelevancy before the Iraq war, may have actually strengthened the UN's legitimacy in the longer term, even in the eyes of Americans. This reversal began to take shape when Bush had no choice but to eat humble pie soon after the Iraq war by returning to the UN to get a "permission slip" to sell Iraqi oil. He had to do so because no company would buy the oil as long as it was illegal under a UN mandate (which the U.S. had previously approved). International law still mattered in the real world, regardless of Bush's anti-UN swaggering and political rhetoric. Bush has again returned to the UN, more than once, to seek assistance and legitimacy in rebuilding the country.

During his election campaign, Bush promised a humble foreign policy. He is beginning to be forced to deliver, very much against his will. It is not the UN's resources that give it the power to humble George Bush. The U.S. Government's budget is over 200 times the size of the UN's budget. It is the UN's widely perceived legitimacy under international law that gives it leverage. In current parlance, this is "soft power," but it certainly is real power. An episode in the hand-over of national sovereignty to Iraq provides an illustration.

In early 2004, the Shiite Ayatollah Ali Sistani, who had real legitimacy in Shiite eyes, scuttled the U.S. plan for caucuses to select Iraqi leaders for a transitional government. A reclusive religious leader had more real power through his perceived legitimacy than all the American tanks and guns and bombs in Iraq. His argument was that the caucus approach was too undemocratic; that only elections would be seen as legitimate. His real political reason was that Shiites constitute a 60 percent majority of the Iraqi population. Democracy is to their advantage. Sistani's Shiite followers agreed that elections were essential and took to the streets in their hundreds of thousands to demonstrate in support of his position. Here was an exquisite irony: In this situation the U.S. appeared to be less committed to democracy than a Shiite ayatollah and his followers, people who are usually thought of as preferring theocracy as a form of government, and who may yet prove that to be true.

Another exquisite irony is the following: The UN had to be called to George W. Bush's rescue (again). The Bush team could not convince Sistani that it was impossible to hold elections before the scheduled end-of-June hand-over of sovereignty to Iraq. Driven by Sistani's suspicions of American motives and truthfulness, the U.S. requested a UN team to explore the matter. A group headed by senior UN envoy Lakhdar Brahimi evaluated the situation, laid out the steps necessary to conduct a fair election, and agreed that it was not possible to conduct elections within the stated time frame. Brahimi talked with Sistani and convinced him of the real impossibility of elections before the designated time, the end of June. Brahimi lent credibility to the U.S. position and at the same time furthered the process of looking for an alternative to the caucuses. So much for the irrelevancy and lack of legitimacy of the UN. The "soft power" of legitimacy triumphed twice over the "hard power" of American military force—once when Sistani balked, and again when the UN persuaded him of the realities surrounding elections.

Though the UN doesn't consistently bend the knee and do the bidding of American presidents, and as a result sometimes draws harsh criticism from them, opponents of the UN among American citizens have consistently been a small minority. Tribalism and fear of any apparent external threat, no matter how unfounded the fear may be, is a powerful motivator of this minority's hostility. Are they wrong? Or are they more perceptive than the majority of their fellow Americans? Their minority status tells us little about the merits of their position or their concerns. Sometimes minorities are right and majorities are wrong. The only rational way to decide is to look at the evidence, pro and con. After considering the pros and cons we will look in more detail at what the majority of Americans think, as indicated by several scientifically designed polls over the past decade.

What's Right With the UN?

As noted above, a peculiar fact of American politics is the reality that the political far right wing is fond of sneering at the legitimacy of the UN or outright denouncing it as a fraud. This outlook is particularly rampant among neoconservatives who advocate an American empire that rules the world, by force if necessary, and that exports democracy to places like the Middle East. It is a viewpoint that deeply swayed the thinking of the Pentagon and the White House as they beat the drums for the second war with Iraq. However, there was a notable ambivalence about international law and the value of the UN in the political rhetoric leading to war. The White House veered from one extreme of denouncing Saddam partly because he flouted the UN to the other extreme of denouncing the UN and flouting it as an irrelevancy to be brushed aside if it didn't go along with the Bush administration's plans for war. The double standard was breathtaking in its audacity. Saddam is a bad guy because he flouts the UN, but as the U.S., we are the good guys, so it's O.K. if we flout the UN.

The denial of the UN's legitimacy has been asserted so often in conservative editorials and op-ed pieces that it has become an article of faith, an essential component of right-wing scripture or political dogma. Since the fall of the Berlin Wall, the UN has taken over the role of the guy with the horns and the forked tail in the absence of the truly dangerous Soviet Union. Of course, the UN has to vie for the demonology crown with real threats such as rogue nations, terrorists, and weapons of mass destruction. Reality insists on intruding. As a consequence of the demonizing drumbeat against the UN, any discussion of its merits for an American audience must tackle at least briefly the question of its legal and political legitimacy as an institution, as well as its practical usefulness to the U.S. and the world.

A decisive indicator of the legitimacy of the UN in the eyes of the world is the fact that the government of every new nation seeks validation of its

234

own legitimacy by applying for membership in the UN. The UN (through its member states) now confers legitimacy on individual nations, and vice-versa. Further, a club that has the whole population (in this case, the whole population of nations) as its voluntary members has *de facto* legitimacy, no matter what its critics say. The U.S. participates actively in the UN and votes on issues before the General Assembly and the Security Council. It is active on a range of UN commissions and committees. Whatever the President or a Senator may say to the contrary, every vote and every committee membership is a U.S. Government acknowledgement of the UN's legitimacy. Given that the UN's political legitimacy is not an issue, what about its legal legitimacy?

The UN Charter is a treaty that was signed and ratified by the governments of all 191 member states, including the U.S., at the time when they joined the UN. These actions by member states are a unanimous and legally binding affirmation, at the highest possible level in the world, of the UN's legal legitimacy. It follows that the UN is quite literally the most thoroughly legitimized organization on the planet. This fact does not in itself prove that its existence is a net benefit to humanity or to the U.S., but it demolishes the specious argument against its legitimacy, a favorite claim of the UN's most vehement critics.

The UN's benefits to the world are a story worth exploring. Former Assistant Secretary of State and U.S. ambassador to the UN, Madeleine K. Albright, sums it up in a striking paragraph:

The United Nations' ongoing relevance is evident in the work of more than two dozen organizations comprising the UN system. In 2003 alone, the International Atomic Energy Agency reported that Iran had processed nuclear materials in violation of its Nuclear Nonproliferation Treaty obligations; the International Criminal Tribunal for the Former Yugoslavia tried deposed Yugoslav leader Slobodan Milosevic for genocide; and the World Health Organization successfully coordinated the global response to severe acute respiratory syndrome (SARS). Meanwhile the World Food Programme has fed more than 70 million people annually for the last five years; the U.N. High Commissioner for Refugees maintains a lifeline to the international homeless; the UN Children's Fund has launched a campaign to end forced childhood marriage; the joint U.N. Programme on HIV/AIDS remains a focal point for global efforts to defeat HIV/AIDS; and the UN Population Fund helps families plan, mothers survive, and children grow up healthy in the most impoverished places on earth. The U.N. may seem useless to the self-satisfied, narrow-minded, and micro-hearted minority, but to most of the world's population, it remains highly relevant indeed.[6]

Restraining War and Negotiating Peace

Not surprisingly, given its mandate to save succeeding generations from the scourge of war, some of the UN's most notable contributions include defusing international crises, resolving conflicts, and peacekeeping. The UN works to prevent conflicts such as the Cuban missile crisis. It has brokered over 100 peace agreements in its 59-year history and it works to correct the underlying causes of war and build a durable peace. In addition to the Cuban missile crisis, dramatic instances include helping to defuse the Middle East crisis in 1973 and negotiating peace at the end of the Iran-Iraq war in 1988. The UN also sponsored the negotiations that led to the Soviet withdrawal of troops from Afghanistan.[7]

Immediately after 9/11 the UN had a contributing role in the American response to terrorism: "When terrorists attacked the United States on 11 September 2001, the Security Council acted quickly—adopting a wide-ranging resolution which obligates States to ensure that any person who participates in financing, planning, preparing, perpetrating or supporting terrorist acts is brought to justice, as well as to establish such acts as serious criminal offences under domestic law."[8]

As regards the war in Iraq, the UN Security Council has been fully vindicated in its skepticism about the basis for the war. The purported weapons of mass destruction that were not found by the UN inspection team before the war also were not found by two U.S. teams after the war. The insurgency in Iraq, the great difficulties getting the infrastructure of the country repaired and up and running in the face of sabotage, and the continuing political instabilities in the aftermath of the war are vindicating the Security Council members' skepticism about the political wisdom of destabilizing an already unstable country in the heart of the Middle East.

Americans who oppose the UN and support the war in Iraq may continue to rage against the UN's refusal to sanction it, but they are ignoring the most salient fact of the situation—the strong evidence in plain sight before Bush launched the war that it was based on a false rationale and a wildly over-optimistic vision of the eventual outcome. The UN Security Council was acting sensibly and responsibly in declining to sanction the war. In retrospect, its refusal offers not a valid criticism of the UN, but an argument supporting it.

Peacekeeping

One of its key tools for bringing peace to troubled countries or regions is sending in peacekeeping forces. After some preliminary movement toward peace has been negotiated between parties to a conflict, often "United Nations peacekeepers, wearing distinctive UN blue helmets or berets, are dispatched by the Security Council to help implement peace agreements, monitor cease-fires, patrol demilitarized zones, create buffer zones between opposing forces, and put fighting on hold while negotiators seek peaceful solutions to disputes. But ultimately, the success of peacekeeping depends on the consent and cooperation of the opposing parties."[9]

Of course, peacekeeping costs money and risks lives. The reluctance of the U.S. to engage in peacekeeping operations is driven partly by these practical considerations. However, these concerns are apt to be extremely shortsighted in view of the way major crises often spin out of control and run up still higher costs and losses of lives than peacekeeping does. Ambassador Jonathan Dean summarized the value of UN peacekeeping and the savings it represents to the U.S. in the following comments at a local-global forum at Hood College:

> If a conflict lasts long enough and is large enough, the United States cannot stay on the sidelines, but has to go in. Otherwise, the damage to our capacity to shape international decisions is very large. Therefore, it is better for the United States to go into UN peacekeeping with other UN states paying 75% of the costs and furnishing 98% of the troops than to do it alone.

> There have been 54 peacekeeping operations from 1948 to now [May 7, 2001]. Today, ninety countries besides the U.S. are contributing military personnel for peacekeeping operations, with a total of 39,000 military and police personnel. Not counting NATO troops in former Yugoslavia, the U.S. has only 44 military personnel and 800 of 7,000 policemen out of this total. This is a good deal for the United States.

237

The United Nations has negotiated over 100 cease-fires or war conclusions, among them the Iran-Iraq War, and the end of the civil war in El Salvador.[10]

The image of the UN in some quarters of the U.S. as a do-nothing organization is vividly challenged by this record. In 1988, UN peacekeeping operations were awarded the Nobel Peace Prize.

Despite the impressive accomplishments of UN peace negotiations and peacekeeping missions, there is a serious problem in the way peacekeeping is managed. When a crisis arises, often debate drags on in the Security Council before a decision to act is taken. Then further delays are occasioned by the ad hoc nature of the system for recruiting peacekeepers. In recruiting, at present the UN has no choice but to rely on voluntary contributions of troops by member states. Nations are often slow to provide peacekeepers and sometimes devastating harm is done in a crisis or conflict situation while the UN is struggling first to decide to act, then to persuade member countries to provide the needed peacekeeping troops and police. The long run result is horrifying loss of life and much greater expense to all UN member countries and to the U.S. Again, Ambassador Dean, speaking to the cost side of the issue, has a powerful summary:

A standing international police force, like the one the European Union is now recruiting but did not exist then, could have prevented the Rwanda massacre and saved the international community the $5 billion plus it has spent on the care of Rwandan refugees.

A UN police force like this inserted into Kosovo early on could have kept the situation there under control and saved the international community $15-20 billion, of which the U.S. has paid about $5 billion.

If a force like this had been used at the beginning of the breakup of Yugoslavia, when Slovenia, the first of the Yugoslav republics to secede, was opposed by the Serbian forces, it could have saved the United States the $20 billion it has spent on the Yugoslav wars and an equal amount spent by the European Union. A preventive force of 800 men kept the peace in Macedonia for four years until it was withdrawn.[11]

Despite the human tragedy and greatly amplified expense resulting from these delays, the UN eventually did succeed in taking action and further tragedy and expense were at least contained. As these events all-too-painfully illustrate, there is wide latitude for improvement, but that can come only by strengthening the UN, not by destroying it or pulling out, as some extreme conservatives advocate.

At the end of the talk quoted above Ambassador Dean commented, "What do all these benefits for our security from the UN cost us? ... The average family in Frederick County [in Maryland, where the talk was given] annually pays $1,247 in taxes for national defense. The cost of the UN services I have described this evening is $7 per person per year."[12] In view of this cost picture, arguments that the U.S. should not spend money on needed peacekeeping operations early in crises involving genocide are at best misguided, at worst dishonest. In view of the much greater costs later and far more importantly, the loss of thousands of human lives, delays based on reluctance to spend modest sums of money to nip such problems in the bud are almost criminally negligent.

Humanitarian Interventions

Peacekeeping may be the best-known of the UN's contributions, but humanitarian assistance is another key element in its work:

In the face of disaster, the UN family of organizations supplies food, shelter, medicines and logistical support to the victims—most of them children, women and the elderly.

To pay for this assistance and deliver it to those in need, the UN has raised billions of dollars from international donors. During 2001 alone, the Office for the Coordination of Humanitarian Affairs launched 19 inter-agency appeals, raising more than $1.4 billion to assist 44 million people in 19 countries and regions.[13]

The UN website details a closely related activity: As the world's largest food aid organization, WFP [World Food Programme] supplies one-third of emergency food assistance worldwide. In 2000, WFP delivered 3.7 million

239

tons of food aid to 83 million people in 83 countries—including most of the world's refugees and internally displaced persons.[14]

The list of humanitarian contributions to human well-being by the UN is all but endless; for the sake of brevity, those provided above will have to suffice as indicative.

Justice and Human Rights

Establishing a global consensus on matters of basic moral and legal principle, justice and human rights, is another of the UN's pivotal contributions to human well-being. Codifying what human rights actually are might seem like a dry, academic exercise to the uninitiated. But the documents that do so, starting with the Universal Declaration of Human Rights and running through a series of 80 other declarations and treaties, have a powerful role to play in protecting people all over the world from oppression and providing them with the legal tools for redress when violations occur. Early in the history of the UN it was an American, Eleanor Roosevelt, who led the world in the conceptual and literary work of drafting the Universal Declaration of Human Rights and in the political work of getting it approved in the General Assembly. It became the foundation stone of a vast edifice of human rights law. It identifies rights to which all people are entitled including the right to life, liberty and nationality; to freedom of thought, conscience and religion; and the right to work and to be educated.

At the philosophical level, globally accepted statements of human rights principles have proven wrong those who would say that morality is relative and changes from one culture to another. These declarations and treaties show that although specific practices and traditions may vary from one culture to another, certain fundamental rights are universal and agreed upon in all or most cultures. And more importantly, widely agreed upon human rights declarations and treaties create strong pressures and norms that over time profoundly influence the behavior of nations. Dozens of countries have included the Universal Declaration of Human Rights as integral parts of their constitutions, giving it a place in their legal system comparable to the Bill of Rights in the U.S. Constitution. And as with the Bill of Rights, no matter how often the practices of these countries may violate the principles embodied in the Universal Declaration of Human Rights, the legal system of the country eventually provides a corrective to violations through precedent-setting lawsuits and conforming legislation. This process is a long one, a saga for the decades and the centuries that will never fully be completed. Nevertheless, it is no less valuable for being inescapably slow. We should remember that women did not get the right to vote in the U.S. until the twentieth century. The following describes a small part of the institutional procedure by which the UN seeks to ensure universal human rights:

> With its standards-setting work nearly complete, the UN is shifting the emphasis of its human rights efforts to the implementation of human rights laws. The High Commissioner for Human Rights, who coordinates UN human rights activities, works with governments to improve their observance of human rights, seeks to prevent violations, and works closely with the UN human rights mechanisms. The UN Commission on Human Rights, an intergovernmental body, holds public meetings to review the human rights performance of States, to adopt new standards and to promote human rights around the world. The Commission also appoints independent experts—"special rapporteurs"—to report on specific human rights abuses or to examine the human rights situation in specific countries.[15]

In addition to highly visible and sometimes controversial functions such as peacekeeping, humanitarian interventions, and development and implementation of human rights instruments, the UN carries out barely visible but vitally important routine administrative functions at the global level such as regulating mail delivery, setting standards for coordination of air travel (a function similar to that of the Federal Aviation Administration in the U.S.), coordinating global use of the electromagnetic spectrum for radio and TV broadcasting, and many others. If you have flown in an airplane overseas, listened to a radio station or watched a TV channel near a border of the U.S., or sent or received mail from a person in another country, you have directly and personally benefited from the work of the UN.

One independent agency of the UN, the International Atomic Energy Agency (IAEA), has been instrumental in constraining the proliferation of nuclear weapons among the nations and in conducting inspections for nuclear weapons and programs. A particularly telling example is the inspections of Iraq after the first Gulf War. Through these inspections the IAEA successfully eliminated Iraq's nuclear weapons program, and under the economic sanctions the UN imposed on Iraq for the next decade it was not feasible for Saddam Hussein to re-start these programs. The world is a much safer place because of the IAEA.

What's Wrong With the UN?

There are serious, well-founded criticisms of the UN and foolish and paranoid objections. Unfortunately the latter cannot be ignored. They have real and harmful effects on American politics and policies toward the UN. It may make sense to dispose of the follies first; they at least have the merit of providing some dark humor. Having cleared the air of toxic gasses, we can then look at the UN's genuine problems and seek solutions.

(1) The Paranoid Fantasies

The sight on TV screens of lightly armed UN peacekeepers with their blue helmets patrolling demilitarized zones or buffer zones between recently warring parties may have conjured apocalyptic visions of immense UN power in a few overactive imaginations. But the benign and pedestrian reality of blue helmets long ago gave way among conspiracy theorists to a much more interesting urban legend: black helicopters. Some extreme and remarkably misinformed (or deranged) ultra-conservative opponents of the UN worry that the UN threatens U.S. national sovereignty and will, if not restrained, soon grow into an oppressive and domineering world government. Their special *bete noirs* are black helicopters designed by UN supporters for the ultimate purpose of taking over the U.S. The details are not well spelled out on how the Herculean task of defeating the world's greatest military power might be accomplished by a few black helicopters (or even a lot of them), but the fantasy persists. Consider this gem, a clarification of the true nature of black helicopters from a web site about them:

> Black Helicopters (BH) are not just helicopters with a black paint-job as you may have been told. They are, in fact, autonomous agents -- *lifeforms* -- created by New World Order agencies via nanobiotechnology. Their purpose is to spy on the activities of North Americans in order to gather tactical information and discover "subversives" who are not bowing to the will of the Liberati's UN-backed Federal Government. Furthermore, when the NWO [New World Order] invasion takes place in the not-too-distant future, they will round

up citizens for internment in concentration camps or carry out the *elimination* of the more vocally anti-Liberati.[16]

Further into the same website several fuzzy photographs of a dissection of a "young" black helicopter are provided, demonstrating that they are artificial biological life forms, not ordinary machines.

Surprisingly, this kind of highly inventive paranoid thinking is a factor in U.S. foreign policy. Congresspersons with constituents who are this off base seem to feel they must be careful what the say and do regarding the UN. And as the news article below indicates, some appear to believe the nonsense about the UN being a threat to the U.S., despite the awesome power discrepancy (hundreds to one) in favor of the U.S. Partly because of these fears, some Congresspersons annually vote to withdraw the U.S. from UN membership. Here's a local example in the state of Utah of the kind of thinking by legislators about the UN that might be funny if it were a joke rather than a fact. While this article happens to document activities at the State level, the same follies are attempted at the Federal level every year. The story is presented with a straight face in the *Washington Times*:

Utah's House of Representatives urged the U.S. Congress last week to withdraw from the United Nations, which it called a threat to American sovereignty.

The nonbinding resolution, which reportedly passed by a 42-33 vote, favors "freeing the nation from a large financial burden and retaining the nation's sovereignty to decide what is best for the nation and determine what steps it considers appropriate as the leader of the free world in full control of its armed forces and destiny."

Conservative lawmakers in Utah long have warned that the United Nations is plotting to take over the United States and create a world government.[17]

Regrettably the article didn't mention whether the purported plot includes black helicopters. At the outset it is worth noting for beginning students of international relations that the UN does not have any army at all.

243

It would therefore be quite a challenge for it to take over the U.S. (Black helicopters alone don't seem adequate to the task.) As noted elsewhere, when the UN Security Council, on which the U.S. has a permanent seat and a veto, sanctions military action at the insistence of its members, it is then necessary to beg and cajole member nations to provide the troops and police to carry out the action, unless of course the U.S. is leading a coalition as it did during the 1991 Gulf War. In that rare case, troops are virtually guaranteed by the U.S. military. Although U.S. foreign policy is sometimes quite illogical and self-contradictory, it seems unlikely that the U.S. would lead a military coalition against itself. No other country or combination of countries comes within orders of magnitude of having enough power to threaten the United States.

It would be interesting to ask the conservative lawmakers of Utah how the staff of 50,000 UN employees, only a handful of whom are soldiers, would overcome the handicap of a U.S. veto in the Security Council and use their $3 billion annual regular budget (25% of which is supplied by the U.S. when it's in the mood) to take over and run the U.S. These UN "forces," who would have to be mostly bureaucrats wearing business suits, would be attempting to control by military occupation a country thousands of miles across with a population of 280 million people. Or they could try to control the country indirectly through the Federal Government, an organization that runs the country through the work of about two million employees using a budget of $2,400 billion ($2.4 trillion) per year, or 800 times the size of the UN budget. The U.S. spends a total of $400 billion of the U.S. budget on its military establishment, a sum 133 times the size of the UN's budget. It would appear that the UN is a bit underpowered and underfunded for the task of taking over and running the U.S. A mouse may spook an elephant, but it's unlikely that the mouse is going to have the elephant for lunch.

Fortunately most of the American people are wiser than the conservative lawmakers in Utah or the purveyors of black helicopter fantasies. According to the website of the Program on International Policy Attitudes (PIPA), among American citizens "there seems to be little fear that the UN might evolve into a world government that could override US sovereignty. In June 1995, ATIF [Americans Talk Issues Foundation] respondents were presented the argument that "The UN might become a world government and take away our freedom." Seventy-three percent rejected this (58% strongly) with just 17% agreeing (11% strongly).[18]

A related question cast light on whether the public has concerns about the UN being too powerful for the safety of American sovereignty. Over two-thirds of the public supported strengthening the UN. Here's the question and the results: "Overall, do you think that in the long run, efforts to strengthen the U.N. (United Nations) would be a good investment or not a good investment? Good investment 68%; Not a good investment 28%; Don't know 4%"[19] Polls focused on politically conservative congressional districts have shown that the percentages of American citizens supporting the UN in those districts are similar to those in the general population. In view of these numbers, clearly the fears of our politicians about the power and numbers of UN-haters among their constituents are exaggerated, as are the fears of the UN-haters about the power of the UN. So two layers of fear-driven myth-making are motivating the anti-UN politics in the U.S. Congress.

Slightly less paranoid and much more specific than the generalized fantasy of the UN taking over the U.S. is the worry that the UN might be taking over plots of U.S. land. Two UN programs carried out by the UN Educational, Scientific, and Cultural Organization (UNESCO) designate, at the request of UN member nations, certain sites as especially valuable culturally or ecologically. If they meet certain criteria they may become World Heritage Sites or Biosphere Reserves. The purpose is both to honor the country and the site so designated, and to encourage preservation of the sites from activities that would destroy their value. At the request of various past presidents, the U.S. has been honored with the designation of 67 such sites. Extremists have argued that this constitutes surrendering U.S. national sovereignty over the sites.

However, the UN and the U.S. State Department make it clear that the UN's encouraging preservation and providing guidelines on how this might be done does not in any way constitute UN control of these sites. The guidelines are advisory. According to the World Heritage Treaty, a World Heritage Site remains under the sovereignty of the country it is located in. If the host country so requests, sites can become eligible for international aid for restoration. In poverty-stricken countries this has the possibility to be of valuable assistance in preserving such treasures. The biosphere and world heritage programs have no legal authority over the host countries or the sites. A 1999 article in the *Washington Times* reported that the US State Department posted a letter two years before "in response to widespread concern about UN meddling in U.S. affairs." The letter stated the following: "The idea that the United Nations is taking over U.S. lands, private and public, is completely false. Neither the United Nations nor any other international body has any authority" over lands designated as biosphere reserves.[20]

Once the overheated political rhetoric is cleared away, the real issue appears to be the possible designation of lands in one or the other of these two UNESCO programs with the recommendation of the Interior Department and the President, but without the say of local people in the state. The more reasonable of the local opponents of the UN designation apparently were concerned about another layer of bureaucracy interfering with their possible economic exploitation of the land, or with the Interior Department using the designation as an "excuse" to prevent such development. For a time this was a hot-button issue in Alaska. Interior Department officials defused the issue to some extent by agreeing that they would not press the UN to designate sites where the action is opposed by local communities or congressional representatives.[21] In a country as decentralized as the U.S., this solution makes good sense. What does not make good sense is getting into a tizzy over purported threats to national sovereignty from such benign and innocuous activities.

(2) The Real Problems

The UN General Assembly (UNGA) represents almost every nation on the planet, but it is often criticized as nothing but a talk shop. It is designed for debate, discussion and policy formulation, but not for making hard decisions and enforcing them. Some debates on difficult issues go on and on, virtually forever. The UNGA's less important decisions are made by a vote of a majority of members, but important decisions, as determined by a majority vote, require a two-thirds majority. Its decisions are implemented only when member nations collectively or individually choose to implement them. However, talk sometimes leads to agreement and progress, so the UNGA serves a useful if modest purpose. It also serves as a venue for diplomats to talk informally behind the scenes and explore one another's views and their country's views on issues that may or may not be on the UN's formal agenda. Henry Kissinger has said that he found this process extremely valuable.

In size and power, the nations of the General Assembly include giants like Russia, China, India, Brazil, and the U.S., and also tiny Pacific island nations such as Palau, with about 15,000 citizens. Members include democracies and dictatorships and all shades of freedom and coercion in between. And each nation has one vote. Obviously this arrangement is highly undemocratic relative to the "one-person, one-vote" principle. There is one vote in UNGA to represent 1.2 billion Chinese (who are not truly represented at all because their leaders constitute a totally undemocratic oligarchy) and one vote for the 15,000 people of Palau. Of course the smaller nations treasure their votes as indicators that the UNGA is in fact democratic, that the weak have a vote as well as the strong. Clearly this is less than half true; weak nations have a voice, but not the vast numbers of globally powerless individuals in heavily populated countries such as China and India.

In sharp contrast with the UNGA, the UN Security Council has exactly the opposite set of problems. It has the unique global authority and responsibility under international law to authorize military action by its member nations for collective security. However, it has no army and military power of its own; it can only authorize the use of military force by member nations. Its power to authorize force, of course, is no threat to the United States because the U.S. holds a permanent membership and has veto power along with the other permanent members.

Though the Security Council has coercive power, it is far less representative and democratic than the General Assembly. At any given time it represents only fifteen of the UN's 191 member nations, and ten of the fifteen rotate onto and off the Security Council randomly, every two years, by position in the English alphabet. Because of their small numbers, individual non-permanent members can be subject to enormous pressure from more powerful nations when a controversial vote comes before the Council. Five permanent members—the U.S., China, England, France, and Russia—have veto power. The other ten have only a vote, not a veto. The five permanent members (P-5) were the great powers when the UN was established in 1945; they were the winners of World War II. Hardly anyone argues that they are still a legitimate power elite who should hold unique authority under international law. But their position in the structure of the UN makes them powerful enough to block any change that would rob them of their permanence on the Security Council and their veto power. Naturally this situation undermines the legitimacy of the Security Council in world public opinion.

The structure of the Security Council, particularly the veto, often gridlocks the Council and prevents any constructive action. It is one of the great stuck places of international law and institutions. The Security Council is arguably the most important international institution on the planet, and everyone agrees that it needs membership reform, but no one has succeeded in forging agreement on an alternative. Debates and discussions about it go on endlessly and fruitlessly. No one has answers on which everyone, or nearly everyone, can agree.

However, two acute needs are clear. One is equitable expansion of the Security Council's membership, and the other is to find a way to limit the use of the veto to extraordinary circumstances such as refusing to sanction war. Any change in the use of the veto would require an agreement among the Permanent Five on what the circumstances of its use might be. This is an awesomely difficult task, especially when American leaders are in a mood to brush aside the UN, and by implication the whole accumulated body of international law, whenever they please. Various schemes to limit the use of the veto have been proposed, but all of them require goodwill and a cooperative attitude on the part of American leaders as well as the other permanent members.

For all its drawbacks, the Security Council has its uses. In a recent example, when Haiti collapsed in February 2004 and its elected leader, John Bertrand Aristide, was forced out of power, rioting, looting, beatings and killings were rampant. During the run-up to Aristide's ouster the police were forced to hide from armed rebel gangs who outgunned them. The gangs burned down police stations and killed the police in several cities. Some degree of civil order could only be achieved by an outside force. The Security Council unanimously authorized action to move in quickly and restore order. Again the Bush administration *de facto* recognized the legitimacy of the UN in securing the authority not only to go in and move to restore order, but to go in with the participation of other countries, notably France. While the outcome of this intervention cannot be fully predicted, it appears likely to be preferable to the violence and chaos that reigned in the weeks before and the day after Aristide's departure.

Among the most notorious of problems with the UN is the inefficiency and corruption of its administrative arm, the Secretariat, and the politicization of the Secretariat and some of its independent agencies. There is no single solution, no silver bullet, that will solve these problems. Multi-pronged efforts and constant vigilance are partial, but not complete solutions. Administrative reforms such as establishing Inspectors General to conduct investigations and root out corruption are among the ways these problems can be dealt with. Whistle-blower protection is vital.

As with other perennial problems such as high crime rates in America's inner cities and corruption of government at all levels, federal, state and local, these problems are partly endemic to human nature and human institutions and must be constantly battled, despite uneven results. Vigilance is the price of freedom; it is also the price of organizational efficiency and integrity. Success is cause for celebration, followed by continued vigilance;

occasional failure is part of the price of doing business, and cause for renewed effort. Occasional failure is not a justification for the cowardly option—to give up and abandon the program unless program effectiveness is hopelessly compromised or completely destroyed. The struggle between good and evil is eternal, and its manifestations in bureaucracies are not an exception.

The UN has a particularly difficult inherent problem with organizational integrity because of the huge discrepancy in income between its normal employee, who makes a salary comparable with that of a government employee in Europe or the United States, and the far more meager incomes available in less developed countries. Compounding this problem is the tribal social structure in some very poor countries where one person with a decent income becomes a cash cow for an entire community. For local employees in these countries, the incentives and social and economic pressures leading to corruption, cronyism, nepotism, bribery, etc. are overwhelming. Social norms in some cultures may actually favor corruption (as defined in administratively disciplined cultures) as a survival mechanism rather than frowning upon it.

Again, there is no solution but the hard, pedestrian work of disciplined administrative practices—well-ordered accounting and human resource systems with well-designed regulations and procedures, alert supervision, and audits to catch and correct irregularities. By itself, training employees in how to do things properly has no favorable influence on corruption. A well-trained thief is a more skilled thief. Administrative controls combined with reliable monetary incentives supporting integrity and sanctions for lack of it (dismissal of offending employees) must be particularly strong and consistently applied. Developing an organizational culture that appreciates integrity and stigmatizes lack of it may help, but in some environments the cultural context outside the organization is likely to be too strong for a countervailing culture inside to succeed as the dominant shaper of behavior.

Member countries of the UN that value integrity in the use of resources, including Europe as well as the United States and many others, obviously have a special responsibility to create pressures in the UN leading to improvements. However, refusing dues owed to the UN and previously agreed to in principle and holding them hostage until improvements are made constitutes blackmail and going back on one's word. These acts are hardly examples of integrity; they merely reinforce lawlessness and brute force and undermine the cause of integrity. In the future the U.S. should pay its dues in full, on time, and without conditions and should use other, legitimate channels to create pressures for administrative reform.

The UN: What Americans Really Think

As noted above, the American public is sharply divided on the UN. A substantial majority supports it, but a vocal minority vehemently opposes it. An extremely vocal and powerful minority of American politicians, those who are in power in the White House and Congress at the time of this writing early in 2004, seem to fear UN infringement on U.S. freedom of action far more than they value any contribution of the UN to the U.S. and the world. They often express open contempt for the UN. Since they share control of the reins of power, the relationship between the U.S. and the UN is a rocky one. They have inherited the mantle of Senator Jesse Helms, who was one of the nation's most vocal and vehement critics of the UN through much of his long Senate career, but who mellowed slightly in the last year or so.

By contrast with these politicians, American citizens, most of whom support the UN, seem to be at least vaguely aware of historical events such as the Cuban missile crisis, and more importantly they are aware that the United Nations represents something both noble and highly practical. The UN is the embodiment of organized cooperation among nations, including mutually agreed upon legal constraints that all or most nations agree to adhere to, in the context of an over-arching aspiration toward peace, justice, and human rights. These goals and ideals of the UN, despite its obvious institutional flaws, have a strong appeal to most of the world's people, including Americans.

What do polls say Americans think about the UN? A substantial number of scientifically designed polls have tackled this subject down through the years. One organization, the Program on International Policy Attitudes (PIPA), affiliated with the University of Maryland, has done notably comprehensive studies and has reported the results of its own polls and other credible polls on its website. These polls, conducted over two decades by several organizations with different emphases and concerns, provide a strikingly consistent picture. In stark contrast to the noisy hostility toward the UN voiced by extreme right-wing American politicians, a strong majority of the American public views the UN favorably on a remarkable array of issues.

A majority of Americans support the UN and U.S. participation in it and would like to see it stronger. Only a small minority feel that a stronger UN might threaten U.S. national sovereignty. Support for strengthening the UN exists even though most Americans grossly overestimate the magnitude of its activities. The following paragraphs are a summary of PIPA's report on "General Attitudes Towards the UN" reported on their website, "Americans and the World: Public Opinion on International Affairs":[22]

In various polls, an overwhelming majority of Americans has stressed that strengthening the UN should be a foreign policy goal for the US. An October 2001 Pew poll found that 92% believed strengthening the UN should be a foreign policy goal, with 46% saying it should be a top priority and 46% saying it should have some priority.

* * *

In a November 1995 PIPA poll, respondents were first presented a pro argument and then a con argument for strengthening the UN. The pro argument said: "For the US to move away from its role as world policeman and reduce the burden of its large defense budget, the US should invest in efforts to strengthen the UN's ability to deal with potential conflicts in the world." Seventy-three percent agreed and 24% disagreed.

The con argument stressed the potential loss of US sovereignty that might result from a strengthened UN: "Strengthening the UN is not a good idea because if the UN were to become stronger, the US could become entangled in a system that would inhibit it from full freedom of action to pursue its interests." Only 37% agreed, while 57% disagreed.

* * *

Respondents...were also presented four concrete options for strengthening the UN all of which received very strong support. These included:

- Improving UN communication and command facilities- 83% in favor
- Having joint military training exercises- 82% in favor
- Having UN members each commit 1,000 troops to a rapid deployment force that the UN Security Council can call up on short notice- 79% in favor

- Allowing the UN to possess permanent stocks of military equipment stored in different locations around the world- 69% in favor

On the congressional hot-button issue of UN dues, a majority of Americans feel that the U.S. spends too much on the UN until they find out what proportion the U.S. actually pays, what the dues payment formulas are, and how much the U.S. pays relative to other countries. When provided this information, most American citizens find our UN dues appropriate. The initial feeling that we are paying too much is based on misinformation.

The National Sovereignty Disconnect

As noted before, a frequent objection to the UN and related international bodies from conservative politicians and op-ed writers is the feeling that these institutions somehow threaten American national sovereignty. Along with other vague but evocative words like "freedom," "national sovereignty" is seldom defined with any degree of clarity in this kind of discourse. Its main purpose is emotional and rhetorical. Strangely, the extraordinary freedom of action on the international scene bestowed by the reality of disproportionate American power seems not to mitigate these concerns. In fact, America's essentially unlimited power makes any supposed loss of American national sovereignty to the UN or to an international court an impossibility unless the constraint is voluntarily accepted, which of course negates the idea that sovereignty is lost.

Particularly controversial with conservatives are two permanent international courts affiliated with the UN system. One is the International Court of Justice, also called the World Court, an old and venerable institution that adjudicates legal disputes between nations, but has no mandatory authority to enforce its decisions. The other is the new International Criminal Court (ICC), a court of last resort which tries individual suspects accused of war crimes, genocide, or crimes against humanity only in situations where they cannot be tried by national courts. These situations arise either because the country where the crime is committed is a failed state with no viable judicial system or because it has been so corrupted it refuses to hold criminals accountable. (Neither of which is terribly likely to apply to the

U.S.)* Although conservatives view the UN and these courts as threats to national sovereignty, polls show that a majority of Americans are not concerned. Again, a few excerpts from PIPA's web site tell the story. The first is about the UN in general; the others are about the international courts:

> PIPA's April 1995 poll ... found low levels of public concern about the UN impinging on US sovereignty. Respondents were asked to choose between two statements about the power of the UN. Only 36% chose the statement: "I am afraid that things like UN peacekeeping are getting so big that the US is losing control of its foreign policy to the UN, while a 58% majority chose: "I am not afraid that the UN is becoming too powerful. The US has a veto in the UN Security Council and therefore the UN cannot dictate anything to the US."

When Americans are asked concrete questions about the U.S. accepting the jurisdiction of courts that are part of the UN, a majority says the U.S. should accept such jurisdiction. In October 1999, a PIPA question described World Court jurisdiction to respondents as follows:

> The World Court is part of the United Nations. It makes rulings on disputes between countries based on treaties the countries have signed. Some countries have made commitments to accept the decisions of the World Court. Other countries decide in advance for each case whether to accept the court's decisions. Do you think the US should or should not make the commitment to accept the decisions of the World Court?

> A modest majority of 53% thought that the US should make this commitment, while 38% thought the US should not do so.

> A stronger majority supported the US accepting the jurisdiction of the proposed International Criminal Court, even though the argument against doing so was spelled out in the question. Sixty-six percent agreed that "the US should support such a court because the world needs a better way to prosecute war criminals, many of whom go unpunished today."

---

* This court is discussed in much more depth in the chapter, "Above the Law" in this book.

Only 29% said that "the US should not support the proposed Court because trumped up charges may be brought against Americans, for example, US soldiers who use force in the course of a peacekeeping operation."[23]

On the question immediately above, though trumped up charges could be brought against an American soldier, the court is designed to assure that such charges would be dismissed long before going to trial, so there is far less danger to American soldiers than the question suggests. Despite this exaggerated implication of threat, two-thirds of Americans supported the court.

Given the lack of concern on the part of a majority of the American public about any imagined threat to American national sovereignty from the UN and these international courts, there is a clear disconnect between a majority of the American public and conservative American politicians who supposedly represent them and currently run the country. Either the politicians are posing for a narrow constituency, or they are a bit paranoid, or both. Evidently the hostility toward the UN expressed by the current crop of American political leaders is a bubble that cannot last forever. It seems likely that eventually democracy will work its magic and politicians will have to yield to widespread public opinion.

Horrors! UN Taxes?

It's hardly news that there is a strong knee-jerk ideological bias against any and all taxes among conservative politicians in the U.S. They seem to think they are representative of all the American people on the matter. But a surprising result of polling on the UN is the discovery that the American public might well favor certain specific kinds of taxes levied by the UN. This idea has been proposed by a number of prominent economists and political analysts, but the discovery that the public might accept it is almost revolutionary. Not surprisingly, the public did not support the idea of a broad authority for UN taxes in principle. But large majorities of Americans were willing to allow UN taxes in specific circumstances for specific purposes.

For instance, "In a June 1995 poll, ATIF [Americans Talk Issues Foundation] tested the proposal that 'the United Nations should monitor and tax international arms sales with the money going to famine relief and humanitarian aid.' Seventy-two percent of respondents supported the proposal."[24] In a later poll, 72% also supported "a charge on international oil sales dedicated to programs...to protect the world's environment."[25] 71% supported "a charge on international sales of tobacco dedicated to programs to...improve health care."[26] 67% supported a "charge on international arms sales dedicated to keeping peace in regional conflicts."[27] Obviously the pattern that is acceptable to American citizens is to tax a harmful activity and use the money to support an opposite beneficial activity. The combination is powerfully attractive, creating a net benefit to humanity on both the revenue collection side and the expenditure side of the equation. But the surprise is that the public does not object to the concept of the UN doing it.

These are extraordinarily encouraging results for the long-term future of the UN. They point to the possibility of UN programs that could be self-sustaining revenue generators, rather than calling on nation-states that may or may not respond to pay dues from the taxes they collect. However, before such programs could be launched and funded, the world's only superpower would have to stop the demagoguery against the UN and against all taxes, whether beneficial (as taxes on international arms or tobacco sales might be) or harmful. In the current irresponsible political climate, that is a tall order—in fact, it is out of the question.

A Major Step Forward

The single most immediate need in beefing up the UN's capability is peacekeeping that arrives on time and has the muscle to actually work. As illustrated by the sudden explosion of chaos in Haiti in February and March of 2004, when the need arises there is no time for delay. Fortunately for Haiti, it is on the doorstep of the U.S., and the U.S. acted quickly. Although neoconservative thinkers often seem stuck in the rut of seeing the U.S. as the only policeman for the world, one of their number, neoconservative military expert Max Boot, boldly proposes a solution that is not exclusively a call for unilateral U.S. action. He asks, "Isn't it about time we got serious about dealing with failed states? If we did, we would have to devise both national and international remedies."[28] He advocates a number of strengthened peacekeeping and nation-building capacities including a U.S. cabinet agency concerned with nation-building, encouragement of additional regional powers for peacekeeping in "their own back yards" such as Australia in East

Timor, and a strong role for international organizations such as NATO. Then he adds the following regarding the UN:

> It's time to resurrect the idea of a standing U.N. army, as a supplement, if not replacement, for the other forces mentioned above. The key to making it work would be eschewing the old U.N. way of doing things, which consists of asking for military contributions from a lot of countries with minimal capabilities, no record of working together and differing strategic interests. This produces low-quality blue helmets that are the laughingstock of thugs everywhere.
>
> The U.N. needs a tough, professional force like the French Foreign Legion that would not quail before Haitian gang leaders or Serbian ethnic-cleansers. Members of such an outfit would have to be recruited on merit and trained together; it could not be cobbled together at the last minute from the military riffraff of Third World dictatorships. To make it work, the U.N. Department of Peacekeeping Operations would have to beef up its command, intelligence and logistical capabilities. The U.N. would also need to improve its ability to run failed states in a Kosovo-style receivership. [29]

Other conservatives will be horrified, of course, at the idea of a UN "army." A more descriptively accurate term would be a rapidly deployable peacekeeping force (RDF). While it should be tough, well trained and equipped, such a force would not engage in full-fledged combat on one side or the other in a conflict. It should be capable of imposing peace where the people who are temporarily in control are undisciplined gangs of thugs, as in the aftermath of the overthrow of Aristide. And, of course, it should be obvious that such a UN force could and should never come within many orders of magnitude of the military power necessary to confront one of the larger member nations of the UN, least of all the U.S. They would exist to restore order where there is anarchy.

Another closely related and promising proposal has been jointly put forward by Citizens for Global Solutions, a dynamic new organization with a self-explanatory name, and Refugees International. It proposes a standing UN Civilian Police Force (CIVPOL) that could be rapidly deployed to restore order in post-conflict situations when criminal activities like looting contribute greatly to the problems of a failed state. The difference from the preceding proposal is that RDF troops are soldiers, not police. They are trained differently and perform different functions. The U.S. military is reluctant to shift to policing (and is not trained to do it), as the aftermath of the war in Iraq demonstrated. In post-conflict situations police are needed for a range of functions extending from arresting looters to directing traffic. The CIVPOL proposal has attracted enough political interest to become proposed legislation in the U.S. House of Representatives. The *UN Reformer* offers the following details about the proposal:

> A coalition of 47 organizations and notables presented a letter to the House of Representatives this fall calling for support of H.R.1414, the McGovern-Houghton International Rule of Law and Antiterrorism Act of 2003. H.R. 1414 calls for the United States to take a leading role in an effort to create a United Nations Civilian Police Corps. While the actual structure of the body created out of H.R. 1414 is not yet defined, it would be used in international operations to maintain the rule of law and promote peace and security in post-conflict situations.[30]

The *UN Reformer* gives the following explanation:

> Supporters of H.R. 1414 see an improved UN CIVPOL as the best way to address the capacity and time gaps that typify international policing efforts. A professionalized UN police force with common training, procedural and behavioral rules, equipment, and a common command and control structure would alleviate current post-conflict problems. As stated in the organizational sign-on letter, "If an effective and impartial police force had been deployed on the heels of coalition forces the violent looting, destruction, and sabotage that followed coalition military action in Iraq might have been avoided."[31]

Of course, to implement either of the plans briefly outlined above would require either a regime change in Washington or a major collective religious conversion in the White House from worshiping exclusively at the church of American military power to a much more team-oriented approach. This approach would have to admit the value of the contributions of others such as the UN, even if they were independent sources of power, not merely *ad hoc* "coalitions of the willing" controlled by the United States. The adverse consequences of the Iraq war, falling mainly as it does on U.S. shoulders, may provide the motive for such a conversion. As a result of the Iraq war, already the stock of the United Nations is rising and that of unilateral American action is declining.

For Civilization: Is There a Future?

In view of the favorable opinions of the UN held by a majority of American citizens, the contempt for the UN often expressed in word and action by America's current crop of political leaders constitutes a noteworthy and dangerous failure of American democracy. Either our leaders are misinformed about what the American public thinks, and thus accidentally misrepresent their views, or they feel they can safely disregard those views because they are not about "bread and butter" domestic issues that control elections. Either way, our "representative" democracy is in fact unrepresentative. It is failing dismally to reflect the views of our people and is behaving in ways that are opposed to their wishes. If the current American political leadership were replaced or were to change course and represent the American people in strengthening and working through the UN, the world could become a planet with a brighter future.

The UN is not an angel, and certainly not a devil, but an essential and benign stabilizing political, administrative, and legal component in the loose institutional structure of an increasingly integrated world. As is often said, if the UN didn't already exist, we'd have to invent it. The UN has a vast, as-yet partially unfulfilled potential for good and an acute need for substantial reform. It too-often looks bad because most of its accomplishments are invisible, but its mistakes and problems make headlines. Reform can come about only if the world's most powerful nation, the U.S., stops obstructing, insulting, and starving the UN financially and leads a coalition of democracies in bold and creative efforts to make it both more democratic and more effective. In working with other democracies to reform the UN (without the blackmail of withholding its dues), the U.S. could act as a genuine world leader, not as a hyper-powered obstacle to progress, as it often does now. Respectful inclusion of the UN Secretary General as a key figure in reform planning and implementation would be essential. Arrogant, unilateral demands would be fatal.

Without a strengthened and reformed UN system, the numerous critical problems the whole world faces, problems that threaten all humanity, cannot be solved or even mitigated. Nations acting alone cannot possibly solve global problems like terrorism, global warming and the spread of deadly diseases and weapons of mass destruction. The number and severity of these problems assure that it is just a matter of time until one or some combination of them brings all human civilization to its knees, as did two World Wars half a century ago. An American empire, a self-interested *Pax Americana* run for the benefit of American business interests, has no potential to solve these global problems. The American military-industrial empire is already a well-entrenched part of the problem. A reformed, democratic, and effective UN, shaped by an organized coalition of democracies and supported and strengthened by its most powerful member, could serve as an instrument through which the people and the nations of the world tackle urgent global problems and steer the planet toward a sustainable course. No other institution or nation has that potential.

---

[1] http://www.americans-world.org/digest/global_issues/un/un_summary.cfm
[2] Idem.
[3] Lizette Alvarez, "Senate Ends Bitter Dispute With the U.N. on U.S. Dues" *The New York Times*, February 7, 2001
[4] Steven Hollaway, "U.S. Unilateralism at the UN: Why Great Powers Do Not Make Great Multilateralists," *Global Governance*, July/September 2000, Vol. 6, #3, p. 361.
[5] Idem.
[6] Madeleine K. Albright, "United Nations" *Foreign Policy*, September/October, 2003, p. 17.
[7] The UN In Brief: What the UN Does for Peace:
http://www.un.org/Overview/brief2.html
[8] Idem.
[9] "UN Fact Sheet: Setting The Record Straight: Peacekeeping" DPI/1851/Rev.9 -- June 1999
[10] This information is excerpted from the transcript of a talk by Ambassador Jonathan Dean at a local-global forum at Hood College, Frederick, MD, on May 7, 2001
[11] Idem.
[12] Idem.
[13] The UN in Brief: What the UN Does for Humanitarian Assistance
http://www.un.org/Overview/brief4.html
[14] Idem.
[15] The UN In Brief: What the UN Does for Justice, Human Rights, and International Law http://www.un.org/Overview/brief3.html

[16] Black Helicopters! Secrets THEY Don't Want You To Know About! Web address: http://zapatopi.net/blackhelicopters.html
[17] http://washingtontimes.com/world/20040208-105646-6639r.htm
[18] http://www.americans-world.org/digest/global_issues/un/un_summary.cfm
Organization: Market Strategies/Greenberg Research/ Americans Talk Issues
Foundation; Sample Size: approx. 500. Date: JUN 21-28, 1995
[19] This polling information was reported on the same web site,
http://www.americans-world.org/digest/global_issues/un/un_summary.cfm. PIPA
conducted the poll. The sample size was approximately 600
[20] Sean Scully, *Washington Times*, February 26, 1999 as quoted in the UN Wire, an
internet wire service.
[21] David Whitney, *Anchorage Daily News*, October 1, 1999 as reported in the UN
Wire
[22] http://www.americans-world.org/digest/global_issues/un/un_summary.cfm
[23] Idem.
[24] Idem.
[25] Idem.
[26] Idem.
[27] Idem.
[28] Max Boot, "Shouldering the Load, and the Rifle" *Los Angeles Times*, February 26,
2004.
[29] Idem.
[30] "Addressing the Need for Civilian Police," *UN Reformer,* Fall 2003 Issue.
[31] Ibid.

Chapter Ten

AN UNNECESSARY WAR

Throughout the globe the United States is becoming associated with the unjustified use of force. The president's disregard for the views in other nations, borne out by his neglect of public diplomacy, is giving birth to an anti-American century.

—John H. Brown, Foreign Service officer resigning in protest against plans for the Iraq war.

Our nation now finds itself on the verge of initiating war against another sovereign nation. We have not been attacked by Iraq, and we have thus far failed to produce convincing evidence that Iraq has aided, or plans to aid, those who have attacked us. If we go to war, we will be the initiators of aggression.

—Talbot Brewer

The horror of September 11, 2001 with its images of the World Trade Center towers collapsing amid clouds of smoke and the Pentagon in flames brought in its wake a worldwide outpouring of sympathy for the United States. Newspaper headlines throughout the world reflected this feeling. The French shared in it as displayed by the headline in Le Monde: "We Are All Americans." Americans and the rest of the world as well soon realized we had been thrust into a new kind of war, an all-out war against international terrorism. The bombings of two U.S. embassies in Africa, the barracks of American troops in Saudi Arabia, and the battleship U.S.S. Cole in the

Yemeni harbor of Aden did not fully wake us up, but the devastation to the World Trade Center and the Pentagon did in spades.

President Bush galvanized a shaken and traumatized nation and led the way with a patient and determined response to the challenge. His approval ratings in polls went through the roof and stayed high for months. Everyone understood that the war on terrorism, whether conceived as a metaphorical war or a literal one (it was actually a little of both), was a real and necessary response. America's allies understood this necessity as well and supported the U.S. and their own security interests by aggressive police work and by sharing intelligence on terrorism-related activities within their borders.

However, one ominous note was a harbinger of problems to come. President Bush announced to other countries a hard-line policy: you're either with us or against us. The eminently sensible purpose, of course, was to muscle ambivalent countries into siding with the U.S. against terrorism. But the unilateral demands and the artificial clarity were not sustainable, and the bullying left resentments. The hijackers were from Saudi Arabia, and some terrorism was known to be supported by the Saudi royal family (though not the government) but as old allies and suppliers of oil to the U.S., the Saudis got a pass. On the other hand, Saddam Hussein, who was in no way involved in 9/11 and had no significant ties with al Qaeda, was immediately mentioned as a potential target. A scapegoat was in the making. Ironically, the irrational rhetoric and the bullying were labeled "moral clarity." However, they did have some of the desired effects.

Even the officials of Yemen, despite its conservative Muslim culture, allowed the U.S. government one of its bolder moves. The CIA fired a missile from an unmanned Predator spy plane to annihilate a carload of alleged terrorists within Yemen's borders. One of the alleged terrorists turned out to be an American citizen. Certainly one could and probably should question the legality of this action. Was it murder? Self-defense? An act of war? If so, war against which nation? In the political arena these kinds of questions were raised with an attitude of thoughtful inquiry, not for the most part with outrage or condemnation. The nature of war itself had changed. The rules of engagement had not caught up with the reality. The enemy was a shadowy trans-national entity. Legal and moral questions aside, the Yemini government's cooperation in this action, taken within its own borders, was indicative of a major change in the world—a tilt toward widespread acquiescence to the demands of the U.S.—at least in the new war on terror.

Another conservative Muslim country, Pakistan, previously ambivalent about terrorism and about alliance with the U.S., openly sided with the U.S.

in the effort to uproot terrorism by Islamist terror groups. Of course, Pakistan received a substantive bonus. The U.S. lifted sanctions it had applied in reaction to Pakistan's development and testing of nuclear weapons. Whether in the long term this will prove to be a beneficial tradeoff remains to be seen.

Investigations revealed that Saudi millionaire Osama bin Laden and his organization were behind the September 11 attack. Gradually it became clear to the American public and the world that bin Laden and al Qaeda were inseparably linked to the brutal rulers of Afghanistan, the Taliban. The American public strongly supported a war in which the U.S., working closely with the Afghan Northern Alliance, overthrew the Taliban and drove al Qaeda and much of the Taliban out of Afghanistan.

There was little global dissent toward this action except from the extreme right wing of the Muslim faith and the extreme, essentially pacifist political left in the U.S. and Europe. President Bush was on a roll. However, two major problems showed their ugly heads as the Afghan war wound down. One was that Osama bin Laden and Mullah Omar, the leader of the Taliban, had slipped the noose and had not been captured or killed. The other was that al Qaeda, while hurt, was alive and active in other countries, and still present, though underground, in Afghanistan. Clearly these facts were an embarrassment to the U.S. military and the Bush administration. In public statements, Bush ceased to mention bin Laden, though he and his organization were clearly still a threat. Wags began to refer to the terrorist-millionaire as "Osama been forgotten." Obviously the forgetting was politically calculated. To continue to look successful in spite of this inconclusive result, Bush needed a distraction or a dramatic next phase in the war against terrorism.

A Year Later

Fast forward a year and a quarter from September 11, 2001 to January 2003. At this time, the U.S. was in the late stages of war preparations against Saddam Hussein. Despite the absence of any specific provocation by Iraq or any solid evidence linking Saddam September 11 or al Qaeda, President Bush had been announcing regularly that he would launch an attack on Iraq, with or without a UN mandate. If the UN did not support the attack, it was irrelevant. Yet there was not even an imminent threat from Iraq, let alone an attack on the United States. President Bush, sounding for all the world like a petulant child, had been snarling that he was "sick and tired" of Saddam's concealments, lies and deceptions about weapons of mass destruction.

Evidently the simple truth—that Saddam might actually no longer have them—never occurred to him or his advisors. Also Bush had been claiming that Saddam was involved with al Qaeda, even though both the CIA and the FBI had discredited the thin thread of evidence for this assertion.

Based on a great deal of rhetoric and small amount of ambiguous intelligence evidence, Bush claimed Saddam to be in "material breach" of UN Security Council Resolution 1441 requiring inspections and calling for Iraq to disarm itself. Therefore, Bush reasoned, use of force to disarm him was justified. Bush was calling up reserves and sending scores of thousands of American troops to the Middle East. Perhaps most importantly, he was repeatedly threatening to form a "coalition of the willing" to attack Iraq in the absence of an explicit UN Security Council sanction.

This threat demonstrated more than just a blithe willingness by the Bush administration to dismiss or ignore international law. The U.S. Constitution states that treaties are the law of the land. Treaties thus carry as much legal weight as any law passed by Congress and signed by the President. The UN Charter is a treaty the U.S. has signed and ratified. And the UN Charter allows countries to attack other countries only in reaction to an attack, in response to an imminent threat, or under the authority of a Security Council Resolution for the sake of global security. For the U.S. to attack another nation without one of these three circumstances is thus clearly illegal both under international law and under the U.S. Constitution. Stated bluntly, such an act is legally unjustified aggression.

In the run-up to the U.S. war on Iraq, it became increasingly evident that Iraq, though led by a deeply evil and dangerous man, one of the world's worst thugs, constituted no imminent threat to the U.S. He had not attacked the U.S. or anyone else in 12 years. Evidence of his weapons of mass destruction was conspicuously missing. So the only legal approach to disarm Saddam by force was to go through the Security Council. The American public overwhelmingly supported this approach. Only thirty percent of Americans felt that Security Council support was not needed. For reasons more related to military and diplomatic strategy than to moral or legal principle or public support, Colin Powell persuaded George W. Bush to give the UN a whirl before attacking Iraq.

Preventive Attacks: Religion, History, and Pop Culture

The moral case for opposing the war was every bit as strong as the legal case. The war won all-but-unanimous objections from church organizations as well as philosophers specializing in ethics.

No one disputed the assertion that Saddam was a notably evil person, nor that Iraq had been in material breach of Security Council resolutions. However, these facts were not enough to convince people concerned with ethics that launching an attack on Iraq, i.e., starting a major international war, was the right thing to do, absent an attack or imminent threat of attack on the U.S. Bush's stance, an extraordinarily aggressive one for an American President toward another country and its leader, was naturally the subject of a great deal of discussion in circles where ethics are matters of special concern, such as American and worldwide church organizations. I'm including below a sample of reactions reported in the press.

U.S. Roman Catholic bishops raised serious moral doubts about the U.S. going to war with Iraq. A November 14, 2002 *Washington Post* article states, "By a vote of 228 to 14 with three abstentions, the bishops endorsed a statement declaring that they 'find it difficult to justify the resort to war against Iraq, lacking clear and adequate evidence of an imminent attack of a grave nature.' The hierarchy said it is 'deeply concerned' about the use of preventive wars 'to overthrow threatening regimes or to deal with weapons of mass destruction.'" Later the Pope himself visited Mr. Bush and expressed his strong ethical and moral objections to the war.

The Catholic bishops were far from unique among Christian religious leaders in their opinion on this subject. Earlier, on September 29th, Henry Brinton, pastor of the Fairfax Presbyterian Church, ran an article, "Can Christians Back This War?", in the *Washington Post's* Outlook section. The article addressed the reactions of other Christian churches to Bush's announced plans.

Here are a few of the more telling observations from that article: "The contrast between President Bush, who is working to drum up support for the war, and Christian leaders from around the globe, who are taking strong stands against it, is quite stark"; "One hundred Christian ethicists from more than 50 schools have signed a petition saying that the president has failed to make a compelling moral case for a preemptive war"; and "At a recent World Council of Churches central committee meeting, 37 church leaders signed a statement urging restraint. And the general secretary of the Middle East Council of Churches, Riad Jarjour, Pope John Paul II and the Archbishop of

Canterbury-designate Rowan Williams all have spoken against resorting to war. For a worldwide Christian church that rarely agrees on anything, this is quite a consensus."

The same article goes on to point out, "One of the criteria of the centuries-old Christian doctrine of a 'just war' is that all possibilities of peace have been exhausted. There is still much that can be done internationally to bring about Iraqi compliance with all U.N. resolutions and to move vigorously to eliminate all weapons of mass destruction."

Not only did organized religion speak out, but press articles also cited American traditions against "shooting first" in American history and even in popular media such as cowboy and western movies. On November 19, 2002 Ken Ringle wrote an article in the *Washington Post* titled, "Duel With Tradition: American Popular Culture Upholds the Notion That We Never Draw First." Love Bush or hate him, Ringle says, "One seldom-discussed aspect of his proposed preemptive strike against Iraq is beyond dispute: It is sharply at odds with this nation's historical image of itself. On the world stage or the silver screen, we have always told ourselves, Americans don't shoot first."

Ringle goes on to illustrate the point profusely from both American history and American movies, where the heroes often take great risks to avoid shooting first. He also acknowledges a very few exceptions, usually accompanied by murky circumstances such as the Gulf of Tonkin incident. He concludes with observations from David Hackett Fischer, author of *Paul Revere's Ride*, and Warren Professor of History at Brandeis University: "It [the American reluctance to shoot first] does not spring from pacifism. Rather from the notion of morality that something done for the right reason must also be done in the right way. *It has been our collective judgement as a nation that something as immensely serious as war should only be embarked on for very clearly defensive reasons. And our culture tells us we depart from that judgment at our peril.*"

Inspectors Return to Iraq

UN Secretary General Kofi Annan made the moral and legal argument on the war that must have been uppermost in the minds of many of the world's leaders. In a speech on February 8, 2003 at William and Mary College he warned that when states decide to use force, not in self-defense but to deal with broader threats to international peace and security, there is no substitute for the unique legitimacy provided by the United Nations

Security Council. He added that the UN is not a separate or alien entity seeking to impose its agenda on others, but rather it is us—you and me. Stated more precisely, it is the crystallized collective will of its member nations.

Fortunately, Secretary of State Colin Powell had earlier seen the advisability of working through the UN and had persuaded President Bush to go that route. In a diplomatic tour-de-force of persuasion and arm-twisting, Powell had secured a unanimous Security Council resolution, 1441, giving Iraq one last chance to accept inspections and to disarm. A material breach of this resolution would leave Iraq subject to "serious consequences," a diplomatically coded term for war. In order to achieve this unanimous vote and to sell Resolution 1441 to the members of the Security Council, Powell had to assure the members that it did not constitute an "automatic" basis for attacking Iraq. Security Council members were assured that the U.S. and England would request a final resolution if it became clear that Iraq was in material breach. On this basis, and this basis alone, the resolution passed unanimously.

Saddam saw the handwriting on the wall and acquiesced. Inspectors were sent in. Surprisingly, Iraq did not block their access to any sites they wished to inspect. The CIA provided the inspectors with information on about one hundred top priority sites where they were most likely to find weapons of mass destruction. What the inspectors found, by and large, were tumble-down ruins. None of the hundred sites contained weapons of mass destruction. The more the inspectors looked, the more they found nothing, or very little. Either Iraq no longer had such weapons, just as it claimed, or it was doing an outstanding job of hiding them. The Bush administration's bellicose rhetoric about these weapons was looking less and less credible. Anti-war sentiment was growing.

According to President Bush, the UN inspection process to search for weapons of mass destruction was leading nowhere. If Saddam did not come clean and voluntarily reveal his hidden weapons of mass destruction, the U.S. will use force to disarm Iraq, with or without an additional Security Council resolution authorizing such action. By clear implication, the inspections need not continue even though they had just begun. According to Bush, enough evidence had accumulated. However, the "evidence" presented at this stage by the Bush administration seemed long on rhetoric and short on facts. Few leaders other than England's Prime Minister, Tony Blair, found the evidence and logic conclusive or persuasive enough to be a cause for war.

Worldwide Anger

A number of American leaders, including well-known journalists, attended a prestigious World Economic Forum in Davos, Switzerland in January 2003. At this time the U.S. was in the late stages of war preparations against Saddam Hussein. The inspectors had found no weapons of mass destruction and had encountered no opposition to their work from Saddam, but Bush was beating the war drums ever-louder. According to attendees at the forum, one of the speakers commented that America was alienating everyone. One solid minute of applause followed this statement. Clearly it was not an isolated sentiment. American journalists such as Richard Cohen and political leaders such as Senator Joseph Biden who attended the forum reported the same intense anti-American feeling implied by the long round of applause. They reported that the official theme of the forum was restoring trust. But the real theme, as Cohen put it in an op-ed piece, was "bashing America." Hardly equivalent to restoring trust. Clearly trust in the U.S. had been seriously damaged, the positive feelings about the U.S. that prevailed after September 11 destroyed. Cohen, backed by other Americans attending the forum, commented on the intensity of anti-American feeling: "In all my years of coming here I have never seen anything like it."[1]

Shockingly, not only at Davos but also across the world a substantial and respectable segment of opinion outside the U.S. in January 2003 held that the U.S. and George W. Bush were the greatest threat to world peace, not Saddam Hussein. American ambassadors around the world were sending cables to the State Department saying this was now the prevailing view in the countries in which they were posted. This view was becoming mainstream, not radical. In two countries, Japan and Germany, candidates in elections for prime minister won elections not by running against their domestic opponents but by running against George Bush's Iraq policy. The contrast with the empathy for the U.S. a year earlier could hardly have been more stark. In one year the world went from a peak of pro-American feeling to a peak of anti-American feeling, or at least, anti-Bush feeling. A priceless resource of overwhelming global public support for the U.S. had been squandered in a single year.

This change of global attitude toward America was accomplished primarily by President Bush's bellicose rhetoric, his dismissive attitude to the UN, and his war preparations against Iraq in conjunction with both his failure to present evidence to back up his claims and the fact that the inspections had just begun. Clearly the inspections had not had time to unearth the information for which they were sent. They were understood by all to be coercive; no one expected that Saddam would disarm willingly. The world did not fail to notice that the inspections Bush had pushed fiercely to establish had barely started before he was asserting that they had failed and war was the only option. Understandably, people weren't buying it. War was not the only option.

During the same month, January 2003, hundreds of thousands of American citizens of all walks of life and political persuasions marched in cities all over the country to protest the coming war. These were not long-haired, wild-eyed hippies, but balding fathers and grandparents and children and soccer moms. The crowds looked like, and indeed were, middle America. The scene was reminiscent of the peak of anti-war feeling during the Vietnam era. Yet this war had not yet started. Support for the war had declined in the polls and few Americans, even among those who supported it because they trusted Bush, were willing to say that he had made an adequate case for it.

Bush was stating emphatically that he would go ahead with or without the UN. By contrast, a majority of Americans felt that the U.S. should seek a UN Security Council resolution sanctioning the war before going ahead, and should not go ahead unilaterally. Major religious organizations such as the National Council of Churches condemned the war as both morally and legally unjustified. Religious as well as secular organizations mounted huge anti-war protests. I remember walking miles along Wisconsin and Connecticut Avenues in Washington DC alongside senior Episcopalian clergy in their clerical robes. These were hardly wild-eyed hippies. Hundreds of thousands of people marched in cities in the U.S. and all over the world. There were demonstrations against the war in 660 cities worldwide, and polls indicated that a majority of people in all countries in the world except Israel and the U.S. were against the war.

Painted into a Corner

Two op-ed pieces written during this period, set side by side, lead to disturbing conclusions about the run-up to the Iraq war. On January 24, 2004 in *The Washington Post*, Charles Krauthammer argued compellingly that there was no turning back politically at that time from Bush's march to war; the stakes in terms of U.S. credibility were too great. The unstated background of his conclusion was the huge numbers of American troops being mobilized and sent to the area combined with Bush's war rhetoric, which had escalated into a virtual declaration of war. Despite Krauthammer's usual exaggeration and bellicosity, he made a convincing case that backing off would be devastating to American credibility, especially with its enemies. Even from my perspective of skepticism about the need for the war, I had to acknowledge that Bush had painted himself and the U.S. into a political corner from which there was no escape without a serious loss of credibility.

Also in The Washington Post, four days after Krauthammer's article, Jessica Matthews, President of the Carnegie Institute for International Peace, argued persuasively on substantive grounds (rather than face-saving political grounds) that war was not necessary. As she stated, "Two supreme questions still demand convincing answers: 'Why war?' and 'Why now?' The reasons that have been offered collapse under scrutiny."[2]

On the "Why now?" question, she argued that Saddam was contained and he knew that if he were to attack another country he would be instantly overwhelmed. Further, the inspections made it impossible for him to further develop weapons of mass destruction without detection. Though she didn't mention this, the containment of his weapons development efforts was especially decisive in the area of nuclear weapons. The inspectors were firm that he did not have such weapons and was not close to developing them. The impossibility of hiding radioactivity in combination with sophisticated monitoring technology gave them confidence that this was the case.

Matthews noted that the administration's answer to "Why war?" was that Saddam has failed to voluntarily disarm, and she reiterated, "Who expected that he would?" "The inspections were never envisioned as an exercise in voluntary surrender. They were undertaken as an attempt at forcibly coerced disarmament just short of war, under conditions much tougher and more invasive of Iraqi sovereignty than anything previously attempted." She continued, "Regarding the timing, a study released this week by the Carnegie Endowment for International Peace reveals that far from being 'exhausted,' as Defense Secretary Donald Rumsfeld described it, the inspection process has barely begun."[3]

Matthews went on to document this claim thoroughly, based on the Carnegie Institute's study. She pointed out that a six-month to two-year time frame is the range every expert and every study cited as necessary for the inspections. The team had received its first bits of American intelligence only three weeks before, and much was still being held back. The first helicopter flight had been carried out only about three weeks before. The inspection teams were not yet at full strength. Overhead surveillance by U-2 spy planes had not yet begun. A war at this stage would make sense only if the goal was not to disarm Hussein but to depose him. If this was the only goal from the outset, then the U.S. was clearly negotiating in bad faith with the UN Security Council when it pushed for Resolution 1441 establishing the inspections regime in the first place. She concluded that a war begun at this time, regardless of the outcome, would bear one of history's harshest judgements, an unnecessary war.[4]

Combining the compelling arguments from both these analyses, we arrive at an unsettling conclusion. The Bush administration had at this stage gone out on a limb and created circumstances in which there was no real political and military alternative but to engage in an unnecessary war that should not have happened before the inspections were given time to accomplish their purpose, if then. Granted, a credible threat of force was necessary to get the inspections started. But to substantiate or disprove violations anywhere near severe enough to justify a necessity for war, the inspectors needed to explore far more deeply the extent to which Iraq had destroyed its chemical and biological weapons or allowed them to deteriorate past usability, as it claimed. No one was arguing that Iraq had the means to launch an effective attack against the U.S. homeland using its chemical or biological agents, if it still had them. The evidence argued strongly that it did not have such a capability.

On the subject of nuclear weapons, the situation was even worse for the Bush administration's credibility. In his State of the Union Address on January 29, 2003, Bush talked about "evidence" that Iraq had a nuclear program. The evidence included Iraqi acquisition of hardened aluminum tubes supposedly to be used as centrifuges in refining uranium. Bush also cited alleged Iraqi efforts to acquire uranium from a source in Niger. Both these allegations had surfaced earlier and had already been challenged by the inspection team report of the head of the International Atomic Energy Agency (IAEA), Mohamed ElBaradei and by other experts.

ElBaradei reported that indeed, as claimed by Iraq, the hardened aluminum tubes were designed for use in conventional rockets and were not capable of use in uranium refinement without significant and costly adaptation. There was no evidence that the Iraqis were engaged in such adaptation. On the contrary, there was evidence that the tubes were being used in rocket engines. Five weeks later, in March, ElBaradei reported that the repeated upgrades in the strength of the tubes was shown to be a necessity driven by failures of weaker cylinders in tests of the rockets in which they were used. This point destroyed a critical argument for American analysts who claimed that the increased strength of the tubes could only be for their use in refining uranium.

Even more troubling is information that came out in early March, that Colin Powell's staff had been briefed about the real use of the strengthened tubes before his famous speech to the Security Council. A key argument for the existence of an Iraqi nuclear program had been destroyed and his staff was aware of it, but the argument was still used in his speech. The Institute for Science and International Security, a Washington-based research organization specializing in nuclear issues reported, "Despite being presented with the falseness of this claim, the administration persists in making misleading arguments about the significance of the tubes." Joby Warrick's article in the March 8 *Washington Post* covering this information also quoted a senior State Department official as saying, "It is not time to close the books on these tubes." His reasoning: Iraq was prohibited from importing sensitive parts, such as the tubes, regardless of their planned use. For this technicality we start a war?

Conclusion: This kind of legalistic hair-splitting provided a key basis for starting a war that would cost thousands of human lives and destroy the economic infrastructure of a country. The thought is simply mind-boggling. With evidence and logic like this behind American leaders' actions, is it any wonder that other countries objected?

In January, ElBaradei also reported that the nuclear inspection team, despite reasonable efforts, was unable to corroborate the allegation that Iraq had attempted to acquire uranium from Niger. Five weeks later, in the same report that annihilated the aluminum tubes as an argument, he dropped an even bigger bombshell. He announced that the documents that supposedly had shown Iraqi officials trying to acquire uranium from Niger were transparent forgeries. The faked evidence, the series of letters between Iraqi agents and officials in Niger, contained crude errors such as names and titles that did not match up with the individuals who held office at the time when they were supposedly written.

Later news reports revealed just how crude these errors were. One of the documents, dated in 2000 and supposedly signed by Niger's president, stated that the proposed uranium purchase was authorized by the country's constitution of 1965. However, Niger had established a new constitution in 1999. Had the president forgotten about the new constitution after only one year? Furthermore, the signature on the letter did not in any way resemble his signature. Another letter was signed by a purported foreign minister of Niger who had left the job ten years before. The letterhead of this purported 1999 document belonged to Niger's military government that had been replaced earlier in the same year. In short, the errors in the faked documents were gross and obvious in the extreme.

A key part of the business of intelligence agencies is to check and cross-check facts to see if they corroborate one another; if they can be relied upon. This is not a sophisticated level of operation, but rather Introductory Intelligence 101. Yet both British intelligence, said to have supplied the documents to the U.S., and U.S. intelligence agents who apparently in good faith supplied it to the inspection team and to the State Department, had failed to catch obvious factual errors that conclusively discredited the information. As with the aluminum tubes, one wonders how a blunder so gross could have happened with information so critical, information presented to the whole world in a speech in the United Nations by the American Secretary of State and used as a key element in the rationale leading to war.

In an attempt to provide evidence of nuclear weapons program activity in Iraq, Bush had stated in an October 2002 speech that satellite photos showed that Iraq was rebuilding facilities where it had nuclear activities in the past. However, ElBaradei's report decisively ruled out these buildings as evidence of such a program. He said that the inspection team's visits to these sites had discovered that equipment and labs at these locations had deteriorated to such an extent that resumption of nuclear activities would require substantial renovation. Such renovation was not under way.

ElBaradei's report to the UN on March 7 stated that an extensive sweep of Iraq using advanced radiation detection had revealed no indication of nuclear weapons activities. Evidently history had been left behind. In the 1970s and 80s Saddam had worked intensively on developing nuclear weapons. But in the 1991 Gulf War, allied bombing extensively damaged his nuclear facilities. ElBaradei reported in January that the previous UN inspections, before they were discontinued, had eliminated the entire Iraqi nuclear weapons program at the time. The discrepancy between U.S. intelligence and the inspectors' findings on the ground shows no bad faith on the part of the Bush administration in its use of satellite intelligence information. However, it does show that there is no substitute for the inspections on the ground for ascertaining what is really going on in Iraq or elsewhere. Satellite photos provide only hints worth exploring. Inspections are needed to do the exploring.

In short, the vaunted U.S. intelligence evidence for Iraqi nuclear activity vanished under scrutiny as the inspections progressed. Significantly, the facts being unearthed by the inspections were undermining the U.S. case for war.

Mark Phillips, a journalist covering Iraq for CBS news, interviewed the inspectors on the ground in Iraq on the subject of the U.S. intelligence provided to the inspection team. In a television newscast he reported disturbing comments by the inspectors on the value of the intelligence provided by the U.S. The inspectors, speaking off the record, were saying that the intelligence in every case was outdated or just plain wrong. It had led to no discoveries and in every case was discredited by the team's on-the-ground findings. According to the inspectors who were in a position to verify the oft-cited intelligence provided by the U.S., the key factual foundation for Bush's case for attacking Iraq, was "garbage after garbage after garbage." Phillips added that the quote had been cleaned up. The inspectors expressed deep frustration at the failure of the American intelligence to add any value to their efforts.

Given that Bush was out on a limb militarily and well beyond the point of no return politically, it is no wonder he was advocating cutting the inspections short by starting the war in weeks rather than months. Not only was desert heat looming in the near future, prospectively making an attack more difficult, but the inspections were working against him in the PR war with Saddam by undermining his claims about Iraqi weapons of mass destruction. Bush's childish petulance in saying that he was "sick and tired" of Saddam's concealments and deceptions takes on added meaning in this context. When people run out of reasons, they begin to snarl and shout.

At this stage, even before the devastating findings of ElBaradei reported on March 3, world public opinion was deeply skeptical of the need for war. So was about half the American public, despite being bombarded by pro-war propaganda from a still-trusted and respected leader. What about the foreign policy experts? What did people think who were deeply informed and thus in a position to think for themselves? These are the people who are not dependent for their opinions on presidential speeches and rhetoric. "Leslie Gelb, president of the Council on Foreign Relations, said there was 'much more skepticism than support' for the administration's Iraq policies among the 4,000 or so members of the nation's most elite foreign policy think tank and debating club. He noted that his own views were more pro-administration on Iraq than those of most council members."[5]

According to Gelb, council members were asking such questions as "Why invade Iraq now?", "What's wrong with containment?", "Where is the hard evidence that Hussein has weapons of mass destruction?", and "What are we doing to plan for the day after an invasion?" He said he was hearing these concerns from Republicans as well as Democrats, including Capitol Hill staffers.[6]

Other major foreign policy and military figures who weighed in publicly with concern and skepticism about the war, to mention a few, included retired General Norman Schwartzkopf, the general who led the U.S. forces in the first Gulf War in 1991; Anthony Lake, former National Security Advisor; retired General Brent Scowcroft, former National Security Advisor to George H.W. Bush; retired General Anthony Zinni, former commander of the U.S. Central Command, which includes Iraq and the Middle East; retired General William E. Odom, another former director of the National Security Agency; and Edward Peck, former U.S. Ambassador to Iraq. These are not people to be dismissed lightly as peaceniks or sissies, or dupes of Iraqi lies and rhetoric.

Op-ed pieces written by neoconservative pundits ridiculed the anti-war demonstrations, but the skepticism about the need for war was mainstream and respectable, and not confined to wild-eyed left-wingers. One might ask, why are so many senior officials in this group of generals and ambassadors retired? The answer is thought-provoking. Though many experts inside the government were said to be against the war by Gelb and others, none of them was in a position to challenge the President in public. To do so would be insubordination, punishable by dismissal at the very least. Among high-level public figures in foreign affairs and the military, only the retired were in a position to speak out.

John Mearsheimer, a foreign policy expert at the University of Chicago, stated that he found abundant support among university foreign policy experts for a statement declaring that it was against the U.S. national interest to go to war with Iraq. Furthermore, he said he was amazed at how much support there was for his position in the military, the intelligence community, and the State Department: "Most people agree that the war on terrorism is more important than a war with Iraq. In order to win the war on terrorism, we must work hand in glove with our allies, but Iraq is driving us apart."[7]

Colin Powell Weighs In

On February 5, 2003, Secretary of State Colin Powell, formerly the Bush administration's foremost (and maybe only) "dove" and one of America's most distinguished generals, gave his famous speech to the UN Security

Council. His credibility was sky-high; he recently had pulled off the remarkable feat of securing unanimous approval of Security Council Resolution 1441. This resolution called for UN inspectors tasked with finding and destroying his weapons of mass destruction and other prohibited weapons in Iraq and "serious consequences" for Saddam if he failed to cooperate with the inspectors.

The issue now, on February 5, was whether the inspections had gone on long enough (though they had barely begun) and Iraq could be declared in "material breach" of Resolution 1441, allowing President Bush's war to topple Saddam to begin. Bush's rhetoric against Saddam had been strident, but little evidence of his weapons of mass destruction or his connections with terrorism, particularly al Qaeda, had been presented. The world was becoming tired of rhetoric without evidence. Even a long-suffering American public, straining to give their President the benefit of the doubt, felt that the case had not been made.

In his speech, Powell detailed U.S. intelligence evidence that had just been declassified for the purpose of his talk. It appeared to show deliberate deception and concealment of weapons of mass destruction by the Iraqi regime. Finally, concrete information about Saddam's concealment of weapons of mass destruction was on the table. Powell made a persuasive case that Iraq had a massive capability, especially in the areas of biological and chemical weapons, and was in "material breach" of Security Council Resolution 1441. He presented modest but seemingly convincing evidence that Iraq had an ongoing nuclear weapons program. He also made a case, somewhat less compelling, that Iraq had ties with al Qaeda, and argued that Iraq was providing al Qaeda with technical assistance with poisons in its terrorist activities. He called on his listeners to "imagine" what would happen if Iraq provided al Qaeda with nuclear weapons. Facts, imagination and fear—a winning combination. His speech was a huge success.

Particularly telling were drawings he dramatically presented based on eyewitness accounts of chemical weapons laboratories on trucks that could be moved around the country, making detection by the inspectors all but impossible. Also telling was evidence through intercepted telephone conversations and satellite photos appearing to show Iraqi quick cleanups just days or hours before the inspectors arrived. The evidence appeared persuasive that Iraqi intelligence had penetrated the plans of the inspectors, anticipated their moves, and hidden evidence just before they arrived.

So impressive was Powell's display of U.S. intelligence on Saddam's activities that a question arose in the minds of some analysts: if we have this kind of detailed intelligence on his activities, how could Saddam get away with plans to launch a surprise attack? The speech made it appear that the U.S. is able to watch his military's every move from space, and even to intercept incriminating phone conversations between Iraqi leaders. Some expert commentators noted that the availability of this kind of intelligence could just as easily have been used as an argument to support containment rather than war.

France, China and Russia followed Powell's talk immediately with speeches of their own that had obviously been written before they'd heard his. They stuck with their insistence that the inspections be allowed to continue. Suddenly, the permanent Security Council members who had previously looked reasonable and peace-loving by advocating continued inspections were the ones looking unreasonable and recalcitrant. They had sought more evidence in the face of noisy Bush administration war rhetoric. Now they were up against seemingly persuasive information, but were not changing their positions. For the moment, at least, the tables seemed to be turned. It was the hawks' great moment. Yet strangely, the boost in American public support for Bush's war plans was modest, up from 57% to 60%. 40% of the American public remained unconvinced of the need for war. And a significant fraction of that percentage was passionate enough about it to get massively organized for protests and march in sub-freezing weather. Also, about half of the sixty percent who supported the war did so conditionally based on support from the UN. This was no public opinion slam-dunk.

Lost in the excitement about all the newly presented and disturbing intelligence were the two supreme questions raised by Jessica Mathews: Why war and why now? These fundamental questions still cried out for answers. It was still clear that Saddam was profoundly evil and it now appeared that he was involved in chemical and biological weapons. Nevertheless, he was still contained and still a relatively minor regional threat. The link to terrorists, particularly al Qaeda, sounded strong in Powell's speech, but serious and respected analysts debunked it. Articles following up on Powell's speech stated that the British intelligence service flatly denied such a connection.

Further, it was crystal clear that Saddam had no nuclear weapons, no way to deliver them long-distance if he had them, and he could not develop them without the world knowing and taking action. Most importantly, he had demonstrated for 12 years that he was a survivor who would not commit suicide by using his deadliest weapons unless he was attacked. Even the CIA explicitly acknowledged this. By contrast, North Korea had nuclear weapons and a fast-growing capability to produce more. It had multi-stage rockets for use as delivery systems. And it was being ignored by the Bush administration. North Korea, the Bush administration insisted, could be contained and dealt with by diplomacy. But the diplomacy wasn't happening. The double standard was dramatic.

With her usual wit, noted columnist Mary McGrory commented,

President Bush is casual about inconsistencies. His policies are highly personal and shamelessly political. On North Korea, he has outdone himself. He insists that the problem with an outlaw dictatorship that has gone nuclear with a vengeance can be solved by diplomacy – but he refuses to talk to North Koreans." Later in the same op-ed she noted, "Kim issues a primal scream almost daily. He threatens all-out war, a first strike against our troops in South Korea. And yet, while every hour that passes increases our President's urge to go to war with Iraq, there seems to be no way he will pay any attention to, much less fire on, North Korea, whose nuclear program is not in the subjunctive [supposition contrary to fact] but unfolding before our eyes.[8]

During the 1991 Gulf War, Saddam did not use his chemical weapons because of fear of massive reprisals by the U.S. American leaders had hinted that the U.S. might use nuclear weapons. In other words, at that time Saddam demonstrated that he was shrewd enough to pull his punches. He survived as a result. In early 2003 he was a weakened but still significant problem and a regional hazard rather than a potentially catastrophic global threat. The CIA had acknowledged that he was not likely to use the potential of his deadliest weapons unless he was attacked. So what did we do? We announced that we would attack him.

But Bush and now Colin Powell had behind them the political momentum of Security Council Resolution 1441. It gave Saddam a last chance to disarm, and in their view, he was not doing it. However, this view was the point of dispute. The inspections were revealing, gradually, that Saddam did not have nuclear weapons, and it was becoming less and less clear that he had the other weapons claimed by the U.S. intelligence apparatus. Much of the rest of the world, except England and Spain, was not convinced that action was required. France, Russia, and Germany—all three on the UN Security Council, and the first two equipped with veto power and the third temporarily presiding over the Council—were notably unconvinced.

278

In Prospect: Winning the War, Losing the Peace

Foreign policy experts and ordinary American citizens alike asked another question that was not answered by Colin Powell's speech: "What are we doing to plan for the day after an invasion?" According to Ambassador Richard Holbrooke in an interview on the Charlie Rose show in early February 2003, the Bush administration was divided at that time, during the run-up to the war, between advocates of two major alternatives. One group, the minimalists, advocated going in, toppling Saddam, and getting out quickly. The maximalists, according to Holbrooke, advocated staying after the war and putting Iraq back on its feet. The severe problems of both these alternatives should have been obvious to anyone who knew the situation in Iraq.

To topple Saddam and leave soon after could create anarchy and civil war between the Kurdish population in the North (possibly wishing to unite with the Kurds in Turkey), the Sunnis in the center, and the Shiites in the South (who would be getting cozy with Shiites in Iran). Because of their links to the neighboring countries, the leftover war and anarchy would almost certainly spread devastation not only within Iraq but also draw in the surrounding countries, especially Turkey and Iran. A lawless environment would also create a haven for terrorists much as the anarchy in Afghanistan did for al Qaeda. The alternative would be a coercive U.S. military presence spread throughout the country. The cost of this on a continuing basis would be enormous.

Obviously, to stay and occupy the country for an extended period would leave U.S. troops with a huge and expensive cleanup job. They would be endlessly vulnerable to sniping and terrorism. A foreign occupying force that topples a tyrant may be popular with the people of the country at first, but soon it is resented and subjected to all manner of insults, resistance and terrorism by virtue of being foreign invaders and having to exercise coercive control. This resentment would be intensified by loss of food supplies, electric power, gasoline, etc. for any extended period. The third, middle alternative of gradually turning over the maintenance of security in the country to the UN or the oft-mentioned "coalition of the willing" would be rendered difficult both by the level of violence to be dealt with and by the reluctance of the international community, particularly the UN with its limited resources, to take on such an impossible mission in such a large and volatile country.

On February 11, 2003, the Pentagon and State Department explained their plans for postwar reconstruction to a worried Congress. The obvious "stay and occupy" decision had been made. The U.S. military would take on responsibility for security, finding and destroying weapons of mass destruction, providing emergency food to millions of Iraqis, rebuilding the country's economy and reshaping its society. The cost would be untold billions and it would take years to complete. At least this was a realistic, if appallingly expensive plan. At the hearings, Senator Joseph Biden (D-Del) noted that Americans had no notion of what they were in for. One wonders if they would have supported the war had they really understood.

Undersecretary of Defense Douglas Feith and Undersecretary of State Marc Grossman were the administration's main presenters of the plan. They were unwilling to discuss cost estimates of the war and the postwar reconstruction because there were too many unknowns. Yet Grossman estimated that Iraqis could regain control of the country in two years. In view of the extreme internal instabilities of this cobbled-together country of three mutually resentful ethnic and geographic enclaves, one had to wonder if this wasn't a gross underestimate. Departure has not been so easy in Bosnia.

Another consideration was that the Shiites in the South, though a majority of the population, were not in control of the country. They have strong ties to Iran, Iraq's eastern neighbor. The Sunnis in the center of the country are a minority population, but were nevertheless in control. Democracy would threaten this control. The Shiites in the South and the Kurds in the North had rebelled against Saddam after the 1991 gulf war, had received little military support from the U.S., and had been put down hard by Saddam. How would establishing democracy work in this situation? Wouldn't the Kurdish North want to break away and join with their Kurdish brothers in Turkey to form an independent Kurdistan? Wouldn't the majority Shiites in the South want to draw strength from Iran and take over Iraq, since they are the majority population?

In view of these transnational problems, the Bush administration considered maintaining the integrity of Iraq's borders essential to the stability of the entire region. The acute problems for making postwar peace, and the probability of a debacle, were evident from the start. Anyone could see that this situation had the makings of a Bosnia in the middle of the Middle East.

The U.S. would have the daunting and perhaps impossible task of holding the country together by force.

In response to intense pressure to demonstrate that it had a detailed plan to deal with the postwar chaos, on February 20, 2003 the Bush administration provided preliminary briefings on a more thorough postwar blueprint. It envisioned U.S. military control at the outset, followed by an American civilian authority once security was restored, possibly to be followed eventually by a multinational administration perhaps run by the UN. A prime early-stage goal would be to make sure the Iraqi people immediately felt themselves to be better off than they were before the war. While this would clearly be essential to make security a possibility and to prevent endless sniping and terrorist attacks against American "protectors," anyone with a smidgen of exposure to such matters knows this sensible and admirable goal to be extraordinarily difficult to accomplish. If this goal were not accomplished, a strong military presence would be required for a long time.

The plan included establishing an Iraqi consultative council and eventually an Iraqi representative government and an Iraqi commission to establish a judicial system. An additional commission would write an Iraqi constitution. A key concern in the design of the plan was an Iraqi government strong enough to hold the country together and prevent other regional powers such as Turkey and Iran from building up client warlords dependent on them and pulling the country apart. Obviously this was an admirable goal, but feasibility, cost, and duration of U.S. involvement were difficult to determine. The plan made more sense than the vacuum that preceded it, but whether it was feasible and whether the U.S. could muster the staying power to implement it was anybody's guess.

An American Empire?

Remarkably, conservative commentator Robert D. Novak, usually a relentless supporter of Republicans and of Bush, saw the dangers and the larger implications of the Iraq war for U.S. foreign policy. He argued in a *Washington Post* op-ed piece on February 10, 2003 that the U.S. is poised to attack Iraq on its own, without UN Security Council authorization, and that "presumed military success projects an American imperium that evokes apprehension among some conservative supporters of President Bush. This imperial mission has staunch proponents in the Bush administration, definitely not including Powell." It would serve one well to pause here for a moment and reflect. A conservative is warning of American imperialism. Not so long ago, it was the communists who warned about American imperialism, not American conservatives.

A few of Novak's other comments: "The International Atomic Energy Agency is expected, several weeks from now, to declare Iraq free of nuclear weapons development. But the U.S.-led coalition will have attacked by then and, probably, driven Hussein from power." Novak quoted an e-mail from a conservative he identified as prominent in Washington's think tank culture: "Once we cross the Tigris and Euphrates we may have started down a road to Pax Americana through an American imperium from which there is no return." He noted also that the administration's confused, underfunded reconstruction approach following military victory in Afghanistan casts doubts on America's willingness to run an empire.

Novak cited a White House briefing a few days earlier in which "Ari Fleischer was asked whether the President was retreating from 2000 campaign opposition to the use of U.S. troops for nation- building. As they are now stationed in Afghanistan, Kosovo and Bosnia and will probably soon be in Iraq. 'No' responded Fleischer, 'the President continues to believe that the purpose of using the military should be to fight and win wars.' Instead, he talked about U.S. relief workers distributing humanitarian aid in occupied Iraq along with 'a variety of international relief organizations.' Watching Fleischer on television, a skeptical Republican in Congress could only chuckle. It will take more than civil servants to bring order to Baghdad after the coming war."

Arch-conservative Novak concluded the following about President Bush: "While disdaining nation-building, he is embarking on empire building." My comment: empire building, once the U.S. has dismantled the government of a country, however unsatisfactory or vicious it may have been, requires nation-building. No wonder the follow-up in Afghanistan is confused. The underlying policy is schizophrenic. It contains two opposite imperatives: do nation-building and don't do nation-building. Mary McGrory was on point when she noted that Bush is casual about inconsistencies. Here he tries to implement contradictions. Ari Fleischer's comments suggest that the policy in Iraq after the war is likely to be equally self-contradictory and therefore equally muddled. But the situation will be much more dangerous and volatile. The consequences of such a confused policy may be far more destructive.

In his article, "Salesmanship in a Skeptical World," David Ignatius made similar observations. He noted that the debate should start with the fact that Saddam Hussein is an international outlaw. He has flouted the UN for over a decade. (Never mind that the U.S. has, too.) Yet, Ignatius said, somehow it's the U.S. that is on the defensive at the UN and in other international forums. The question, he noted, for President Bush is how to get the debate "back on track" so that Hussein's arrogance, rather than that of the U.S., is the issue.[9]

Further in the same article he came to the crux of the problem, ideological arrogance: "What's enfeebling U.S. Iraq policy now is that it's carrying too much baggage. For neo-conservatives, it's a test of America's willingness to act unilaterally to achieve its global goals—and thereby create the structure of what amounts to an American empire." He went on, "That unilateralist argument is wrong. American power remains rooted in the global institutions that the United States created after 1945, especially the United Nations. America cannot weaken those institutions without also weakening itself. The 'soft power' of American economic, cultural, and political life remains as important as our 'hard' military power – and a lot less expensive."[10]

Hubris and Aggression as Guides to Policy

At the heart of the debate about Iraq is the Bush administration's radical new policy regarding warfare and the circumstances under which the U.S. may initiate war. Essentially it authorizes preventive strikes against other nations by the U.S. even if the U.S. has not been attacked and there is no imminent threat of attack. In U.S. policy, international law, and the ethical analyses of outstanding philosophers down through the centuries, these two conditions—defending against an attack or an imminent threat of attack—have always been critical in justifying war.

A third condition, military action under a resolution of the UN Security Council for the purpose of establishing or maintaining global security, was added with the founding of the UN. When the United States signed and ratified the treaty establishing the UN, the UN Charter, it formally incorporated this new element of international law into its own legal framework. Under the U.S. Constitution, a ratified treaty has the same legal force as any domestic law. Nevertheless, from the beginning of his rush to war with Iraq, President Bush has stridently asserted that he will launch the war with or without UN approval. In short, from the beginning he announced his contempt for the UN and for international law and *de facto*, for the constraint of the U.S. Constitution. Customarily, contempt for law and law enforcement has been thought of as the purview of thugs, not U.S. Presidents.

Judging from Bush's behavior, the new policy allowing preventive strikes without an imminent threat had guided his thinking about Iraq for months before it was published in September 2002 as his new National Security Strategy. When it finally was published, it raised immediate alarms throughout the world. Essentially, it gives a central place to the extreme advantage of U.S. military power over all rivals and places military power at the center of U.S. foreign policy. Tragically, this policy, if consistently applied, is a formula for a new chapter of American and global history, "America the Bully."

Allowing preventive attacks against regimes that might be dangerous at some time in the future not only constitutes a radical departure from international law and contradicts American moral, legal, and cultural tradition, but it is also extremely dangerous. It is a formula for unnecessary wars, and quite possibly endless war and international anarchy. If other countries practiced this new policy as well, following the American example, the world would soon revert to the international anarchy that prevailed in the 19th century and led to the unforgettable legacies of World War I and World War II. The policy is an explicit repudiation of the very foundations of international law as it applies to war and peace, the foundations that have given us a half-century without a third world war.

This central policy change is almost always misstated in the press as allowing "preemptive" attacks. A "preemptive" attack is a legitimate military initiative under imminent threat. It is authorized under international legal tradition and under the UN Charter. In other words, for example, when a nation has stationed troops and tanks at your border and has announced its intention to invade, it's O.K. to attack first. "Preventive" attacks, by contrast, are military actions that anticipate dangers from another nation even though there is no imminent threat of attack from that country.

The other notable item in the Bush administration's National Security Strategy is a determination to maintain military power without rival, including not only building up the U.S. military but also dissuading potential adversaries from building up their military power. Together these two changes constitute a tilt toward maintaining U.S. dominance by military might. It has caused concern among both liberals and conservatives. Writers Thomas Ricks and Vernon Loeb quote concerns from both ends of the political spectrum side by side. "Harvard University foreign policy expert Stanley Hoffman recently wrote in the liberal magazine *American Prospect* that 'the Bush doctrine...amounts to a doctrine of global domination' that also is 'breathtakingly unrealistic.'"[11]

The article continues, "In the *American Conservative,* Boston University political scientist Andrew J. Bacevich, a retired Army colonel, worried about a new 'militarization of foreign policy.' The Bush administration, he wrote, regards the use of force not as a last resort, but as the nation's 'most effective instrument of statecraft.' In summary, he warned, 'The Bush administration's grand strategy reeks of hubris.'"[12]

Military force is not the only kind of coercive force the Bush team has used to get its way with adverse effects. In his article, "Forceful Tactics Catch Up With the U.S.," journalist Glen Kessler documents the diplomatic strong-arm tactics the U.S. has used on other countries and one of the effects these actions have had. They have led to resistance on the Iraq war question. He quotes a diplomat (nameless for obvious reasons) who hails from a country that publicly supports the U.S. position on Iraq: *"The U.S. team often acts like thugs. People feel bullied, and that can affect the way you respond when someone makes a request."*[13]

The article points out that America's allies have been repeatedly jolted by Bush's go-it-alone actions such as the abandonment of the Kyoto Protocols on global warming, his "unsigning" the treaty on the International Criminal Court, his brush-off of North Korea's sunshine policy of rapprochement with North Korea, and his withdrawal of the U.S. from the Anti-Ballistic Missile Treaty. But America's allies are also distressed by the administration's apparent willingness to destroy long-standing international institutions in the process of toppling Saddam Hussein. Even a senior Bush administration official, referring to his own team, complained that "There are people here who are trying to destroy institutions that have served us well since WWII – and still have some utility—and they have no obvious replacement but raw American power." In fact, this replacement is the explicit goal of many of the neo-conservatives who surround George Bush. Their literature makes it clear that they openly want to establish a new American empire, a Pax Americana.

Straining Alliances and Undermining the UN

As of mid-February 2003, France, Germany, Belgium, China and Russia were expressing strong reservations about the U.S. initiative to attack Iraq before the inspections had time to run their course. As permanent members of the UN Security Council with veto powers, France's, China's, and Russia's acceptance of a resolution that in effect authorized an immediate invasion of Iraq, or at least their reluctant acquiescence by abstaining, was essential to the U.S. in achieving political legitimacy and legality under international law for the effort. Further, Germany, though lacking a veto, held the rotating Chairmanship of the Council at the time. The combination of these pressures created an uphill battle for the U.S. in securing a resolution sanctioning the attack.

The U.S. at first pinned its hopes on a report of the UN inspection team that was scheduled for February 14. When the great moment came and the inspection team's leaders, Hans Blix and Mohamed ElBaradei, made their Valentine's Day report to the Security Council, the U.S. got an unpleasant surprise. Hoping against hope that the inspectors would present enough evidence against Iraqi cooperation to tip the scales toward immediate action for war, American leaders heard something quite different.

The report was a measured and balanced presentation that made it clear that Iraq was improving its cooperation, however modestly. It concluded that more time was needed. Blix recommended further work by the inspection team. He also questioned some of the evidence presented in Colin Powell's statement to the Security Council, including his key claim that Iraq was working with al Qaeda.

ElBaradei's report on nuclear weapons was particularly telling. Bush's original launching of war rhetoric and diplomatic maneuvers against Iraq was based first and foremost on the prospect of Iraq soon acquiring nuclear weapons and then possibly providing those weapons to al Qaeda. In short, the nukes and terrorism connection were the whole basis of his case against the containment status quo with Iraq. So ElBaradei's report was particularly important as a verification or falsification of Bush's rationale for war.

Without any evident political bias or reference to Bush's original arguments, the distinguished head of the International Atomic Energy Agency reported that the team had found no evidence of nuclear activity at suspected sites in Iraq and debunked evidence, including the aluminum tubes cited by Colin Powell, that Iraq had a nuclear program. He argued that there was in fact no such evidence. The tubes were clearly designed for and being used for a different purpose, conventional rocket engines. ElBaradei and Blix both noted that the U.S. was still not providing all its relevant intelligence to the inspection team. His final observations: "We have to date found no evidence of ongoing prohibited nuclear or nuclear-related activities in Iraq.... I would underline the importance of information that states may be able to provide to help us in assessing the accuracy and completeness of the information provided by Iraq."[14]

The speeches by members of the Security Council after the inspection team's report made it clear that most members favored giving more time to the inspections, feeling that alternatives to war were not exhausted and that the inspections were making progress. A number of countries the U.S. had thought were in its corner joined in calling for Council unity and patience. Guinea, Chile, and Angola were among those who jumped the fence away from the U.S. The Angolan ambassador even said that Blix's report was "a beacon of hope that we can indeed save the world from an imminent conflict."[15] The U.S. efforts to cobble together a majority for a resolution authorizing war unraveled. The Russian and French foreign ministers even received applause for their remarks opposing the U.S. position. Applause is said to be a rarity in the staid Security Council, and was taken by the diplomats present at the meeting as a clear sign of the unpopularity of the American position and style in dealing with the situation.

On a related front, in NATO, France, Belgium and Germany balked at providing defensive military assistance requested by Turkey in anticipation of the war. Since NATO operates by unanimous consent, even one of these countries balking would have paralyzed the alliance. These three countries felt that it was premature to signal that war with Iraq was inevitable by supporting Turkey. They were not willing to act on an assumption of definitive failure for efforts at peace or for postponing military action while the inspectors did their work. U.S. officials were furious. Refusal of NATO members to help protect an ally? This was disgraceful!

The controversy placed a considerable strain on the alliance. Strangely, the U.S., which carried the responsibility for initiating a war which its leaders intransigently insisted upon starting within weeks, blamed France, Belgium and Germany for the crisis. The U.S. message was the following: We're determined to create this mess (the war and its aftermath), and you are behaving disgracefully if you don't agree to act in advance to admit its inevitability and help us clean it up or contain it.

Nobody on the American team acknowledged that the NATO alliance is designed to be defensive, not offensive. Who was attacking a NATO member? Are NATO allies required to help when a member country (the U.S.) attacks a non-member country (Iraq)? Are members obliged to help if an attack on an outsider by a member nation (in this case the U.S.) puts another NATO member (Turkey) in jeopardy? Are member nations obliged to signal acceptance of a war of aggression by another NATO nation even before the war has begun? Evidently France, Germany and Belgium thought the answer was "no" to the last three of these questions. Nothing in NATO's charter would suggest otherwise. Yet the U.S. officials (who were "shocked, shocked") tried to cast them as the bad guys who were blocking help for a NATO ally.

Eventually NATO solved the problem in two stages. The first stage was referring the issue to its Defense Planning Committee, which did not include France in its membership. (France had pulled out of NATO's integrated military command in 1966.) Then during the course of arduous negotiations, Belgium designed compromise language that made it explicit that NATO was not acquiescing to the inevitability of a war on Iraq. The statement said that its decision relates only to the defense of Turkey and is without prejudice to any other military operations by NATO, and later decisions by NATO or the UN Security Council. NATO had achieved agreement, but experts warned that the damage to internal harmony in NATO could be lasting.

Perhaps the most curious aspect of these clashes in the UN Security Council and NATO was the outlandish arrogance of the U.S. position. The moral dimension of the Bush administration's stance can be summed up by stating its position baldly, without the usual halo of fuzzy euphemisms and diplospeak. The argument goes something like this: "We are going to start this war with or without you, and thus with or without legitimacy under international law. Saddam tramples on international law and flouts the UN, so he is a bad guy. We are the good guys. We are planning to trample on international law and flout the UN to destroy him if you don't go along with us. We are willing to destroy the credibility and effectiveness of two great institutions of peace and diplomacy that have served the international community for over 50 years to get this thing done. You must serve as a rubber stamp of our policies and go along with us despite your objections or you are being obstructionist and causing the destruction of these institutions." To state it bluntly, this borders on hostage-taking. "We will destroy these institutions and hold you responsible for destroying them if you don't go along with our aggressive plans."

Fareed Zakaria, an astute commentator on international relations for *Newsweek*, grasped the perspective shift this situation requires to be understood. He writes, "The debate is not really about Iraq, it's about the United States. Many in Europe worry more about America than Iraq. For them Iraq is a tactical issue. The strategic issue is what are they going to do about America, the dominating power in the world today."[16]

Later in the same article Zakaria adds,

A world with fewer rules and restraints is one in which America will do just fine. It is the rest of the world that benefits most from these institutions. If some European countries have been slow to recognize the realities of American power, so has Washington. The Bush administration came to office determined to demonstrate that it was not constrained by treaties and international institutions. It has also spoken ill of old allies, eager to prove that it has freedom of action. But it's obvious that Washington has total freedom. That's why it would be wiser not to mention it every few days. When your power is obvious and overwhelming, you need to show not that you *can* act alone, but that you *want* to act with others."[17]

Zakaria's conclusions are far-seeing and also ominous. He observes that the crisis between the U.S. and Europe is partly a result of bad diplomacy, with the U.S. conveying an arrogance that speaks not of leadership but of domination. Unless the bad diplomacy changes, the anti-war and anti-American demonstrations in Europe will "mark the opening of a salvo of a new politics of protest." He continues, "Europe, instead of being America's leading partner, will become its most energetic opponent. This will be bad for the entire world. After all, when the West has been united it fostered peace. When divided, the result has always been war."[18]

In summary, America the almighty is becoming a problem for the whole world, not only because of the power imbalance, but also because of arrogant and bullying behavior.

Motivating Terrorism and Alienating Arab Allies

Critics of the U.S.-led war on Iraq predicted that it would aggravate terrorism. An unprovoked attack on a predominantly Muslim country, they noted, was bound to be interpreted by extremists and by many moderates in the Arab world as another example of U.S. hostility and aggression, a kind of American crusade against Muslims and their faith. America's long-standing financial and political support for Israel set the stage for this erroneous interpretation of U.S. motives. An attack on Iraq could be reliably predicted to increase the Islamist terrorist/extremist's recruitment base. Legions of new recruits for terrorist activity would be a natural outcome. It would also provide Islamist terrorists with a recruitment tool, an argument to rise up and take action against the infidels. Further, it would strain American relationships with friendly or neutral Arab nations on which anti-terrorism efforts depend.

Anger in the Arab streets in reaction to the American attack could make counter-terrorist cooperation with the U.S. more difficult politically for moderate Arab countries. It might even result in their governments falling and being replaced with radical governments. This change, in turn, could result in radicals exercising political control of crucial oil supplies, creating tremendous strains economically and strategically on developed countries, and possibly leading to further war. Of course, American control of Iraqi oil could in the longer term mitigate this problem since Iraq sits on the second-largest oil supply in the world, after Saudi Arabia. Critics of the Bush administration and the war have not overlooked this convenient fact about Iraqi oil. They have made unkind speculations about motives, fed by the Bush administration's exceptionally close ties to the U.S. oil industry.

The predictions that an attack on Iraq would play into the hands of terrorists were not long waiting for fulfillment. Even before the war against Iraq, al Qaeda leader Osama bin Laden used the prospect of the war to launch a propaganda diatribe against the U.S. and possibly to signal a terrorist attack. He released a speech on tape that was broadcast on the Arabic language al Jazeera satellite network. In it he called on Iraqis to carry out suicide attacks on Americans. Intelligence officials warned that the tape was authentic and that similar communications have preceded terrorist attacks in the past.

Simultaneously, based on other indicators, intelligence sources were warning that al Qaeda might be planning attacks with poisons, viruses, or radioactive "dirty bombs" in the U.S. or against American interests abroad. Newspaper reports noted that the tape reinforced warnings from intelligence officials that an invasion of Iraq would prompt attacks by al Qaeda and other terrorist groups against the U.S. The FBI told the Senate that there were several hundred Islamic extremists in the U.S. that have links to al Qaeda.

In his efforts to make the case for international military action against Iraq, Colin Powell argued that bin Laden's statement placed him in partnership with Iraq. But, on the contrary, in the statement bin Laden scorned Iraq's leadership as an infidel government. Rather than allying himself with the Iraqi government, he argued that the Iraqi people should oppose American aggression to counter a latter-day western crusade against Muslim peoples. Bin Laden's point was terrorist recruitment propaganda for a popular audience inside as well as outside Iraq, not a declaration of alliance with an "infidel" like Saddam Hussein, an arrangement that would be anathema to a Muslim fanatic.

Perhaps the saddest and most disturbing impact, even in prospect, of the U.S. war against Iraq was its effect on the opinions of Arab moderates and pro-American Arabs. Anthony Shadid reported the sense of bitterness and betrayal of well-educated Arabs who had strong ties with the U.S. and had been pro-American for years. Quoting one such person, he writes, "An invasion, he says, serves only Israel and a clique within the Bush administration 'whose ignorance is matched only by their greed.'" "I feel we have been deceived about the nature and character of the United States of America," he goes on to say. This from a man who quotes the Declaration of Independence and whose son is an American, whose personal library is stocked with works by Thomas Paine, Thomas Jefferson, James Madison, and other great founders of the U.S.[19]

In the same article, Shadid adds the following:

> 'The upper class used to be extremely loyal to the American ideal. It always saw the United States as the incarnation of its own ideals,' said Mohamed Sayed Said, deputy director of Cairo's Al-Ahram Center for Political and Strategic Studies. 'Now they share the same negative view of the United States, that it targets Arabs and Muslims. That's a new element.' ... Said and others said that their disenchantment springs not from a fear of American power, but from a sense of betrayal of ideals.... Powerful and once sympathetic voices have turned decisively against U.S. policy. Reda Hilal, a columnist for Egypt's leading newspaper, the English language *Al-Ahram Weekly*, was once a stalwart defender of U.S.-Arab ties. He now talks of America's arrogance of power.[20]

A final comment from the same article, this one by a former Qatari ambassador to the United States who said that his three children were graduates of George Washington University: "Believe me and write this ... Nobody hates America. America used to be a great example, it was not a colonial power in the region. Our sons and brothers work with American businesses. I am very sorry that American policy is threatening the human relations between nations. The Americans are antagonizing their friends."[21]

A few weeks later, in April 2003, reports began to surface stating that moderate and secular Pakistanis, upset by the war, had started turning to

291

religious parties and stating that the war was making them more radical. The religious parties in Pakistan have close ties to the military and the intelligence services, which are generally more conservative and anti-American than Pakistani leader Pervez Musharraf. They also, paradoxically, have allied themselves with the cause of democracy in Pakistan, a move that tends to delegitimize and undermine Musharraf's military rule. As they gain power, he loses power. His close ties with the U.S. become a greater political liability.

A Rosy Vision of Iraq's Future

As Bush pressed for a Security Council vote on a final resolution authorizing the impending war by declaring Iraq in "material breach" of Resolution 1441, the picture looked grim for approval. Toward the end of February 2003 he had definitively lost the struggle for world public opinion and appeared to be losing the diplomatic struggle for approval of the war in the Security Council. The arm-twisting that had succeeded in passing 1441 was no longer working. In fact, leaders and ambassadors of other countries no longer believed in the sincerity of Bush's original decision to work through the UN. His short-lived support for inspections quickly followed by a call for them to halt so the war could commence gave the appearance of a con job, a bait and switch. Leaders of other countries who voted for 1441 felt manipulated and deceived.[22]

On the UN Security Council, France and Germany were vocally and consistently opposed to the war. Russia and China were cautiously with them in opposing war, and only England, Spain and Bulgaria were supportive of the war and any new resolution that might sanction it. Polls showed overwhelming majorities of the populations in the permanent five Security Council countries except the U.S. vehemently opposed to the war. Unprecedented millions of people were marching in anti-war protests in cities all over the world. U.S. ambassadors were reporting to Washington that in the countries where they were posted, Bush, not Saddam, was considered the enemy. Clearly Bush needed a major boost in global public opinion.

On February 26, flanked by American flags, he made a televised speech before members of the ultra-conservative and Bush-friendly American Enterprise Institute. The audience applauded almost every line. He painted a glowing picture of a free and democratic postwar Iraq that would serve as a

An Unnecessary War

dramatic example of freedom for other nations in the region and bring hope and progress into the lives of millions. To those who had derided the possibility of quickly establishing democracy in a country that had no history or experience with it, he argued that the same was said about Germany and Japan before U.S. occupation, and called it "presumptuous and insulting" to think that the Muslim world would not welcome freedom and democracy, and that these would not easily or quickly take root in Iraq. For some reason, he failed to suggest to leaders of the other Arab countries that they might want to try a similar shortcut to democracy—a takeover by the U.S., which could then shove them aside and quickly set things right. Without that, it seemed hardly likely that they would be inspired to establish democracy in their countries and step down from power.

In ironic counterpoint to Bush's words, at almost the very moment of his talk there were hints in the news that the world was not turning out as splendidly as he was envisioning. As a conciliatory gesture to the Arab world, he mentioned the need to establish a Palestinian state and to bring about an eventual end to Israel's settlement activity in the occupied territories. But as he spoke, in Israel Ariel Sharon was piecing together out of political necessity (labor had abandoned him and he lacked a legislative majority) a coalition government of ultra-right wing political parties adamantly opposed to a Palestinian state. While Bush appeared to be lurching to the left in his speech, Israel was lurching to the right in practice.

Also at the time of Bush's glowing speech, Afghanistan's new leader, Hamid Karzai, was visiting the U.S. and diplomatically voicing concerns about the inadequacy of the U.S. support for his fledgling government. This after a takeover of his country similar to that proposed for Iraq. The U.S. had refused to provide security outside of the capitol city of Kabul, and warlords were regaining control of much of the country. By a remarkable coincidence, one of those moments that tempt one to believe in a divine order behind events, the very day after Bush's speech two American experts, one of them the Dean of the George Washington University Law School, published an analysis of the situation in Afghanistan. In it they stated, "We have spent billions of dollars and lost precious lives to vanquish the Taliban. Yet the groundwork is being laid in Afghanistan for a regime that may be almost as repressive as the Taliban, particularly with regard to religious freedom. This is occurring with consent and in some cases, help from the United States."[23]

The analysis goes on,

There are disturbing reports that an extreme and strict interpretation of Islamic law, or *sharia*, is being nurtured in the post-Taliban era. Moreover, attempts are being made to include some of the harshest and most discriminatory elements of *sharia* in the new constitution and judicial system. The notorious Ministry for the Promotion of Virtue and Prevention of Vice, which enforced religious conformity and meted out harsh punishments under the Taliban, has re-emerged in a supposedly gentler guise. Abuses against women and girls continue, apparently with the support of police and the courts. Women and girls finally have the opportunity to go to school, but recent attacks and threats against schools for girls are keeping many away.

Human rights concerns reported in the article included, to mention a few, judicial endorsement of amputations, coercive measures including on-the-spot beatings for failures to follow specific religious practices and dress and behavior codes for women, blasphemy charges against reformers, and torture of prisoners. The report further states, "Several key cabinet posts have gone to leaders or members of extremist groups or ruthless warlord factions. Some of these appointments were made on the advice of the U.S. Government." The final paragraph casts a telling light on Bush's glowing speech about the future of Iraq: "What we do in Afghanistan is a prelude to Iraq."[24]

Similar concerns were expressed two days earlier by Iraqi expatriates talking with Deputy Defense Secretary Paul Wolfowitz, one of the Bush administration's lead advocates for attacking Iraq. The predominantly Shiite group of about 300 people asked tough questions about the shape of a postwar Iraq: "Members of the audience repeatedly expressed concern that the United States, looking for a quick exit, would settle for having the country ruled by an Iraqi general, and also would leave in place much of the ruling Baath party. Wolfowitz repeatedly sought to dispel these worries."[25]

The article continues, "But moderator Maha Hussain, an Iraqi American doctor who is president of the Iraqi Forum for Democracy, pointedly asked why such reassurances should be trusted, 'considering the history of the United States government' in not supporting the 1991 uprisings, among other things."[26]

"Wolfowitz seemed momentarily nonplused by the question, but then responded by noting that the U.S. government repeatedly came to the aid of embattled Muslims in recent years, first in Somalia, Bosnia, and Kosovo, then in Afghanistan, and probably soon, he said, in Iraq. 'I know there's a lot of history,' he added. 'This is not the time to look to the past, but to the future.'"[27] The article doesn't mention whether anyone observed that the past is prologue.

As of March 2003, Bush administration officials had estimated that it would take two years after the war to have Iraq ready to hand back to the Iraqis. They cannot have made this estimate with the President's glowing vision of Iraq's democratic future in mind. Realistically, one could see in advance that it would take at least two years, probably much longer, to have Iraq ready to turn back to another strong man, soon to become a dictator. But establishing democracy for the first time after decades of violent oppression requires a profound cultural change and is sure to take much longer than two years. As seen from the vantage point of early March 2003, before the declared beginning of the war, the pieces of the postwar puzzle were not fitting together. Two years to utopia sounded just a bit unrealistic. It takes decades to build the institutions and the trust that make democracy work.

On Bush's glowing picture, Senator Edward Kennedy commented, "He painted a simplistic picture of the brightest possible future—with democracy flourishing in Iraq, peace emerging among all nations in the Middle East and the terrorists with no place of support there. We've all heard of rosy scenarios, but that was ridiculous."[28] Stating the point more bluntly, Bush and his team were promoting a fantasy for the sake of mustering support. In some circles this would be called a con job. One wonders who believed him besides his applauding audience (if indeed they did) at the American Enterprise Institute. Perhaps President Bush himself did, a possibility almost as disturbing as the alternative.

Likely Postwar Realities: The View from Before the War

The lives of the Kurdish people in northern Iraq present an illustration, plainly visible before the war, of the extreme difficulties for peace and democracy in a postwar Iraq. After the 1991 Gulf War the U.S. established no-fly zones in northern and southern Iraq to protect the Kurdish people in the North and the Shiite people of the South from the worst depredations of Saddam's government. Over the 12 years since that time, the Kurds inside Iraq have learned to manage their own affairs with little interference from Saddam and have reveled in the freedom and relative prosperity they have achieved.

Across their northern border are millions of brother Kurds within the boundaries of Turkey. They have a long history of resistance and rebellion against the Turkish government and have been pounded by countervailing oppression and human rights violations by the Turkish government. One of Turkey's greatest fears is the widespread desire by their Kurdish population to break away and create an independent state, ideally including the Kurds of Iraq and Iran.

One of the Bush administration's oft-repeated postwar goals for Iraq is the maintenance of its territorial integrity. Clearly this goal is vital for stability in the Middle East. Fighting between the Kurds and the Turks, possibly on both sides of the Turkish-Iraqi border, is one of the possibilities likely to make this goal difficult. Another problem for both the noble dream of postwar democracy in Iraq's future and for its territorial integrity is the population in the South.

The oppressed Shiite population in the South constitutes a majority of the Iraqi population. Any shift toward representative democracy in the country would also shift power from the dominant Sunni center of the country toward the Shiite South. The Iraqi Shiites have strong ties with the Shiites of Iran and have little love for the minority Sunnis who live in central Iraq and who have for decades controlled the country by brute force with Saddam in charge. Will the Iraqi Shiites want to break away? Join with Iran? Will they want to settle old scores? Certainly they will want the whip hand of majority power. Given that they will, how will it be possible to get the minority Sunnis and Kurds to agree to genuine democracy in Iraq? It may well be that in the short to medium term, only strong-arm tactics will hold the country together. And the U.S. will be the only force in the country with strong enough arms. Of course, a backlash of resentment against the U.S. will inevitably follow.

To sum up the grim prospect, before the war it is evident that it will be a long-term challenge for American forces to prevent the country from fissioning violently into multiple pieces with bloody, multi-ethnic Balkan-style civil wars and tribal bloodbaths, not to mention numberless individual war crimes. It could also be difficult to prevent the war from spreading into Turkey and Iran and possibly other neighboring countries. In the course of controlling these fragmenting tendencies, scores or hundreds of thousands of American troops would most likely be necessary, probably for far longer than two years. These American troops would be resented as foreign, non-Muslim occupiers and for restraining the impulses of factions that may at first welcome them as liberators. These are hardly circumstances conducive to the trust and cooperation necessary for establishing viable democratic institutions in a postwar Iraq.

A subject for discussion before the war was how many American soldiers will it take to keep the lid on this volatile situation? General Erik K. Shinseki, the Army's Chief of Staff, estimated that "several hundred thousand soldiers" could be necessary for peacekeeping duties after the war. Deputy Defense Secretary Paul Wolfowitz, the civilian driving force behind the Bush administration's plans for the Iraq war and postwar recovery, publicly brushed aside this estimate, calling it "way off the mark."[29] However, like General Shinseki, Retired Army Major General William L. Nash, who commanded the first Army peacekeeping operations in the Balkans in 1995, estimated that 200,000 U.S. and allied forces would be needed to stabilize Iraq.[30] A week or two after Wolfowitz's rejection of General Shinseki's estimates, the general reiterated his high estimate before Congress. I checked with friends in the military and their comment was, Shinseki is a man of vast military experience and notably high integrity; they said he was the one to believe. Events proved him closer to the mark than Wolfowitz was. The 130,000 troops the U.S. had on the ground after the war were not enough.

Ivo H. Daalder, a senior fellow at the Brookings Institution, noted that recent history shows that 60,000 peacekeepers were necessary in Bosnia just to separate warring ethnic factions. This type of action would be only one of the missions that the Army would have to carry out in postwar Iraq. Furthermore, Bosnia's population is 4 million, about one-sixth of Iraq's population.[31]

Of course, the Bush administration was planning to do its best to divide the costs and responsibilities of postwar peacekeeping and reconstruction in Iraq with allies, if there were any left after the war. But the precedent of Afghanistan was instructive. Bush has had modest luck in getting other nations to provide substantial help. However, the U.S. action in Iraq was far more unpopular in world opinion than was the war in Afghanistan. It was easy to see before the war that the U.S. would most likely be left holding the bulk of the bag, and a messy bag it would be.

Some of the doom and gloom predictions before the war were wildly off the mark. One was the likelihood that there would be huge floods of refugees into other countries such as Jordan, countries that could ill-afford to feed and house them. Again, the UN struggled to prepare and expressed alarm at the lack of readiness and funding to handle these refugee flows. According to an article by Kenneth Bacon, former Pentagon TV spokesperson, and George Rupp, President of Refugees International, the UN estimated that in a "medium impact scenario," a two or three month conflict involving ground troops, 1.45 million refugees would try to reach neighboring countries and 900,000 people would be newly displaced within Iraq. The UN High Commissioner for Refugees, Ruud Lubbers, stated that when people flee their countries, his agency lacks the resources needed. Before the war the refugee office had raised $20 million of the $60 million it expected to need for tents, stoves, blankets, etc. for refugee camps. As a result the agency had positioned only 20% of the equipment needed in the region.[32] Note that this was the state of affairs less than two weeks before President Bush's deadline for starting the war.

Blessedly, thanks partly to the extraordinary effectiveness and speed of the U.S. military and partly to the weakness of the Iraqi military, the war took a much shorter time than the scenario predicted and relatively few refugees rushed out of the country. Ironically, after a very short period of major combat, the flow of people across the Iraqi borders was in the other direction. It consisted of outside terrorists coming into the country to attack American soldiers whose patrols of Iraqi cities made them sitting ducks conveniently available to terrorists in a Middle Eastern shooting gallery. The war turned out to be a boon to terrorists who had previously lacked easy American targets.

Another off-the-mark prediction before the war was the expectation that, as in Kosovo, there would be bloodbaths of revenge killings against ethnic "others," e.g., Shiites killing Sunnis who had oppressed them under Saddam. This was touted in the press as likely to be a difficult problem for American troops. After the war, revenge killings did happen, but they were a relatively minor problem. The far greater problems the U.S. troops were totally unprepared for, were widespread looting, then a ferocious ongoing anti-American insurgency. The history of takeovers of other countries predicted looting, but the U.S. military was unready. American soldiers stood by and let the looting happen; they had no orders to stop it.

A Balsa Wood "Smoking Gun"

In an especially exciting moment in the run-up to the Iraq war, the UN inspectors found an Iraqi unmanned drone airplane that caused a great stir. It was touted as Iraq's newest and largest remote controlled airplane. The inspectors reported that Iraq had not declared the drone as required under two separate Security Council resolutions. The Bush administration, always at the ready to declare Iraq in material breach of UN resolutions, jumped on the discovery. Here was an opportunity to bolster its increasingly shaky arguments that Iraq was flouting UN disarmament rules. John D. Negroponte, U.S. Ambassador to the UN, suggested that the drone could travel beyond UN-imposed limits, 93 miles or 150 kilometers. Not to be outdone, Colin Powell added that it might be able to dispense biological and chemical weapons and "should be a concern to everybody."[33]

These announcements were a heaven-sent opportunity for the government of Iraq. The whole episode may constitute evidence that God has a sense of humor. (Theologians take note.) Iraqi officials proudly displayed the plane for reporters. This formidable weapon of mass destruction turned out to be a prototype drone built of cannibalized aviation parts and craft shop materials including fabric and balsa wood wings and duct tape. The fuselage was made from a dinged-up torpedo-shaped fuel tank from a larger aircraft. One of the charms of this dangerous weapon was that it could be disassembled and reassembled at will, like a child's toy. A UN official privately noted to reporters that it had neither the guidance system capabilities nor the cargo carrying capabilities to travel long distances or to drop chemical or biological weapons. It had not been flown more than two miles and could not be guided from more than five miles away. It was designed for reconnaissance, jamming, and aerial photography—all purposes within UN guidelines.

UN officials admitted they erred in denying that the plane had been declared. The drone had been declared to the inspectors but the wingspan was erroneously reported as 13 feet rather than the actual 24.5 feet. The Iraqi official in charge of the plane stated that the error was a typo that had been corrected in a letter to the inspectors on February 18. Perhaps the wingspan error was the reason the UN inspectors failed to recognize the newly discovered plane as the one Iraq had already declared. All in all, these findings must have been a sad moment for U.S. officials, who apparently thought at last they had the goods on Saddam, the long-sought but elusive "smoking gun."

The total picture here is stark. One has to ask, what is happening when American officials at the genuinely high stature of Colin Powell are so desperate for small shreds of proof that they stumble and damage their credibility over such ridiculously inadequate evidence? The aluminum tubes, the faked documents on uranium acquisition, the erroneous conclusions from satellite photos of supposed weapons production plants, and the dinged up balsa-winged reconnaissance plane, all suggest the same story of an administration lacking verification for its case and desperate to grasp at any straw. Even after this kind of "evidence" had been thoroughly discredited,

Vice President Cheney continued to make speeches citing items such as the purported uranium purchases as evidence. To put it bluntly, unless he was isolated from news reports and writing his own speeches on the back of an envelope, he had to be lying. I wondered, can it be that our leaders, with their busy staffs and talented speechwriters and their access to classified information, are less informed than I am as an ordinary citizen reading the newspaper?

Who Are We Trying to Embarrass?

The evidence used by the Bush administration to try to persuade the world of Saddam's weapons of mass destruction has been a major embarrassment. However, there is a related story that is also important but much less visible. Why did the UN inspection team find the intelligence provided by the U.S. to be "garbage after garbage after garbage?" A quite disturbing possibility—much more disturbing than mere errors and lack of evidence—was revealed by a news report on March 16. It presented evidence that the U.S. was withholding its best evidence from the inspectors for political reasons in order to undermine the inspections, even after claiming it had passed along all its information. "Some [U.S.] officials charge that the administration is not interested in helping the [UN] inspectors discover weapons because a discovery could bolster supporters in the UN Security Council of continued inspections and undermine the administration's case for war. 'We don't want to have a smoking gun,' a ranking administration official said recently. He added, 'I don't know whether the point is to embarrass Blix or embarrass Saddam Hussein.' Another official familiar with the intelligence said, 'Not all the top sites have been passed to the inspectors.'"[34]

The same article continues, "Administration officials, in making the case against Iraq, repeatedly have failed to mention the considerable amount of documented weapons destruction that took place between 1991 and 1998, when the previous U.N. Special Commission on Iraq had inspection teams in the field. In that period, under U.N. supervision, Iraq destroyed 817 of 819 proscribed medium-range missiles, 14 launchers, 9 trailers and 56 fixed missile-launch sites. It also destroyed 73 of the 75 chemical or biological warheads and 163 warheads for conventional explosives."[35]

In addition, "U.N. inspectors also supervised destruction of 88,000 filled and unfilled chemical munitions, more than 600 tons of weaponized and bulk chemical weapons agents, 4,000 tons of precursor chemicals and 980 pieces of equipment considered key to production of such weapons." The article goes on to document significant, but less comprehensive, destruction of biological weapons.[36] In this context, it should also be remembered that ElBaradei, the head of the nuclear part of the UN inspection team, had stated that the previous inspections destroyed all of Iraq's nuclear program at that time. And as noted before, he had found no evidence of rebuilding and substantial evidence that rebuilding had not occurred. A scan of the country using sophisticated detection technology revealed nothing that would suggest that a nuclear weapons program existed.

No set of facts could be further from the picture the Bush administration has been at pains to project to the American public—that the previous UN inspections did not work, that they were abject failures that did nothing to rid Iraq of weapons of mass destruction. In fact, as the above-stated facts show, they were actually quite successful until they were discontinued, though there was plenty more work to be done. It should be noted here that the reason they were discontinued was not because Saddam threw the inspectors out, as is often erroneously reported. Saddam did engage in outrageous obstruction tactics, and finally the UN had to withdraw the inspectors because the Clinton administration decided to do a bit of bombing to send Saddam a message. It was the U.S. decision to bomb, not Saddam's noncompliance, that triggered the pull-out of the inspection team.

In the run-up to the 2003 war, the Bush administration's undermining of the new UN inspections by not providing the most powerful intelligence on Iraq's WMDs appears tactically rational in the context of its relentless inspection-bashing. The better Hans Blix looked, the worse George Bush looked. Any success by the UN inspectors in finding Iraq's WMDs would make Bush's rush to war look even more irrational and premature. Considering the highly dubious and often flatly wrong evidence presented to the American public about Iraq's weapons of mass destruction, as well as the evidence swept under the carpet about the success of previous inspections, it is difficult to avoid the impression that the American public was being lied to, or at the very least, cynically manipulated.

What Are We Trying to Do?

During the run-up to the war, discussion in the press about the mystery of the real reasons for the war abounded: given that Saddam's threat to American national security is not nearly as real as the Bush administration claims, what is the real motive for this war? Is it merely a huge mistake based on faulty intelligence, a mistake with a life of its own, a momentum that cannot be reversed without too great a loss of face? No one seemed to know the real motive. One wondered if even George W. Bush did.

Steadiness of purpose and political rhetoric are things Bush does well. But self-awareness and consistency of rationale are unfamiliar territories to him. He admits to making decisions instinctively rather than rationally. And he sees Saddam as evil, so let's go after him. But events suggested there was a place for reason in this mix. Bush's objectives and rationales changed with the wind, often quickly going in the opposite direction from where they started as circumstances changed. First he would take military action to remove Saddam without Congress or the UN. Then the Congress must be consulted. Then the UN Security Council was consulted. When the Security Council proved balky it was pronounced irrelevant unless it rubber stamped Bush's goals. However, despite being irrelevant, the UN would be needed to help clean up afterwards. At the outset, the goal of the war was regime change. Then it was disarming Saddam. Then it was both or either. Then it was a humanitarian intervention to liberate the Iraqi people and establish a glowing model of democracy in the Middle East.

In the context of these dizzying changes in methods of approach and goals for the war, the anti-war protesters can be excused for assuming one of the most cynical of all reasons, the desire to control Iraqi oil. After all, as they like to point out, Iraq has the world's second-largest oil fields, and the top echelon of the Bush administration is extraordinarily tightly linked to the oil industry. So much so that they are willing to fall on their swords politically to espouse the unpopular goal of drilling for oil in a magnificent and pristine Alaskan wildlife sanctuary. The combination of the administration's close ties to oil and the vast reserves of oil in Iraq seem too dramatic to be coincidence. The inference that oil was the real motivator may or may not have been true, but its plausibility was so transparent that the situation read like the clunky script of a contrived play or novel. It was the unacknowledged elephant in the drawing room.

Without denying or agreeing with control of Iraqi oil as a contributing motive, my own guess is that the original motive that jump-started the war was psychological, not rational: a political impulse to demonstrate America's continuing strong global leadership in a time of great uncertainty and fear after 9/11. At first, the demonstration of leadership had gone quite well. Initially Bush's war on terrorism traced the events of that terrible day to bin Laden and al Qaeda, and then unseated bin Laden's hosts, the rulers of Afghanistan. Soon that country's brutal Taliban regime was falling to the

Northern Alliance with the aid of U.S. pinpoint bombing, and all seemed to be going very well indeed.

But gradually the war in Afghanistan wound down, never quite ending, and bin Laden and Mulla Omar were still not captured and their whereabouts remained unknown. The inevitable lull followed, an uncertain and boring period that was still dangerous, after the initial excitement and success of the Afghan war. Al Qaeda's continuation was a threat and the failure to capture bin Laden an embarrassment to Bush. Before and during the Afghan war, bin Laden was Bush's favorite bogeyman. After the war inconclusively slowed down, Bush stopped mentioning him. It must have been sad for bin Laden to lose all that free publicity. Bush had helped to make him an ever-bigger hero in the Arab world.

To sustain the demonstration of America's strong global leadership after 9/11, something more dramatic was needed to keep up the political and psychological momentum. A war on an obvious villain, Saddam Hussein, who was thought to be connected to terrorism and al Qaeda, must have looked like the perfect solution. Highly placed officials in the Bush administration such as Paul Wolfowitz were obsessed with Saddam and had long advocated his overthrow. He seemed to be an ideal next target. He also represented an opportunity to use America's overwhelming military superiority to win a quick war and further demonstrate America's strength to the world, enhancing U.S. prestige and power still further, to the point of *de facto* complete dominance. Wolfowitz and other influential neo-conservatives had long held as their political Holy Grail this American hegemony over the rest of the world. This goal squared well with the views of other, less overtly ideological conservatives such as Vice President Cheney and Defense Secretary Donald Rumsfeld.

If a demonstration of American leadership was the intent of going after Saddam (in addition to dubious concerns about national security), the effort went disastrously awry. World public opinion quickly evolved into overwhelming opposition to the war.

Newsweek, hardly known for its radicalism, ran an uncommonly bold cover headline in the March 24, 2003 issue: "Why America Scares the World, and What to Do About It." Inside, the feature story was headlined, "The Arrogant Empire." In a time of flag-waving super-patriotism, for a major, politically moderate American news magazine to call the United States or the Bush administration an "arrogant empire" is itself newsworthy. The article itself was outstanding for its candor, accuracy and scope of vision during a period in which American journalism had become deeply dominated by tribalistic groupthink. For these reasons I have included a number of excerpts below.

In its campaign against Iraq, America is virtually alone. Never will it have waged a war in such isolation. Never have so many of its allies been so firmly opposed to its policies. Never has it provoked so much public opposition, resentment, and mistrust. And all this before the first shot has been fired.

Watching the tumult around the world, it's evident that what is happening goes well beyond this particular crisis. Many people, both abroad and in America, fear that we are at some kind of turning point, where well-established mainstays of global order—the Western Alliance, European unity, the United Nations—seem to be cracking under stress. These strains go well beyond the matter of Iraq, which is not vital enough to wreak such damage. In fact, the debate is not about Saddam anymore. It is about America in its role in the new world. To understand the present crisis, we must first grasp how the rest of the world now perceives American power.

Fareed Zakaria, the author of the article and a respected and moderate foreign affairs analyst for *Newsweek*, concludes the first part of the four-part article with these words:

...the administration is wrong if it believes that a successful war will make the world snap out of a deep and widening mistrust and resentment of American foreign policy. A war with Iraq, even if successful, might solve the Iraq problem. It doesn't solve the America problem. What worries people around the world above all else is living in a world shaped and dominated by one country— the United States. And they have come to be deeply suspicious and fearful of us.

Zakaria goes on in the second part of the article to remind us of our history of generosity after World War II, including as "exhibit A" the Marshall plan to rebuild Europe. What is striking is the contrast between U.S.

behavior at that time and the current pattern of blatant self-interest and lack of consideration for the rest of the world.

A couple of concluding sentences sum up Zakaria's outstanding article and condense much of the message of this book: "Does America really want a world in which it gets its way in the face of constant public anger only by twisting arms, offering bribes, and allying with dictators?" And finally, Zakaria addresses the idea that the U.S. must act to rebuild its relations with the world:

> But above all, it must make the world comfortable with its power by leading through consensus. America's special role in the world—its ability to buck history—is based not simply on its great strength, but on a global faith that this power is legitimate. If America squanders that, the loss will outweigh any gains in domestic security. And this next American century could prove to be lonely, brutish, and short.

Unfortunately, American leaders had already squandered the world's somewhat shaky trust in the legitimacy of its power by the totality of its self-interested and domineering behavior, starting before the Bush administration came into power and culminating in the war on Iraq. There is no sign that the Bush administration grasps the scope of this damage to America's legitimacy as a leader in the eyes of the world or is willing to reverse course as needed, both in action and at a basic policy level. Whether a new set of leaders following the Bush administration can restore some measure of trust in the good will of the U.S. and the legitimate uses of American power will be the great question facing U.S. foreign policy during the next few years. Especially challenging will be restoring some minimal level of trust within the Muslim world.

Malice in Blunderland: Tribalism at Work

Fareed Zakaria based the hardheaded and well-reasoned article discussed above on polls and on interviews conducted all over the world. He relayed what people told him of their fears about an out-of-control superpower. His article must have offered little comfort to the flag-waving hyper-patriots who believe in America's manifest destiny to push the world, by war and violence if necessary, kicking and screaming into a glorious Pax Americana. By

305

contrast, remarkable distortions of fact and logic, driven by tribalism and groupthink, were colorfully visible like exotic birds in the op-ed pages of the newspapers just before the war. They reached a zenith of rhetorical intensity and resentment toward France and the UN during the time just after Bush and Powell failed to get Security Council ratification of the war and before its ugly realities began to hit home.

It's both painful and amusing to look at some of the richer absurdities of these opinion pieces, but doing so provides an object lesson on the extent to which tribalism or ultra-nationalism in the U.S. can turn reason and common sense upside down. From a plethora of possibilities I've selected one piece as exemplary. It's headlined "UN Absurdity" by George F. Will, published in the *Washington Post* on March 13, 2003.

But first, for context, some observations on tribalism. As noted at the beginning of this book, its positive side is a strongly felt sense of obligation to protect members of the "tribe" (one's country, religion, extended family, etc.) from genuine external threats. This side of tribalism is admirable; it plays an essential role in the survival of innumerable human communities.

The negative side of tribalism is exaltation of one's own "tribe" and vilification of the "other" if the "other" disagrees or gets in the way, or is merely strange and different. It is an extension of protection of "one's own" to unreasoning fear and loathing of the "other. It is one of the chief causes of both war and genocide. Even if one's own tribe or group, for which one is waving the banner, is out of step with a much larger social context, it follows that "we" in our group are in step and therefore the rest of the world must be out of step. In the case of the war with Iraq, though overwhelming majorities of people in every other country except Israel opposed the war, they must still be wrong, and only we Americans are right about the need to attack Iraq. Further, our might makes us right. We are less than five percent of the world's population, but we have more military clout than all the rest of the world combined. So we can do as we please; we can play policeman of the world and pick our targets at will, without anyone else having a say. This arrangement is O.K. because our military might inescapably places the responsibility to act on our superpowered shoulders. Rudyard Kipling's "white man's burden" has become the neoconservative American's burden.

This tribalistic attitude, viewing the rest of the world as out of step because the U.S. is by definition in step, is of course an occasion for a great deal of American anger toward the rest of the world. How can "they" be so wrong-headed? How can they possibly oppose our righteous plans and actions? They must be cowardly, have sinister motives, or be hostile to us.

However, it's essential for the unconscious tribalist to not admit anger with the whole world, since admitting that would raise questions about why our group's opinions are so out of sync. So one must find a much more modest-sized focus for the anger—a symbol or scapegoat. (This mental process is unconscious and automatic, of course; it doesn't happen at the level of conscious reasoning, where it is transparently ridiculous.)

These irrational reactions exactly describe the situation of a certain fraction of American citizens and newspaper pundits who support the war in Iraq not with reason (by which it might be, with great difficulty, supported) but with the fervor of a passionate and unreasoning "patriotism." For these people, France and the UN are the obvious scapegoats. The French are the ones who articulated and mobilized the UN Security Council's opposition to the war. Never mind that this was a cakewalk since the whole world was against us. Since the French opposed us, we eat "freedom fries" and "freedom toast" rather than "French" products at the congressional cafeteria. We pour French wines into the gutter. A person who can't laugh at this is woefully lacking a sense of the ridiculous. What the French, Germans, Russians and the UN really did was to articulate an overwhelming majority of world public opinion. In particular, the UN, despite its flaws, was doing exactly what it was designed to do by its founders, including the U.S.—to express global opinion and to seek an effective alternative to war.

The kind of American tribalism or overheated patriotism that rages at France and the UN for expressing global public opinion contrasts with a mature patriotism that is balanced with reason and a recognition that the highest value is the value of all human life. One can love one's country and at the same time recognize that its government's policies are sometimes wrong. The pundits, conservative and liberal alike, who write op-ed pieces usually feel quite free to criticize government policies without feeling they are thereby being unpatriotic.

However, the prospect of war and the UN attempting to stand in the way has apparently unhinged some of them. Enter George Will's classic demonstration of the negative side of tribalism in his editorial, "U.N. Absurdity." Like Bush, for whom clarity means ignoring very real nuances and shades of gray, he claims to value clarity: "War precipitates clarity as well as confusion, and the war against Iraq has clarified this: The United Nations is not a good idea badly implemented, it is a bad idea."[37] The rest of the article is a diatribe against France and more emphatically, the vehicle of its momentary influence, the UN. According to Will, the UN is unaccountable and irresponsible. It lacks legitimacy because it lacks certain characteristics. These happen to be the characteristics of an extremely powerful democratic nation-state like the U.S. A key, he says, is that its internal political authority is legitimized by the recurring consent of the governed: By contrast, "inebriated by self-approval, the United Nations is grounded in neither democratic consent nor territorial responsibilities, nor independent fiscal means, nor the material means of enforcing its judgements."[38] In other words, the UN is not legitimate because it is not the United States.

Will's denial of legitimacy to the UN conveniently overlooks several decisive points. The UN's legitimacy is based on the ratification of its Charter by 191 member nations, essentially all the nations in the world, including the United States. Their continued participation in its activities, including their debates and votes in the General Assembly and the Security Council, constitute a clear continuation of consent to its legitimacy. Member nations, including the U.S., are affirming the UN's legitimacy with every one of their votes. In both political and legal terms, the United Nations is the most massively legitimized institution on the planet. I wonder if it is lost on the deniers of the UN's legitimacy that the first thing every new nation does to establish its own legitimacy is to apply for membership in the UN.

The UN Charter, ratified by all the world's nations, states clearly that there are only three legal reasons for a nation to go to war: the nation has been attacked; it is subject to imminent threat of attack; or the UN Security Council has determined that the action is needed for the collective security of the member nations. Since the U.S. Constitution makes treaties signed by the President and ratified by the U.S. Senate the law of the land, these criteria for the legality of war constitute U.S. law as well as international law. So American law, among other sources, legitimizes the UN's definition of what constitutes a legitimate reason to go to war.

This rock-solid legal legitimacy, the strongest possible in international and domestic American law, is the reality Will's "U.N. Absurdity" denies when he mocks the UN as "inebriated with self-approval."[39] Who is the "self" here except the collective will of the UN's member nations? He ridicules the very idea of a community of nations in his article, but then attributes to this supposedly non-existent entity the "self" approval of the UN, which is in reality nothing more than the embodiment of the community of nations. The moral and legal authority of the UN rests on the U.S. Constitution and the constitutions and laws of every other nation in the world. Can someone offer a more substantial form of legitimacy?

In the article's comments about the war with Iraq, the influence of tribalism is richly, almost comically apparent. First, a little context: George Bush was voted into office by less than half the voting population of a nation consisting of less than 5% of the world's population. Doing the math is easy. He holds the immense military power his questionable election gave to him by a vote of substantially less than 2.5% of the world's population. His power thus "legitimized," Bush has anointed himself policeman of the world and announced that with or without the concurrence of the rest of the world as expressed through the UN, he will use military force to depose the head of state of another sovereign nation. This is legitimacy?

During the months before the war began Bush declared war on Iraq again and again, in effect announcing his defiance of international law and his determination to flout the UN and attack Iraq even if the UN didn't rubber stamp his decision. The UN must agree with him or doom itself to irrelevance. His rationale for attacking Iraq is that Saddam violates international law and flouts the UN. Then Bush does the same thing.

This breathtaking arrogance has a Grand Canyon-like magnitude. If such things could be measured, it would stand out as the hands-down winner of the *Guinness Book of World Records* award for hubris and double standards. Yet in the inverted perspective of tribalism, from which our leader can do no wrong and anyone who impedes him is therefore out of step, Will announces, "...for America, the imperative of disarming Iraq will soon be supplanted by the imperative of insulating U.S. sovereignty from U.N. hubris." In other words, U.S. sovereignty allows us to freely violate the sovereignty of any other nation, and Bush's hubris is really the UN's hubris, since it fails to bow to his ready-made decision. The consequent result: inversion of reality completed. Reasons need not be given, lest they be recognized as preposterous. Wondrously, the upside-down values of tribalism make the transparent contradictions invisible to the author. From the passion of his rhetoric it is impossible to doubt his sincerity.

In view of Bush's frequent declarations of war on Iraq and his repeated announcements that he would defy the UN and go ahead with his war plans even if the UN didn't cave in to his demands, remarkably, Will's article blames France and the UN for making war inevitable. One wonders what planet the author was visiting while Bush was announcing almost daily that war was inevitable if Saddam didn't do what the leader of any nation would refuse to do under threat from another—unilaterally disarm or go into exile. The answer can only be that Will was visiting the inverted Alice-in-Wonderland world of planet tribalism. I don't recall seeing any op-ed pieces by George Will eating humble pie when immediately after the war, Bush had to go to the UN to legalize U.S. sale of Iraqi oil.

Tribalism in the Media

During the run-up to the Iraq war, the 40% of Americans who opposed it often found themselves looking under rocks and in closets and attics for reports from the news media on even the most conspicuous and dramatic evidence, logic, speeches, and demonstrations against the war. Innumerable stories that were clearly newsworthy were not reported or were merely mentioned in passing. Why? The first mysteries were the surprising flimsiness of the rationale for the war and the unsuccessfully answered questions, "Why war, and why now?" The second mystery became why the "free" American news media were ignoring the very vocal opposition to the war and the logic against it.

Hawks may have wanted to believe that the media's failure to report dissent on the war was just a fantasy of the political left. But there is abundant evidence that it was no fantasy. For example, Michael Getler, the Ombudsman of the *Washington Post*, having received a good deal of mail about the *Post*'s neglect of opposition to the war, did his homework on the subject. He wrote an article on March 16, 2003 that makes the reality clear. He begins by mentioning the *Post*'s long delay in publishing the letter of resignation by State Department Foreign Service Officer John Kiesling. He acknowledges that the letter was a powerful expression of dissent against the war. Then he says, "What makes the *Post*'s treatment of it [the letter] noteworthy ... is that it is part of a perplexing flaw in coverage that has persisted throughout this long run-up to a controversial war and that contrasts with the many fine reporting efforts" of the paper.

Getler then lists other examples. Looking back, he says, "There is a pattern in the news pages of missing, underplaying or being late" on public dissent or uncertainty about the war. These lapses

started last August with the failure to record promptly the doubts of then-House Majority Leader Richard K. Armey (R-Tex) and of Brent Scowcroft, the first President Bush's national security adviser. The first public hearings on the implications of the war, held by the Senate Foreign Relations Committee, got just a few paragraphs at the end of stories. In September, there was no spot coverage of the testimony of three retired four-star generals before the Senate Armed Services Committee warning against an attack without exhausting diplomatic options and gaining United Nations backing. Soon after, a widely reported speech by Sen. Edward M. Kennedy (D-Mass) got one line in the Post, and large antiwar rallies in London and Rome went unreported the next day. In October, when more than 100,000 people gathered in Washington to protest war, the paper put the story in the Metro section. Then came complaints about a major speech by Sen. Robert C. Byrd (D-W.Va.), one of the few Senators who has taken a strong antiwar position, was missed and that the story about the most recent bin Laden audiotape failed to point out bin Laden's description of Iraqi leaders as 'infidels.'

Getler goes on,

A rare story last month estimating the cost of the war, which was front-page news elsewhere, ran on page A19. The congressional testimony the following day of Deputy Defense Secretary Paul D. Wolfowitz, who discounted those costs and who described as "wildly off the mark" previous testimony by the Army chief of staff that hundreds of thousands of troops might be needed for occupation duty, was not reported.

This is an impressive catalog of journalistic oversight, neglect and delay, all by one highly respected newspaper (a reputedly liberal newspaper at that) and all concentrated on neglect of the same point of view—news about opposition to the war or questioning its wisdom. How is it possible that this consistent pattern is accidental?

The pattern becomes even more suspect when one considers the editorial position of the *Washington Post*. Despite its reputation as a liberal paper, the *Post*'s editorials supported the war from day one. The *Post*'s ombudsman resists the seemingly obvious conclusion that the editorial bias may have affected news reporting and states that "I am very confident that the *Post* news coverage is straight, tough and fair, and that the wall between news and editorial is solid." As an outsider, one cannot realistically second-guess Getler's knowledge of what goes on inside the *Post*. But one can see that there is a serious problem. Maybe there is bias in the selection of the news in the newsroom, specifically the selection of stories among various competitors for copy space, quite independently of the views of the editorial page staff. In any case, a strong bias was unmistakably at work, whether it was deliberate or not.

The public did not get the full story of the downsides and objections to the war from this source, and the *Post* was far from alone. My personal experience with media neglect of a story included marching in a protest against the war on a blustery, sub-freezing Saturday in January in Washington DC. I was part of an immense crowd that filled the National Mall; there were thousands of people as far as the eye could see, a veritable ocean of humanity. My own visual scan and that of others confirmed that they were a cross-section of American society, parents with children in strollers, grandparents, teenagers, classic "soccer moms," young couples, the kind of people you might see at the Fourth of July fireworks display on the Mall. They were the opposite of a few eccentrically dressed extremists, which was what the op-ed pieces of the hawks claimed. Many (myself included) said they were demonstrating against a war for the first time in their lives, because they saw this war as different and unjustified.

Similar demonstrations flooded the streets with people in every major city throughout the country, arguably involving millions of people. The marches were not limited to the U.S. There were demonstrations against the war that day in 660 cities all over the world. The estimates of the size of the crowd in Washington DC were in the 100,000-200,000 range. Speakers at the podium included big-name politicians and Hollywood celebrities. Among other people there, I met and chatted informally with CBS journalist Joie Chen and saw her cameraman, so I know at least one national network was on the scene. Yet there was hardly a mention of it in the national television news, including, so far as I could tell, the CBS Evening News. My friends, who are more avid TV-watchers than I, told me that so far as they could tell only CNN reported it nationally. I wondered, what's wrong with this picture? A hundred thousand people or so march in Washington DC on an extremely cold and windy day, with celebrities on the stage, against a war that hadn't started yet and it's not news? During the Vietnam War, crowds like this were news. They have always been news. What has changed?

A theory offered by the most liberal end of the media spectrum, journalists and commentators like *Pacifica*'s Amy Goodman, was that the mainstream media are controlled by a handful of major corporations and these corporations were suppressing dissent. They were telling the news anchors what not to talk about. This view quickly became the far left's orthodoxy on the subject. However, there are problems with this theory.

One is motive. The war's impact on the economy might be catastrophic rather than beneficial. Large corporations move slowly and thus need a fairly predictable economic environment. Would they, for economic reasons, really bet on a wildly unpredictable war, with potential downsides such as oil price spikes, huge government budget deficits, etc.? Certainly the vendors of weapons and supplies to the military would benefit, but are they the same corporations that control the media? If I needed to, I could easily muster the cynicism to believe that the media-owning corporations were behind the biased war coverage, but the theory wasn't on its face very convincing. Of course, the news media would have a ready-made compelling story for months. TV viewership would go way up. They would see advertisements. That could be a plus. But still the unpredictable potential influence of the war on the economy made me wonder.

Another problem with the corporate-control-of-the-media theory is that the mainstream journalists denied vehemently that their corporate owners were telling them what to say, or influencing them in any way. They added or implied that if the corporate sponsors or owners tried to control them, they—the journalists—would rebel. Of course, if the corporate conspiracy theory were true, one would expect denials. American journalists feel a strong traditional responsibility to maintain at least the appearance of objectivity or freedom from bias in news reporting. But there would have been leakage about illegitimate influence if it were happening, and there no was no such leak. By contrast, even the Pentagon, despite an organizational culture of discipline and one of the world's strongest chains of command, has leaked like a sieve during the war about the dissent in the ranks on the wisdom of the war plans. If the Pentagon can't suppress internal dissent and stay on message, how could the news media with its fragmentation and fierce competition among rival news sources hope to accomplish such a feat? Corporate control didn't add up.

An alternative explanation for the undeniable bias of the media is that the newsrooms are also infected, like the general public, with the post-9/11 viruses of fear, anger, and tribalistic rally-round-the-flag emotional reactions to events. After the World Trade Center buildings went down, President Bush gave a few stirring and thoroughly tribalistic speeches and suddenly morphed from a small man in a big job, a man of limited intellect who hilariously mangled his words and syntax, to a knight in shining armor who would deliver us from the evils of terrorism. His poll numbers skyrocketed.

The news media was the vehicle through which this near-miraculous transformation was carried out. Of course, they had to report his speeches

313

and decisions. Suddenly they could not attack Bush, formerly one of their favorite punching bags. Now to attack him would be unpatriotic, divisive behavior in a time of national crisis. The public was lapping up what he had to say and idolizing him. After criticizing him, the next-best thing for holding the attention of the public was to make him a hero. The war in Afghanistan went well and involved few American casualties, thus reinforcing his stature as a wartime leader. The proposed war on Iraq was also his baby, wrongly portrayed as a continuation of the war on terrorism, and therefore not to be questioned lest one appear unpatriotic.

The American news media almost never displays the courage to criticize a President who is running high in the polls. They know what slings and arrows of outrageous fortune will come their way if they do. Also, they know that to challenge the popular wisdom of the moment could lower ratings, as people turn in disgust from stories they disagree with to other sources of news. So stories challenging the war and Bush's advocacy of it could safely be given short shrift in the midst of fierce pressures for copy space in the papers and time slots in the evening television news. The TV anchors and newspaper editors didn't need their corporate masters to tell them what to say; they knew the political lay of the land themselves. Their job was to get on the bandwagon, to beat the tribal war drums. This was a really big football game, and football games need cheerleaders. Of course, it should be stressed that this reaction, while quite real, is not necessarily conscious and deliberate. No one expects Dan Rather or Tom Brokaw to deliberately don a pleated skirt and wave pom-poms. It is equally unlikely that George T. Will was aware of the ridiculous tribalism driving his thinking, obvious though it is to an outsider, in his "U.N. Absurdity" article.

Just in case directors of news programming were not shrewd enough or cynical enough to figure out on their own that beating the war drums and muffling dissent was not only "patriotic" (read jingoistic) but also financially advantageous, there were consultants around to tell them. The following headlines cited by Paul Farhi illustrate: "Consultants Tell Radio, TV Clients That Protest Coverage Drives Off Viewers"[40] and "Skip Protests, Media Advisers Tell Stations."[41] Money talks. Here's a telling comment from Frank N. Magid Associates, an influential TV-news consulting firm: "Covering war protests may be harmful to your bottom line."[42] These same consultants advocate playing patriotic music, visiting military bases, interviewing veterans of the Gulf War, and engaging in other pro-war programming. Whip up that tribalism, even if it rationalizes killing people; it pays in advertising revenue.

314

Does this consulting message prove the point about the concentration of corporate control over the major American news media? No, quite the opposite, but paradoxically, it might as well. Who are the clients of these consultants? According to Farhi, "Their influence is considered strongest in the smaller markets, where many radio and TV stations have smaller staffs and less experienced management than their network or big-city brethren."[43] So the conclusion is clear. The major media outlets have savvy internal news staff who know that playing down dissent against the war will keep their ratings up, and the smaller outlets are told the same thing by consultants. Either way the financial interests that control the media—both major and minor, diverse and concentrated—have aligned with a tribalistic public reaction. These forces in conjunction are calling the shots and increasing the war fervor. Tribalism begets more tribalism, and money greases the skids. One simply must not risk lower ratings and consequent loss of advertising revenue to present the unpopular news of opposition to the war.

The TV coverage of the Iraq war by British Broadcasting Company (BBC) World News provided an exception that proved the rule. Alone among the purveyors of TV news that regularly reached a national audience in the U.S., BBC showed no pro-war bias or tendency to play down anti-war dissent. It reported the war and world public opinion as it was, warts and all, favorable and unfavorable. The show's origins in England, revealed not only by its name but also by the English accents of its reporters and anchors, tell the story.

England has no public opinion bias in favor of the war, despite Tony Blair's valiant efforts to persuade the British public to go along. The anti-war opinions (or at least relative absence of pro-war opinions) among the British people are naturally mirrored in their premier broadcast medium, even though they also have a substantial American audience. Amusingly, the BBC reports have been subject to criticism by the American news media for their occasional, modest displays of skepticism about the war, expressed in the types of questions anchors ask in interviews. The American media's message: "You're not objective because your bias is different from our bias."

David Greenberg, an historian and visiting scholar at the American Academy of Arts and Sciences, analyzed the wide discrepancy between American news reporting and that of other countries during the run-up to the war. He concluded that the American press and the American public alike have blind spots that stem from an historic shift away from the post-Vietnam and post-Watergate cynicism, national self-criticism, and suspicion of our leaders to the opposite extreme of post-9/11 flag-waving faith in our leaders.

315

The overseas press was caught up in no such fervor, of course. Foreign audiences and foreign press find American military power and a trigger-happy willingness to use it deeply alarming. Greenberg cited the shift in American attitudes illustrated by several episodes such as the fraudulent evidence for Iraqi uranium acquisition used in Colin Powell's speech supporting the war. He comments, "Not long ago the U.S. media would have treated these recent episodes as huge scandals—the equivalent of the Pentagon Papers or My Lai or the 18½ minute gap in Richard Nixon's Watergate tapes."[44] Yet they got so little play most Americans are unaware of them. "What did Colin Powell know and when did he know it?" is not a question anyone was asking in the press.

Fallacious Assumptions

Two questions haunt anyone studying the diplomatic fiasco leading up to the U.S. failure to get UN Security Council backing for the war: how did we get so far out on a limb? How did this widespread global abandonment of American leadership, with a majority of citizens in every nation except Israel and the U.S. opposing the war, come about? James Mann, a former diplomatic correspondent for the *Los Angeles Times* and a senior writer-in-residence at the Center for Strategic and International Studies has some convincing answers.

Mann notes, "For more than two years, indeed even before President Bush took office, the members of his foreign policy team have repeatedly advanced a series of optimistic, self-justifying ideas about America's relationship with its friends and allies—namely, that these nations' growing estrangement from U.S. foreign policy wasn't real, wasn't serious or wouldn't last. Now the administration is belatedly discovering that both its beliefs and its underlying assumptions were wrong."[45] Mann hints at, but doesn't mention Bush's brusque and blatantly selfish ("not in our interests") departure from global treaties such as the International Criminal Court and the Kyoto Protocols on global warming. These actions were major background sources of allied discontent. The war piled on to these other stresses and multiplied them many times over. For America's alienated allies, perhaps, it was time to take the American "hyperpower" down a peg or two. The unpopularity and blatant illegality of the war (but for a Security Council resolution they could easily block) provided an irresistible opportunity.

Bush ran for President emphasizing the importance of working with our allies. Yet the neo-conservative foreign policy team he put together believed openly in preventive war, a radical departure from anything explicitly avowed before. Briefly, the policy was based on the notion that the U.S. could legitimately start a war where it perceived its interests to be threatened, without first being attacked or being subject to an imminent threat. In short, it's O.K. for the U.S. to be an aggressor if it feels threatened. Mann comments, "It is almost as if the administration has been running its foreign policy out of two sides of its brain. On one side, it has been developing a whole new set of principles, centered on the doctrine of preventive war. On the other, the administration has clung to and operated with more traditional views about the continuing importance of our friends and allies, who do not accept the administration's new doctrines.

Mann continues, "The result of the administration's disjointed approach has been plain to see. Over the past few months, Americans have been stunned to discover that some allied governments and large numbers of people overseas are focusing upon the power of the United States – rather than upon Saddam's programs for weapons of mass destruction – as the main problem."[46]

Mann identifies two assumptions that led us down this primrose path: the strength hypothesis and the follower hypothesis. Behind them was Deputy Secretary of Defense Paul Wolfowitz. Wolfowitz criticized President Clinton for a weak policy against Iraq, and argued that this weakness was the reason the U.S. coalition against Iraq was gradually getting weaker. He argued for what Mann calls the "strength hypothesis," that the more strength the U.S. displayed in its opposition to Iraq, the more support it would have.

Mann labels another aspect of Wolfowitz's thinking the "follower hypothesis"—if America led, its friends and allies would follow. Echoing the widespread belief of the time that the U.S. was the "indispensable nation," Wolfowitz argued that if America led, even to the point of willingness to act unilaterally, allies would follow. The Bush administration charged ahead, embracing these assumptions and failing to see that other nations would become worried about excessive unilateral American power, resulting in a backlash, and that other nations would be insulted by the demand that they just get into line and stop grousing. Both assumptions were arrogant, and both, carried too far, proved to be wrong. As Joseph Nye points out in his book, *The Paradox of American Power*, when too much brute force is applied, diplomacy breaks down and the U.S. loses the attractive power of its culture and values. President Clinton avoided this mistake and treated America's allies with at least an appearance of respect. Conversely, Bush made the mistake in spades, and paid the diplomatic price of a major, historic breakdown in our traditional transatlantic alliance.

A leader (if not a dictator) can only lead where others want to go, and then must do so with tact, diplomacy and respect. Bush tried to lead the world where his presumed followers (other nations and their people) did not want to go, namely war with Iraq, and he did so with aggressive rhetoric, a bullying style (bribing some countries and threatening others with loss of American economic aid and other unspecified consequences), and with little regard for the feelings and opinions of the people and the leaders of other nations. As a result, it became a positive political advantage to other world leaders in dealing with their own populations to stiff-arm the United States. They did so with glee, and made great political gains with their people by doing so. From their point of view, the moral high ground and the political high ground converged in opposition to the war. This is a combination few politicians can be expected to resist.

On the future of the UN and our alliances, Mann's prognosis is pessimistic. He states, "The diplomatic battles over Iraq have created dynamics and crystallized perceptions that are likely to endure. Many Europeans have developed their own set of illusions about the United States. Some now believe erroneously that American foreign policy is in the grip of a right-wing cabal, a misperception that fails to explain why many Democrats and liberals have supported (or are not opposing) war in Iraq."[47]

I agree with Mann that the damage may be lasting, especially if the U.S. Government doesn't drastically change the substance and style of its policies. However, I disagree on one vital point. The truth is that American foreign policy is indeed very much in the grip of a small, extreme and unrepresentative right-wing group of people. Calling them a cabal is of course wrong, since their identities, aims and ideology are out in the open. A cabal or conspiracy is usually considered secretive. Neoconservative ideologues have for some time been openly advocating an aggressive, militaristic, "America first" foreign policy that was bound, if put into practice, to alienate U.S. allies and launch wars. Until the second Bush administration, the neoconservatives had held no reins of political power. They were present in the administration of Bush, Sr., but he deliberately restrained their ambitions for U.S. global domination, evidently considering them too extreme in their views.

For most of the period after the Cold War, the great majority of Democrats and the few remaining moderate Republicans have been consistently positive and cooperative in their foreign policy views and opposed to the lone-ranger foreign policies of a Republican-dominated Senate Foreign Relations Committee and a Bush-dominated White House. An overwhelming majority of Democrats have supported the treaties on the rights of children and women, the International Criminal Court, landmines, global warming, etc.

But on the run-up to the war, it was some of the Democrats, not other countries, who fell into the trap of Wolfowitz's two assumptions, the "strength hypothesis" and the "follower hypothesis." As regards the war, an event that usually whips up a lot of not-very-rational patriotism, during the run-up to the 2002 House and Senate election many Democrats did not want to stand up to a popular President. They were afraid to be labeled "unpatriotic." As a result of their lack of leadership, their internal divisions and their "me, too" stance on the war and other issues, they lost control of the Senate in November 2002. This was a mid-term election in which historical statistics suggest they should have gained seats. They lacked the courage to stand up to the war, and they paid a heavy price. But Howard Dean's candidacy for the Democratic nomination for President revealed how strong the resistance to this kind of foreign policy was among Democrats. What the people want will make a difference in the longer term; the neoconservatives are a small minority.

Mann's belief that European perceptions are likely to endure is persuasive because the arrogant unilateralism that plagued U.S. foreign policy well before Bush took office may outlast him. The U.S. Government may go on thumbing its nose at the progressive views of a majority of Americans on these issues if decisive electoral action is not taken by that majority. This is a clear, if difficult, test of American democracy. Every time the U.S. stiff-arms Europe on matters such as global warming, curbing landmines, demanding exemptions of U.S. troops from the jurisdiction of the International Criminal Court, abrogating yet another major arms treaty, etc., the European image of the U.S. as an arrogant, bullying superpower is reinforced. If American citizens wake up and vote based on their foreign policy views as well as their domestic concerns, these behaviors of their government will change, and relations with Europe and other allies will improve.

A look at the foreign policy preferences of Americans shows that a three-fourths majority is thoroughly multilateralist in their outlook—supportive of the UN, supportive of major arms control treaties, and supportive of coordinated action on global problems such as the rights of women and children, global warming, landmines, etc. These attitudes have been consistent for years, as revealed in repeated polls over time by a variety of pollsters. The most thorough and recent of these polls are those of Steven Kull of the University of Maryland, but there are many others with corroborative results.

Seemingly, the Democrats had eight years to put a distinctive multilateral stamp on U.S. foreign policy. Why wasn't the Clinton administration more decisively multilateralist? The short answer is that for the latter six of the eight years of the Clinton administration, U.S. foreign policy was partially hijacked by one of the most extreme conservatives in the Senate, Jesse Helms, who served as Chair of the Senate Foreign Relations Committee. He maintained a vindictive dictatorship over policy. The committee ceased to be a place for policy debates and discussions. It became a one-man-playing-hardball show in which pre-determined, extreme conservative policies were the only permitted subjects for consideration. If at first Helms didn't get his way, he blocked nominations for ambassadorships and other needed Senate action until he did. Nothing got out of his committee that he didn't like, and he disliked the UN and multilateral treaties.

Now that Helms is gone, we have another power center controlled by another extreme conservative, George Bush Jr. as President working with a closely divided Senate. It takes the President forwarding a treaty to the Senate and a two-thirds majority voting "yes" to ratify a treaty. Neither of these actions will be taken on progressive multilateral treaties under the present U.S. leadership. These are the unfortunate flukes of circumstance that have for ten years prevented the U.S. Government from representing the foreign policy beliefs and values of a majority of Americans. Yes, Mr. Mann, the nation's foreign policy has indeed been hijacked, as the Europeans think it has, by a tight-knit group of ultra conservative politicians who do not represent the majority views of the American public. However, it seems unlikely in a democracy that such an unrepresentative foreign policy can last indefinitely. Concerned citizens in the U.S. and in Europe can only hope that it will change soon. Americans can work toward that end by organizing and by voting.

The Shoe on the Other Foot

The claim that history repeats itself is a bit too facile, but sometimes it turns out to be true. After the defeat of the Ottoman Empire in World War I, England and France divided up the Middle East, enjoying the benefits of their control of Middle Eastern oil, while the U.S. stood on the sidelines and criticized their colonialism. As a part of these events, Iraq was "liberated" from the Ottoman Empire in 1917 by the British, who took the country militarily with some difficulty, and announced that they were liberators. They led the Iraqis to expect a substantial degree of self-rule, but disappointed them with considerably less than full control of their own affairs. For England, the Iraq war of 2003 was the second time around, but this time in the shadow of American power, whereas for the U.S. it's a role reversal. During its first occupation of Iraq England had to use military force to put down rebellions, the largest in 1920. Eventually England allowed Iraq formal independence in 1932.

The colonialism of that era is or appears to be a thing of the past, and the U.S. has shown little appetite for nation building—far too little, if Afghanistan is any indication. However, the temptations of control of Iraqi oil and the possibility of having military bases in Iraq from which to exert coercive pressures on other Middle Eastern nations may make American political leaders loathe to let go of a costly prize. Wolfowitz's vision of the takeover of Iraq as a first step in remaking the Middle East suggests an expectation of a continued strong U.S. presence, if not outright control. Aside from these longer-term considerations, the U.S. will have to stay in Iraq long enough to establish some semblance of order and at least some reasonable appearance of self-rule. History suggests that this will be neither a short stay, nor an easy one.

Democracy in Iraq may prove to be as self-terminating as it was in Algeria, where elections would have voted in an anti-democratic Muslim theocracy had the Algerian military not truncated the election process. The horrific result in Algeria of this start-stop movement toward democracy was a seemingly endless mix of civil war and terrorism. Thousands of civilians were slaughtered in mindless, pointless massacres. Tragically, this may also be the future of Iraq. (Eventually, after years of bloodshed, Algeria did find political stability and in March, 2004 held a successful election.)

During the period of English control of Iraq after WWI, Iraq was newly carved out of pieces of the Ottoman Empire by the European powers. It had no history as an independent nation. However, even at that time Muslims resented being governed by non-Muslims, as they do if possible even more vehemently at the beginning of the 21st century. In addition to that cultural and religious dynamic, many of the Iraqi people have a sense of national pride that is bound to be offended by a foreign invader determining the fate of the country. It is only natural that they should rejoice at being liberated from the terror of Saddam's rule, and then turn on the foreign invaders in order to oust them. The terribly difficult balance for the U.S. will be to stay long enough to establish some degree of stability, but not so long as to leave hastily in a hail of gunfire from resentful Iraqi rebels. It may be impossible to achieve the goal of stability; there may be no equilibrium point. If there is not, civil war with the potential to destabilize the whole region would seem to be the grim alternative. Going into Iraq was a strategic blunder from the start.

---

[1] Richard Cohen, "Bush, the Bad Guy" *Washington Post*, January 28, 2003.

[2] Jessica Matthews, "War Is Not Yet Necessary" *Washington Post*, January 28, 2003

[3] Idem.

[4] Idem.

[5] Michael Dobbs, "On Iraq, Chorus of Criticism Is Loud but Not Clear" *Washington Post*, February 3, 2003.

[6] Idem.

[7] Idem.

[8] Mary McGrory, "Fuzzy-Headed on North Korea" *Washington Post*, February 9, 2003.

[9] David Ignatius, "Salesmanship in a Skeptical World" *Washington Post*, January 28, 2003.

[10] Idem.

[11] Thomas E. Ricks and Vernon Loeb, "Unrivaled Military Feels Strains of Unending War" *Washington Post*, February 16, 2003.

[12] Idem.

[13] Glenn Kessler, "Forceful Tactics Catch Up With U.S.: Efforts to Build Support on Iraq Stymied by Two Years of International Resentment," Washington Post, February 16, 2003.

[14] "'Without Evidence, Confidence Cannot Arise' Excerpts from Statements by Hans Blix and Mohamed ElBaradei at the UN," *Washington Post*, February 15, 2003.

[15] "U.S. Meets New Resistance at UN" *Washington Post*, February 15, 2003.

[16] Fareed Zakaria, "This Isn't About Iraq Any More" *Newsweek*, February 24, 2003.

[17] Idem.

[18] Idem.

[19] Anthony Shadid, "Old Arab Friends Turn Away From U.S.," *Washington Post*, February 26, 2003

[20] Idem.

[21] Idem.

[22] Joseph Cirincione, director of the Non-Proliferation Project at the Carnegie Endowment for International Peace was quoted as saying this in an article by Glenn Kessler and Mike Allen, "Bush Faces Increasingly Poor Image Overseas," *Washington Post*, February 24, 2003.

[23] Felice D. Gaer and Michael K. Young, "Remember Afghanistan: The U.S. is still far from achieving a lasting humanitarian victory," *Washington Post*, February 27, 2003.

[24] Idem.

[25] Thomas E. Ricks, "A Pitch to Iraqi Americans," *Washington Post*, February 24, 2003.

[26] Idem.

[27] Idem. (ref. Ricks, footnote 16)

[28] Colum Lynch, "Annan Urges Council Members to Make War a Last Resort," *Washington Post*, March 5, 2003.

[29] Vernon Loeb and Thomas E. Ricks, "For Army, Fears of Postwar Strife" *Washington Post*, March 11, 2003.

[30] Idem.

[31] Idem.

[32] Kenneth Bacon and George Rupp, "Unready for the Aftermath," *Washington Post*, March 7, 2003.

[33] Rajiv Chandrasekaran, "Iraqi Officials Proudly Exhibit A Disputed, Dinged-Up Drone," *Washington Post*, March 13, 2003.

[34] Walter Pincus, "U.S. Lacks Specifics on Banned Arms," *Washington Post*, March 16, 2003.

[35] Idem.

[36] Idem.

[37] George F. Will, "UN Absurdity" *The Washington Post* , March 13, 2003.

[38] Idem.

[39] Idem.

[40] Paul Farhi, "For Broadcast Media, Patriotism Pays," *Washington Post* Style section, March 28, 2003.

[41] Idem.

[42] Idem.

[43] Idem.

[44] David Greenberg, "We Don't Even Agree On What's Newsworthy," *Washington Post* Outlook section, March 16, 2003.

[45] James Mann, "Bush Wanted His Doctrine And the Allies Too," *Washington Post* Outlook section, March 16, 2003.

[46] David Greenberg, "We Don't Even Agree On What's Newsworthy," *Washington Post* Outlook section, March 16, 2003.

[47] Idem.

Chapter Eleven

THE WAR AFTER THE WAR

In the lead-up to the Iraq war and its later conduct, I saw, at a minimum, true dereliction, negligence and irresponsibility; at worst, lying, incompetence and corruption. If there is a center that can hold this mess together, I don't know what it is. Civil war could break out at any time. Resources are needed; a strategy is needed; and a plan is needed.

—Marine General Anthony C. Zinni (Ret.)

The speed with which the initial military outcome of the 2003 attack on Iraq became clear to all, including the Iraqis, was breathtaking. Three weeks to the day after March 20, 2003—the beginning of Gulf War II—or whatever history will call it, Iraqis were celebrating the Americans' arrival in the streets of Baghdad. They were whacking the head of a fallen statue of Saddam Hussein with their shoes, kissing American soldiers, relishing their freedom to express their true political opinions for the first time in decades, openly looting and burning government buildings, hospitals, schools, and some of the world's greatest museums and libraries, and engaging in revenge killings against Sunnis, Baath Party officials, and mullahs who took the wrong side or said the wrong thing. Despite the jarring and sometimes lethal civil chaos, it was mainly a time for celebration. The end of such a despicable, vicious regime seemed to leave an open moment in history for something better for the Iraqi people. There was also at least a possibility of starting to heal the bitter divisions the run-up to the war had created between the U.S. and the rest of the world, especially the UN and NATO.

The Iraqis who demonstrated their elation at the fall of Saddam were conspicuous on the TV cameras. Those who had reservations about the likely motives of the foreign invaders and the future of the country were not so visible, but blessedly were not afraid to speak their minds to journalists. The new freedom the invasion had suddenly thrust upon them was illustrated by that lack of fear. On the other hand, civilians who lost limbs or eyes or loved ones in the bombing had reservations, if not extreme anger. A week or two after the fall of Baghdad, tens of thousands were demonstrating against the American presence in Iraq. It didn't take long for resentment to arise and express itself. Foreign military domination is seldom appreciated for very long, no matter what it replaces.

Both sides, those who welcomed the Americans and those who felt humiliated and feared for the future of their country, had legitimate feelings, concerns, and points to make. None had the only "right" answer. The evidence for doubt about how delightful the outcome really was came not only from the Iraqis' uncertainties about American intentions, but also from the hospitals filled with the dead and dying from American bombs and the crossfire of gunfights. The hospitals were barely able to provide minimal medical services because they had been looted of equipment and supplies and had neither water nor electricity. Their doctors worked 20 hours per day, performing major surgery such amputations without anesthesia. The patients screamed in pain and the doctors wept as they worked, but the amputations had to be done. The wounded streamed in faster than the hospitals could respond. Despite the pinpoint bombing and the quick outcome of the war, there were thousands of civilian casualties. They were brand new, blessedly unintentional (but inevitable and predictable) American additions to the endless thousands of casualties of Saddam's reign of terror.

Americans who opposed the war as well as those who supported it were glad major combat operations did not drag on and lead to a prolonged humanitarian catastrophe even more horrific than the one already unfolding on everyone's TV screen. To the surprise of the pro-war people, after the war many Americans who opposed the war felt they had little reason to apologize or back away from their opposition. The fall of Saddam in itself, taken out of context of how it was achieved, was a good thing. But it was achieved by violent methods that failed to pass the most rudimentary tests of morality and legality, and left deep scars and devastation behind. The future of Iraq was still a huge question mark, with an anti-American insurgency a high short-term probability and civil war a dark cloud on the longer-term horizon.

The UN and NATO, institutions of international cooperation that had maintained the stability of the world for half a century, had been severely damaged. American credibility was in tatters since the factual basis for the entire war enterprise, the Bush administration's claims that Saddam had weapons of mass destruction and a cooperative relationship with al Qaeda, was still highly questionable, and getting more so by the day. Like the pot of gold at the end of the rainbow, the evidence for WMDs was always vanishing over the horizon. Every day U.S. military search operations for these weapons were coming up empty-handed. Neither chemical, nor biological, nor nuclear weapons were anywhere to be seen. The UN inspectors who could find nothing before the war had the last laugh, given that there was nothing to find, but the situation was too grim for laughter.

Obviously, in this wide-open moment, the future was deeply uncertain, and crucial decisions had yet to be made. The future was in the hands of a regime in Washington DC that had displayed great military skill and disastrously little diplomatic wisdom and finesse during the run-up to the war and during the war itself. Having shown itself long on arrogance and short on patience on the diplomatic front, having charged ahead with a war that was clearly illegal under international law, and having decisively lost world opinion in the process, the Bush administration now needed to reverse gears and display immense, almost superhuman humility and patience in the political and economic reconstruction process inside Iraq. Additionally, they had to try to regain lost diplomatic ground by getting democratic allies Bush had stiff-armed before the war and whose populations were opposed to the war to provide risky and expensive assistance with security and reconstruction.

At the same time, the administration needed to be decisive and effective in delivering humanitarian aid, or quickly making it available through the agency of others. Rebuilding the utility infrastructure quickly was critical. Millions of people were without water and electricity. Hospitals had no water, electricity, or medicine. All institutions had been stripped clean by looters who could have been stopped, but the American soldiers stood around and watched it happen, lacking orders to stop it. The humanitarian situation was desperate, yet there were still firefights in the streets, making security inadequate for delivery of essentials. Could the U.S. government be humble and patient, yet decisive and effective at the same time? No one knew the answer, including the Americans. But history was not encouraging on the humble and patient side of the ledger.

Iraqis and the world wondered about the American flag briefly draped over the face of Saddam's statue before it was pulled down. Was this the new reality, a foreign military occupation, or was the reality the quick change in which it was replaced with the Iraqi flag? The Arab and Muslim world, upon seeing on Al Jazeera the image of the American flag going up, saw American jingoism, not "liberation." Could this quick-change artistry, first the U.S. flag, then the Iraqi flag, be the first symbolic cover-up of a de facto American imperialism? Most people in the Arab world thought so. Establish American control of Iraqi oil, and pretend it was all for the good of the Iraqis. Whether this cynical perception was right or wrong mattered less than the fact that it was widespread and associated with intense hostility toward the U.S.

During the reconstruction of Iraq, Muslims, who constitute more than a billion people worldwide, or one-sixth of the world's population, and who were already distrustful and resentful of the U.S., would be watching every American stumble and placing hostile interpretations on even the most benign American actions. Fortunately only a small percentage of these billion people are extremists ready to die in a suicide bombing, but a long-term increase in terrorism stemming from increased resentment seems inevitable. To pick an arbitrary number to illustrate, if only one percent of Muslims tend toward extremism in their views, one percent of a billion people is ten million, a huge potential field for the recruiters of terrorism. Islam is, in essence—as George Bush wisely proclaimed—a religion of peace. But one suspects that the number of Muslim extremists or tribalists lurking among their more peaceful brethren may exceed one percent.

The momentary expression of understandable pride by the American troops who made the flag blooper and quickly corrected it demonstrated the larger ambivalence of American leaders on how postwar Iraq should be governed. They agreed in their rhetoric that the Americans should get out of Iraq, or at least turn over as much power as possible to the Iraqi people, as quickly as possible. They weren't stressing the point that "as quickly as possible" would probably be years.

Hawks' Vindication?

Regarding the war itself, still ongoing at a lower level of intensity, American officials were cautious about their optimism except for Dick Cheney, who threw caution aside to do an early "pre-victory lap." And of course President Bush did a bit of strutting in a flight suit on an aircraft carrier under a sign that read, "Mission Accomplished." One suspected he would regret this over-the-top photo-op later. Aside from the indulgence of Bush and Cheney, the expected crowing of the administration's war hawks in the op-ed pages was surprisingly muted. Perhaps they sensed that the difficulties ahead were far greater than those the U.S. had already faced and overcome in the active combat of the war itself.

However, innumerable commentators who had supported the war and who were stronger on tribalistic emotional reactions than on clarity of thought, took the cheering behavior and smiling faces of "liberated" Iraqis in Baghdad as vindication of the U.S. action. These Iraqi smiles, most definitely cause for celebration, were held up as evidence that those who opposed the war were either stubbornly wrong-headed, or at least naïve about the horrors of the Saddam regime. The attitude seemed to be, now that we've gotten rid of this evil regime, isn't it obvious that this was the right thing to do? I begged to differ. At this early stage after major combat operations we had not yet begun to see the chickens come home to roost from the evils we had perpetrated in launching an unnecessary war. I was confident that we would live to regret it.

The UN—Not So Irrelevant

In the aftermath of the war, or better stated, the war after the war, what would be the real role of the UN? It has nation-building and humanitarian relief expertise the U.S. lacks. The UN would have a "vital role" Bush declared after soul-searching talks with Tony Blair, but what would that mean in reality? An aircraft carrier could steam through the gaps between the possibilities. Clearly Bush did not mean the lead role, which would be reserved for the U.S.

Just before the war Bush had displayed his contempt for the UN—and by implication the member nations of the Security Council—by declaring it to be "irrelevant" if it failed to rubber stamp his war plans. It did refuse to do so, since the evidence was not corroborating the claim that Saddam had weapons of mass destruction, and there was plenty more work for the inspectors. However, immediately after the war, Bush could no longer dismiss the UN. Oil companies filling their tankers with Iraqi oil would not deliver it to customers until they were sure of the legality of what they were doing. They didn't want to risk losing huge sums of money by delivering oil that was later judged to be illegal. On the other hand, selling Iraqi oil was an essential step in reconstructing the country.

The UN Security Council held the keys to the legality issue, so the UN didn't look so irrelevant any longer. The U.S. needed it to lift the sanctions against Iraq, but the opponents of the war in the Security Council were saying, "Not so fast." They wanted assurances that the UN would play a large role, perhaps a lead role, both for the protection of their interests in Iraqi oil and for international acceptance and legitimacy of the enterprise of rebuilding Iraq. They also wanted the inspection team headed by Hans Blix to return to Iraq and validate any findings of (or lack of) weapons of mass destruction. The U.S. was adamantly opposed to the larger UN role and the return of the inspection team. The U.S. got its way, but paid a high price.

Tony Blair had stretched his leadership of his Labour Party to its elastic limits and risked the demise of his political career to support Bush. He had troops on the ground in Iraq, and he had contributed English blood and treasure to the war. Politically, Bush had to take him seriously in the postwar reconstruction phase. And Mr. Blair was determined to promote a strong role for the UN in the post-war reconstruction, both for legitimacy and to move toward his vision of a more cooperative world order, a vision massively different—almost opposite—from the Bush administration's chauvinistic vision of American global dominance. For Bush, openly threatening and scorning the UN as he had before the war was no longer an option, but the negotiations were clearly going to be difficult.

Bush worked out a vague role for the UN having mainly to do with humanitarian aid and little to do with the monumental task of rebuilding the country politically. In view of the substantial experience with the difficult art of nation building acquired by the UN on multiple fronts in the previous decades, critics observed that this decision was a waste of experience as well as the "soft power" of legitimacy. The UN began to build up its staff in Iraq despite the weak and somewhat unclear role it had been assigned. Tragically, its involvement in Iraq was abruptly ended by a car bomb that took advantage of inadequate security and killed Sergio Vieira de Mello, the stellar UN executive heading the team, and numerous other staff members. Clearly the anti-U.S. insurgents were not looking to the UN to provide an alternative to American governance of the country.

A Close-to-Home Analogy

An analogy to the ethics and legality of the war based on closer-to-home realities of everyday American life might be helpful for perspective. The details of this analogy may sound artificial because it is fictional, but it will serve to illustrate the moral, legal, and practical issues surrounding the war on a personalized scale people can readily understand.

In a small town, there is one extremely rich person, a multi-millionaire who owns about a quarter of the town's money, houses and property. He is a forceful person who doesn't hesitate to use the power of his wealth when he decides he wants to. Though often resented for his power and his occasional hardball tactics, he is usually a law-abiding citizen, and is respected by many of the townspeople and is generally not deeply feared. He is a very influential member of the town council.

In the same town is a terribly evil man who beats his wife, abuses his children, and feuds with his neighbors. He has an arsenal of guns in his home and is reputed to have bombs stored in his basement. Everyone fears and dislikes him. When he gets into a feud with the town's only millionaire, this is the last straw. The millionaire is deeply worried about his own safety and decides he must rid himself and the town of this evil man.

He gets the police to use the rumors of bombs in the man's basement to go to a judge and get a search warrant to search the evil one's house. They find no bombs. The town's assumption is that they are hidden, maybe in a trunk in storage somewhere, or maybe in a concealed room off the basement that the police missed in their search. The man's wife and children are too terrified of him to testify against him about his abuse and thereby to get him arrested. The town's police and sheriff can or will do nothing.

The millionaire decides to take action. Using the rougher contacts he has through members of his personal security guard, he arranges for a hit man to take out the evil one. The "hit" goes a little awry. It succeeds in killing the evil man, but the wife is wounded, the house is burned down, and the children are traumatized. Sympathetic acquaintances of the wife, visiting her in the hospital, can't help noticing that she is remarkably cheerful despite her wounds, the loss of her house and her husband, and her children's lingering fear. They whisper, and some say openly, that she's better off without her monster-husband. Though shaken by the violent and illegal means by which he was dispatched, they are glad he is gone. The wife is known to have job skills that will probably enable her to support herself and the family, after receiving some initial help from the townspeople.

Did the millionaire do the right thing? Regardless of the future possible well-being of the wife, the millionaire is in point of fact a murderer. If a higher legal authority than the relatively powerless townspeople and police catches him, he will be tried. And if the evidence is good, he may be convicted for murder. In the story, morally and legally he did commit murder. He is hardly a hero by any reasonable standard, since his motive for the murder was self-interested rather than humanitarian. His action may have had a benign long-term effect on the family but what he did was nonetheless grossly wrong. The relief of the family would hardly stand up in a court of law as excusing the murder.

In my mind's eye I can see the critics of this analogy turning red in the face and spluttering that what the U.S. did in Iraq in no way resembles murder and that this is a grossly unfair analogy. Actually, however, it is quite accurate. Saddam and a handful of top people in Iraq were openly targeted for death. They were not put on trial in any court such as the new International Criminal Court (which the U.S. has opposed). In addition to eventually capturing Saddam, the U.S.-led war killed an estimated ten to fifteen thousand other people.

Thousands of those who died were civilians. And many more civilians were severely wounded and traumatized. They are scarred for life. As a tactical matter, kudos are genuinely in order to the U.S. military for developing the "smart bomb" technology to hit targets precisely and minimize civilian casualties, and for their efforts to spare civilians. This technology and the political will to use it are major humanitarian advances in the ghoulish art of warfare. Yet a "war of choice"—as this one is euphemistically called—remains a choice to kill thousands of innocent people. The U.S. decided to do this despite its inability to legitimize the war under international law. Whether Iraq will be better off in the long run is an open question. It is likely to sink into civil war and anarchy despite the efforts of the U.S. to hold it together, but there is a small theoretical chance that it may become a democracy. More likely, after a period of civil war and extreme human misery, it will end with another, perhaps less destructive dictator.

Responsibility

Shortly after the war a thoughtful and witty friend of mine was speaking to a group of people in Washington DC and said, "Welcome to the capital of [he paused thoughtfully] Iraq." The quip was greeted with groans and uncomfortable, rueful laughter. It went straight to the heart of the problem. With victory in war and the military occupation of a country comes responsibility. Duck reality by calling it something other than occupation, but it adds up to the same thing. Under international law the U.S. as an

331

occupying force became responsible for providing humanitarian aid and for rebuilding the damaged infrastructure of Iraq, at least until other authorities could take over. Defense Secretary Rumsfeld's denial of this responsibility at the time did not change the facts.

On the ground in Iraq this responsibility meant everything from immediate questions such as how to get electricity and water flowing again to longer-term questions such as how to get Iraqi oil sales back on track. The goal, of course, was to help millions of civilians rebuild shattered lives, on the way to establishing a democratic government. The problems were huge. A week after the takeover of Baghdad, no one could figure out how to get the electricity back on. The Americans blamed Saddam's government for shutting it down, and the Iraqis blamed the Americans for bombing the power grid, which the Americans denied. Meanwhile, vital products and services such water, gasoline, and hospital services, not to mention lights and air conditioning in desert heat, were arrested because electricity was not available to run the machinery. Lack of medical services for people injured in the war was particularly problematic. Now that the U.S. had launched a war that had caused thousands of additional horrors, despite the best technology and the most sincere efforts to minimize civilian casualties, would the U.S. be able to do something commensurate with the extent of the damage?

A Month After Major Combat Operations

The seeming hopelessness of repairing the damage of war, the out-of-control looting, and the years of misrule by Saddam that aggravated these conditions were painfully illustrated by the experiences of some of the American soldiers in Baghdad. An Army sergeant whose unit patrolled Baghdad told of a situation in which

Countless Iraqis beseech the troops for help delivering water or electricity or providing security ... and others approach a police station that his unit has been guarding and ask for jobs or salaries unpaid since before the war. 'I have no answers for the people,' he said. 'I feel like a paid liar. To look these people in the eye and say, 'tomorrow, you'll have electricity.' And then, tomorrow, they look you in the eye and say, 'when?'[1]

Babies didn't stop being born because hospitals were incapable of meeting their medical needs and those of their mothers. A glimpse into an Iraqi hospital one month after the U.S. takeover of Baghdad tells the story. An upper middle class woman, Mona, brings her baby, sick and yellow with jaundice and unable to nurse, into the hospital. It doesn't have an incubator with the special light needed for treating jaundice. It doesn't have clean water. It also has no vitamins or calcium supplements.[2]

Throughout the Al-Alwiyah Children's Hospital ... tiny patients wail, their bellies distended and hot to the touch. Of the 160 children here, most are suffering from diarrhea. They drank contaminated water. Mothers and grandmothers, many in full-length black abayas, crouch over the children, panicked and praying. They haven't seen a doctor for several hours. Some clutch precious stocks of bottled water and canned milk – enough, perhaps, to keep the babies alive through the night." Some of the babies die. The grandfather of Mona's baby, "normally a placid man, flares with anger: 'There's no milk, no medicine, no salaries, no safety in the streets. What kind of freedom are you talking about? Under Saddam it was better than now!' He collects himself, seems to regret the outburst and continues, 'I don't know if tomorrow I will find my granddaughter dead.'[3]

* **

During Saddam's regime, medications were readily available, distributed by quota at sate-run neighborhood health centers. Patients, pharmacists, and hospitals last received allotments in March. Everyone is running low. Where is the United Nations, where are the Americans, people demand to know. It's coming soon, the officials say, but many Iraqis no longer believe that. 'We hear about humanitarian aid, but that's only for the TV and the pictures' says one Iraqi. 'You can see with your own eyes, we are not receiving anything: Nothing from Bush, nothing from the European leaders, just talk about freedom.'[4]

Of course, any postwar situation is bound to be a tragic mess, and reconstruction a long and difficult road. But the impatience of Iraqi parents beside the beds of their dying babies cannot be dismissed. A brilliantly planned reconstruction process did not follow the brilliantly planned military attack that toppled Saddam's government. A woefully inadequate process followed it as American troops wandered the streets of Baghdad watching looters clean out everything, including hospitals and banks. The troops, of course, could do nothing without orders. Why were the orders not coming? Looting is always rampant when a repressive government falls and a power vacuum is created. Even a minimal postwar planning effort would have anticipated this outcome.

Finally, after everything in even the most vital institutions such as hospitals, schools, nuclear facilities and oil industry facilities had been stripped clean, right down to the light fixtures and electrical wiring, the troops were ordered to arrest looters. The horse was already out of the barn. It should not have been a surprise to American war and reconstruction planners that Iraq's economy was centrally controlled, and that when the government collapsed, anarchy would prevail and the economy would collapse. Nor should it surprise anyone that looters would run wild in the ensuing anarchy. Substantially, before the war the socialist government of Iraq *was* the economy. A plan to deal decisively with the impending reality of its collapse would seem to have been a moral and practical obligation of planning for the takeover of Iraq. The fact that reconstruction planning was less than minimally adequate raises serious doubts about the post-combat political rhetoric saying how this war was for the freedom of the Iraqi people and for democracy in the Middle East.

A month after the U.S. military's takeover of Baghdad, "An engineering professor at Basra University, surveying his destroyed campus, said 'this is chaos, not freedom.' On a drive through Basra, southern Iraq's largest city … it is nearly impossible to find a concrete improvement since the resistance by Baath militia men was silenced April 7th."[5]

The government infrastructure is barely functioning. And in southern Iraq, nearly everything of consequence was run by the government. Offices and banks stand gutted and abandoned. Contracts, work orders, financial records and employee rolls have been lost or destroyed. Equipment has been stolen. A grain trader, Walid Khaled, said too few trucks remain to haul vegetables to market or grain to silos. Purchasing agents have no money to pay the producers, he said. Government distributors burned out of their offices cannot complete the paperwork to keep track of distribution. [6]

Still referring to a month after the American takeover,

> Civilian officials have struggled to fulfill their pledge to dole out
> emergency payments to millions of cash-strapped Iraqi government
> workers. Restoration of services, particularly electricity and water, has
> been spotty, despite promises to get things working fast. At the same
> time, U.S. officials have yet to fully address fuel shortages that have
> exasperated Iraqis forming mile-long lines at gas stations – in a country
> that was a major oil producer. 'The planning was ragged,' lamented a
> senior U.S. official here, 'and the execution was worse.' Providing public
> services, security and stopgap payments were supposed to be the easy
> part.[7]

During their planning, officials made some key assumptions that proved
incorrect, chief among them that government employees would be able
to quickly return to work in their offices, people involved in the process
said. They failed to foresee the wave of looting and arson that struck the
capital in the days after it fell, rendering most government buildings
uninhabitable. Military commanders also have complained that although
Defense Secretary Donald H. Rumsfeld's desire to fight the war with
smaller numbers of fast-moving troops may have been a wise battlefield
strategy, it has left them with too few personnel to police a California-
size country of 25 million people.[8]

A Year After Major Combat Operations

During the few months after the invasion of Iraq there was a gradual
reduction in the frequency of attacks against U.S. forces and this change
allowed modest progress in rebuilding the country. Eventually, after
agonizing delays, electricity came back on at approximately pre-war levels,
water started running again, and oil started moving through the pipelines
toward destinations that permitted foreign sales, despite spectacular instances
of sabotage. However, insurgents regularly blew up American humvees in
convoys with roadside bombs called "improvised explosive devices (IEDs)
and rocket propelled grenades (RPGs) and sniped at American soldiers in

dozens of attacks every day. Losses of American lives climbed slowly but steadily. American soldiers fought back and caused substantial Iraqi casualties, and inevitably incurred Iraqi resentment as they did so.

Eventually the insurgents, realizing that they were taking unacceptably heavy losses from directly attacking American troops, began to attack Iraqis who worked with the Americans and foreign civilians involved in reconstruction. Car bombs wreaked havoc at police stations and mosques in southern Iraq. Suicide bombers caused devastating damage in political offices in Kurdish northern Iraq in attempts to foment civil war. Security for reconstruction became enormously expensive and the dangers made such work extraordinarily difficult. Much of the money for reconstruction could not be spent, and much of what was spent went to American companies rather than to Iraqi recipients.

During the month of April 2004, one full year after major combat operations in Iraq began, an explosive increase in the scope and intensity of the Iraqi insurgency against the U.S. presence brought about more than 130 deaths of American soldiers. This one-month total exceeded all American deaths during the three weeks of major combat operations that had started in March 2003. Clearly, after an entire year, the war was far from over. If anything it was worse than before. Iraqis no longer filled the streets cheering the demise of Saddam Hussein; those who weren't openly fighting the U.S. were struggling with shortages of jobs and spotty electrical service.

American forces captured Saddam Hussein in December 2003, and this event momentarily boosted the morale of the U.S.-led coalition and those Iraqis who were glad to be rid of his vicious rule. His capture also provided some useful intelligence against the insurgency. However, the effect of Saddam's capture appeared to be short-lived and the insurgency continued. Former Saddam loyalists morphed into Iraqi nationalists and Muslim fanatics, and the struggle went on.

During this first year after the invasion of Iraq the Bush administration was paying a rising political price domestically for the continued expense and loss of life in Iraq, and a presidential election was looming ahead. Part of the solution—not likely to succeed, but desperate times call for desperate measures—was to arrange a handover of political power or sovereignty to the Iraqis as soon as possible, and certainly before the November 2004 election. June 30 was the date selected. Apparently there was magic in the date because it was the only thing that stayed fixed in the increasing chaos of the months leading up to it.

As the magic June 30 date for handover of power to Iraqis approached, American political efforts to win the support of the Iraqi people were going badly. The Iraqi exiles the U.S. appointed as the country's leaders, the Governing Council, were outsiders despised by most Iraqis and gaining little political traction. They were derisively referred to as Ahmed Chalabi and the twenty thieves. (Actually there were 25 members.) Chalabi had been convicted of bank fraud in Jordan some years earlier; whether or not he was actually guilty, the huge blot on his reputation didn't help. Toward the end of the watershed month of April 2004, news reports spoke of allegations of kidnapping and theft and fabrication of intelligence by the Iraqi National Congress, the organization headed by Chalabi. Whether these allegations are true or not, they were of little help in securing Iraqi support for the occupation.

During the months before the eruption of violence in April, pulling together an interim constitution or set of rules for governing Iraq until an election could be held at first proved daunting for American leaders, then impossible. The U.S. drafted an interim constitution and a process involving regional caucuses for selecting interim leaders. After great difficulties and many changes, the Governing Council approved it. However, the Grand Ayatollah Ali Sistani, a revered Shiite leader, objected to any system of governance not based on direct elections. Supporting his position, vast numbers of Shiites demonstrated in the streets, and it became evident to the Americans that the new arrangement had come unraveled. Shiites constitute a majority of Iraqis and are more supportive of the occupation than the Sunnis, who stand to lose their privileged place in the Iraqi power structure. When the Shiites bailed out, it was clear that the deal was off. As a result of Sistani's position, the new interim constitution lacked an essential minimum of popular support. And there was not yet any prospective government to whom the Americans could hand over the keys of power on the magic date of June 30th.

337

Who Has Legitimacy?

How could one reclusive Ayatollah scuttle a deal between the U.S. and the new Iraqi Governing Council? Historian Fareed Zakaria frames the question another way: "What does this man have that the United States doesn't? Legitimacy. Sistani is regarded by Iraqi Shiites as the most learned cleric in the country. He is also seen as having been uncorrupted by Saddam's reign."[9] Zakaria goes on to assess the legitimacy of the U.S. occupation:

> From the start, the Pentagon planners (or nonplanners) believed the United States would have no legitimacy problems in Iraq. 'We will be greeted as liberators,' Vice President Cheney famously predicted. When urged after the war to transfer some authority to the United Nations to gain legitimacy, administrative officials were dismissive in public and scathing in private. 'We have far more legitimacy than the UN,' one senior official told me last June. To discredit the idea of internationalization, Defense Department officials kept insisting that their goal was to transfer power not to the United Nations, but to the Iraqis. 'No foreigners can be in charge of [determining how elections will be held],' said Paul Wolfowitz.[10]

Under intense time pressure and seeking a go-between who could persuade the reclusive Sistani that it was impossible to hold elections in the needed time frame, the U.S. turned to UN Secretary General Kofi Annan. He and his envoy, Lakhdar Brahimi, demonstrated that the "foreigners" Wolfowitz didn't want involved had some legitimacy after all. Brahimi first persuaded Sistani that elections were impossible before June 30. Another constraint determined what kind of a plan could be implemented. The existing interim government of Iraqi exiles imposed by the United States lacked legitimacy in the eyes of the Iraqi people, and would not be accepted as an interim government, even if it was expanded as some suggested.

Brahimi quickly formulated the rough outlines of a plan for an interim government that could be accepted by the Americans and Sistani. It consisted, essentially, of governance by non-political technocrats who could run the country administratively but could not make laws that would be binding after the elections planned for January 2005. It balanced power among the three major groups, the Shiites, Sunnis and Kurds. It was a foregone conclusion that the interim technocrats would have no control over the U.S. military, which would continue to struggle to maintain (or rather establish) security. Critics at the time noted that a government that can't make laws and can't control security is not much of a government. But is seemed better than nothing, which was the alternative, given Bush's insistence on the handover date. Given the continued presence and independence of the U.S. military, the shift of power was bound to be a bit of a charade. American leaders began speaking of it as a gradual process rather than an abrupt and complete shift.

Major Trouble

A radical young Shiite cleric, Ayatollah Moqtada al-Sadr, had been building a militia in Sadr city, a slum in Baghdad named after his illustrious father. His militia was rapidly gaining strength in organization, numbers, and arms. The U.S. and coalition forces eyed him nervously, but in the absence of any specific violent acts initiated by his militia, they took no military action against him. However, he was beginning to incite violence against the American occupation through his newspaper. American military leaders decided to act, and closed down the newspaper. They also announced that al-Sadr was wanted for the murder of another Shiite cleric several months earlier, raising legitimate questions about the timing and motive of the arrest warrant.

The result, predictably, was a violent confrontation with al-Sadr's militia. Although they were only a few thousand strong, they were scattered throughout several southern Iraqi cities. Suddenly the U.S. and the U.S. led coalition were fighting a two-front war. One front was the ongoing struggle against the Sunni insurgency in the Sunni triangle west and north of Baghdad, and now a second front had opened in the south against an increasingly angry Shiite population. Sunni and Shiite leaders began making common cause against the United States. This situation was the worst nightmare of the leaders of the American occupation.

The Americans' announced intent to capture or kill al-Sadr was rendered all but impossible by a maneuver by his militia. They moved him to a mosque in the holy city of Najaf, perhaps the holiest of the Shiite sites. For the Americans to invade this city would be more than a simple provocation against the southern Iraqi Shiite population; it would be a desecration of a site revered throughout the Muslim Shiite world. It would inflame Shiite feelings against the U.S. throughout the Middle East, as well as—probably decisively and fatally—in southern Iraq. Al-Sadr's maneuver constituted a stalemate, if not a checkmate, for U.S. efforts to capture or kill him.

To make matters worse, four American contractors were killed in the Sunni city of Fallujah, west of Baghdad, and two of their bodies were burned and strung up on a bridge while residents of Fallujah cheered and celebrated. TV pictures of the event were broadcast throughout the world. The anti-U.S. insurgency had always been at its most intense in Fallujah, and as a result the American forces had agreed to stay out of the city to minimize hostilities and presumably also to minimize American casualties. So the city was unusual in being self-governed by local Iraqi leaders. But the attack on the American contractors was an escalation and a provocation that American military leaders could not ignore. They announced military action to capture or kill the insurgents who had committed the atrocity and began taking steps to surround the city and invade it.

American military leaders negotiated a peace deal with local civilian political leaders that would result in the insurgents giving up their heavy weapons and allowing American and Iraqi troops to patrol the city streets, but the ability of the civilian leaders to bring about disarmament compliance from the insurgents was doubtful from the start. It didn't succeed. The result was escalating violence. American military leaders wanted to avoid an all-out assault on Fallujah, first because urban fighting—especially on the enemy's home turf—would incur extremely high loss of life for American soldiers; second because it is impossible in such a battle to avoid killing large numbers of civilians; and third because such fighting was certain to inflame the rest of the Iraqi population against the American occupation.

Fallujah was a no-win situation. To invade the city and fight was to lose large numbers of American lives and lose the hearts and minds of much of the rest of the Iraqi population; to decline to fight would signal weakness and invite more aggressive attacks from the insurgents. The Americans fought their way into part of the city, but the going was rough, and the reaction from the population in the rest of Iraq was extremely negative. Eventually a breakthrough came in the form of a decision to back an Iraqi general who would police Fallujah with an Iraqi militia that would presumably be more acceptable to the Iraqi population. The Marines pulled back, and the insurgents and rebellious citizens of Fallujah celebrated victory. The future was unclear. A further embarrassment for the Americans came with the discovery that the general they had put in charge had a shady past and could not be approved by the vetting process in the Pentagon. A new different general would be needed to lead the local militia. These highly visible reversals left an impression of an American chain of command in disarray. Nevertheless, after a few days the new arrangement in Fallujah seemed to be holding.

Simultaneous with these damaging events in Fallujah and Najaf, the horror of American soldiers abusing and humiliating Iraqi prisoners of war burst into the public eye in the most vivid possible way: unforgettable photographs on national and then international television of hooded and naked Iraqi prisoners stacked in a pyramid and other pictures of them naked, apparently being taunted by a female soldier. In a culture that is extremely conservative about nudity and about male-female relationships, such pictures could only cause extreme horror and rage, while vindicating the worst stereotypes of American amorality and bad intentions toward Iraqis. Verbal reports from credible sources of other, even worse abuses are also spreading like a dark stain across the world. The image of American good will and legitimacy in its efforts to rebuild Iraq, already at a disastrous low everywhere and especially in the Arab and Muslim world, had received yet another possibly fatal blow. The intensity of anti-American feeling ratcheted up a step higher, a seemingly impossible achievement. The political price tag on the Iraq war, already high, was going through the roof. Is it worth it?

The Disappearing Rationale

The state of affairs in Iraq was grim a month after the fall of Baghdad. In some ways it was even grimmer a year later. These facts, in combination with the self-serving stances of American leaders about who should be allowed to rebuild the country, strongly recommend revisiting from a post-war perspective the mystery of the real basis for the war. The Bush administration's constantly changing rationales leading up to the war and their disconnect with the available evidence originally provoked the question. It seems sensible to think that the real reasons for the war, in contrast to the political pretenses, wouldn't shift and fade like a ghost or disappear like a Cheshire cat. After all, the determination to initiate the war did not change.

After the war the Bush administration touted the fall of Saddam as a great thing for the Iraqi people; they were freed from the tyranny. In short, though Bush never used these words, the war morphed into a humanitarian intervention. The problem, of course, is that this change was an after-the-fact rationalization, and the evolving facts on the ground after the war suggested at the very least that this rationale was unrealistic. Initially the war was presented as self-protective, preventive. First Bush said he wanted the war because of Iraq's links to terrorism. The CIA and the FBI both said that Iraq had no ties with al Qaeda and no involvement with 9/11, but these dissenting reports were conveniently cast aside. Bush and Cheney were sure there must be some connection. Then it was said to be necessary because Iraq had a nuclear program that could produce a bomb in a few months or years. It turned out there was no nuclear program at all, let alone one so far along as that. When that rationale was discredited, he wanted the war because of biological and chemical weapons.

The CIA identified one hundred locations where these were most likely in preparation. The inspection team checked them out and found ruins, not weapons manufacturing plants. On this point the CIA was wrong one hundred times out of one hundred, a remarkable record little noted by a jingoistic press, and still the Bush administration's faith in Saddam's chemical and biological weapons remained unshakable. As these weapons proved elusive to the first set of inspectors, the goal of the war was finally touted as bringing democracy to the Middle East. Columnist Richard Cohen points out after the war in a clever *mea culpa* on his own support for it, that in retail sales these kinds of changes are called "bait and switch."[11] Get people to come to the war for one reason (fear and national insecurity); then once they're in the door, switch to another reason and another goal.

It was late in the pre-war game when Bush gave a speech at the American Enterprise Institute, his tribalistic home base, giving a rosy picture of the splendid world of freedom and democracy that would open up to Iraqis and the Middle East generally as a result of the war. It is hard to believe that this idealistic afterthought was a major motive for attacking Iraq, but if so, it was incredibly naïve. First, the likelihood of Iraq becoming a democracy was low on the face of it, given its history and cultural divides; second, there was no reason to think that this success, if it happened, would change the rest of the Middle East. Turkey is a democracy, and we haven't seen other Middle Eastern countries rushing to emulate it. The undemocratic majority of Middle Eastern countries have their own internal problems, not least of which is the possibility that a popular vote might bring radicals into power who would further destabilize the Middle East and possibly choke off Western access to oil. We should be careful what we wish for; we might get it.

Bringing democracy to the Middle East does seem to have been a large element in the thinking of Paul Wolfowitz, who along with Vice President Cheney was a key architect of the war, but it was not the rationale that other members of the Bush team found acceptable. Rescuing Iraq and the Middle East from oppressive rulers is a strange motive in view of the Republican history of strenuously objecting to humanitarian military interventions, especially when launched by liberals. The rationale for the war Wolfowitz could sell inside the administration was the combination of terrorism and weapons of mass destruction—in other words, the post 9/11 fear factor for the American public. Both of these fears were supported by dubious evidence and both proved to be false.

Despite the lack of evidence, even weeks after the war President Bush was still claiming a link between Saddam and al Qaeda, and even September 11, especially when speaking to military audiences. Trying to make an emotional link between 9/11 and Saddam since a rational or factual link could not be made, Bush said in his famous "mission accomplished" speech on the aircraft carrier that the invasion of Iraq was just one battle in the War on Terrorism that began on September 11. Eventually, much later, when directly challenged during a TV interview, he had to eat his words. "Only in September 2003, only after occupying Iraq, only after Vice President Cheney had stretched credulity on *Meet the Press*, did the President clearly state that there was 'no evidence that Iraq was involved in the September 11 attacks.'"[12]

As for the Iraq war being an integral part of the war on terrorism, aside from the 9/11 attack, the evidence that Saddam was involved with al Qaeda was flimsy from the start. There was a group of al Qaeda-linked terrorists in northern Iraq called Ansar al-Islam, but the region was completely out of Saddam's control, protected by American airplanes maintaining a no-fly zone against Saddam. The area was politically managed by a budding Kurdish democracy. Saddam had zero influence there; all he could do was hover on the borders as a threat. Another item of supposed evidence was a photograph of one of Saddam's people meeting in the Czech Republic with a person thought to be Mohammed Atta, one of the 9/11 hijackers. The meeting was assumed to imply a connection. Later the CIA and the FBI, whose investigative records showed Atta elsewhere at the time, discredited this seeming evidence. The Czech government withdrew its claim that the second person in the picture was Atta. After the CIA and the FBI had debunked this item, Vice President Cheney continued to cite it in speeches as proof of the connection between Saddam and al Qaeda. It would have been flimsy evidence, even if it had been true. One meeting is hardly proof of an extensive system of cooperation. Yet another item sometimes cited as proof of Saddam's involvement with terrorism was the presence of terrorist Abu

Nidal in Iraq, where Saddam had him killed. But Nidal was not an al Qaeda member and given his fate, he was evidently not Saddam's best buddy. In short, there was simply no evidence of a collaboration between Saddam and al Qaeda.

President Bush or at least his staff must have known the claims were insupportable. He continued to imply the link, but not to state it explicitly. On the other hand, in public speeches Cheney continued to refer explicitly to the discredited photograph as evidence that Saddam had links with al Qaeda. Logically, these persistent misstatements suggest one or more of three possibilities: either Bush and Cheney were knowingly lying, or they were ignorant of the facts and flying on auto-pilot while using old discredited material in their speeches, or (more likely) their staffs were writing the speeches and they were either incompetent or lying. None of these alternatives were possibilities the news media and the public wanted to face.

Liberal Theories on War Motivation

While all this Bush administration manipulation of the facts was under way before and during the war, and in the glaring absence of any sound rationale for it, liberals who opposed it were creating their own plausible but unflattering and unsubstantiated theories about the real motives behind it. Their assumptions seemed a bit too cynical. One theory was that Bush wanted U.S. control of the vast oil resources of Iraq. The strong orientation toward the oil industry in the backgrounds of virtually every key person on the Bush team who was involved with decision-making on the war provided ammunition for this suspicion, though not specific evidence. Argument *ad hominem* can be suggestive, but it hasn't ceased to be a logical fallacy. Bush's attempts to drill for oil in Alaska's pristine wildlife sanctuaries was another point supporting this theory. Clearly he would pay almost any political price to get more oil, even small amounts of it. Any price, that is, except conservation (by far the most effective way to extend the useful life of available fossil fuels), or developing and implementing alternative clean technologies.

Another liberal motivation theory was that Bush and his team wanted to establish U.S. military bases in Iraq from which the U.S. could project greater military power throughout the Middle East. The problem with this theory was the presence of military bases already established in nearby places such as Qatar. These bases were already capable of projecting the power that facilitated the swift defeat of Iraq. The bases in Saudi Arabia were awkward for the Saudi royal family and hence were soon to close, but other bases were available. In support of the argument, the close proximity of U.S. bases in Iraq to both Syria and Iran would be a plus for the U.S. military.

Both liberal theories, oil and military bases, were not only overtly cynical (which might actually increase their plausibility) but also they were based partly on opposition to the war and dislike for George W. Bush. As such they invited skepticism, though they had some degree of plausibility. The problem was verification. How can we know the Bush administration's real but unstated motives for the war? Events would prove suggestive, but not definitive.

Who Controls the Spoils—The Oil?

The main overt rationale for the war, of course, was national security. Iraq was said to have weapons of mass destruction and would sooner or later give them to al Qaeda for use against the U.S. This rationale has been decisively and irrefutably discredited by events. It may or may not have been sincerely believed, but it was wrong. Iraq posed no such threat to the U.S. As noted above, the U.S. launched a war against another country that cost billions of dollars and thousands of lives based on intelligence that was flat out wrong—either erroneous or fraudulent.

Surprisingly, the American public is undisturbed by this shocking fact. The reason may be that they saw something even more shocking. They were mesmerized by the visceral impact of another kind of evidence on American TV screens. Everyone has seen the evidence of Saddam's atrocities against Iraqi civilians, the mass graves with thousands of moldering packages of human bones. We have seen Iraqi relatives weeping for their lost sons and daughters, brothers and sisters. The horror and tragedy of this reality cannot be overstated. Along with the torture chambers we have also seen, these pictures convey an intensity of human pain comparable to the horrors of the Holocaust in Europe before and during WWII. Toppling Saddam because he created these monstrosities was a worthy goal, if not exactly the original rationale. It is strange indeed that doing so was an accidental byproduct of a national security concern that proved completely unfounded. But it satisfied the emotional need of the American public to feel that the war was worthwhile. Considering the extremely large number of American troops involved and the fact that a large proportion of the U.S. public is closely associated with one or more of them, it is understandable that Americans have a strong need to find some sort of justification for the war so as to avoid the realization that their loved ones have been placed in harm's way for false or unacceptable reasons.

People who opposed the war from the beginning and still feel that it was the wrong thing to do feel both joy at the toppling of Saddam and at the same time an understandable sense of frustration with the American public's acceptance of the rationale shift. It hardly needs to be said that everyone is glad Saddam is out of power, and with him the Baath party, who together caused tremendous amounts of human suffering. That fact is worthy of unmitigated, unqualified celebration. One can wholeheartedly celebrate this good news and still have a strong sense of foreboding about the future of Iraq and the U.S. role in it. The following two key questions hung in the air after the dust of initial combat operations settled: Would the Iraqi people really be better off in the long run, or were they "out of the frying pan, into the fire" of civil war? And given that the war proved unnecessary for U.S. national security, was that claim a cover for something else?

One of the stories about the follow-on to the war is the contest over who would control Iraqi oil and revenues. Top-level American officials such as Bush, Rumsfeld, and Powell had all repeatedly insisted with great sincerity in their voices that the oil belonged to the Iraqi people. It would be used for the reconstruction of Iraq. To those like myself who had grave doubts about the altruism of the takeover of Iraq, this had a comforting sound. Probably people who were dogmatically cynical about it simply disbelieved these statements from the start. In any case, these statements were nice rhetorical gestures, seeming to imply that the hearts of American leaders were in the right place.

In this context, naturally the world reacted with suspicion when the U.S. submitted a resolution to the UN replacing the sanctions and the oil-for-food program with a built-in insistence that Iraqi oil and revenues be handled not by the UN, but by the good ol' USA. Apparently American honor and integrity were so obvious to American leaders that they believed that exclusive U.S. control of Iraqi oil and money was synonymous with honesty and impartiality, and would be recognized as such by all. Setting up advisory and audit teams with promises of transparency was clearly intended to reinforce this view.

There is another possibility: maybe it was just a naked power grab. Motives can be hard to fathom, but the very early decision to award a major oil industry reconstruction contract without competition to an American company, Haliburton—Vice President Cheney's old company—seemed a hint. Clearly the spoils of war were going to the victor and the victor's corporate friends. Is that a surprise? Did anyone believe it likely that French companies would have an equal chance at reconstruction in Iraq? If not, what does this say about integrity and impartiality? Transparency, yes; the whole world knows. But impartiality? Who will believe it, especially, who in the Arab world?

The nations who opposed the war in the Security Council could have once again opposed the U.S. in this seizure of control of Iraqi money and oil, but the bruising battle over the legitimacy of the war itself had done its work. They were too exhausted and too concerned about repairing their damaged relationships with the all-powerful U.S. to be willing to fight another battle. Furthermore, Bush and company had them over a barrel—an oil barrel. It was essential for the benefit of the Iraqi people to lift the UN economic sanctions against Iraq, particularly sanctions on oil sales. The need for the sanction was clearly gone. Yet in Security Council Resolution 1483 the U.S. had indissolubly linked lifting the sanctions to U.S. control of Iraq and its oil and money. France, Germany, Russia, and other nations in the Security Council picked at the details of the resolution but eventually let it go. They had no stomach left for another major fight with the world's only superpower.

Was the original Bush administration plan to attack Iraq motivated primarily or even substantially by a grab for Iraqi oil? No one but the people planning the attack know for sure, but after the war, one thing was clear. The grab had occurred. The UN, the obvious and only legitimate (i.e., international and not self-interested) institution to control Iraqi oil, was cut out of the action. Sometimes the best way to judge the motive of an action is to look at the result. Facts at the end of a chain of events outweigh rhetoric at the beginning. The theory about military bases in Iraq forming a key motive will have to await much longer-term U.S. behavior. Whether long-term establishment of bases there is feasible is certain to be affected by the great difficulty the U.S. is having establishing security in Iraq.

In addition to taking over Iraqi oil fields, three other bonanzas to American business emerged after the war. Apparently even the most strident critics of Bush and the war were not cynical enough to think of these ahead of time. Bombs dropped and other military equipment destroyed or used up have to be replaced, boosting military spending in politically key districts and states back home. Further, the Iraqi economic infrastructure devastated by the war has to be rebuilt, boosting yet another set of American companies. U.S. big business wins coming and going. If this sounds too cynical, may I ask, does anyone seriously expect French or German companies to get major reconstruction contracts? They have been relegated to minor roles as subcontractors. In addition to advantages for business, jobs were created by the sudden surge in military spending. Since jobs are a key campaign issue for the November 2004 presidential election, this circumstance is a plus for President Bush's reelection. Whether planning was in the driver's seat at the front end of these events, clearly opportunistic exploitation of the effects of the war will play a large role at its conclusion and beyond.

Economists have not failed to notice that the stimulus of the deficit spending provoked in part by the war may help pull the U.S. economy out of its slump before the 2004 elections. Of course it would be far too cynical to even consider this as a possible conscious motive for the war. However, a general pro-military tilt is stronger in parts of the country where troops are stationed and where jobs are often military-related. Military spending has often been used as a caffeine jolt for the American economy, and war is the surest driver of military spending. Boosting military spending and using military power generously in dealing with international problems go hand-in-hand; they are predispositions of the same ideological and political grouping. Both are pervasive tendencies in the Bush administration. The link does not have to be a direct and cynical one to be a reality.

Excessive military spending is not healthy economically in the long run because it drains brainpower from private sector productivity that puts products in American hands rather than putting bombs on targets in other countries. It is possible to make a lot of product improvements in cars and computers or to create brand new products with the engineering time and brainpower it takes to design a new aircraft carrier or fighter jet. But military spending is a stimulant. It does get the economic wheels turning in the short run. The ordinary American citizens and younger generations in particular who have to pay taxes to cover the cost of the war and the reconstruction and the deficit they aggravate, are the losers in the midst of this artificial business bonanza. Bush's simultaneous decision to cut taxes (mainly for the rich) merely aggravates the problem and shoves it into the future. Our children and grandchildren will pay.

Where Are Those Weapons of Mass Destruction?

After the war, the evidence that Saddam had no weapons of mass destruction became steadily stronger, eroding the credibility of American intelligence and the rationale for the entire enterprise. The UN inspection team, using U.S. intelligence tips, had found nothing before the war. It was sent home at the beginning of the war, before it could complete its work. It had acquired extensive data that might have been useful in continuing the search. Nevertheless, scorned by the Bush administration, Hans Blix and the UN inspectors were not invited back into Iraq after the war.

Instead a fresh, all-American team (and thus, in keeping with tribalistic assumptions, presumed to be more competent or more honest) was sent in. They too struck out. One headline tells the story of the end of the second effort to find WMDs: "Frustrated, U.S. Arms Team to Leave Iraq: Task Force Unable To Find Any Weapons."[13] The article goes on to say, "The group directing all known search efforts for weapons of mass destruction in Iraq is winding down operations without finding proof that President Saddam Hussein kept clandestine stocks of outlawed arms, according to participants.... The group's departure, expected next month, marks a major milestone in frustration for a major declared objective of the war."[14] Another quote captures the significance of the story: "Task Force 75's experience, and its impending dissolution after seven weeks in action, square poorly with assertions in Washington that the search has barely begun."[15]

The fact was that the team had searched the high priority sites and found nothing incriminating, and little that was even slightly suggestive of weapons of mass destruction. They found swimming pools, rooms full of vacuum cleaners, empty warehouses, open fields and high school chemistry experiments, but no WMDs. One exception was a truck carrying a rig that might have produced chemical weapons, but the chemicals and weapons themselves were nowhere to be seen, and the mobile facility had apparently not been recently used. Later analysis suggested that the equipment may have been used in producing hydrogen. Expecting to find a mountain range of evidence, the team had found a tiny molehill, or nothing at all.

In explaining this puzzling absence of evidence, much was made of the looting that had decimated the suspected sites. Destroyed files couldn't guide searchers to purported or assumed hidden caches of weapons. But many of the sites surveyed were assumed in the original intelligence analyses to be actual locations where the weapons hardware existed, not just offices where there might be records of weapons. It hardly seems likely that the expected thousands of warheads loaded with anthrax or VX were carried away by looters. No one on the search teams claimed this. Looters did carry uranium yellow cake from one site, spreading radiation sickness, but the team ascertained from what was left that it was not nearly weapons grade. Serious questions also lingered about why the U.S. military failed to post adequate security in such vital locations immediately after the war. Perhaps they were

349

stretched too thin, but if security was not important at these places, then where? The UN inspection team had already surveyed these sites repeatedly. Is it possible that the military brass suspected there was really nothing there and didn't want to spend valuable resources guarding nothing? If so, we're back again to the question, why did we fight the war?

Journalists interviewed members of the search team for their perspective. "Intelligence agencies had a far less accurate picture of Iraq's weapons program than participants believed at the outset of their search, they recalled. 'We came to bear country loaded for bear and we found out the bear wasn't there,' said a Defense Intelligence Agency Officer here who asked not to be identified by name.'"[16] "The stymied hunt baffles search team leaders. To a person, those interviewed during the weeklong visit to the task force said they believed in the mission and the Bush administration accusations that prompted it. Yet 'smoking gun' is now a term of dark irony here."[17]

David Kay's Bombshell

This team's departure was followed by a still larger team taking over the search, a small army of 1,400 people headed by veteran weapons inspector David Kay. Despite the evidence accumulated by the two previous teams, Kay set out expecting to find weapons of mass destruction. What he found confirmed the results of the other teams. When he resigned from the leadership of the team in January 2004, his colleagues thought he would go quietly into the night, but instead he made quite a splash. He testified in a variety of venues including the Senate Armed Services Committee, where he stated that on Saddam's weapons of mass destruction, "We were almost all wrong—and I certainly include myself here."[18]

He declared prewar intelligence on Iraq a sweeping failure.[19] "After months of searching Kay and his 1,400-member team found none of the chemical or biological weapons Bush cited as a key reason for the U.S.-led invasion to oust Iraqi dictator Saddam Hussein."[20] However, he defended the Bush administration, arguing that it was provided with faulty intelligence. He stated that he "had extensive conversations with intelligence analysts, [and] said he found no evidence that the White House pressured analysts to tailor findings to support the administration line."[21] In view of his defense of the White House, clearly his statements were not a political attack on President Bush.

The results of Kay's inspections are simply staggering. What they say is that the entire war was based on a falsehood—either an outright mistake or a fraud. This was a war for which the U.S. alienated world opinion, infuriated the Muslim and Arab worlds (thereby providing new recruits for terrorism), tore vital alliances to shreds, and spent scores of billions of dollars and lost the lives of hundreds of American soldiers and about fifteen thousand Iraqi soldiers and civilians. All to get rid of a threat that did not exist.

Important questions linger about the intentions and causes behind the spectacular failure of intelligence on which this war was supposedly based. Was this huge intelligence blunder the product of innocent errors or a product of exaggerations under pressure? David Kay provides one answer, holding the intelligence agencies responsible and exonerating the White House, but an investigative study done six months earlier suggests another answer.

> Vice President Cheney and his most senior aide made multiple trips to the CIA over the past year to question analysts studying Iraq's weapons programs and alleged links to al Qaeda, creating an environment in which some analysts felt that they were being pressured to make their assessments fit with the Bush administration's policy objectives, according to senior intelligence officials.[22]

One intelligence official stated to reporters that visits from Cheney and his chief of staff, I. Lewis "Scooter" Libby, "sent signals, intended or otherwise, that certain output was desired from here."[23] Other agency officials denied that they were influenced by the visits. It may or may not be significant that they did not deny that there was pressure, but merely said they were not influenced by it. Other sources also noted intense pressure:

> Former and current intelligence officials said they felt a continual drumbeat, not only from Cheney and Libby, but also from Deputy Defense Secretary Paul D. Wolfowitz, Feith, and less so from CIA Director George C. Tenet, to find information or write reports in a way that would help the administration make the case that going into Iraq was urgent.

> 'They were the browbeaters,' said a former defense intelligence official who attended some of the meetings in which Wolfowitz and others

pressed for a different approach to the assessments they were receiving. 'In interagency meetings' he said, 'Wolfowitz treated the analysis work with contempt.'[24]

The pressure from the neoconservative hawks would not have been necessary if the unbiased conclusions of highly professional analysts—based on evidence and logic rather than ideology or politics—had pointed to Iraq as a threat. It is difficult to escape the conclusion that Cheney and the hawkish political appointees who were pressuring the CIA and other intelligence agencies were being intellectually dishonest, at the very least.

Clueless in Washington

The contrast between the neoconservative hawks' approach to intelligence data and that of retired Marine General Anthony Zinni, the former Chief of the U.S. Central Command in the Middle East, could hardly be more dramatic. He has made revealing public comments on the intelligence regarding his observations on Iraq and the rationale for the war. His overall assessment, as reported in a December 2003 news article, was the following: "He didn't think Hussein was much of a worry any more. 'He was contained,' he says. 'It was a pain in the ass, but he was contained. He had a deteriorated military. He wasn't a threat to the region.'"[25] Zinni was alarmed at Cheney's oft-stated certainty that Saddam was amassing weapons of mass destruction and planning to use them against the U.S. and its allies.

Cheney's certitude bewildered Zinni. As chief of the Central Command, Zinni had been immersed in U.S. intelligence about Iraq. He was all too familiar with the intelligence analysts' doubts about Iraq's programs to acquire weapons of mass destruction, or WMD. 'In my time at Centcom, I watched the intelligence and never—not once—did it say, 'He has WMD.'"[26]

Commenting on his more recent access to intelligence information, Zinni states, "'I did consulting work for the agency [a code word for the CIA], right up to the beginning of the war. I never saw anything. I'd say to analysts, 'Where's the threat?' Their response, he recalls, was 'Silence.'"[27] Zinni sat on the stage as Cheney gave a speech on the immediacy of the threat from Saddam and the urgency of attacking him. "Zinni's conclusion as he slowly walked off the stage that day was that the Bush administration was determined to go to war. A moment later, he had another, equally chilling thought. 'Those guys don't understand what they're getting into.'"[28]

Events in Iraq during the year following the U.S. entry into Iraq have powerfully vindicated Zinni's chilling thought. After the military's skillful and dramatically successful major operations to take over the country, it was all downhill. The looting caught them off guard; the total disappearance of the Iraqi security structure, both police and army, surprised them; they intensified the insurgency and aggravated the lack of security by dismissing the leaders and troops of Saddam's army without the pensions they had expected under Saddam; the complete collapse of the Iraqi economic infrastructure caught them unprepared; they were surprised by the ferocity, sophistication and durability of the insurgency; the problems sabotage created for the reconstruction were unexpectedly severe; the surge of anti-American violence a full year after the war surprised them according to Defense Secretary Rumsfeld's own admission; they failed to anticipate and prevent the humanitarian and public relations disaster of the abuse of prisoners of war; and on and on.

General Zinni's foreboding that they didn't know what they were getting into was understated; they were clueless. Most—though not all—of these problems had been predicted by experts, but the experts and their pessimistic scenarios had not been consulted. Cheney and Wolfowitz believed we were going to be welcomed as liberators. We were for the first week. The State Department had done postwar planning, but the Pentagon ran the show and didn't consult the State Department.

Carnegie Endowment: We Were Misled on WMD

In a 107 page report, "WMD in Iraq: Evidence and Implications," the Carnegie Endowment for International Peace, one of the nation's most prestigious think tanks on international relations, conducted an in-depth analysis of the use of intelligence leading to the Iraq war. This report, issued in January 2004, states unequivocally that "Administration officials systematically misrepresented the threat from Iraq's WMD and ballistic missile programs." A preview summary sheet listing key findings states that intelligence on Iraq both "failed and was misrepresented."[29] It goes on to explain that the "intelligence community overstated the chemical and biological weapons in Iraq;" the "intelligence community appears to have been unduly influenced by policymakers' views," and "officials misrepresented threat from Iraq's WMD and ballistic missiles programs over and above intelligence findings."[30]

The report concludes that Iraq WMD was not an immediate threat; that Iraq's nuclear program had been suspended for many years; Iraqi nerve agents had lost most of their lethality as early as 1991; and Operations Desert Storm and Desert Fox, and UN inspections and sanctions effectively destroyed Iraq's large scale chemical weapon production capabilities.[31]

The report documents the Bush administration's muddling together three very distinct potential threats, nuclear, chemical and biological weapons, thereby distorting the cost/benefit ratio of the war. It also points out that there was "no solid evidence of a cooperative relationship between Saddam's government and al Qaeda," and "no evidence to support the claim that Iraq would have transferred WMD to Al Qaeda and much evidence to counter it."[32]

On the popular theory that WMD couldn't be found because Saddam hid them or shipped them to another country, the report concludes, "It is unlikely that Iraq could have destroyed, hidden or sent out of the country the hundreds of tons of chemical and biological weapons, dozens of scud missiles and facilities engaged in ongoing production of chemical and biological weapons that officials claimed were present without the United States detecting some sign of this activity before, during, or after the major combat period of the war."[33]

The report's findings on the Bush theory of preemptive warfare are especially interesting in the aftermath of the Iraq test case. "The National Security Strategy's new doctrine of preemptive military action is actually a loose standard for preventive war under the cloak of legitimate preemption [military action in the face of imminent attack]."[34] And further, "In the Iraqi case, the world's three best intelligence services proved unable to provide the accurate information necessary for acting in the absence of imminent threat."[35] In short, reaching around the world and attacking anybody we may think is a threat is not a good idea. Especially since, in the case of Iraq, we were wrong in thinking they were a threat.

In short, the Carnegie Endowment's analysis convincingly annihilates just about every shred of the Bush administration's rationale for the Iraq war. It also proposes a series of recommendations for U.S. policy and for international action. Among those for U.S. action are: to create an independent non-partisan commission to establish a clear picture of what the intelligence community knew about Iraqi WMD and to consider the question of political pressure on analysts and agencies' responses to it; to raise the priority of protecting nuclear weapon stockpiles and materials; to deter transfer of WMD from nations to terrorist organizations by announcing our resolve to use overwhelming force in such a case; and to revise the National Security Strategy to eliminate the doctrine of unilateral, preventive war in the absence of imminent threat.[36]

Was The War Good Military Strategy?

Once the U.S. decision to go to war in Iraq was made and the military capabilities were positioned, the swift success of the American military takeover of the country was impressive, to say the least. The pinpoint bombing of selected targets to maximize "shock and awe" and minimize civilian casualties was also impressive. The conduct of these operations certainly seemed, to a lay person, like a brilliant piece of military strategy. Nothing can alter the fact that the American military performed superbly in this huge operation. The achievement it represents, taken on its own terms, should not be diminished or belittled in any way. The American soldiers and their leaders who conducted this operation deserve high praise for a job well done. Whether we agree with the rationale for the war or not, it is imperative that all American citizens honor the heroism, the risks, the hard work, and the sacrifices of our troops and the hardships of their families. The troops did not create the war, but they fought honorably in it.

Still, there is a major problem, one of wider military strategy, one created at the political level, not at the level of our professional military. The U.S. Army War College published a study in December 2003 that raises serious strategic questions, not so much about this one swift and successful campaign, but about the entire Iraq war and its place in the larger war on terrorism. Military strategy is about more than moving troops around and making sure they are adequately supplied and are able to achieve their military objectives, no matter how large those objectives may be. It is about selecting broad war objectives that are clear, achievable, that actually enhance national security, and can be accomplished by means that do not exhaust national resources. These are practical tests that have little to do with questions about the morality or legality of the war. On these practical tests of military strategy the Iraq war flunks, and so does the war on terrorism as a whole.

The War College study is so important I include its entire summary below verbatim to assure myself and the reader that I'm not distorting what it says in any way. I make no claims to expertise as a military strategist, so I let Dr. Jeffrey Record, one of the country's foremost experts, do the talking. I should note that the U.S. Army War College cleared this study for public release and unlimited distribution, but stated that the study does not necessarily reflect the official position of the Army, the Department of Defense, or the U.S. Government.[37] Clearly it does not reflect the policies of the Bush administration. Here is the summary:

In the wake of the September 11, 2001, al-Qaeda terrorist attacks on the United States, the U.S. Government declared a global war on terrorism (GWOT). The nature and parameters of that war, however, remain frustratingly unclear. The administration has postulated a multiplicity of enemies, including rogue states; weapons of mass destruction (WMD) proliferators; terrorist organizations of global, regional, and national scope; and terrorism itself. It also seems to have conflated them into a monolithic threat, and in so doing has subordinated strategic clarity to the moral clarity it strives for in foreign policy and may have set the United States on a course of open-ended and gratuitous conflict with states and nonstate entities that pose no serious threat to the United States.

Of particular concern has been the conflation of al-Qaeda and Saddam Hussein's Iraq as a single, undifferentiated terrorist threat. This was a strategic error of the first order because it ignored critical differences between the two in character, threat level, and susceptibility to U.S. deterrence and military action. The result has been an unnecessary preventive war of choice against a deterred Iraq that has created a new front in the Middle East for Islamic terrorism and diverted attention and resources away from securing the American homeland against further assault by an undeterrable al-Qaeda. *The war against Iraq was not integral to the GWOT, but rather a detour from it.*

Additionally, most of the GWOT's declared objectives, which include the destruction of al-Qaeda and other transnational terrorist organizations, the transformation of Iraq into a prosperous, stable democracy, the democratization of the rest of the autocratic Middle East, the eradication of terrorism as a means of irregular warfare, and the (forcible, if necessary) termination of WMD proliferation to real and potential enemies worldwide, are unrealistic and condemn the United States to a hopeless quest for absolute security. As such, the GWOT's goals are also politically, fiscally, and militarily unsustainable.

Accordingly, the GWOT must be recalibrated to conform to concrete U.S. security interests and the limits of American power. The specific measures required include deconflation of the threat; substitution of credible deterrence for preventive war as the primary vehicle for dealing with rogue states seeking WMD; refocus of the GWOT first and foremost on al-Qaeda, its allies, and homeland security; preparation to settle in Iraq for stability over democracy (if the choice is forced upon us) and for international rather than U.S. responsibility for Iraq's future; and finally, a reassessment of U.S. military force levels, especially ground force levels. The GWOT as it has so far been defined and conducted is strategically unfocused, promises much more than it can deliver, and threatens to dissipate scarce U.S. military and other means over too many ends. It violates the fundamental strategic principles of discrimination and concentration.[38]

Remarkably, the bottom line judgement on attacking Iraq looks the same—a bad idea—from every perspective. Church leaders and experts on ethics condemn it on moral grounds. Legal scholars point out that it was a clear violation of international law. Politically it has been a disaster that has angered and frightened our allies, intensified the hatred of our enemies, and has gravely damaged international institutions whose job it is to keep the peace in the world. Fiscally, the war constitutes a high, damaging, and ongoing cost to the nation at a moment when the deficit is ballooning and baby boomers are soon going to retire, putting a huge strain on social security and medicare. And finally, as the War College study shows, launching the war was an instance of bad military strategy, a detour from the war on terrorism that motivated increased terrorism and siphoned off funding that was more urgently needed for homeland security.

Giving al Qaeda a Recruitment Tool

Richard A. Clarke's is one of the nation's foremost terrorism experts, and served in the White House during the aftermath of September 11 and during the run-up to the Iraq war. His book, *Against All Enemies,* hit the Bush administration and the U.S. news media like a five hundred pound bomb. One of Clarke's key messages was that President Bush did not take the terrorism threat from al Qaeda seriously before 9/11; he and the White House were asleep at the switch. This was an electrifying claim in the context of Congressional hearings on failures to prevent 9/11, especially coming from a person with his expertise and vantage point.

But Clarke had another message that was, if possible, even more damaging. In a moment everyone will remember who watched the evening news on TV that night, as he testified before the 9/11 commission he commented on the Iraq war. Asked why his earlier testimony to the commission had not included the criticism of the President he included in his book, Clarke replied, "In the 15 hours of testimony, no one asked me what I thought about the President's invasion of Iraq. And the reason I am strident in my criticism of the president of the United States is because by invading Iraq...the president of the United States has greatly undermined the war on terrorism."[39] Clarke's statement was greeted with stunned silence, a moment so striking that television news anchors commented on it. The Iraq war, supposedly a part of the war on terrorism, actually undermined it? This statement, coming from one of the nation's foremost terrorism experts, was no small matter.

Clarke, in his book, echoes other accounts, such as Ron Suskind's book on former Treasury Secretary Paul H. O'Neill, that key administration officials appeared unduly focused on Iraq in the months before the September 11 attacks—and then leapt to the conclusion that Iraq was somehow involved.

Clarke depicts the President as intensely demanding that his staff look for links between the Sept. 11 attacks and Iraq. He charges that, for Bush and his advisers, attacking Iraq was 'a rigid belief, received wisdom, a decision already made and one that no fact or event could derail.' In the end, through the Iraq war, we delivered to al Qaeda the greatest recruitment propaganda imaginable.[40]

Of course, the White House deployed all its public relations capabilities to counter Clarke's statements, launching a storm of attacks and attempts at character assassination. In their rush to attack Clarke and deny the truth of his statements, several representatives of the White House, including Condoleezza Rice and Dick Cheney, failed to coordinate their stories and made mutually contradictory statements and even contradicted themselves. For once the press was on top of its game and pointed out the contradictions. Aside from their factual mistakes, their main point was that Clarke was disgruntled and partisan; that he had an anti-Bush axe to grind. He was therefore not to be believed.

Unfortunately for the credibility of the White House in its attacks on Clarke, four highly respected terrorism experts chimed in, supporting what he had said. Rand Beers, who served as counterterrorism chief after Clarke, publicly agreed with him. Beers stated specifically that Arabic-speaking Special Forces officers who were doing a good job of tracking bin Laden in Afghanistan and could have caught him were pulled off in March, 2002 to prepare for Iraq.[41] Flynt Leverett, a former CIA analyst and Middle East expert also agreed, saying, "Clarke's critique of administration decision-making and how it did not balance the imperative of finishing the job against al Qaeda versus what they wanted to do in Iraq is absolutely on the money."[42]

Jessica Stern, an expert on religious militants and terrorism, also agreed with Clarke. "It was a distraction on the war on terrorism and made it more difficult to prosecute because the al Qaeda movement used the war in Iraq to mobilize new recruits and energize the movement."[43] Pat Lang, who had headed Middle East and South Asia intelligence in the Defense Intelligence Agency, said the resources, especially the Special Forces, committed to Iraq were subtracted from the war on terrorism. He said he did not believe Iraq war was connected to the war against the jihadis.[44]

We learned a terrible truth on September 11, that there are people in the world who not only hate us as a nation intensely enough to want to do us great harm, but some of them have the means to accomplish their aims. The hatred that al Qaeda and thousands (if not millions) of other Islamic extremists feel toward the U.S. is not directed at "civilization" in general nor at "our freedoms" as President Bush vacuously suggests in his political rhetoric. Certainly the worldwide spread of our secular and sexually licentious culture are factors in the hatred that Islamic extremists direct our way, but they are far from the only sources of the problem.

The U.S. comes in for special attention and hatred because of more specific motives. The hostility toward the U.S. is directed at specific patterns of American international behavior such as our unbalanced and almost unconditional support for Israel and our corresponding indifference to Palestinian suffering. It includes our support for corrupt and oppressive rulers of Arab countries that provide us with the lifeblood of our economy, oil. And it is reinforced by specific conditions in the Muslim world such as financial support for madrasses by wealthy members of the Wahabbi sect in Saudi Arabia. Madrasses are Islamic schools, many of which teach an extreme and distorted version of the Muslim religion, including hatred for the U.S. These schools are often the only source of minimal education for poverty-stricken young people in countries such as Pakistan. They spread a particularly virulent and hate-filled ideology all over the world, indoctrinating children with an ideology that may stay with them for a lifetime.

Richard Clarke's book recognizes these realities and suggests that we could have pursued a much different approach to dealing with the forces that created September 11. "The second agenda item post-September 11 should have been the creation of a counterweight ideology to al Qaeda, the fundamentalist, radical version of Islam because much of the threat we face is ideological, a perversion of a religion."[45] He compares the real struggle, one that would, if engaged, last many years, as did the U.S. ideological struggle with Communism for half a century. "We found ways of assisting Christian Democratic parties in Europe and Latin America.... We found or created spokesmen, leaders, heroes, schools, books, films, development programs. That effort did as much to win the Cold War as did the U.S. Army tanks in West Germany."[46]

However, we did something exactly opposite in its effect on Muslim public opinion.

Rather than seek to work with the majority in the Islamic world to mold Muslim opinion against the radicals' values, we did exactly what al Qaeda said we would do. We invaded and occupied an oil-rich Arab country that posed no threat to us, while paying scant time and attention to the Israeli-Palestinian problem. We delivered to al Qaeda the greatest recruitment propaganda imaginable and made it difficult for friendly Islamic governments to be seen working closely with us.[47]

President Bush repeats the mantra that if we had not fought the Iraq war, Saddam would still be in power, as if this possibility were the ultimate horror. Given that he was contained militarily (the no-fly zones) and economically (the UN sanctions) had no weapons of mass destruction and no contacts with al Qaeda, this is not such a horrifying alternative to the mess we have now. Bush fails to mention that without the war we would have 800 American soldiers alive rather than dead, 4,000 soldiers whole rather than wounded, well over 150 billion dollars in the U.S. treasury for more constructive purposes, and far fewer enemies in the world. Clarke has the following observations, after acknowledging the terrible evil of Saddam:

> I know that in one sense the world is better off without him in power, but not in the way it was done, not at the cost we have paid and will pay for it; not by diverting us from eliminating al Qaeda and its clones; not by using the funds we needed to eliminate our vulnerabilities to terrorism at home; not at the incredibly high price of increasing Muslim hatred of America and strengthening al Qaeda.[48]

He wrote these words—and published his book—before the most damaging blow yet to America's credibility and moral authority, if it had any left—the photos of smiling American prison guards, including young women, terrorizing, torturing, and sexually abusing Iraqis at Abu Ghraib prison. These photos and the reality behind them were also costs of a war that should never have happened and has produced a seemingly endless stream of woes for the U.S. and for the world.

Abusing Prisoners

Brushing aside international law as if it were a minor inconvenience or a menu from which leaders of the U.S. may pick and choose (an approach sometimes called *á la carte* multilateralism) is a habit and an ideology of the Bush administration. The White House seems almost to have a preference for thumbing its nose at international law as a way to demonstrate the superiority and impunity of the United States. Aside from these whims and preferences of politicians, the reality of international law is much more structured and more tightly integrated. Under the U.S. Constitution, treaties that have been signed by the President and ratified by the Senate are the law of the land, as

361

legally binding as any domestic law. But never mind, it seems there is always a way around a treaty if one of our leaders wants to find it or wishes to assert it.

So it was no surprise when Donald Rumsfeld brushed aside the Geneva Conventions on treatment of prisoners of war.

Beginning more than two years ago, Mr. Rumsfeld decided to overturn decades of previous practice by the U.S. military in its handling of detainees in foreign countries. His Pentagon ruled that the United States would no longer be bound by the Geneva Conventions; that Army regulations on the interrogation of prisoners would not be observed; and that many detainees would be held incommunicado and without any independent mechanism of review. Abuses will take place in any prison system. But Mr. Rumsfeld's decisions helped create a lawless regime in which prisoners in both Iraq and Afghanistan have been humiliated, beaten, tortured and murdered -- and in which, until recently, no one has been held accountable.

The lawlessness began in January 2002 when Mr. Rumsfeld publicly declared that hundreds of people detained by U.S. and allied forces in Afghanistan "do not have any rights" under the Geneva Conventions. That was not the case: At a minimum, all those arrested in the war zone were entitled under the conventions to a formal hearing to determine whether they were prisoners of war or unlawful combatants. No such hearings were held, but then Mr. Rumsfeld made clear that U.S. observance of the convention was now optional. Prisoners, he said, would be treated "for the most part" in "a manner that is reasonably consistent" with the conventions -- which, the secretary breezily suggested, was outdated.[49]

The direct consequence of this casual dismissal of international law and the fundamental principles of human rights have been catastrophic for thousands of individual human beings, for the last shreds of American moral authority, and probably for U.S. success in establishing stability in Iraq.

Despite the triteness of the concept, there really are moments when a picture is more powerful than a million words. The pictures that surfaced in May 2004, first on TV, then in newspapers, of horrifying and despicable prisoner abuse at Abu Ghraib prison in Iraq transcend language and even imagination in the impact they have had throughout the world. Mental and emotional torment, extreme sexual humiliation in the context of a culture that is hyper-sensitive—at least by comparatively casual American standards— about sexual activity and nudity, may well be worse than physical torture. But physical torture was shown in the pictures too, as illustrated by one in which a naked man is shown with his arms pulled tight behind him and his back arched over the sharp edge of an iron bed frame. This position would become excruciating in minutes. One wonders whether he was kept in it for hours.

Everyone has seen these terrible pictures; I need not dredge up the muck yet again by describing them in gratuitous detail. But there are certain salient points about them that have gotten surprisingly little attention in the American press. One is the nature of the young women shown sexually humiliating naked Iraqi men in the first few pictures. These women, separated for a moment from the context of what they are doing, do not appear to be female thugs or hard-looking prostitutes; they are the girl next door, the young woman you expect to see behind the counter at your local grocery store. They might be anybody's wife or sister or daughter. They are middle America, suburban and small-town America.

Looking at them, one suspects instantly that they are products of a system or a culture that called on them to do what they did, or at least encouraged it. This does not excuse what they did, but it does put it into a larger context. They simply do not look like the type to seek out on their own initiative opportunities to torture and humiliate people. Of course, appearances can be deceiving. But interviews with their families confirmed the impression of ordinariness gone horribly awry. These women and the roles they played suggest two things: that quite possibly large numbers of people have the capacity to commit such evil, though few people do; and that unusual circumstances must have unleashed the potential.

Research conducted at Stanford University[50] casts a bright and disturbing light on the potential for ordinary, normal people to become sadistic in circumstances in which they were under pressure to exercise complete control over others. In 1971 Psychologist Philip Zimbardo set up a situation that simulated prison conditions and called for paid volunteers to serve as either guards or inmates for two weeks. The experimental subjects were college men who showed no abnormalities in the way they reacted or tested; others were screened out. The two groups, guards and inmates, were selected randomly from among the normal volunteers; there was no systematic difference between them. The test was designed to go on for two weeks, but it had such destructive effects on the subjects it had to be terminated early. In less than six days prisoners became helpless, dependent, depressed, socially isolated from and suspicious of one another. Called by numbers rather than names and required to wear identical stocking caps and gowns without underwear, they quickly lost their sense of individual identity. After a few days some broke down completely, crying hysterically, screaming, etc. (After initial reluctance in which they were mistakenly thought to be faking, they were released from the study.)

Inmates with a strong authoritarian streak did best at handling the role of inmate, presumably because they were comfortable with accepting arbitrary orders and controls. Initially some inmates rebelled, but eventually all succumbed to harsh dominance by the guards except those who broke down and were released. Prison "guards" decided how to deal with problems such as prisoner rebellions. They spontaneously fell into groups, some being nice and doing prisoners favors; some becoming sadistic. Faced with occasional resistance and rebellion, guards became obsessed with control and quickly became skilled at intimidating prisoners and breaking down their resistance to control and their social solidarity by techniques such as arbitrary punishments and making them suspicious that other prisoners were informants. Punishments for rebellious behavior included short periods of deprivation of clothing, food, comfortable beds, solitary confinement, etc. The punishments were very effective at controlling behavior. Some guards began to deal with boredom by secretly sexually mistreating prisoners at night. Guards did not quit the experiment or demand overtime pay for extra hours, and they always arrived for work on time. They objected when the experiment was discontinued early. Apparently they thrived on the power the role gave them, just as the prisoners wilted under the relentless dehumanization.

While not all of the guards in the experiment became sadistic, about a third of them did so on their own, without any prompting or any Abu Ghraib-like expectation that they "soften up" inmates for interrogation. The psychologists conducting the experiment could find no correlation between this change toward sadism and personality characteristics noted before the study.

The contrasts and similarities to Abu Ghraib are striking. However, there the guards are said to have been given instructions and encouragement to soften up detainees for interrogation. It appears that the pressures and expectations on the Abu Ghraib prison guards were far more supportive of abuse than those of the Stanford experiment.

In the context of the study described above, the news reports on Abu Ghraib make it possible to infer that the guards too, not only the prisoners, were victims of a system. Evidently they were not just sadistic perpetrators of terrible crimes purely on their own initiative, as the politicians desperately want the American public to believe. Soldiers are trained to take orders without asking questions, even if doing so means risking their lives. Volunteer soldiers may be on the job at least partly to serve their country. The guards, ordinary people, were given a job to do by their superiors, whose business was interrogation, not merely warehousing prisoners. The interrogation occurred in the context of an Iraqi insurgency that was costing American lives. The pressure to extract information from these detainees must have been intense, and the basis for rationalizing harshness was clear. Some reports noted that as the insurgency became more violent and deadly, the treatment of the prisoners in an effort to extract information also became harsher.

The interrogators are said to have tasked the guards with "softening up" the prisoners for interrogation, to make sure they were predisposed to answer questions. News reports indicated that prisoners who were cooperative and answered questions voluntarily were given as "privileges" treatment required of all prisoners by the Geneva Conventions for prisoners of war such as food and clothing and more-or-less comfortable circumstances for sleeping. Those who were not cooperative in answering questions were denied even necessities like clothing and sleep and were treated harshly until they became more cooperative.

It seems likely that the guards who were softening up the prisoners were told that the information the prisoners provided could save the lives of Americans by leading to the capture of more insurgents. In short, these prison guards appear to have been doing on a micro scale and under orders, exactly what the war as a whole is doing, i.e., committing a great evil in the hope or expectation that a greater good will come of it. Ironically, people who are knowledgeable about torture often say that the quality of information extracted by such methods is poor. Having disgraced the U.S., and undermined the remaining goal of stabilizing Iraq, the work of the guards is a ghastly failure as an effort to do something constructive, and so, probably, will be the war itself.

Nevertheless, it is almost self-evident that the guards should have been trained in the Geneva Conventions and reinforced in their efforts to implement these standards, rather than being encouraged to violate them at every turn. Even more than the guards, the interrogators, the people directing the guards, should have known the Geneva Conventions and should have defined and adhered to what was acceptable and unacceptable treatment of prisoners. They and their superiors are the people who carry the primary responsibility for the mistreatment of the prisoners. Scapegoating the guards misses the point, or rather, constitutes a failed attempt to let the chain of command off the hook, up to and including Rumsfeld and Bush.

Why those two, so far removed from the action? Again, they established a lawless policy by dismissing international law as irrelevant. If the assertion that the interrogators should have been trained in and required to follow the Geneva Conventions seems naïve, consider the stakes: the behavior that they allowed and encouraged (or possibly ordered) destroyed not only the credibility of the U.S. in general, but more specifically, it destroyed the contrast between the U.S. and Saddam. Given that Saddam had no WMDs and no contact with al Qaeda, if we appear to be no better than he was in our treatment of Iraqis, then the last semblance of political legitimacy for our being there has vanished. Already, many in the Arab and Muslim world have concluded that we are no better than Saddam; that nothing has changed except that the cruel overlords of Iraq are now hated aliens from America rather than hated insiders. That this belief is a major misperception does not change the increasingly adverse political realities in the Middle East.

Though the actions of the prison guards illustrate the moral paradox of the war as a whole, they were of course in no way typical of the majority of tens of thousands of American troops, many of whom are helping Iraqis rebuild their shattered country, as President Bush quite rightly insists. Conversely, it is equally important to recognize that these prison guards were not just a handful of sadistic individuals getting out of control in one prison. The problem of mistreatment of prisoners is or was widespread and systemic, as indicated by Red Cross and Amnesty International officials and other humanitarian groups as well. And this systemic abuse continued for months, possibly more than a year, despite repeated warnings that it was inhumane and violated the Geneva Conventions on treatment of prisoners of war.

We Americans are, by our presence and our inescapable role as occupiers in Iraq, forced to kill more and more Iraqis in an effort to bring them the blessings of freedom and democracy. The irony is almost too painful to contemplate. The good we do as we rebuild schools and hospitals and the rest of the wrecked infrastructure of the country is constantly being undermined by the violence we perpetrate while attempting unsuccessfully to defend our troops and contractors and the Iraqis who work with us. We cannot escape the ugly reality that we are aliens who are not Muslims, do not speak the language and do not understand the culture, and we are forcing our national will on other people, many of whom feel resentful and humiliated by our dominance. This reality is a given of the war and the occupation; we cannot change it except by leaving. Yet it seems we must stay and establish stability in the country if we can. But the longer we stay, the more the liberation of the Iraqis from the tyranny of Saddam fades into the background and the violence we are forced to perpetrate against the insurgency moves into the mental and emotional foreground. Having deposed and replaced Saddam, we are forced to become Saddam.

The pictures are not only symbols of the moral paradox of the war itself (doing evil that good may come of it), but they are also turbo-charged psychologically for more obvious reasons. The differences between the sexual morays of Americans and conservative Muslims is amplified a thousand-fold by pictures that are outrageous even by American standards. For the entire Middle East and possibly the whole world, the pictures become a sort of real-world horror show merged with sadistic pornography.

Symbolic meaning, horror and pornography all rolled up into one potent package: these are likely to make a lasting impression, one that digs deep into the subconscious fears and unwelcome desires of the Iraq people and of Muslims generally, intensifying and making more durable the already strong incentives to hate America. In short, these images are indelible; we will live with them for years. Their circulation may constitute the tipping point, the event that makes it impossible to accomplish even the modest goal of stability, let alone the higher goal of democracy, before we leave Iraq. Also, any future efforts by the U.S. to indulge our habit of lecturing other countries about human rights abuses will most likely be met with angry derision. Maybe that is a plus.

Knowledge that abuses of prisoners were happening was fairly widespread; it was not limited to the military chain of command. I myself knew something about terrible but not quite so horrific abuse of detainees and civilian non-combatants in Iraq by August 2003, nine months before the infamous pictures emerged. I knew these things despite being far removed personally from the CIA and the U.S. military, and having only distant connections to the humanitarian organizations such as the Red Cross that were concerned with monitoring treatment of detainees. Here are a few excerpts from an e-mail I received on August 20, 2003. It describes, not

367

specific abuses of specific prisoners, but the general conditions in a hellish prison camp near the Baghdad International Airport.

Each prisoner receives six pints of dank, tepid water a day. He uses it to wash and drink in summer noonday temperatures of 50 degrees Celsius. [About 120 degrees F.]

He is not allowed to wash his clothes. He is provided with a small cup of delousing powder to deal with the worst of his body infestation.

For the slightest infringement of draconian rules he is forced to sit in painful positions. If he cries out in protest his head is covered with a sack for lengthy periods.

This is daily life in America's shameful Gulag - Camp Cropper on the outskirts of Baghdad International Airport.

Only the International Red Cross are allowed inside. They are forbidden to describe what they see.

But some of its staff have broken ranks to tell Amnesty International of the shocking conditions the 3000 Iraqi prisoners are held under.

None had been charged with any offence. They are listed as suspected "looters" and "rioters". Or listed as "loyal to Saddam Hussein".

Every day more prisoners are crowded into the broiling, dusty compound.

Surrounded by ten-foot-high razor wire, they live in tents that are little protection against the blistering sun. They sleep eighty to a tent on wafer-thin mats.

Each prisoner has a long-handled shovel to dig his own latrine. Some are too old or weak to dig the ordered depth of three feet. Others find they have excavated pits already used.

The over-powering stench in this hell-hole is suffocating.

"Added to sleep deprivation and physical abuse, you have highly degrading conditions which are tantamount to torture and gross abuse of human rights," said Curt Goering, deputy director of Amnesty International, the London-based human rights watchdog.

He confirmed that Amnesty had received "credible reports" of detainees who had died in custody, "mostly as a result of shooting by members of the coalition forces."[51]

There is plenty more, but this is enough to convey a picture that is in its way almost as horrific as the photos from Abu Ghraib that have created such an uproar. It follows from the existence and the date of this document that abuse of detainees and denial of their basic human rights—such as access to legal representation—was an open secret, even reaching some members of the public, for the better part of a year. It just hadn't yet achieved enough visibility to create a political disturbance. When the reality finally did become visible in the form of the pictures, it created an earthquake that will adversely affect the ability of the U.S. to attract the help of other nations and international organizations and to stay in Iraq long enough to create stability.

Countering the moral outrage that has been widely expressed in the media about prisoner abuses in Iraq is an attitude I have encountered in some news articles and also among some acquaintances. It is essentially a tribalistic rationalization of the prisoner abuse. A certain fraction of the U.S. public is saying, in effect, "Oh, well, war is war. Besides, these are terrible people, insurgents who were killing Americans. They deserve anything that happens to them. Why should we go out of our way to treat them well?"

This rationalization overlooks one of the most disturbing facts about the treatment of prisoners. "In a report in February, the Red Cross stated that some military intelligence officers estimated that 70 percent to 90 percent of 'the persons deprived of their liberty in Iraq had been arrested by mistake.' Of the 43,000 Iraqis who have been imprisoned at some point during the occupation, only about 600 have been referred to Iraqi authorities for prosecution, according to U.S. officials."[52] In other words, if we do the math, somewhere in the range of 30,000 to 39,000 innocent Iraqis have been imprisoned and may have been subjected to horrors similar to those of Camp Cropper, if not the even greater horrors seen in the pictures of torture and humiliation.

The magnitude of the injustice to tens of thousands of innocent people beggars the imagination. When the U.S. commits such atrocities in the name of liberating Iraq, it is difficult to imagine how we can ever hope to establish any semblance of legitimacy there. There is no way to rationalize this as a few bad apples among guards, or tough handling of criminals. Our leaders have made our nation the perpetrator of a great crime. We may forget, but Iraqis who were no part of the insurgency and yet have suffered at our hands, and their families and friends, will not forget. We may have just created the next generation of anti-U.S. terrorists. Certainly we have strengthened the insurgency.

All this for the privilege of casually brushing aside international law and moral principle.

Democracy or Impending Civil War?

Long before Bush took office the neoconservatives who were calling the policy shots in the White House and the Pentagon during the lead-in to the Iraq war wrote visionary foreign policy articles expressing their desire for a military takeover of Iraq. For them, this takeover was part of a larger strategy to reshape the entire Middle East to America's advantage and to install democracy. Military force was a key part of this vision. It would all be part of a new American century, one in which American dominance was the great force in the world for democracy and free market capitalism. Diplomacy was best backed by force or trumped by force, and the UN was at best a tool of American power to be used when needed or brushed aside when inconvenient. Perhaps there would be no departure from Iraq, despite the pre- and post-war rhetoric. At the very least, military bases there would be useful in projecting further coercive power throughout the Middle East.

But Colin Powell and the State Department did not share key elements of the neoconservative vision. For them, diplomacy mattered, and the UN was an important component in legitimizing the war at the beginning and in carrying out and legitimizing postwar reconstruction. It would become more so as time passed and the U.S. found its task increasingly daunting.

Iraq is proving to be a painful test case for this neoconservative vision. The architects of war are finding it a catastrophic illustration of their theories in action. It may become their well-deserved complete undoing. It seems unlikely that democracy and freedom can be quickly imposed from scratch and from the outside by brute force and violence on a country that has no history of democracy and indeed no history of benign social order. Thirty-five years of violent oppression and corruption are not promising foundations on which to hastily build democratic institutions. Democracy is almost always a product of a long, gradual evolution. It entails a slow building of trust and values and ideals in the minds of millions of people. And if it is to include one of its key components, religious freedom, democracy entails acceptance of a diversity of value systems and separation of church (or mosque) and state, or at least explicit tolerance of religious diversity.

These ideals and "habits of the heart" develop gradually and cannot be imposed in a matter of months or even a few years on a society torn by intense ethnic rivalries, seething with religious and tribal passions, and traumatized by decades of genocidal dictatorship. Further, control of the country's single great natural resource, oil, confers economic control of everything else. Oil is therefore a potent source of strife as different groups compete for it, and then a source of tyranny if one group controls it. None of this bodes well for democracy in Iraq.

Henry Kissinger put it well when he said,

> Compressing the evolution of centuries into an inappropriate time frame risks huge unintended consequences. Where societies are divided by faith or ethnicity, our practices run the risk of ratifying a permanent distribution of power based on those divisions. Where the minority has no prospect of becoming a majority, elections may often result in civil war or chaos—the very breeding ground for militant terrorist organizations.
>
> Because democracy must be rooted in domestic factors, it will thrive only where it reflects cultural, historical and institutional backgrounds.[53]

The neoconservatives' comparisons of Iraq with Germany and Japan after World War II are remote and far-fetched. Germany was a democracy before Hitler, and after WW II it was ready to turn away from dictatorship and its consequences and back toward democracy. Japan had been orderly, stable and unified culturally and politically. After the war it was guided toward democracy by a towering leader, General Douglas MacArthur. The emperor, its revered symbol of power and source of political legitimacy, was allowed to stay on in a ceremonial role. He encouraged obedience to the occupation forces. As a result, Japan was not afflicted by the type of violent insurgency that devastates Iraq and the U.S. efforts to rebuild it. Both Japan and Germany had accepted the fact that they were defeated and occupied, however reluctantly, and neither had an influx of foreign terrorists with a fanatical dedication to thwarting the American goal of rebuilding the country.

The exact opposites of these situations pertain in Iraq: a leadership vacuum, a despised, deposed and imprisoned former leader, an ethnically diverse, traumatized and turbulent population with no habit of voluntary social order, and key elements among the fragmented emerging leadership (e.g., Moqtada al Sadr and his followers) that successfully advocate violent resistance to the American presence. Foreign terrorists, local religious fanatics, resentful Saddam loyalists, and fanatical Iraqi nationalists are a volatile mix all bent on attacking foreign troops, relief workers and Iraqis who cooperate with the occupation. These forces have succeeded in creating chaos and retarding reconstruction.

During April 2004, Sunnis and Shiites, often at each others throats, temporarily united against the humiliation of a military occupation by a non-Muslim power. It is not clear whether they will continue to cooperate against the occupation, but when that external power is gone, they will most likely turn against one another. At the same time the Kurdish population in the north may seize the opportunity of disorder to drive for their own independence, additionally trying to take over the oil-rich city of Kirkuk. In short, thanks to the U.S. military intervention, the future political situation in Iraq is all but completely untenable. A naïve and self-contradictory neoconservative dream of violence and coercion leading to freedom and respect for human rights may have been a key factor in luring the U.S. to attack and take over Iraq, but natural and cultural forces such as local tribalism and ethnic divisions far beyond U.S. and allied control are most likely to determine the final outcome.

A Probable Future

Declining to fight when attacked is felt by Iraqis to show weakness and encourages more attacks. Fighting kills people and makes enemies, thus encouraging more attacks. The result either way is a vicious circle of escalating violence. As fighting in Iraq continues and as public distrust of the U.S. intensifies, we may reach a point of diminishing consent, a possible tipping point where a majority or a lethal plurality of the whole Iraqi population opposes U.S. presence. In this matter the largely symbolic handover of power scheduled for June 30th may prove to be almost irrelevant. Much of the real power will continue to reside with the American occupiers as long as they stay.

Upon passing a certain point of diminishing consent to *de facto* U.S. power, the situation could spin completely out of control, becoming untenable for the occupation or liberation of Iraq no matter how much force and military prowess is brought to bear. If this possibility comes to pass, there will be no point in U.S. staying against the will of Sunnis and Shiites united against us. Civil war is the most likely next step for Iraq after our departure no matter how long we stay, and is likely to draw in Turkey and Iran and destabilize rest of Middle East. It is easy to imagine such a war inflaming the hostilities between the Shiites and Sunnis elsewhere in the Middle East, such as Pakistan, creating further unpredictable instabilities. Oppressive governments that are friendly to the U.S. may fall and be replaced by governments that are also repressive but are not friendly to the U.S. War creates chain reactions no one can control, or even predict with confidence.

Though civil war appears to be the most likely outcome for Iraq, with incalculable and probably horrific consequences for the region and the world, the paradox of the U.S. position now is that we can only delay this probable outcome by staying and trying valiantly to establish some sort of stability. If we stay, as we must so long as there is a slim chance of a better outcome than civil war, we will continue to run up staggering costs and casualties, borne mostly by the U.S., and will continue to intensify the hatred of the Muslim world and the alienation of much of Europe. By going into Iraq in the first place, we seem to have painted ourselves into a no-win corner.

Can the UN and NATO Help?

On its own the UN completely lacks the military and policing capability to contribute to security in Iraq. Those capabilities can only be provided by its member states, and they are pulling out of the U.S.-led coalition rather than joining the effort. Adding a UN umbrella would not change the allies' reluctance to risk lives and lose political support from their citizens as a result of staying in Iraq. The tragic car bombing of UN headquarters in Iraq demonstrated that its considerable experience with nation building cannot be harnessed there until there is much more stability and security in the country than appears possible with the insurgency intensifying and spreading out of the Sunni triangle into the South. Security is the essential requirement for progress in Iraq, and the U.S. cannot provide security, nor can the much weaker UN.

NATO could make substantial contributions to security in Iraq if it wished to, but NATO works by consensus, not by vote, and both France and Germany are against a NATO role. Their reluctance is completely understandable. Their populations were against the war from the start, and their governments do not wish to oppose their own populations and put the lives of their own soldiers at risk and spend vital national treasure on a project they opposed from the start and that may in the end in dismal failure.

As Bush has discovered, getting help from the UN in planning Iraq's future may add some degree of legitimacy, or more accurately, it may marginally diminish the illegitimacy of America's *de facto* control of Iraq. But in the context of an impossible security situation, the UN can do little more than offer political guidance, subject to U.S. concurrence. UN envoy Lakhdar Brahimi has contributed valuable impartiality and negotiating skills in planning the structure of an interim government to receive power at the time of the "handover of sovereignty" from the U.S. on June 30, 2004.

To summarize the situation, in the volatile religious, political and military context of the country, the transition government is a paper boat perched atop a volcano. It could be blown away by events at any moment. It is unclear whether military backing from the U.S. will help or hurt this structure on the way to planned elections in 2005, nor whether it is realistic to hope that such elections can actually happen. American military backing would give the interim government coercive muscle but undermine its legitimacy. At present, the two kinds of power are inversely correlated. As with Iraq's ethnic structure, this circumstance makes progress toward stability difficult.

In short, by taking over Iraq the Bush administration seems to have boxed the U.S. into an untenable, no-win situation. Those who believe in prayer had better pray fervently. We need a miracle.

Are there solutions?

Bush and his team bear unique and exclusive responsibility for the war in Iraq. No one made them do it; they chose to do it. Even most supporters of the war apparently no longer dispute that it is a war of choice. Most of the world outside the U.S. opposed it from the start. Further, Bush seems incapable of seeing the increasingly plain reality that the war and the failed rationale for it are debacles of colossal proportion. In his speeches he still clings to the forlorn hope that WMDs may yet be found in Iraq, perhaps on a turkey farm somewhere, as in Libya. (One wonders if the White House isn't the turkey farm.) By aggressive questioning he was forced to admit on TV that there is no evidence of a link between Saddam and 9/11, but he has never admitted that there is also no evidence of any collaboration, 9/11-related or not, between Saddam and al Qaeda. Furthermore, even as evidence mounts that the mistreatment of prisoners was systemic and widespread in Iraqi prisons, he delivers speeches in which he implies that the crimes were perpetrated by a handful of sadistic individuals. Persistence is one of his strong suits; realism and candor in the face of bad news is not. And genuine collaboration with others outside his extremely secretive inner circle of advisors is a rare event.

Bush often refers to September 11, 2001 as a turning point in his view of Iraq. He is often praised for his handling of 9/11; before it he seemed a man far too small for the job. After it his leadership commanded more respect; he seemed more presidential. He pulled the country together, delivered stirring speeches, and took actions (sometimes pushed by Congress against his will) that were required by the magnitude of the event and the threat it represented. In a sense, these were no-brainers, actions any competent leader would have taken. However, the one momentous action he took that was not required was the attack on Iraq. Richard A. Clarke states it well:

> Any leader whom one can imagine as president on September 11 would have declared a "war on terrorism" and would have ended the Afghan sanctuary by invading. Almost any president would have stepped up domestic security preparedness measures. Exactly what did George Bush do after September 11 that any other President one can imagine wouldn't have done after such attacks? In the end, what was unique about George Bush's reaction to terrorism was his selection as an object lesson for potential state sponsors of terrorism, not a country that had been engaging in anti-U.S. terrorism but one that had not been, Iraq. It is hard to imagine another president making that choice.[54]

Most of the rest of the world sees this reality and shudders, but half the American public, still swayed by presidential rhetoric and misinformed on the facts, does not. With the war on Iraq, preceded by other actions stiff-arming the rest of the world such as his dismissal of the Kyoto Protocols on global warming, President Bush has turned the world against himself and the U.S., with the exception of a handful of leaders like Tony Blair and Ariel Sharon. In this dismal situation, what can be done to restore American credibility generally and to resolve the Iraq war in a way that is other than catastrophic?

Is there any chance that Bush and his key aides can muster the flexibility to change course dramatically? If they could, which seems highly unlikely, it is even more unlikely that the rest of the world would trust Bush's sincerity enough and muster enough goodwill toward him to work with him in collaboratively developing and implementing new courses of action. His approach has been to by-pass collaboration and consultation and simply announce ideologically-driven solutions and then try to sell them to or force them on the rest of the world. This combination of arrogance, habitual lack of collaboration, isolation from the mainstream opinion in the international community, and ideological bias is a key element of the problem.

As a result of the Iraq War and the other demonstrations of a go-it-alone and force-it-on-others style documented throughout this book, the depth of hatred and distrust toward Bush in the world outside of the U.S. is almost impossible to overstate. The good news is that much of the rest of the world is still clinging to a positive view of America but blaming the problems on George Bush. If Bush is reelected, it will be increasingly difficult for them to give the U.S. a pass and blame the leader. The world's widespread temporary anger with America may harden into lasting hatred, gravely undermining our national security.

Realistically, there is no chance that President Bush can suddenly start exercising effective and collaborative leadership in a world where he is all-but-universally despised and distrusted. His only remaining way of dealing with the world outside the borders of the U.S. is pressure and coercion, and he has overused that option beyond the point of exhaustion. Doing so has led him to the unprecedented low point in world esteem he has reached now. It follows that for real progress, for real healing in the relationships between the U.S. and the rest of the world, regime change in Washington DC essential.

A different American president with the opportunity to establish credibility by contrasting with Bush could move swiftly to reverse both the policies and the processes that have led the U.S. into this extraordinary mess. Such a president could establish from day one that collaboration with other world leaders and institutions would be a priority, and that trying to dictate to them is a thing of the past. Such a commitment, acted out boldly and consistently, would almost immediately reverse the worldwide free-fall of respect and goodwill toward the United States and its leadership.

To begin to restore goodwill and respect for the U.S., a number of key actions would be essential. One of the first would be to repudiate immediately the ideological foundation of the Iraq war, the Bush doctrine declaring America's freedom to launch preventive wars without having been attacked or subjected to imminent threat of attack and without UN sanction. Packaged with this, a new president would need to drive hard (but still flexibly and collaboratively) for reform of the UN Security Council to resolve the widely acknowledged problem of the narrowness of its membership and to deal creatively with the structural problem of paralysis by veto.

A new president could act on a commitment to collaboration by meeting with world leaders, especially Arab and Muslim leaders, preferably with groups and organizations as well as with individuals. He could discuss problems with them and listen respectfully, taking their suggestions seriously, as an informal leader among equals might do, rather than behaving as a dictator announcing his own preconceived plans for the way ahead. (In the light of the abuses of Iraqi prisoners at Abu Ghraib and other prisons, Bush's unilateral plans for reforming and democratizing the Middle East, previously given little support, must certainly be dead, having had its credibility annihilated not by arguments, but by indisputable facts.) A new president could, among other responses to the feedback he would certainly get from these meetings, develop collaboratively and begin to implement an even-handed policy in dealing with the Israeli-Palestinian problem. He could work to make continued material aid to Israel contingent on real and serious negotiations and action steps toward peace and toward human rights for Palestinians.

He could begin to explore creative alternative solutions to the Iraq problem by expanding on bold experiments such as General Abizaid's win-by-losing approach to Fallujah—giving power to local Iraqi leaders who develop collaborative solutions to local security problems—even if they in turn collaborate with the insurgency to get it done. The U.S. will have to leave Iraq some day; the sooner we turn real power, including security, over to the Iraqis, the sooner we can leave gracefully, or at least, non-catastrophically. At the end of the first month after it was initiated, the Fallujah experiment appears to be successful. Of course, no one knows if its success will last. And no one knows whether it or something similar can be replicated elsewhere. But it is a start.

"Loosing" in Order to Win

The experiment in Fallujah, if its apparent success holds, brings up the most creative and realistic approach I have yet seen to solving the exit strategy problem—how to leave Iraq without leaving a hopeless mess that descends into civil war and destabilizes the whole region. The proposal, a long shot that would require exceptional wisdom and humility, is the only one I've seen that appears to have any chance of working. It was outlined in the Washington Post's Sunday Outlook section on May 9, 2004 by John Brady Kiesling, the Foreign Service officer who had the courage and the integrity to resign from the State Department in protest as the Iraq war approached. In addition to these qualities, he appears, judging from the article, to be a provocative strategic thinker.

His article begins by stating an unconventional but indisputable principle of military strategy. "The deadliest illusion about warfare is that the aim of war is military victory. The true aim of war is to accomplish the political, economic or security goals for which it was fought."[55] He adds, "in a war like the one in Iraq, which is based on assumptions since proven false, we cannot win by being victorious."[56] The challenge now, he points out, is to create a viable Iraqi state, given that we lack perceived legitimacy in the country and have no magic toolkit for creating democracy.

His argument is simple in principle: we need to choose to allow an Iraqi leader who is the lesser of the available evils to "win" in chasing the U.S. out of Iraq. He could thus become a national hero. Rallying around such a perceived hero, Iraqis just might pull together rather than flying apart. On this scenario, the Iraqi nationalism that is now creating huge problems for the U.S. could become a force for Iraqi coherence after the U.S. leaves. As he puts it, "The alternative to virtual defeat is real defeat.... Once we leave, whether tomorrow or in 10 years, the resulting failed Iraqi state will be not simply a reproach to American competence, but a danger to the whole planet. And Iraq will fail unless we validate a credible leadership and a new national myth."[57] The psychological realism of this idea is stunning. The dream of quickly transforming such a fractured and traumatized society as Iraq into a functioning democracy was always a fantasy, but leaving behind a leader who is effective and more benign than Saddam is a real, though somewhat distant, possibility.

The first and probably fatal difficulty, of course, is finding such an Iraqi leader. The available crew are not promising. Moqtada al Sadr is the most visible anti-U.S. military activist, but he appears to be a half-crazed leader of an undisciplined gang of thugs rather than a promising statesman. The Ayatollah Ali Sistani looks like a moderate, wise, and strong-willed statesman, but he is reclusive and seems to show little desire for worldly position. Certainly he is taking no military action. Both, being Shiite clerics, would be problematic as leaders to the Sunnis and the Kurdish population. In short, the leader the U.S. might wisely yield to is at present missing. Whether such a person will emerge remains to be seen, and if he does, whether the U.S., even a new president, will be able to muster the wisdom and humility to let him "win" and withdraw from the country leaving him in control remains to be seen.

The Longer Term

A new American president, having moved forcefully and convincingly toward resolving the most acute problems between the U.S. and the Arab and Muslim world such as the Israeli-Palestinian problem and—if we're very fortunate and he is very skillful—the Iraq War, and having thus bought some time and credibility, could work to establish improved longer-term relations in the wider Middle East by developing political and administrative institutions designed to promote mutual understanding, designed to promote mutual understanding with the West and to provide financial support for programs that would directly benefit people, programs such as locally and culturally appropriate poverty relief, medical treatment, non-sectarian primary education, and similar initiatives in collaboration with friendly countries in the region such as Pakistan and Egypt.

For such programs to be useful would require a difficult integration of two elements that are naturally in tension with one another. These are consultation and work with national and local governments (as well as civil society organizations) to assure that assistance to the target populations really happens, and maintaining financial and operating policies and procedures that prevent or minimize corruption. Doing both simultaneously would be a challenge, but investing substantial funds and efforts in concrete programs to improve relationships with the people, not just the governments, of the Middle East would be more effective in the long term than allowing anti-American hatred and terrorism to flourish or only using violent (and thus self-defeating) methods to counter it.

A new president who was not himself a creature of the oil industry could move toward long-term solutions to American dependence on Middle

Eastern oil first by emphasizing conservation using such means as ratcheting up gasoline efficiency requirements for cars and especially SUVs. Detroit has the technology to make substantial gas economy improvements, but car manufacturers are under no pressure to implement the new technologies. Hybrid gas and electric cars are inching their way into the market; this trend could be greatly accelerated by sensible government support through tax incentives and/or through regulation. Conservation as a matter of public policy is not just a stop gap or a minor improvement; it has a potential for huge effects on both gasoline consumption and air pollution.

Another set of steps that were essentially brought to a halt by the Bush administration when it took office is aggressive pursuit (possibly by tax breaks or subsidies or both) of alternative energy technologies such as wind, solar, geothermal, hydrogen, and natural gas. Merely promoting new inventions in these technologies is not the answer; government support and partnership with private-sector implementation on a large scale will be the key. As nature's oil supplies dry up, as they will begin to do in the next few decades, market forces will eventually drive us to wean ourselves from our addiction to oil. This may be a bumpy ride or even an abrupt plunge off a cliff. Getting ahead of this forced change by government-backed gradual change could minimize more abrupt and wrenching change later. Subsides at present are upside-down in their effects. We subsidize the oil industry. Drying up this particularly dysfunctional form of welfare for the rich would be difficult politically, but it would create huge long-term gains for the country both in reducing dependence on Middle Eastern oil and reducing environmental damage such as carbon dioxide emissions.

As for promoting democracy in the Middle East, the most a new President could do would be to promote improved harmony and cooperation rather than strife and discord in the region. Doing so would be a complete reversal of the present inharmonious and coercive policies, and could promote long-term conditions under which democracy can evolve naturally.

---

[1] Rajiv Chandrasekaran and Peter Slevin, "Iraq's Ragged Reconstruction: A Month After Baghdad's Fall, U.S. Efforts Flounder," *The Washington Post*, May 9, 2003.
[2] Richard Leiby, "Birth Pangs" *The Washington Post*, May 5, 2003.
[3] Idem.
[4] Idem.
[5] Peter Slevin, "A Sense of Limbo In South: Iraqi Power Void Results in Chaos," *The Washington Post*, May 5, 2003.
[6] Idem.
[7] Idem.

[8] Idem.

[9] Fareed Zakaria, "Bowing to the Mighty Ayatollah," *Newsweek*, January 26, 2004

[10] Idem.

[11] Richard Cohen, "Baghdad Bait and Switch," *The Washington Post*, April 29, 2003.

[12] Richard A. Clarke, *Against All Enemies*, Free Press, NY, 2004, p. 268.

[13] Barton Gellman, "Frustrated, U.S. Arms Team to Leave Iraq," *The Washington Post*, May 11, 2003.

[14] Idem.

[15] Idem.

[16] Idem.

[17] Idem.

[18] John Diamond, "'We Were Almost All Wrong,'" *USA Today*, January 29, 2004.

[19] Idem.

[20] Idem.

[21] Idem.

[22] Walter Pincus and Dana Priest, "Some Iraq Analysts Felt Pressure From Cheney Visits," *The Washington Post*, June 5, 2003.

[23] Idem.

[24] Idem.

[25] Thomas E. Ricks, "For Vietnam Vet Anthony Zinni, Another War on Shaky Territory" *The Washington Post*, December 23, 2003.

[26] Idem.

[27] Idem.

[28] Idem.

[29] Jessica T. Mathews, George Perkovich, and Joseph Cirincione, "WMD in Iraq: Evidence and Implications, Summary of New Carnegie Report, to be released January 8" Published by the Carnegie Endowment for International Peace.

[30] Idem.

[31] Idem.

[32] *WMD in Iraq: Evidence and Implications*, Published by the Carnegie Endowment for International Peace, January 2004, p. 7.

[33] Idem.

[34] Ibid., p. 9

[35] Idem.

[36] Ibid., pp. 10 & 11.

[37] Jeffrey Record, "Bounding the Global War on Terrorism," Strategic Studies Institute, U.S. Army War College, December, 2003. Internet: *www.carlisle.army.mil/ssi/*

[38] Idem.

[39] Glenn Kessler, "Clarke's Critique Reopens the Debate on Iraq War" *The Washington Post*, March 28, 2004.

[40] Idem.

[41] Idem.
[42] Idem.
[43] Idem.
[44] Idem.
[45] Richard A. Clarke, *Against All Enemies*, Free Press, NY, p. 262.
[46] Ibid., p. 263.
[47] Ibid., p. 264.
[48] Idem.
[49] Editorial, *The Washington Post*, May 5, 2004,
http://www.washingtonpost.com/ac2/wp-dyn?node=admin/email&referrer=email article
[50] Philip Zimbardo, the Stanford Prison Experiment, www.prisonexp.org
[51] Gordon Thomas, "America's Gulag for Iraq's VIP Prisoners," www.globe-intel.net email Gordon Thomas at gthomas@indigo.ie, August 20, 2003.
[52] Rajiv Chandrasekaran and Scott Wilson, "Mistreatment Of Detainees Went Beyond Guards' Abuse," *The Washington Post*, May 11, 2004.
[53] Henry A. Kissinger, "Intervention With a Vision" *The Washington Post*, April 11, 2004.
[54] Clarke, op. cit., p. 244.
[55] John Brady Kiesling, "To Win the Peace, We Must 'Lose' the War," *The Washington Post Outlook,* May 8, 2004.
[56] Idem.
[57] Idem.

Chapter Twelve

DESIGN SPECS FOR A BETTER WORLD

The 27 fortunate souls who have ventured outward to lunar orbit have all gazed upon a single, borderless, breathtaking planet suspended among the blazing stars. They were perhaps the first humans to have the opportunity to grasp that the whole Earth was more than the sum of its parts, that it was something singularly deserving of our loyalty, our allegiance, our planetary patriotism.

—Tad Daley[1]

Design engineering at its most creative builds a new reality not by tweaking an existing design, but by asking the question, "What purpose, what end goal, do we want to achieve?" What do we want to accomplish, regardless of how we accomplish it? Is there some drastically new way we can accomplish it? If we start with a flexible and broadly defined description of the goal or end result we desire without specifying the means to achieve it, the way is open for innovation. A simplistic example: if we start with the goal of building a better car, we will end up with another car. But if we start with the goal of a better way to move people from one point to another, we leave the way open to invent a helicopter or a motorcycle or an airplane.

Seldom is this kind of creativity, the kind that produces a major breakthrough, brought to bear on the problems of human civilization as a whole. One reason is obvious—usually no one has the power to implement a major change. The world's leaders, paralyzed by the magnitude of the task and the intransigence of the U.S. and of other political forces, are trying to tweak the system, to build a better car, not to introduce design innovations. Yet in the face of the problems threatening human civilization, innovation is almost certain to be essential.

Intractable Problems

The world as a whole is now on the edge of a cliff, or several cliffs. A number of global problems with potentially devastating impacts seem intractable. Some of them have already been mentioned often or discussed in detail in this book. A few of the problems are war and genocide; terrorism; the spread of weapons of mass destruction; global warming and other environmental problems such as rapidly dwindling fresh water resources; loss of topsoil and loss of biodiversity; widespread, acute poverty; and the wildly unstable movements of money in the international monetary system. There are two basic reasons for their seeming intractability. One reason is the level of anarchy in the world and, as a part of that, the fragile, incomplete, and undemocratic way human civilization is now structured for solving transnational or global problems.

The other, intimately related reason for the intractability of these problems is the current foreign policy of the world's most powerful nation. American leaders adamantly oppose the development of global mechanisms by which these kinds of problems might be solved. It is painfully clear that American foreign policy is making the situation worse, not better. To zoom in on just one example, President George W. Bush abruptly and summarily rejected the Kyoto Protocols on Global Warming, leaving America's allies in shock. This treaty, though it is weak and insufficient by itself to fully solve the problem of global warming, is better than nothing—a step in the right direction.

Given the attitude indicated by the President's dismissal of Kyoto, it is virtually inconceivable that current American leadership would allow, let alone take a leading role in, establishing an international institution to tackle an array of global environmental problems in a serious way. Such an institution is obviously needed, but knowing what the response would be from American leaders, other countries don't even consider proposing its establishment. Their own inertia and reluctance to take on a daunting problem is reinforced by that of the U.S. American global dominance and current hostility to such institutions makes it all but impossible to even mention such a proposal without a loss of credibility or at the very least, a loss of power to shape events.

The current U.S. policy, in a nutshell, is to maximize American freedom of action by blocking development of needed international institutions and by tearing down the alliances and international organizations that the U.S. and much of the rest of the world spent a half-century building after World War

II. These global structures have provided a certain degree of stability, though they are by no means ideal. Still, they constitute the only set of mechanisms—if strengthened and made more democratic, focused and effective—through which there is any hope of solving the most dangerous global problems. One hundred ninety-one different nations going off in all different directions cannot possibly solve these problems.

The U.S. policy is to replace the insufficient but useful and stable system of alliances and institutions we already have with a series of *ad hoc* "coalitions of the willing" in a world dominated by the U.S. These sometimes turn out in practice to be coalitions of the unwilling who are bought or bullied into joining, as in the Iraq war. The policy is based on an assumed American moral superiority backed by military force (always a euphemism for violence), coercion, and economic clout. In this view, the U.S. is "'a city on a hill,' a beacon of morality and justice, and a fit model for other nations."[2] Hence the slightest constraint on U.S. freedom of action is contrary to the good of all. "We are the good guys," so the rest of the world should do as we do. If they fail in willingness, we will force them to follow. The policy includes a missionary zeal to spread the benefits of the American way to the rest of the world. American-style freedom, democracy, morality and justice must be imposed by force, if necessary, on a benighted and reluctant world. The inherent contradiction and hypocrisy of imposing freedom and democracy by violence and coercion is conveniently overlooked. This is the "morality" of the neoconservatives who control the White House.

This "America must brook no constraints" policy, as noted before, has also meant the abrogation of several key arms control treaties, the refusal to sign the Kyoto Protocols on Global Warming, the systematic war on the International Criminal Court, the opposition to human rights treaties the rest of the world embraces, and on and on. Not surprisingly the policy behind these actions is hated and reviled by the rest of the world. The moral principles it denies (while implicitly claiming American moral superiority), the cooperative mechanisms it undermines or destroys and the resentment and fear it generates destabilize the world and reduce the chances of cooperative solutions to looming global crises.

Anarchy or Order?

Aside from specific crises that may be looming, what kind of a world do we live in, if we stand back and view it whole? A world of anarchy or of order? Would a creature from another solar system, viewing it overall, be impressed with its peacefulness, its democratic institutions, the freedom and prosperity of earth creatures? Or would this creature be horrified by its anarchy, disorder, violence, poverty and oppression?

The answer, viewed from this wide angle, is obvious. Half of the world's population has some degree of freedom and prosperity, and the other half lives in the direst poverty. Among a population of six billion people, roughly one billion live on less than a dollar per day, and over two billion live on less than two dollars per day. War, genocide, and terrorism are commonplace. One hundred ninety-one nations, many heavily armed, make war on one another when they please, unless restrained by regional arrangements like NATO and the European Union. Sometimes the UN manages to prevent conflict, though more often it sponsors peace negotiations and provides humanitarian aid after conflicts.

Hundreds of millions of people live under the thumbs of repressive governments. Many of these same governments are sitting on the planet's most valuable resource, oil. And many of them are harboring extremists who are determined to wreak havoc on other countries and their own. Nations around the world, ranging from Cambodia to Somalia to Lebanon to Yugoslavia to Haiti collapse and sink into devastating chaos, causing millions of people to die and providing havens for terrorists and drug lords.

On the other hand, about half of the world, the developed half, shows signs of order and varying degrees of prosperity. About a third to half of the world's people, live in at least some degree of comfort and prosperity. However, they are contributing disproportionately to the severe environmental degradation that hangs over the planet like a sword of Damocles, and they are largely oblivious to the danger. Their lifestyle—our lifestyle—is not sustainable without major changes that are not happening.

Global organizations such as the UN system are intended to address the world's problems, but by and large they are ineffective. Viewed overall, despite significant and promising pockets of order and prosperity, the state of the world seems tilted toward chaos and anarchy, or at best is about fifty-fifty.

People and nations are understandably reluctant to make sacrifices for the common good unless there is some system to distribute those sacrifices more-or-less fairly. Voluntary action, while noble and often helpful, is virtually never comprehensive and reliable. Although it sometimes works, usually an orderly distribution of shared sacrifice can only be accomplished by formal agreements and by institutions. There are always those who opt out. Given this intrinsic limitation of human nature and human cooperation, the global problem is, at its core, a shortage of effective and democratic laws and institutions for solving a whole range of global problems that certainly will not be solved by individuals or nations acting separately.

As implied earlier, two major structuring or organizing forces are at work in the current global setup. On one hand we have an anarchic nation-state system partially cowed but not subdued by an increasingly domineering American military and economic empire, and on the other hand we have a slow and fitful evolutionary movement toward global integration and systematic cooperation. These forces are partly in collusion, partly in collision. It's not clear which will prove to be the more powerful force over the long haul.

In a classic head-on confrontation between these two forces—the run-up to 2003 Iraq war—the forces of global integration expressed themselves in the refusal of the Security Council to sanction the war before the arms inspectors had completed their work. The objective was to let international law and institutions do what they were designed to do. It was also, of course, to tweak the nose of the American empire by those who were not happy with its overbearing behavior. Global public opinion, as reflected in polls as well as demonstrations all over the world, was overwhelmingly against the Iraq war and in favor of continuing with the inspections. This global consensus expressed itself accurately in the Security Council. But the impulse to global integration proved unable to stop the juggernaut of the American military empire, which proceeded with the war. Score one for the military empire. However, the victory proved to be short-lived. Circumstances repeatedly forced President Bush to return to the UN for help with non-military matters like selling Iraqi oil and rebuilding the country. In the usual sequence, arrogance was followed by a generous helping of humble pie. This archetypal head-on conflict between global order and the American global oligarchy is far from the whole story, of course.

In the past fifty years the U.S. has contributed enormously to the building of the partial world order we have, including the UN, NATO, the World Bank, the International Monetary Fund, the World Trade Organization, the International Atomic Energy Agency, the World Health Organization, and many others. However, right now the leadership of the U.S. tries to have it both ways, at one moment defying and undermining the global system of cooperation and at another moment relying on it.

Given the enormous power of the U.S., the rapid-fire contradictions between building up and tearing down international order leave the leaders and the people of the rest of the world confused and alarmed. This inconsistent, erratic approach has a harmless-sounding name under the Bush administration— "*à la carte* multilateralism"—as if the international legal order the U.S. and the rest of the world struggled for sixty years to build were a restaurant. As if adherence to mutually agreed upon laws were equivalent to placing an order at McDonalds. Do we allow American citizens to pick and choose which laws they will obey? If we did, would this be a good way to operate?

In practice, "*à la carte* multilateralism" means that one day we will act like a rogue nation trampling international law and pursuing only our own selfish interests, and the next day we will make nice to the rest of the world and harness international law to our own ends when expediency calls. Naturally the rest of the world becomes wary when American leaders suddenly shift into collaborative mode. Trust has been destroyed. The net effect undermines American leadership rather than enhancing it. The end result is a net increase in global anarchy, chaos and violence. The world becomes a more dangerous place for everyone, including Americans.

The stock political rejoinder to any objection to "*à la carte* multilateralism" is the red herring that the U.S. must be able to defend itself against external threats. This statement is true, but it misses the point. Defensive warfare in response to an attack or imminent threat of attack is well within the boundaries of international law. It is not a part of "*à la carte* multilateralism," which means in practice violating international law when it suits us. Let no one pretend that this book or this author denies the importance of genuinely defensive military action. Such action may well be necessary, as it was when the U.S. went after al Qaeda in Afghanistan, and in the process defeated the Taliban, al Qaeda's conjoined twin. War in legitimate self-defense does not constitute one of the contradictions in U.S. foreign policy that I'm discussing. However, preventive war—launching a war against a country that may or may not be a threat five or ten years in the future—is clearly a violation of international law and moral norms generally, and is definitely a part of the problem.

In his excellent book, *The Choice: Global Domination or Global Leadership*, Zbigniew Brzezinski, one of the nation's leading foreign policy thinkers and a former White House National Security Advisor, presents the issue starkly:

The potential self-isolation of the only superpower could plunge the world into escalating anarchy, made all the more ominous by the dissemination of weaponry of mass destruction. With America—given the contradictory roles it plays in the world—fated to be the catalyst either for a global community or for global chaos, Americans have the unique historical responsibility to determine which of the two will come to pass. Our choice is between dominating the planet and leading it."[3]

Will American citizens choose leaders who shift toward a global win-win game of cooperation and teamwork, while in the process providing global leadership in creating a sustainable world? There is no more pressing question for all humanity. A high level of creativity and a widespread willingness to empower and democratize global organizations that address the world's problems is an absolutely essential prerequisite for the future of the planet. Nation-states and especially the United States cannot continue to monopolize power and cripple global institutions if the world is to survive the multiple crises into which we are headed. Individual nations acting alone and going off in all different directions, no matter how powerful one or another may be individually, cannot solve global problems and crises. These are much more likely to be manageable when transnational laws and democratic institutions that address the problems exist or can be created to manage them and the horses of the nation-states all pull the carriage in the same direction.

It seems unlikely that the current crop of American leaders is capable of such a major shift in ideology or mindset. They are deeply committed to the present erratic and self-centered approach. If future American leaders follow the course of promoting increased global integration, they will have to display the self-control of true leadership and patiently accept the occasionally annoying constraints on their behavior that participating in this integration entails. Democracy and cooperation both necessitate self-discipline. In the short run they are not as much fun as always getting your own way, but in the long run they make the world better for everyone. At present, American leaders try to teach the art of negotiation and compromise to the Iraqi leaders, while refusing to practice it themselves in the international arena. One wonders if the Iraqis notice the contradiction. Certainly the rest of the world does.

Circumstances seem to be (partially) educating American leaders where common sense, logic and moral intelligence do not. As noted earlier, in Iraq the Bush administration has been forced to move toward more cooperation with global institutions such as the UN and away from opposition and confrontation. But these choices are tactical retreats; they don't represent a change of heart or ideology. The key leaders in the Bush administration, Colin Powell partially excepted, still show every sign of seeing the world in tribalistic terms as a win-lose game that we must win decisively, creating a long-term American dominance that cannot be challenged. There is even a strategic military term for this goal: "full spectrum dominance." It is the goal of the American military, which in turn, when it wishes to, has a dominant say in American foreign policy.

By definition, a world order structured this way is an oppressive global oligarchy run for the benefit of the powerful and wealthy few without regard for the consequences to the many. If America stands for freedom and democracy, this is a strange way to express it. If the U.S. succeeds in achieving still greater dominance of the world, it will find itself dominating a world that is increasingly unmanageable, collapsing on multiple fronts and generating increasing terrorism, regardless of efforts by force to stop it. Eventually the U.S. will find that controlling a collapsing world by force is inherently impossible.

The Great Disconnect

Strangely, one of the central problems of American democracy is seldom recognized or commented upon. It is the great disconnect between what the American public believes in, often based on widely accepted moral principle, and what American leaders do in the foreign policy arena. When the Senate voted on the Comprehensive Nuclear Test Ban Treaty (CTBT), roughly 80% of Americans supported it when presented with a straightforward, unbiased summary of the essentials of the treaty. Yet, driven by conservative leaders and an influential anti-arms control bloc of Senators, the Senate voted it down. Senators who voted against it evidently did not fear that their vote would harm them in the next election. This kind of event, now common in the U.S. on the foreign policy front, constitutes a huge failure of democracy. How is it possible that our elected leaders can not only fail to represent us, but thumb their noses at public opinion and still get re-elected?

The problem, simply put, is that the American public votes mainly on domestic issues and seldom considers foreign policy in the polling booth. Problems at home trump seemingly remote matters like treaties abroad. The exception comes when disaster strikes or threatens from abroad. When disaster does strike, the voting decisions tend to be fear-based, hostile and angry rather than sober and farsighted. And even then important foreign policy issues may still be trumped by domestic concerns of dubious relative importance. Although foreign policy under America's present leadership is radically disconnected both from the deeper values of the American people and from the longings and concerns of the rest of the world, there is no reason why this disconnect cannot be reversed.

Beginning to Re-Connect

The first step out of this dilemma and toward creating a viable, integrated and sustainable world is for American policy thinkers and political organizations to beat the drums for a different policy. Much of the present destructive policy pattern started in the op-ed pages of the newspapers; more rational voices must be heard in such public venues. The second is for American citizens and political organizations to press politicians to begin emphasizing key international issues in their campaigns, along with domestic issues. And the third step is for the public to learn from debacles such as the Iraq war and to elevate the relative importance of international relations at the voting booth.

It is totally consistent with American values for citizens to wish to assure that their country, the world's most powerful nation, is moving cooperatively toward the goal of a better world, rather than battling blindly for its own supremacy in a self-created win-lose game. If the record of the Bush administration were ambiguous or divided on this score, the Bush White House might be influenced by persuasion or political pressure. However, its record of global non-cooperation is so consistent, as shown in this book, that regime change in Washington is the only realistic answer.

However, changing presidents is far from a complete answer, because the U.S. Senate under its present leadership has also shown a remarkable, long-term political will and capacity to obstruct global progress and assert U.S. dominance. Ratifying a treaty requires a two-thirds majority in the Senate, and getting even a fifty percent majority for globally constructive treaties can be a struggle. Ratification of even the most transparently benign and cost-free global (i.e., multilateral) treaties is out of the question with the current Senate. However, the good news is that a president who is willing to sign treaties and to work in good faith to implement those that have already been signed, even without ratification, can make significant headway. Merely changing presidents would make a huge difference, if only a preliminary one.

Based on the totality of discussions in this book, the items below are a few common sense immediate actions a new president could carry out, without the supermajority (two-thirds) of the Senate required to ratify treaties. Taking these actions would signal to American citizens that the President is returning American foreign policy to action based on rock-solid values that were first expressed in the Declaration of Independence and the Bill of Rights of the Constitution, and are still espoused by American citizens. It would send the world a signal that the U.S. is engaging constructively with the community of nations rather than scorning and trying to dominate it. As with the chapter topics in this book, this list is illustrative and not in any way complete. Much more could be done, but these would be a start.

- Affirm the commitment of the Executive Branch to the treaties on the rights of women and children and take substantive action to strengthen U.S. participation in international efforts to implement them.
- Repudiate George W. Bush's "un-signing" and re-affirm President Clinton's original signing of the treaty on the International Criminal Court. Explore the ways in which maximum U.S. cooperation can be established with the court short of ratification, which would be impossible with the current, backward-looking Senate. Work to change the thinking and the membership of the Senate to improve its stance toward international cooperation.
- Sign the Kyoto Protocols on Global Warming and move toward regulations and tax incentives to promote fossil fuel conservation, e.g., by encouraging use of hybrid cars that use electricity as well as gasoline. Focus serious efforts and resources on exploring and implementing clean and renewable technologies that do not create greenhouse gasses. (A simple example might be to encourage restoration of wind power as one of several clean sources of electricity.) A part of the mix could be government/private sector partnerships in developing operational versions of clean technologies and substantial tax incentives for shifting to them.
- Reaffirm the commitment of the U.S. to existing arms control treaties and bring U.S. practices into alignment with those the U.S. is presently violating.
- Move as far as possible toward internationalizing the rebuilding of Iraq, while continuing to support the effort militarily and to build up

indigenous Iraqi security capabilities. Develop a realistic and flexible multi-year military withdrawal schedule explicitly tied to Iraqi successes in cultivating self-government and civil order. Affirm the applicability of the Geneva Conventions to Iraqi detainees and establish systems to assure that these norms are implemented. Rescind the policy rationalizing preventive strikes against other countries that led to the attack on Iraq.

• Shift the Cold War holdover emphasis of U.S. military spending away from super-redundant capabilities to defend against non-existent or feeble nation-state enemies. Shift spending toward beefing up intelligence cooperation with other nations to defeat al Qaeda and its offshoots, tightening homeland security and tracing and preventing the spread of weapons of mass destruction. In this context, deal with regional threats such as North Korea by means of firm and flexible negotiations, not insults, threats, and hostile confrontation.

• Further promote an excellent idea already being discussed at the United Nations: formation of a democracy caucus that could provide leadership for constructive change without getting hijacked by dictatorships. Use the caucus to make reforms like revamping requirements for membership in the Human Rights Commission to exclude human rights abusers.

• Begin promoting, with the UN and progressive democracies, the possibility of establishing (1) a standing multinational peacekeeping force capable of swift deployment by the Security Council for preventive action in situations like the genocide in Rwanda or the recent anarchy in Haiti and (2) a rapidly deployable police capability to restore civil order in post-conflict situations. The latter is needed because armies are generally not trained in or skilled in police work, and post-conflict anarchy can do as much damage, or more, than war itself, as the looting in Iraq demonstrated.

An Easy, Half-Right Answer

Political ideologies abound that purport to answer how the world would best be structured. The current ideological answers of the American leaders who control U.S. foreign policy are a combination of democracy and free-market capitalism. By these catch-phrases they mean democracy inside countries, not, heaven forbid, at the macro or global level, and laissez-faire capitalism, not the regulated capitalism that now operates successfully inside the U.S. and other developed countries.

In practice, their vision promotes global-level anarchy loosely guided by an American military and economic empire, and robber-baron capitalism, the dynamic but also chaotic non-system we currently have at the global level. Needless to say, this arrangement is wonderful in the short term for large multinational corporations, but not so good for human beings, nor for the long-term viability of the planet and of human civilization. The current non-system, though infinitely better than its dying and disastrous alternative—communism—is still part of the problem, not the solution.

One of the great appeals of the combination of nation-state democracy and free market capitalism is that they make the rich richer, and the rich are in power. The senior members of the Bush administration are a collection of millionaires, mostly oil millionaires. To this super-elite club, non-millionaires need not apply. The rich and their friends are the people who benefit from globalized robber-baron capitalism. The hard truth is they are the new robber-barons. It is not an accident that the Bush family is close friends with the Saudi royal family, nor that members of that family were allowed to fly out of the U.S. after 9/11, even though the airports were closed to other traffic. The robber-barons have common interests and thus hang together in a crisis.

The wider appeal of nation-state democracy and free-market capitalism, of course, is that the concepts of democracy and free-market capitalism are partially correct. No form of government works better than democracy in the long run. Democracies usually don't go to war with one another whereas dictatorships do. And communism, the polar opposite of capitalism, proved to be a comprehensive disaster. Socialism in combination with democracy, as practiced in the Scandinavian countries, is much better than communism but is still relatively sluggish and lacking innovative vitality by comparison with capitalism. Its partial success stems partly from the elements of capitalism embedded in it, as well as the comfortable if not-very-adventurous life it provides for its people. Both free market capitalism and democracy have been successful in the United States, or at least so the mythology claims. Hence we have among the rich who prosper from them a missionary zeal to export them to the rest of the world, where even greater profits can be made.

The historical reality, of course, is that true free-market capitalism—the laissez-faire, robber-baron capitalism of the nineteenth century—did not work well for people other than the rich, and is far from the reality inside the United States and other economically successful countries in the twentieth and twenty-first centuries. American capitalism is restrained and regulated in a variety of ways, partially curbing excesses such as monopolistic practices, exploitation of workers, insider stock trading, boom and bust cycles, and the like. Without the variety of regulatory institutions we have, American capitalism would be far different—and far less stable and benign—than it is.

Successful capitalism requires a context of a stable and effective democratic government that in turn requires at least a minimal degree of honesty and integrity in transactions and has the power and flexibility to make course corrections when capitalism spins out of control. American democracy has begun to make course corrections in reaction to huge corporate scams such as Enron and Global Crossing, but it has a way to go. When the rich gain full control of the government, the safeguards are eroded, but the rest of the American people can vote to take the country back. At least the capacity to establish and maintain safeguards is in place.

So the relative success of the American model, and that of Europe, Japan, and the other Asian economic powerhouses, comes at least partially from a context of more-or-less effective and more-or-less democratic government, not from anarchy. By contrast, the anarchy in some parts of Africa illustrates how essential effective governance is in making capitalism a viable system. Where gangs of thugs fight over diamond mines there is not much room for orderly and profitable business enterprises to take root and thrive. If we turn to a very different example, in a "country" (really just a land area) lacking a government such as Somalia, if you wish to transport goods in a pickup truck from one side of a city to the other, you must hire a group of heavily armed thugs to protect the truck from other gangs of heavily armed thugs who would otherwise seize it. Needless to say, this is an expensive and risky way to run a business. Visitors report that Somalis are working to establish a government; they aren't all thrilled to be living in a chaotic and violent environment without one.

What Actually Works

On the question of how the world should be organized, clearly the simplistic answers, democracy (inside states) and free-market capitalism are a start, but they are far from complete and satisfactory. A better answer will have to contain other elements as well. A better quick answer might be *global democracy with capitalism regulated for the benefit of all the world's people.*

Conservatives will recognize (with horror) that this change in a few words proposes a major paradigm shift, not just a minor adjustment. Yet it is a shift that carries with it the essentials of success from the nation-state level to the global level. Though it may sound radical, it is really just a "politically incorrect" application of common sense. It suggests a shift toward structures at the global level, to recognize the need for both more democracy and more democratically controlled regulatory capacity at that level, explicitly limited to solving otherwise intractable global problems rather than continuing the current global anarchy. There is simply no other way to solve pressing global problems. They will not be solved by the dominance of an American for-profit empire, nor by 191 different countries pulling in as many different directions. This solution is, in fact, a "no-brainer." It leaves globalized capitalism in place, but subject to common-sense regulation by and for human beings, not running wild and trampling on people and the environment for the exclusive benefit of corporate profits.

In this shift, an increase in democracy and an increase in order at the global level would have to be inseparable. An undemocratic order, a global tyranny, would not only be a horror no one would want; if it could be established (a supposition contrary to fact), it would be radically unsustainable. Any global order has to be held together by international consensus or near-consensus. A global order that became tyrannical would destroy that consensus and would lead almost immediately to political rebellion and breakaway or outright war. Among nation-states, democracies endure and dictatorships eventually collapse because dictatorships engender fierce resentments and fail to be responsive to the needs of people and systems. The same dynamic would be more true at the global level because the larger and more powerful nation states are democracies and would not willingly stay subject to a tyrannical system. Further, freedom of information is intrinsic to the modern wired world, where everyone can talk to everyone else on the internet or listen to radio or watch TV broadcasts from all over the world. No one has a serious chance of controlling the content of the internet or the airways on a worldwide basis. And freedom of information is automatic death to tyranny.

So, given the diversity of the world and the relative power of the world's largest democracies, the conservative's nightmare of a tyrannical global order would be impossible to establish in practice. In a sense, every empire in history has been an attempt to establish a global tyranny by military force. And every empire has failed. In the end empires exhaust themselves in a fruitless effort to force the world to yield to their power. The current unconventional (i.e., non-territorial) American empire will also quickly exhaust itself if it continues to move toward military dominance rather than shared responsibility for global stability with other nations and with international organizations. The $150 plus billion the U.S. has had to spend on Iraq in a single year of war and occupation and the tremendous strain the war has placed on U.S. alliances and the U.S. military illustrate the radical unsustainability of this approach. A full-fledged global tyranny cannot and will not happen, not even exercised by the most likely candidate, the American hyperpower. The world is just too big and diverse; democracy and democratic ideals are too deeply ingrained in the most powerful nations, and information flows too freely.

The suggested shift in thinking and action toward global democratic institutions raised in these paragraphs is not as great a novelty as it may appear at first glance. The world is evolving toward it out of necessity, and will almost certainly continue in the same direction, barring catastrophic collapse. The World Trade Organization (WTO) is an example of an already existing and very imperfect institution regulating some dimensions of free-market capitalism at the global level. It is only partially democratic, at best, with a one-nation one-vote rule of governance that creates serious inequities. It is far more responsive to powerful nations and large corporations than to people, but the small nations represented at least give it some diversity of viewpoint. While cumbersome and only partially democratic, it is better than no regulation of trade, which is why it exists.

The Solution's Driving Force

Until this chapter, this book has focused primarily on global moral and legal issues such as human rights, justice, sustainable prosperity, and the problems for peace that are aggravated by the global imbalance of excessive American military power. Why the sudden shift to economic globalization? The answer is that for all the problems it has generated—and they are numerous and acute—economic globalization contains within it the germ of the solution to the other problems this book addresses. Where economic activity goes, political and administrative controls inevitably follow. This process is always slow, fitful, and painful, with numerous setbacks. But in the end it must and will happen. Political and administrative controls on the excesses of capitalism at the global level will have to be established, given that economics has in fact globalized. It is not a question of whether this will happen, but only of when and at what pace, barring a collapse of the global system. Unfortunately, a partial collapse such as a devastating worldwide depression may be the only circumstance that can force the needed changes.

Illustrating the natural flow from economic to political union, the European Union started by uniting at the economic level in the original form of the European Economic Community, but in the end economic union inescapably brought administrative institutions such as the European Commission and the European Parliament to regulate and coordinate business and European policy in its train. These institutions sometimes fail to protect people and are insufficiently democratic, so now the Europeans are forced by the citizens of their various democratic nation-states to revamp their political map to make their systems more democratic, transparent, and politically responsive to citizens.

Given the foundation stones of democratic nation-states, the dynamics of this sequence are inescapable. However, the process is incredibly difficult; the structural and power-sharing problems are hugely complex. Establishing such structures is more daunting at the regional level (e.g., European) than at the national level, and will at some point be more daunting still at the global level. Nevertheless, in the long run, the structural problems at the global level will have to be dealt with and solved, or catastrophic collapse from ecological or economic instability is almost a certainty. Sustainability is not just a catchword; it is a survival issue for human civilization. And it will happen neither by accident nor by divine fiat. It will happen, if it happens, by human design.

Specific Institutions

Despite the huge problems it has engendered, the trend toward economic globalization or global economic unity is a resistless flood. Those who protest against it and would try to stop it are taking arms against a sea of trouble, whacking away with rhetoric and demonstrations at a rising tide. They are wasting their time. The challenge is how to harness globalization for human benefit by developing institutions to regulate it politically, just as business is (imperfectly) regulated in the U.S. to prevent the worst excesses of exploitive behavior. This is a never-ending but absolutely necessary process, as Enron and Global Crossing demonstrate.

The question for humanity is how to shape and guide these unstoppable forces into something that serves humanity rather than destroying it. We must learn, collectively, to curb the drawbacks of global capitalism such as monetary instability, environmental destruction, extreme maldistribution of wealth, predatory and anti-competitive business practices, and exploitation of labor (e.g., backbreaking work at starvation wages in unsafe working conditions). Controlling these terrible negative aspects of economic globalization will require international or global institutions that are effective, not just cosmetic gestures of hope in dealing with these problems.

Curbing these drawbacks means, for example, a democratically run global environmental institution with real teeth, a labor organization that really protects workers, an institution that can regulate and dampen down the now-out-of-control and extremely unstable flows of global capital as it chases speculative bubbles, and a poverty-fighting development organization equipped with adequate funding and a realistic program for dealing with the economics and politics of fighting extreme poverty. These have pathetically weak and ineffectual counterparts in the UN now, but they will need to evolve or be replaced by organizations and systems with regulatory capability and political legitimacy and clout. Clearly these improved or revamped institutions will not rise up overnight, especially with American leaders broadly opposing institutional progress on all such fronts, and fiercely opposing any progress, domestic or global, that entails regulation. There is some faint hope in the fact that even the U.S. does selectively, though modestly, support specific international goals such as AIDS prevention in appreciation of the dangers it poses to national security. The U.S. has also been surprisingly compliant with decisions of the WTO, presumably because even the current leaders recognize the necessities created by global free markets.

The Bigger Picture: A Thought Experiment

In the short- to medium-term the only way badly needed shifts in the institutional structure of the world could be accomplished would be gradual evolution with occasional jumps to a new level as new treaties are signed. However, in the longer term, the entire, hopelessly cumbersome process of forming essentially unanimous agreement by member states on global treaties will eventually have to change to something more efficient and effective. Treaty-making can deal with a dangerous worldwide problem like global warming only when its member nations are willing to admit there is a problem and cooperate in solving it. If one or two powerful nations assumes a head-in-sand posture and refuse to cooperate, little or nothing worthwhile can be done.

While the treaty-making process may be the best the human race can do at the present historical juncture, it is clearly not satisfactory, and getting less so as the problems become more numerous, urgent, and controversial. It seems likely that eventually (in the very long run) a democratic system will be needed that requires compliance from all nations without requiring unanimous agreement among them. It will have to change to some form of democratic global legislature that is more representative than the UN Security Council and is both more democratic and more powerful than the UN General Assembly. This is an idea so shocking in its implications that mainstream political writers and theorists of international relations dare not speak it, though it is actually fairly obvious.

The idea of a true global legislature, no matter how well-delineated and limited its powers, is revolutionary for one main reason: it places the well-being of the entire human race and the planet above the sacrosanct principle of national sovereignty. Some nations would be subject to international laws their representatives voted against. Obviously, to be even minimally workable, this kind of global legislature would have to be widely agreed upon as a system that is constrained by well-defined and widely agreed limitations on its powers. These powers would have to be explicitly limited to those arenas where the collective well-being of all nations and peoples is severely challenged. And the system would have to exclude, as much as possible, cultural biases just as the U.S. Government is designed for separation of church and state.

I do not imagine for a moment that such a profound and wrenching change in the world's political structure can be achieved easily or soon, if ever. But the thought experiment is worthwhile because it calls attention to the need to transcend the theoretical absolutism of national sovereignty that rules the current system as a paradigm. In reality, nation-states are already ceding small degrees of control over their individual destinies for their own benefit as a part of a larger whole. In Europe, this process is advanced, while in other places, it is light years behind. But this shift must come eventually if the planet is to move into an era in which now-pervasive horrors such as war, genocide, and lethal or catastrophic environmental degradation can at least be curbed and diminished. The present fragmented international system is completely unable to cope with these evils, and it cannot go on forever by ignoring them or resisting them ineffectually.

Moments of Opportunity

Through a Darwinian process of survival of the fittest in the art of getting elected, U.S. politicians tend to be masters of the moment and the irrational. For the most part they are lawyers accustomed to dealing with issues on a case-by-case basis. They get elected by espousing with passion whatever they think the people want to hear in relation to dramatic recent events or momentary pain (e.g., fear from 9/11, or the economic pinch from job scarcity). Rhetoric and showmanship matter more than substance. Ideology, dogma, and slogans substitute for real thinking. Proposed legislative programs are hastily concocted and quickly abandoned. When politicians speak of foreign policy, the headlines of the moment are the matters they tackle. The approach is almost entirely reactive; it allows for little or no long-range thinking.

These facts are both unfortunate and perfectly normal. They constitute both the strengths and the weaknesses of democracy. Elections respond to the immediate needs of the people (a very good thing), but they are seldom farsighted. We claim to value the wisdom of the statesman, but we often vote for the momentary appeal of the crowd-pleaser. Fortunately, politicians with seriously wrong answers to public policy problems eventually fall from grace and get voted out of office when their folly catches up with them—and the rest of us. But sometimes damage is already done and is difficult or impossible to repair. Then we veer off in a new direction that may be more sensible or may be just as irrational in a brand new way.

Few, if any, politicians bring to bear the discipline of an engineer or a scientist on public policy problems. Seldom does even an American president dare to tackle the terribly important question that should be obvious to any design engineer: What does human civilization *as a system* need to look like *in the long run* to be peaceful, humane, just, and sustainably prosperous? This seemingly overwhelming and intractable question may be too large for anyone in the political arena. Yet in the past there have been stellar moments of opportunity and creativity when something radically new was designed and tried out. These were moments of acute crisis.

The American Constitutional Convention and later the creation of the League of Nations and the United Nations illustrate historic moments when breakthrough creativity in the political sphere was both possible and necessary. A power vacuum created by the inadequacies of the American Constitution's predecessor, the Articles of Confederation, drove the first. This weak arrangement was failing, and the leaders of the colonies could see

401

a need for change. They rose to the occasion, and the end result was the Constitution of one of the greatest nations in human history.

The creation of the League of Nations and later the UN were driven by two worldwide breakdowns of civilization, the two world wars. The people who came through with the needed innovation were American presidents, in cooperation of course with many other world leaders. In all three cases the leaders saw that they had to break out of the box, to think in larger terms and create a higher level of structure than had existed before. They saw that a refinement of hopelessly fragmented existing structures simply would not work. Those structures were the problem. Such great innovations don't always succeed, of course. The League of Nations failed and the jury is still out on the United Nations. But almost anyone, if given a choice, would rather spend a lifetime in the second half of the twentieth century, with the UN and NATO in place, than in the first half, living through the ravages of two world wars. It would be difficult to argue that there has been no improvement.

Farsighted and intellectually honest people recognize global warming as a threat that could create a major global crisis, and AIDS may also present such a global threat. Certainly it is already a full-blown continental crisis in Africa. But the full impact of either crisis on the world as a whole may be a few decades off. So we are not at a painful moment of stark necessity for profound and sweeping change. Though we are not at such a moment, there may be some utility in developing concepts that describe broadly what the world will have to look like if the future of humanity is to be bright rather than grim. The best time to change is before the crisis, in an effort to prevent it.

Though we cannot create a different future whole cloth, still if we have a realistic vision of a possible healthy future for the planet we can move toward it somewhat more directly than we do now. After thinking through what world civilization will have to look like, roughly, to be viable, the far more difficult problem is how to move the world in the right direction. If we know broadly where we're headed, maybe we can do better than zigzagging randomly in reaction (or overreaction) to short-term problems, and in the process creating new short-term problems. Motion without a concept of a destination may, by trial and error, get us to a desirable goal, but even exploratory and meandering motion with a broad concept of a sensible goal is likely to get us there sooner, with a lot less pain.

Design Concepts

Writing a prescription for what the world should look like in the hope or expectation that everyone will hop to and follow it would be the height of folly, hubris squared or cubed. However, in the spirit of intellectual adventure, it can do no harm to fuse common sense and human experience with imagination to project a vision of a probable future global institutional setup that would or could be (to a far higher degree than today) peaceful, just, humane, and sustainable. Aside from what difficulties the world might encounter in trying to get there, let's consider what this setup would have to look like in very broad outline. Such a world would not be a utopian ideal, but would be the best that flawed human beings can devise, as are the most successful nations we have now. Despite their glaring flaws, these nations are laboratories for what is possible in large-scale social organization.

The following is an example of a set of concepts that are flexible enough to cover the key requirements, and still meaningful in terms of implementing actions that could be taken:

We know we have global problems that can only be solved by nations and non-state actors working collectively, rather than separately. Therefore we know we need a world in which democratic processes create global laws (at present, mainly multilateral treaties) and global organizations that are empowered to work with nations and non-state actors (individuals, corporations, non-government organizations, etc.) to solve global problems. The World Health Organization is one of several successful examples. A majority of nations would have to endow these global institutions with enough power to bring to bear heavy pressure on a few recalcitrant states when their behavior threatened the well-being of all. Naturally getting nations—especially the U.S.—to delegate this power is the hard part. An America that was "behaving itself" and cooperating in the formation and execution of international law would have little to fear from pressures created by such institutions, though it would sometimes have to adjust to them, as it presently adjusts to decisions of the World Trade Organization.

We also know that it is vital for the people of the world, with their diverse cultures and traditions and religions, to maintain a maximum degree of internal autonomy for nation-states to operate in accordance with their own preferences, histories, natural resources, and economic conditions. Unnecessary encroachment on these freedoms is almost as undesirable as failing to solve global problems. (I say "almost" rather than placing them on a par because a collapse or drastic decline of global civilization would cause

403

people more pain than the discomfort of giving up or readjusting some of their cultural uniqueness.) Stated concisely, the two strategic design requirements are establishing a minimum of democratic global muscle necessary to solve specific global problems while maintaining a maximum degree of national autonomy within the broader constraints of global necessity. These two requirements are inescapably in tension with one another, but are not necessarily irreconcilable.

All over the world and throughout recent history human societies have developed a variety of strategies to reconcile varying degrees of central control with varying degrees of local autonomy. This is not a new problem for the human race. Sensible solutions to the problem range from loose confederations such as the UN to very strong federations such as the United States and Germany. In a confederation such as the UN, only nation-states or other aggregates are represented and are held responsible to law, not individuals. By contrast, in a federation individuals as well as aggregates are represented and are held responsible to law.

The United Nations system has until now been almost exclusively a confederation of nations drawing up treaties and other kinds of agreements on how they will govern their relations with one another. However, this global system has recently taken a tiny baby step toward dealing with individuals. The result has been enthusiastic support from much of the rest of the world and explosive resistance from extreme conservatives in the United States. The step I'm referring to is the establishment of the International Criminal Court (ICC). Whereas the long-standing International Court of Justice (ICJ or World Court) adjudicates only disputes among nations, the treaty establishing the ICC holds individuals accountable to a very narrow sliver of international law. This small bit of international law pertains to especially egregious instances of war crimes, genocide, and crimes against humanity. Obviously these are among the greatest crimes a human being can commit, comparable to mass murder and 9/11-style terrorism.

The need for a permanent court is transparent, given the repeated instances of ad hoc tribunals having to be set up for crimes in the former Yugoslavia, in Rwanda, Cambodia, Sierra Leone, etc. The problem with this court for people who are fanatical about state sovereignty may be that dealing with individuals is a tiny step toward federation and away from confederation by the UN system. Because the court deals with individuals, an eminently sensible step for the global community is a neuralgically sensitive step for the most extreme and tribalistic American conservatives. Senator Jesse Helms was apoplectic over the court, and left a remarkably pervasive legacy of misinformation about the court in the Senate. Statements on the record in Senate hearings and debate, even by highly respected Senators, are full of blatant falsehoods about the court.

Whether the set of global institutions needed to solve the global problems discussed in this book is classified as a confederation or a federation or something in between the two, clearly what the world needs at this stage in human history is an arrangement both more democratic and more effective than the United Nations, but far less centralized and intrusive than the United States Federal Government. Democracy at all levels, central and local, is an essential ingredient in the mix.

Despite the horrified protestations of the globo-paranoids at the thought of a global institutional system stronger than the UN system, no one advocates a global tyranny, and no one has anything approaching the power to implement such a monstrosity. The UN certainly does not, given that it often proves too weak to carry out its modest mandate. However, at the national level, the dictatorships and oligarchies of the world (e.g., North Korea and China), though dwindling in number and power, are still an acute problem for any movement toward a more democratic and effective set of global institutions. No one (except Chinese leaders) wants an undemocratic country like China to have a more forceful say in world affairs than it already has with its veto on the Security Council. However, even China yields to necessity when a problem that threatens the whole world intrudes on its affairs, as the spread of the deadly SARS virus—Severe Acute Respiratory Syndrome—illustrates.

As an example of a workable global institution, the World Health Organization (WHO) out of necessity has the power to work with governments to fight diseases in any country to prevent their spreading to all. Virtually everyone recognizes that traditions in a particular country that prevent the WHO from doing its job must take a back seat to the imperative of preventing a lethal worldwide epidemic. Hence WHO can bring to bear highly effective natural-consequence pressures such as travel restrictions on a country or region. There may be controversy about specific applications of that pressure, but seldom do people argue that the capacity to apply it is not needed in principle. I have not heard conservatives fulminate over the loss of national sovereignty the U.S. accepts by embracing membership in the WHO.

One might object to the simple concepts about international institutions in the paragraphs above as "just common sense." Indeed they are, but such common sense does not now prevail in discussions of foreign policy in the

United States. In Congress, passionate, red-faced declamations about national sovereignty begin immediately at the mere thought of any new global institutions or any global influence that might create pressure on the U.S. to change course the slightest bit.

In summary, what we are talking about here is moving the world in the general direction of carefully limited and democratically controlled global institutions that are empowered, as the World Health Organization is, to solve global problems. These institutions must be limited to areas where global problems require them, and must at the same time be designed to protect a maximum degree of national autonomy. If democratic global institutions were established and endowed by the nation states with the capability to move decisively in solving the most important problems looming ahead, the result would be a greatly reduced chance of global catastrophe.

Obviously at this point in history no one with any real implementation power is going to sit down and comprehensively design the necessary changes to the existing global system all at once, as a team of engineers might design and then build a prototype of a new product. Surprisingly, there actually are a few visionaries who call for a global constitutional convention to create a new world order. They are not sinister power-mongers; they are idealistic naïfs. The political reality is that a proposal attempting to add even a single, badly needed international organization such as a global environmental protection agency to the list of existing global organizations would produce vehement American objections, thunderous rhetorical shots that would be heard 'round the world. Even if no one else in the world objected, conservative American leaders would scuttle such an effort in a hot minute and rave on and on about encroaching global tyranny. So the advocates of an exponentially more bold initiative such as a global constitutional convention are dreaming currently impossible dreams.

Almost certainly incremental change will rule, as it usually does, until the shaky and incomplete global system we have built either improves or collapses. If it collapses, God forbid, millions will die and the survivors may recognize that a whole new approach is required, as they did after World War II. The world's leaders might then begin to think about designing a more systematic and realistic approach to global problem-solving, a successor to the UN system that is both more democratic and more effective.

However, if the current world civilization does not collapse, why even think in terms of "design specifications" for a better world? Maybe the current arrangement's survival will mean we're muddling through successfully.

The answer is that incremental changes need not be random, need not be "muddling through." Desirable results would probably be better designed and come sooner if they were intelligent and purposeful parts of a larger vision.

If at least some political elements in the U.S. create steady pressure in pursuit of such a world, there is a better chance that it will come about. If significant numbers of politically active American citizens think, lobby, and vote in these terms, the odds will improve that American foreign policy will lead toward a more democratic, peaceful, humane, just, and sustainable world. Such a world is vastly preferable to the one that is now evolving—an unstable world of ad hoc coalitions of the bought and bullied, dominated by a self-interested American empire that is fiercely resented by the rest of the world.

We can meander toward positive global goals by a random series of events and reactions through a series of painful, if not catastrophic, consequences. Or we can develop a vision of a better world and consciously advocate specific policy decisions that lead in the right direction. The vision is an essential step, but it is not enough. Action is also needed.

One of the problems with democracy at the global level is that a global polity, a self-conscious mass of people who are concerned with the well-being of all, or at least of themselves *en masse*, does not yet exist as an entity. Journalists and scholars speak of the American public, but they never speak of the global public. Ironically, perhaps the first glimpse of a massive global public consisting of millions of people erupted into view when people in cities all over the world protested against the prospect of George W. Bush's war in Iraq. Galvanized by a common cause and connected by the internet, millions of people who had no leader and no common country joined in protesting a political action that was seen as a threat to the stability of the entire planet. The sudden crystallization of this movement suggests that the potential is there that could be activated repeatedly if the threat were sufficient. Ironically, America's worst moment of imperial overreach since the Vietnam war may have triggered the creation of a global polity, a self-aware global community of individuals.

Another more stable but still embryonic beginning of a self-aware body politic is the rapid global rise of non-government organizations (NGOs). These organizations successfully joined hands by the thousands all over the world to press for the creation of the International Criminal Court. They succeeded in spite of the foot-dragging and eventual opting out of the country that at one time carried the standard for justice in the world, the U.S. A global polity is beginning to form, both on the internet and in the meeting rooms of NGOs, but it will be severely handicapped if it encounters nothing but resistance from the world's sole superpower. Citizens within the U.S., especially, need to get organized if the world is going to have a future we all want to live in.

Citizens Making Change

Individuals voting one by one may not be enough to change American foreign policy and thence to change the world. Voting is an essential start, but a single individual has only one vote, and the airwaves are filled with misleading advertisements meant to sway the votes of thousands of people. The resulting individual feeling of helplessness is one of the motives for not voting. Yet any American citizen who cares about the future of the country and the world can readily muster more power than a single vote. Clearly though, it will take organized effort by large numbers of citizens to overcome the well-organized and well-funded armies of industrial selfishness and national jingoism that now control American politics.

The good news is that organizations of American citizens actually exist that formulate and promote a vision of a better world and advocate the step-by-step policy decisions by the U.S. Government that are needed to contribute to more effective global cooperation. The bad news is that these organizations are not yet very powerful politically. However, they are vastly more powerful than any single individual voting alone. They give hope, encouragement and the strength of solidarity to individuals who wish to make a constructive difference in U.S. foreign policy. They also provide valuable information to voters who wish to know more about the candidates on international issues that are little-discussed in the campaigns.

They lobby legislators on Capitol Hill on specific legislative issues related to global structures and on specific issues such as global warming or support for the International Criminal Court. They struggle to make their longer-range message heard amid the uproar in the news media about the latest terrorist bombing or the latest election results. Sometimes they get through, and sometimes they influence a vote in Congress. These organizations are not a fantasy, nor, as the paranoids of the far-right imagine, are they a sinister conspiracy. Their work, carried out by volunteers who are both idealistic and practical, is out in the open for all to see. They make every effort to publicize it.

In my judgment, the best of several such organizations are Citizens for Global Solutions and the United Nations Association. Both have websites anyone can visit to find out about them.* American citizens who are dismayed by the current destructive and self-centered policies of American political leaders can join either or both of these organizations and contribute as little as modest annual dues or as much as volunteer activism at the local or national level. Both organizations are supported and guided by volunteer members and have small salaried staffs at the national level who are paid mainly from dues and donations of members. Occasionally a well-respected national foundation helps out in response to a grant request. Neither of these organizations has any hidden agenda or sources of support that cannot be ascertained by simply looking at their financial records or talking with their staffs. They are, by law and by preference, committed to transparency as a policy and mode of operation. From its website,

> ***Citizens for Global Solutions*** envisions a future in which nations work together to abolish war, protect our rights and freedoms, and solve the problems facing humanity that no nation can solve alone. This vision requires effective democratic global institutions that will apply the rule of law while respecting the diversity and autonomy of national and local communities. We are a membership organization working to build political will in the United States to achieve our vision. We do this by educating Americans about global interdependence, communicating global concerns to public officials, and developing proposals to reform and strengthen international institutions [such] as the United Nations.

Two especially useful products of this organization are a Global Solutions Rating Guide and a political candidate questionnaire. The Rating Guide lays out the voting records of Senators and Representatives on specific issues related to the great divide: Will the U.S. move toward global cooperation and teamwork, toward building up international laws and institutions designed to solve global problems, or toward global domination and coercion? Every two years, as national elections approach, Global Solutions also develops a questionnaire to use in asking political candidates for their views on these issues. Their answers can be a valuable tool in voting and supporting candidates, especially in those cases where a new candidate does not have a voting record.

Also drawing on its website, Citizens for Global Solutions has the following five program areas:

---

* www.globalsolutions.org and www.unausa.org

- **U.S. Global Engagement:** Promoting a multilateral foreign policy. We advocate for a foreign policy that makes us stronger and safer through teamwork, cooperation, and effective global institutions.
- **Peace and Security:** Advocating collaborative approaches to prevent and resolve conflicts and establish effective peace operations. We promote an empowered, efficient and accountable UN peacekeeping capacity to meet the challenges posed to the world by post-conflict regions.
- **International Law and Justice:** Strengthening laws and institutions that protect human rights and help nations resolve disputes peacefully. We promote U.S. cooperation with the International Criminal Court to prevent atrocities and help bring to justice future Hitlers, Pol Pots, and Idi Amins.
- **International Institutions:** Proposing reforms to make international decision-making more effective, transparent, accountable, and democratic. We seek practical reforms to improve the United Nations and support a UN democracy caucus, encouraging democratic nations to lead UN decision-making bodies.
- **Health and Environment:** Supporting global cooperative efforts to confront environmental and public health challenges. We want to see the U.S. resume its leadership role in protecting the global environment. We promote the establishment of an international system to help countries work together to protect the environment and manage shared natural resources.

Citizens for Global Solutions is set up legally and organizationally to empower it to participate actively in elections, endorsing and financially supporting candidates who are constructive on the international issues that confront the Senate and the House.

By contrast, the United Nations Association, because of its tax status as an educational organization, cannot participate directly in getting candidates elected. However, as with Citizens for Global Solutions, its volunteer members lobby legislators on international issues. Often legislators, on first encountering citizens lobbying for a more constructive foreign policy, comment that it is refreshing to encounter people who are lobbying for a constructive cause, not for their own self-interested financial or political gain. According to its website:

UNA of the United States is dedicated to enhancing U.S. participation in the United Nations system and to strengthening that system as it seeks to define and carry out its mission. UNA-USA's action agenda uniquely combines education and public research, substantive policy analysis, and ongoing U.S.-U.N. dialogue.

UNA-USA is a leading center of policy research on the United Nations and global issues such as peace and security, health, development and human rights. With more than 20,000 members nationwide, UNA-USA combines broad grassroots outreach with high-level policy studies involving scholars and government officials from many parts of the world to identify fresh ideas and areas of potential cooperation. Through a series of programs, UNA-USA continues to pioneer efforts to involve the American public in the discussion of foreign policy priorities as well as to provide information and educational materials for Congress, the executive branch, the corporate community, NGOs, the general public and the media.

Both these organizations, Citizens for Global Solutions and the United Nations Association, and many others, are promoting a vision of the well-being of all humanity and striving to build the concrete political and administrative realities at the global level that will implement that vision in the long, hard slog of day-to-day human activity. They fuse idealism with hard-headed practicality. With these two qualities working together, progress in creating a better world is possible; without them both, no progress is possible.

A Momentous Challenge

The world will always be subject to crime, conflict, stress, and crisis; there is no utopia when imperfect human beings are in charge, and saints and angels are in short supply. There will always be a struggle with these forces, the perennial human struggle between good and evil. This book is not intended to envision a utopia or to claim that it is possible. However, it *is* meant to claim that the world can be improved substantially, as it has been since the end of the Cold War; that it can be made more orderly and more democratic at the global level, with far-reaching benefits for all humanity. The U.S. has so much power that American citizens and especially their leaders have a key role and responsibility in making improvements.

The question for American citizens is whether we will move our leadership and our human future toward or away from catastrophes such as major international wars or global economic collapse; whether we will establish global institutions that are effective in restraining horrors such as genocide and terrorism; whether we will move the world toward responsible control of weapons of mass destruction, global control of environmental pollution, and economics that benefit the poor as well as the rich.

The answer to the question, "Which way will the world go?" can be determined nowhere else but in how we, the human race, organize ourselves at the global level—for democratic law, order, and cooperation, or for war, cutthroat competition, and perpetually unstable coalitions of the unwilling. With a number of terrible exceptions, much of the rest of the world is struggling toward law, order, and cooperation, and is using transnational organizations, both regional and global, as key elements in this effort. Europe is the prime example. However, in the U.S., key neoconservative American leaders explicitly consider "moral" action to include violent overthrow of other countries to force the American way of life on uncomprehending and resentful foreign cultures. The result of this arrogance and violence is extreme danger for global stability.

Contempt for the United Nations and the hopes and aspirations it imperfectly embodies are corollaries of their nationalistic selfishness. In these respects they do not represent the views and preferences of a majority of the American public. This temporary failure of representative American democracy must be changed. Awakened and aroused American citizens can change it. It is possible to take back our country from the militarists, the handmaidens of the oil and coal industries, and the apocalyptic nightmares of religious extremists. We, the moderate majority of American citizens, are the ones who must choose to act.

If there is a worthy vision for the United States and for human civilization at this stage in history, it is larger than avoiding various possible disasters, though that is a first step. It's about exercising the courage and imagination to build a tremendously difficult future, about taking off our nationalistic blinders, letting go of our tribalistic selfishness and doing the hard-headed work of creating transnational laws and institutions to bring an entire planet into increasing rather than diminishing harmony and cooperation. It's about the world's most powerful nation supporting the establishment of global institutions such as the International Criminal Court and renouncing violence as a tool of foreign policy except in defense against attack or imminent threat of attack. It's about creating and reinforcing democratic global structures that make human rights and justice realities for all humanity, mirroring progress that has already taken place within the boundaries of the great democracies. And it's about leading global efforts to treat this fragile planet on which we depend for our lives, not as a disposable resource to be pillaged and despoiled for the enrichment of the few, but as a treasure to be preserved for our children and our grandchildren.

Summation: Our Values, Our Power, Our Choice

During the years after World War II the U.S. took the lead role in building the existing fragile, incomplete, and only partially democratic global order. The Cold War held in check to some degree any U.S. tendency to overt global dominance. By contrast, since the end of the Cold War and far more since 9/11, American leaders have engaged in resistance to further development of international order and in reckless actions that tear it down. They have explicitly stated and acted on a preference for unstable and constantly shifting "coalitions of the willing" created and dominated by the United States, and contemptuous of international law and institutions. The result is an increase in global anarchy and a decrease in stability.

A better way forward at the beginning of a new century and a new millennium would be to embrace the global order we once led in building and to work to reform and further develop it, making it both more democratic and more effective. Just as war should be a last resort, so any unilateral action that undermines international law and institutions should also be a last resort. When American leaders act as trigger-happy cowboys, turning the U.S. into a super-powered maverick that casually tramples on international law and refuses to cooperate in its further development, the U.S. in the hands of those leaders becomes a loose cannon, the most dangerous influence on the planet.

On the other hand, because of its colossal power, the U.S. has the potential to be the most constructive influence on the planet. It can do so if it chooses to act as a consistent collaborator and leader in the effort to make the world more democratic, orderly, lawful, and systematically cooperative at the international level. This choice will require the U.S. sometimes to relinquish voluntarily a modest degree of its power to act alone in ways that are not beneficial to the interests of other nations.

This choice will require that the U.S. play the "game" of international relations as a win-win game that benefits everyone. It requires that American leaders resist the temptation to use disproportionate power to seize unfair advantage. The choice to make collaboration and win-win diplomacy and the strengthening of international law and institutions the heart of our foreign policy is quite possibly the most important single policy decision in human history. At present, U.S. leadership is squarely and openly on the wrong side of this choice. Real moral clarity, not the bogus kind used in political rhetoric, requires a reversal of course and a active choice for long-term global cooperation and teamwork, not American dominance.

Given where American leaders stand now, for the U.S. to drift in the same direction and fail to change policies is in effect a choice for a mixture of global oligarchy and global anarchy rather than democratic order. It is urgent that American citizens work to elect leaders who choose peace over war and support international laws and institutions that embody fundamental moral principles such as human rights, justice, and sustainable prosperity. Our children and grandchildren deserve to inherit a planet we have improved, not one we have destroyed by our greed. And all human beings in all countries deserve what we Americans believe in for ourselves. They too are created equal. Life, liberty, and the pursuit of happiness are rights not only of Americans, but of all humanity. These values are not likely to be realized by a self-interested American empire of global military power and economic coercion. They are far more likely to be realized by democratic global cooperation under law.

---

[1] Tad Daley, "Choosing a Flag to Unite a Planet." *International Herald Tribune*, January 29, 2004

[2] Alan Brinkley, "Battle Formation" *The Washington Post Book World*, March 14, 2004, p. 7.

[3] Zbigniew Brzezinski, *The Choice: Global Domination or Global Leadership*, Basic Books, New York, 2003 p. xi.

INDEX

417

418

421